LEABHARLANNA CHONTAE
FINGAL COUNTY LIBRARIES

Items should be returned on or before the last date shown below. Items may be renewed by personal application, by writing or by telephone. To renew give the date due and the number on the barcode label. Fines are charged on overdue items and will include postage incurred in recovery. Damage to, or loss of items will be charged to the borrower.

Date Due	Date Due	Date Due
08. FEB 05		
APR 05.	MAR 06	
12. MAY 05		
16.	02. MAY 06	
	16. JUN 06	
10. SEP 05	10th July 06	
18. OCT 05		
03/12/05	07. NOV	
06		WITHDRAWN FROM STOCK
MAR 06	03 MAR	
	27. MAR	
	13. AUG 07	

of related interest

A Strange World – Autism, Asperger's Syndrome and PDD-NOS
A Guide for Parents, Partners, Professional Carers, and People with ASDs
Martine F. Delfos
Foreword by Tony Attwood
ISBN 1 84310 255 2

Asperger's Syndrome
A Guide for Parents and Professionals
Tony Attwood
Foreword by Lorna Wing
ISBN 1 85302 577 1

The AD/HD Handbook
A Guide for Parents and Professionals on
Attention Deficit/Hyperactivity Disorder
Alison Munden and Jon Arcelus
ISBN 1 85302 756 1

Promoting the Emotional Well Being of Children and Adolescents
and Preventing Their Mental Ill Health
A Handbook
Edited by Kedar Nath Dwivedi and Peter Brinley Harper
Foreword by Caroline Lindsey
ISBN 1 84310 153 X

Asperger Syndrome in Adolescence
Living with the Ups, the Downs and Things in Between
Edited by Liane Holliday Willey
Foreword by Luke Jackson
ISBN 1 84310 742 2

Understanding and Supporting Children with Emotional
and Behavioural Difficulties
Edited by Paul Cooper
ISBN 1 85302 666 2 pb
ISBN 1 85302 665 4 hb

Relationship Development Intervention with Young Children
Social and Emotional Development Activities for Asperger Syndrome,
Autism, PDD and NLD
Steven E. Gutstein and Rachelle K. Sheely
ISBN 1 84310 714 7

Relationship Development Intervention with Children,
Adolescents and Adults
Social and Emotional Development Activities for Asperger Syndrome,
Autism, PDD and NLD
Steven E. Gutstein and Rachelle K. Sheely
ISBN 1 84310 717 1

Children and Behavioural Problems

Anxiety, Aggression, Depression
and ADHD – A Biopsychological Model
with Guidelines for Diagnostics and Treatment

Martine F. Delfos

Jessica Kingsley Publishers
London and Philadelphia

Information about Conduct Disorder (pp. 79–80), ADHD (p. 147) and Hyperactivity/Impulsivity (p. 148) reprinted with permission from the *Diagnostic and Statistical Manual of Mental Disorders, Text revision,* Copyright © American Psychiatric Association, 2000.

http://home.wanadoo.nl/mdelfos

The right of Martine F. Delfos to be identified as author of this work has been asserted by her in accordance with the Copyright, Designs and Patents Act 1988.

First published in 2004
by Jessica Kingsley Publishers
116 Pentonville Road
London N1 9JB, UK
and
400 Market Street, Suite 400
Philadelphia, PA 19106, USA

www.jkp.com

Copyright © Martine F. Delfos 2004

Library of Congress Cataloging in Publication Data
Delfos, Martine F.
    Children and behavioural problems : anxiety, aggression, depression and biopsychological model with guidelines for diagnostics and treatment / Martine F. Delfos.
        p. cm.
    Includes bibliographical references and index.
    ISBN 1-84310-196-3 (pbk.)
    1. Behavior disorders in children. 2. Behavior disorders in children--Treatment. 3. Attention-deficit disorder in adolescence. 4. Adolescent psychopathology. I. Title.
    RJ506.B44D45 2004
    618.92'8914--dc22

                                                                2004003158

British Library Cataloguing in Publication Data
A CIP catalogue record for this book is available from the British Library

ISBN 1 84310 196 3

Printed and Bound in Great Britain by
Athenaeum Press, Gateshead, Tyne and Wear

Contents

Preface

In this book a biopsychological model of behavioural problems of children is presented. Behaviour is deeply imbedded in the biosocial differences between men and women and boys and girls. To discuss differences between men and women is often difficult because we are reluctant to accept that those differences could have deep biological roots. One reason for this reluctance is the emancipation of women the basis of which is the idea that men and women are alike. Another reason is that we have all observed that men and women are very similar overall in behaviour. The third reason is that we have the prejudice that if behaviour is biologically founded it is impossible to change it. This is not true at all. On the contrary: if we accept that some behaviour is biologically founded then we know how and from where we should change behaviour if necessary. It is because we do not accept the biological foundation of behaviour that we continue trying to change behaviour without any success. Our perspective is wrong and our help is coming from this wrong perspective.

So it is very important to discern the nature and nurture aspects of behaviour, in order to adapt our help effectively. We also must take into account another factor, the maturation of the central nervous system, which is particularly important with problematic behaviour and psychiatric disorders.

The model presented in this book encompasses much scientific research and goes a step beyond as the work of a postmodern scientist is expected to. This leads to – I hope – a clear theoretical image with practical consequences for helping children and their parents.

I thank Marijke Gottmer who helped me find all the research I needed, and I thank my family in supporting my scientific endeavour.

Martine F. Delfos
Utrecht, The Netherlands

1

Introduction

There are two parts to this book. In the first I present a *biopsychological model*, where *aggression disorders* and *anxiety disorders* together with *depression* are placed in one explanatory framework alongside *ADHD* (*Attention Deficit-Hyperactivity Disorder*). For an explanatory model about autism I refer to *A Strange World – Autism, Asperger's Syndrome and PDD-NOS:*[1] *A Guide for Parents, Partners, Professional Carers, and People with ASDs* (Delfos, 2004a). Depression will be discussed because it can follow on from anxiety problems. ADHD will also be discussed because with a number of children it occurs in combination with conduct disorders. The second part of the book discusses the practical effects of this model for diagnostics and professional care for children and their parents.

Confusing terminology

'Aggression' and 'anxiety' are two terms used to refer to conduct difficulties with children and youngsters. When these occur with adults, they are described in more detail (for example naming a specific fear such as *agoraphobia* or *social phobia*) or in terms of personality disorders (for example *antisocial personality disorder*).

With 'conduct disorder' a specific group of behaviours is meant, namely those where social codes are structurally violated or not followed out of fear, and disorders such as autism and bedwetting are not included. Use of the term 'behaviour' is more general and is, in principle, free from value judgements. The term 'conduct' refers more to 'behaviours', that is to say behaviour towards something or someone. There is a moral side to the use of 'behaviour', as well as an indication of how one is expected to behave.

---

1   Pervasive Developmental Disorder – Not Otherwise Specified

There are two important diagnostic handbooks: *ICD-10* (World Health Organization 1992), an *International Classification of Mental Disorders and Conduct Disorders*, which is the most used international classification for mental disorders, and the *DSM-IV* (American Psychiatric Association 1994), the *Diagnostic and Statistical Manual of Mental Disorders*. In these handbooks 'conduct disorder' is understood to refer to children's problems where social codes are violated in a specific manner for a long period of time. Another term is 'oppositional defiant disorder' (ODD), the child's defiance of rules and authority.

In this book I will try to create clarity regarding the various terms. I will classify behaviour according to the source of the behaviour, which may be controlled both by predisposition and by the environment. Both factors always play a part, in joint interaction, but the emphasis often lies either on the predisposition or on the environment. I will try to make a distinction, in the sense of unravelling whether certain behaviour is more directed by predisposition or by the environment. It is risky to try to make this distinction, because it is not always easy to deduce the source of the behaviour. However, in daily practice everybody from parent to diagnostician decides whether something is environmental or predispositional. In fact, a remark like 'the child's behaviour is not surprising with such parents' means that the behaviour is attributed to the environment. The intention in this book is to research methodically the distinction between predisposition and environment and to give handles for diagnosing behaviour in terms of predisposition or environment. Because both factors always play a part, it will be a matter of weighing the factors and mapping their interaction. In addition to the factors of predisposition and environment the *maturation of the central nervous system* (CNS, brain and nerve tracts,) plays an important part, as we will see.

A new conceptual framework

I will introduce a new conceptual framework using familiar terminology, by placing the differences between the problems in a co-ordinating framework. In this way I will try to do justice to the nature and the source of the problem controlled by predisposition, environment or maturation of the central nervous system. I will use the term *conduct difficulties* as a co-ordinating concept. Here I distinguish two forms: the conduct *disorder*, which arises and is nurtured mainly proceeding from predisposition, and the conduct *problem*, which arises and is maintained mainly as an effect of the environment.

For a long time 'conduct disorder' only included those behaviours where the person involved came into conflict with his or her environment: the aggressive, externally directed form. This problem only included the socially problematic behaviours such as aggression, stealing or arson. Achenbach and Edelbrock (1978) also include in 'conduct disorders' the group of behaviours where there is no aggression but there is extreme shyness and anxiety. They are in fact two ways of expressing underlying problems. I therefore also class them under conduct difficulties. Achenbach mentions an *externalising*, aggressive, outwardly directed form and an *internalising*, anxious, inwardly directed form. This terminology is particularly suitable to classify the various behaviours and I will therefore use this terminology in this book, refined according to the source of the behaviour.

There is some confusion surrounding the concept of 'conduct disorder' because ADHD (Attention Deficit-Hyperactivity Disorder) – hyperactivity – is also listed under 'conduct disorders' in a lot of literature. We classify this disorder as a conduct *difficulty* and I shall try to make the difference clear.

The purpose of this book is to create clarity in the field of conduct difficulties. The book includes many tables summing up the characteristics of the various conduct difficulties and ADHD. The book can therefore be used by professional carers as a reference book.

In order to create clarity I will categorise conduct disorders and anxiety problems as *conduct difficulties* – this is the co-ordinating concept. In this I make a distinction between conduct *disorders* and conduct *problems*. The disorders are mainly steered from the *predisposition* of the child and the *maturation*, the problems chiefly by the *environment*. The deciding factor is the dominance of the influence, because it is always a matter of both influences. In this book I will use the terms *disorder* and *problem* systematically. With both forms I will make a distinction between aggressive, *externalising* behaviour and anxious, *internalising* behaviour. By way of illustration I have set out the various forms in Table 1.1.

Table 1.1 Conduct difficulties: externalising and internalising		
	Externalising	*Internalising*
Predispositional	Externalising conduct disorder or aggressive disorder	Internalising conduct disorder or anxiety disorder
Environmental	Externalising conduct problem or aggression problem	Internalising conduct problem or anxiety problem

Depression may follow naturally from anxiety problems. Predisposition and environment also play a part here. In this book I will use the terminology that is commonly used for depression in which the concept of predisposition versus environment is expressed by the terms endogenous versus exogenous. I will therefore speak of *endogenous* (coming from within, predisposition or maturation) depression and *exogenous* (coming from outside, environment) depression.

Table 1.2 Depression	
Controlled by predisposition or maturation	*Controlled by environment*
Endogenous depression	*Exogenous* depression

In addition to conduct difficulties I will discuss ADHD. As we will see with any problem, it is important to find out to what extent predisposition and environment play a part; the same applies to ADHD. The term 'ADHD' will be used for the delayed or limited maturation of the central nervous system, as a problem controlled by predisposition.

One of the characteristics of ADHD is *hyperactivity*. Overactive children are, however, sometimes wrongly regarded as children with ADHD. I want to limit the use of the term 'ADHD' to those where it is a problem with the maturation of the central nervous system. When children show overactive behaviour for another reason, for example because they have received a less than adequate upbringing or have problems which they want to express through hyperactive behaviour, I will use the term 'hyperactivity'.

Table 1.3 ADHD and hyperactivity	
Controlled by maturation	*Controlled by environment*
ADHD	Hyperactivity

The source of the behaviour and the strategy for professional care

Making the distinction between predisposition and environment is tricky. It is for a good reason that it is often not made explicitly, or that an extreme point of view is taken where everything is attributed to the predisposition, or on the contrary to the environment. Moreover, the continuous interaction between both aspects does not make matters easier. Various theories, such as *transactional analysis* (Berne 1996), employ an interactionistic view and thus try to show the interaction between predisposition and environment.

In addition, we have to realise that the predisposition of a child does not exist in a vacuum. When the predisposition has been passed on genetically, the child has received it through his or her parents. If a child struggles with conduct difficulties which are mainly genetic, then there is a good chance that one of the parents or other members of the family also struggle to a greater or lesser extent with similar problems. In the case of conduct problems, predisposition and environment c. cause a cumulative effect, causing the persons involved not to be able to 'see the wood for the trees'. Scarr and McCartney (1983) has already said that a child shapes its environment from his or her predisposition. In the case of conduct difficulties we can see that very poignantly. A child with a conduct *disorder* which is chiefly genetic shows very problematic behaviour and because of this problem influences his or her parents' behaviour. In this way the child 'creates' 'difficult parents'. This then means that the parents will show problematic behaviour towards the child. As a result, the child will also develop conduct *problems* in addition to the conduct *disorder* – the latter from the predisposition, the former as a result of the reaction of the parents to the child. The child subsequently does not only struggle with his or her predisposition, but also with parents who, from their predisposition, can only provide a less than optimal upbringing. In addition, it is often the case that people who have a genetic predisposition which makes them less able to function adequately socially live and end up in circumstances which are far from optimal. The environment factor becomes more important. As a result, unravelling the various factors becomes even more difficult.

In addition it is also the case that 'difficult' parents can cause conduct problems in their children, irrespective of the predisposition of the child. The principal aim of this book is to try to unravel the various sources of influence on behaviour and subsequently to assist with finding adequate professional help.

I chose to make a distinction between predisposition and environment, no matter how arbitrary, because this has enormous consequences for the diagnostics, the treatment and the prognosis. Attributing behaviour to predisposition or environment has important effects on professional help. With 'predisposition' as the source, the professional carer often feels powerless and has the impression that he or she has to resign themselves to it and can, at best, make some changes to the situation by means of medication. This is completely wrong. Taking predisposition as a starting point to stimulate a behavioural change can prove to be successful. However, in the case of behaviour induced by predisposition, an approach taking the behaviour to be caused by environmental factors will fail.

Problematic behaviour arising from predisposition cannot be changed essentially through professional help; people can, however, learn to live with it optimally. In this way the problematic behaviour can even disappear.

It should, in principle, be possible to restructure conduct problems controlled by the environment. Professional help should in that case be aimed at changing the environment or treating the effects of the environment's influence. The distinction made is therefore of vital importance to ensure the correct professional help.

From a scientific point of view, forming a model based on the material which is available at the moment is possibly premature. A lot of what is presented in this model will have to be examined further. The first actions to that end have already

... Asperger's
... within the
... that the child
... well how to
... social interaction, as a result
of an inadequate me–other differentiation. Treatment aimed at developing the me–other differentiation
and empathy teaches the child to
interpret social interaction. When
we are dealing with a child who has
adequate intellectual powers, then
this quality can be employed, and it
can be possible that after some time
the child is able to interpret the
social interaction properly intellectually, instead of sensitively. The
problematic behaviour disappears as
a result of that, without removing
the source. This difference between
thinking and feeling is supported by
brain research. People with autism
do not use the amygdala, associated
with feeling and intuition, to make
judgements about social interaction,
but the frontal and temporal parts of
the brain, associated with thinking
and planning (Baron-Cohen *et al.*
1999).

been taken. We are, however, always building
models based only on scientific material which is
available up to that moment. It is not possible to wait
for end results, which we know will never become
available or will not become available in time to
provide more effective professional help. It is,
moreover, necessary to process new views in order
to refine old ideas and strategies for professional
help. This book will be an attempt to do so. It will be
described how predisposition and environment can
be distinguished, including details of the behaviour,
in order to have handles to investigate methodically
the question that everyone is asking. Although
separating predisposition and environment has its
disadvantages, it is my belief that ignoring this
problem will do children and their parents wrong.
One is, after all, in that case inclined to use either
one as a guideline, and to take predisposition or the
environment as a starting point, without
researching this methodically. In addition, I should
point out that, with the conduct difficulties I discuss
in this book, the starting point of professional help
is almost always, and often wrongly so, the belief
that the environment is the only, or the most
important, factor. If, however, the problems are
mainly caused by predisposition, and if professional carers and parents use the idea
that the behaviour is caused by the environment, then this often means that for a
long time they try to make changes and become extremely discouraged if they fail
to bring success. It seems that the tide is turning with ADHD now that scientific
research shows that ADHD is a disorder which a child already carries due to
predisposition. The problem here is, however, that the genetic factor can be
exaggerated and the environment factor can then be overlooked, causing children
to be diagnosed as ADHD when their behaviour is not controlled by a genetic
factor, but is hyperactive behaviour, controlled by the environment. When I discuss
ADHD I will pay attention to this.

A biopsychological model

Drawing on current research into behaviour, I will develop a *biopsychological model*
for conduct difficulties in this book and formulate the consequences for diagnostics and treatment.

In the model conduct difficulties will be looked at and I will consider both predisposition, with its physical processes, and the influence of the environment. With corporal processes I do not mean to refer only to the physical aspect, for body and mind cannot be separated.

We are used to speaking in terms of body and mind, especially since Descartes (1633/1963). Nevertheless, Descartes indicated that he only applied this distinction as an act proceeding from logic in order to be able to discuss the subject. In reality such a distinction does not exist; Descartes himself was convinced about that. Psychological problems are embedded in physical processes; a thought exists by virtue of transference of substances in the brain.

The model incorporates biological factors in addition to, and in co-operation with, psychological factors, with attention to the educationalist framework. Attention to both the biological and the psychological aspects means discussing the subject of anxiety while paying attention to both the psychological impact of a traumatic event and the effects of stress hormones such as adrenlaline; or treating the subject of empathy by discussing both the way to bring up a child as a caring member of society and the brain structures necessary for empathic thinking.

> A recent example of the co-operation between body and mind is the research into the hormonal activity of men whose wives are pregnant. Men who live together with their wives who are pregnant produce an increase of hormones which enables them to assume a more caring attitude towards the woman and the child (Storey 2000).

> The statement 'cogito ergo sum' ('I think therefore I am') derives from Descartes. This statement expresses the inextricability of body and mind.

The necessity of a biopsychological model lies in the fact that the three factors *predisposition*, *environment* and *maturation of the central nervous system* all play a part. Making an overview of those factors is of fundamental importance for respecting a person the way he or she is and helps in understanding that person and offering the right professional help.

The distinction between the factors of predisposition and environment with regard to professional care is used very little in literature and in scientific research. However, more research is made into the physical factors. Usually, the theoretical starting point is that conduct difficulties are caused by the environment and by the upbringing by the parents in particular. Wrong conclusions can be drawn from such unilateral research with regard to professional help for children and their parents. Professional help strategies offer different possibilities in the case of environment problems from those offered in the case of predisposition problems. It is even the case that a certain form of help in the case of a predisposition factor can have a contrary effect, while it is very suitable when the environment factor is of overriding importance. Van Acker (1995) warns of this danger with poor diagnostics for conduct difficulties:

> Without clear definition of these disorders and problems or without con-
> currence in the classification thereof, one easily talks about various groups
> of problems without being properly aware of them. This is even more dan-
> gerous with an intervention because, just as with medical science a certain
> medicine is only effective in treating certain illnesses and symptoms, one
> method of treatment can be good for one behavioural problem and remain
> ineffective or even be harmful for other problems or disorders. (p. 22)

Within professional care for children and youngsters conduct difficulties are the
most common reason for requests for help. Most requests for help concern boys
with conduct difficulties, in particular the aggressive, outwardly directed form.
Boys on the whole show more disorders than girls (Delfos 1996a; Gomez 1991;
Zlotnik 1993). One can immediately wonder to what extent this is a biological
principle or a result of *socialisation*. But apart from outward appearances, the prevalence and occurrence of diseases such as muscular dystrophy in boys show that
there is a difference between boys and girls in a biological sense. We will examine
to what extent biological information can be made understandable in the case of
conduct difficulties and how they can be placed within the context of socialisation.

The prevalence of disorders also shows clear differences between boys and
girls, and also between men and women. In Table 1.4, the differences in occurrence
of disorders in boys and girls according to the *DSM-IV* are stated. It is not an
exhaustive list, because the epidemiological data is not always available. The
terminology comes from the *DSM-IV* (American Psychiatric Association 1994).

Many psychiatric disorders occur more often with boys than with girls.
ADHD, for example, occurs three to five times as often with boys than with girls
and the various forms of autism occur from four to eight times as often with boys
than with girls. The outwardly directed form of conduct difficulties which occurs
more often with boys than with girls causes problems for their environment and is
as a consequence more often the reason for making an appeal for professional help.
The typical form for girls is anxiety, directed inwards and sooner causing problems
for themselves. The indication that help is needed with children comes first from
the adults around them. Given the trouble boys can cause, they are more likely to be
presented as needing help during childhood than girls. The conduct difficulties
with girls are more likely to lead to them asking for help themselves when they are
adults.

The biopsychological model is meant to give a start to a possible structuring of
conduct difficulties, making it possible to formulate clearer handles for both
scientific research and for professional help. I am aware that forming a model
always leads to simplifications and does injustice to the complexity of human
behaviour. Nevertheless, simplifications are necessary in order to understand
behaviour and to set out professional help strategies.

Before I examine the conduct difficulties in detail, I will describe a general view of the sources of origin: predisposition, environment and maturation of the central nervous system (Chapter 2). This will be followed by a chapter about the differences between men and women (Chapter 3). This biological explanation is essential for a better understanding of the various behavioural problems. The anxiety model is presented in Chapter 3, where anxiety, aggression and depression are placed in one explanatory hormonal model which takes gender into account. The somatic counterpart to anxiety and stress is placed in a model of all psychosomatic diseases, which are put together in a hormonal system of balance between androgenic and adrenergic hormones.

After that the various forms of conduct difficulties will be discussed: conduct disorders (predispositional) in Chapter 4 and conduct problems (environmental) in Chapter 5, both externalising and internalising. I will discuss the subject of depression following anxiety disorders in Chapter 4. In addition, ADHD will be discussed (Chapter 6). A separate chapter is devoted to the typical behaviours which play a part in conduct difficulties (Chapter 7). After the theoretical description of the various conduct difficulties, ADHD and the connected diagnostic aspects (Chapter 8), the accompanying forms of treatment will be discussed (Chapters 9 to 12). In addition there are two appendices. Appendix 1 contains a psychosomatics model, the physical counterpart of the psychological model (anxiety-aggression-depression) presented in Chapter 3. Appendix 2 offers an example of a behaviour contract discussed in Chapter 11.

Table 1.4 Gender differences in occurrence of children's disorders	
Disorders which occur more often in boys than in girls	*Disorders which occur more often in girls than in boys*
Enuresis (bedwetting)	Anorexia
Encopresis (soiling)	DIS (dissociative identity disorder)
Pavor nocturnes (night terrors)	Selective mutism (not speaking)
Sleepwalking	Trichotillomania (pulling hair out)
Talking in their sleep	Auto mutilation
Narcolepsy (falling asleep at any moment)	Anxiety disorder and phobias
	Rett's disorder
Tics	Depression
Gilles de la Tourette's syndrome (multiple tic disorder)	
Stereotypical movements	
Banging	
Aggression	
Obsessive-Compulsive disorder	
Language disorders	
Learning disorders	
Dyslexia	
ADHD	
Autism	
Asperger's syndrome	
Conduct disorder	
Delinquency	
Schizophrenia	
Drug abuse	

Part 1

The Model

2

Disorder versus Impediment

The development of the child is influenced by various factors. Since the beginning of developmental psychology a classification into the factors *predisposition* and *environment* has been employed. This classification originates with the first theoretician in this field, John Locke (1632–1704), who saw the environment as the most important factor, and Jean-Jacques Rousseau (1712–1778), who saw predisposition as the fundamental factor. Following Francis Galton (1822–1911), Charles Darwin's (1809–1882) cousin, the predisposition–environment controversy is indicated as the matter of *nature–nurture*. It has become clear that both factors play a part, and that because of the mutual interaction it is often difficult to gain insight into the working of each factor separately. In addition to these two factors we have to mention a third factor: *the maturation of the central nervous system.* The central nervous system consists of the brain and nerve tracts. This system has not yet fully matured after birth and the brain has not yet developed all its functions. The fontanelle provides space for further growth. The maturation of the central nervous system is determined by the first two factors; it is partly predispositional and is partly influenced by the environment. The fact that both factors play a part in the maturation originates in the fact that the maturation does not only take place inside the womb, but continues after birth.

Apart from the above-mentioned three factors – predisposition, environment and maturation of the central nervous system – food is an important element in the growth of children. It is not only an element that maintains the body, but also one that directly

Children who were undernourished during the first year of their lives are at risk of their central nervous system not maturing sufficiently with no chance of this being reversed at a later stage. As a result these children may have to struggle with disorders. It cannot be said that this is due to predisposition, because it happened as a consequence of a lengthy process after birth. At the same time it is an irreversible process that cannot be cured and will influence the child for the rest of its life. It also cannot be said that it is the result of the environment factor, although this does play a part. The child is struggling with a structural problem, where the maturation of the central nervous system factor is the determining factor – a maturation which could have been normal with regard to predisposition, but is restricted by an environment factor.

influences the human's behaviour. More and more research shows that taking certain substances or not taking certain substances influences our behaviour to an important degree.

Predisposition

The predisposition factor, which allows the child to start with a number of characteristics, contains various elements. The most important aspect is hereditariness based on genetic material. The hereditary element is stored in the *DNA* (*Deoxyribonucleic Acid*), of which half comes from the father and half from the mother. In each sperm cell a unique selection is made of 23 out of the 46 chromosomes of the father. The same happens in the ovum of the mother. Then at conception they, together, form 23 pairs of a total of, again, 46 chromosomes. This chromosome pattern forms the unique pattern of the new human being.

Genetic material is stored in the 30,000 genes that people have. The genes are grouped in a DNA cell. *DNA* (*Deoxyribonucleic Acid*) is in fact a collection of programmes. Each gene is a programme in which it is registered how a certain substance, a protein, has to be made. In this way, using all these programmes, it is arranged how a cell of the body has to develop. The genes are assembled in the DNA which in its turn, together with proteins, is classified according to chromosomes. A chromosome is a package of programmes that belong together. The human being has 23 pairs of matching chromosomes, in total 46. Of each pair, one chromosome comes from the father and one from the mother.

Plomin and his assistants at the Colorado project in America (Plomin 1994; Plomin and McClearn 1994) describe how the research into monozygotic and dizygotic twins shows overall that the predisposition, especially in the sense of genetic make-up, is of vital importance for the appearance and behaviour of the human being. Harris (1998) uses the extensive research in the field of heredity to underpin that the importance of the childrearing by the parents fades into nothingness with this factor and emphasises especially the influence of association with peers. In addition to the DNA the environment inside the womb is also of great importance for the child's development – that is to say the circumstances inside the womb during pregnancy and the events during and around the childbirth.

It is customary to include the effects of the mother's influence on the child, during the growth inside the womb, in the predisposition. This influence could be a metabolic disorder of the mother, a drug or alcohol addiction, and also, for example, the amount of the hormone testosterone that is produced by the mother during the pregnancy. The same goes for the effects of complications before, during or directly after birth (*pre, peri* or *post-natal*). Although the predisposition essentially refers to the genetic aspect, the hereditary constitution according to the child's DNA, influences in the womb and complications around birth are usually classified under predisposition and not under environment.

The child's development inside the womb receives a lot of attention because of the increase of scientific knowledge and the availability of new measuring techniques. Money (1980) discovered that the basic form of the embryo is that of a woman. After a signal from the y-element in the xy-chromosome pair, the development is 'branched off' to become the male form after a few weeks. As a result an increased production of androgenic hormones occurs, notably testosterone. From six weeks onwards the *gonads*, the sex glands, of the genetic male embryo develop into testicles, after which the production of testosterone increases enormously. The gonads of the female embryo remain neutral until 12 weeks in order to develop subsequently into ovaries. If the signal from the y-chromosome is not given, the embryo will develop into a female. Interferences in this signal could result in deviations in the gender identity, the experience of being a 'man' in a woman's body or the other way round. Research by Swaab and Hofman (1995) with transsexuals shows that 'women' who feel 'trapped' in a man's body in fact have 'female' brain structures. The development into a man seems to have been set in with these male transsexuals, but not been fully completed.

Complications during childbirth can cause important defects. For example, in the past, the element of a lack of oxygen with the baby during birth was the reason for the diagnosis *MBD* (*Minimal Brain Damage*), which was later replaced to an important extent with the diagnosis *ADHD* (*Attention Deficit-Hyperactivity Disorder*). But now research has proved that it is the baby who produces the hormones causing the birth to start (Swaab 1999). A baby who does not produce enough hormones, or who produces hormones at the wrong moment or produces hormones at the wrong pace, could play a part in a problematic birth. Starting from that information it is conceivable that a complicated birth is not necessarily the cause of a disorder in a child, but it is possible that a child with a disorder initiates a difficult birth.

Many characteristics of children, not only external characteristics, are determined by the genetic material. Rutter and Casaer (1991) point out that research shows more and more often how important the genetic factor is for the development of psychiatric disorders, whether it concerns autism or hyperactivity. Research by, for example, the Autism Consortium (International Molecular Genetic Study of Autism Consortium 1998) shows that with autism there is a deviation of various chromosomes (4, 7, 10, 16, 19 and 22), where Chromosome 7 is the most significant. Research by Barrett *et al.* (1999) supports the importance of Chromosome 7 with autism. Research by Gayan *et al.* (1999) shows that with *dyslexia* there is a deviation of Chromosome 6. Also, research by Fisher *et al.* (1999) indicates this. There are also clear indications that hereditariness plays a part with disorders such as *anorexia nervosa* and *obesity*, while for a long time it was thought that we were dealing with problems controlled by the environment (Rutter *et al.* 1990; van den Heuvel 1998; Vink *et al.* 2001).

We have seen that most *disorders*, whether they concern autism or bedwetting, occur more often with boys than with girls. With disorders I mean the conditions

Research into regulating the amount of food taken is progressing. There exists an *adiposestat* in the brain, a kind of thermostat that arranges the amount of food intake. It has now been discovered, by means of research on mice and DNA of rats and humans, that the hormone MCT (Melanin-concentrating hormone) plays an important part in the regulation of the amount of food taken in. The absence of this hormone was related to thinness. Both *obesity* and *anorexia nervosa* seem to be connected to the presence of this hormone (Chambers *et al.* 1999; Saito *et al.* 1999; Shimomura *et al.* 1999). A genetic cause is generally thought of here. The complexity of food regulation in the human being is so considerable, however, that research will have to be extended. In the case of anorexia you can speak of a too finely tuned body; in the case of obesity, of a body that is not tuned finely enough.

The hereditary condition muscular dystrophy is located on the x-chromosome. Women are carriers of this condition, but when a women has this chromosome with the gene for muscular dystrophy, this is corrected by the second x-chromosome. When a boy receives an x-chromosome from his mother, this cannot be corrected, because he received a y-chromosome from his father as counterpart. This disorder is fatal, but girls can be a carrier and not become ill, while when boys receive the genetic material they will contract the disorder and, after some time, die from it.

which are mainly predispositional. From the starting point of the development of a male child as a branching off of the basic female form, this may not be so surprising. A development which can take its own course possibly runs a smaller risk than a development that is branched off to start a different growth. In addition, the combination xy is more vulnerable than the female component xx. When a certain condition is attached to the x-chromosome, this can, with a woman, be corrected by the complementary x-chromosome. Should the pair consist of an x and a y-chromosome, which is the case with men, then this correction is not possible.

In addition to psychological disorders, testosterone also has consequences for physical conditions. The large production of testosterone during the development into a male has as a consequence that the development of the immune system is inhibited, causing, as we will see in the next chapter, men in general to have a weaker immune system than women and to be more susceptible to various diseases (Zlotnik 1993).

Boys can therefore be regarded as the vulnerable sex, even though in physical competition they are the stronger (Delfos 1996a). At any age, even in the womb, the boy runs more risk of dying than the girl or the woman. He has a slower development and has more chances of diseases and psychological disorders. The chance that a boy may need special education is many times greater than for a girl.

The development inside the womb also depends largely on hormones. Maccoby and Jacklin (1980) have already observed that intelligence is related to the amount of hormones, notably testosterone, in the blood of the newly born, and also that this amount decreases with a second child, especially when children succeed each other quickly. A few months after birth the level of testosterone goes down to about one fifth of what it was at birth (Donovan 1985). This finding supports the idea that has been researched repeatedly, notably that firstborns and only children, on average, have a higher degree of intelligence. Research by, among others, Tan and his assistants (1990a, 1990b, 1990c, 1991; Tan, Akgun and Telatar 1990) into the influence of testosterone on IQ shows that this hormone plays an important part here. Non-verbal intelligence, such as spatial perception, seems to correlate positively with the level of testosterone. That means to say that the higher the level of testosterone, the higher the non-verbal intelligence. Recent research into the influence of hormones on thinking and emotions shows that administering testosterone ensures an improvement of the spatial perception in addition to more aggression and more sexual feelings (Slabbekoorn 1999). The hormone testosterone is related to the production of the growth hormone, and research by van der Reijden-Lakeman (1996) shows that with children who lagged behind in growth the administering of the growth hormone resulted in an increase in intelligence, especially with spatial perception. We will see in the next chapter that testosterone has a restraining effect on the development of the left hemisphere of the brain, which is strongly verbally oriented. Non-verbal intelligence is mainly associated with the right hemisphere. Administering testosterone will therefore not cause an increase in verbal intelligence because it restrains the development of the left, verbal, hemisphere.

Kaplan (1990) indicates that the degree of stress experienced by a pregnant woman, and the amount of testosterone and stress hormones – especially adrenocorticotrophic hormone (ACTH), adrenlaline, noradrenlaline and cortisol – which she produces on the basis of this stress, determines the level of testosterone in the blood of the foetus. He states that the environment inside the womb is of overriding importance for the development of the child's sexual inclination. The level of testosterone could, according to him and other researchers, have as a consequence that a homosexual tendency could actually be expressed. Williams *et al.* (2000) discovered that with lesbian women the right ring finger is larger than the right index finger; this could be attributed to the influence of testosterone during growth in the womb. With male homosexuals it was also proved that the ring finger–index finger proportion deviated from that of heterosexual men.

Testosterone does not only affect the intelligence but also the child's emotional structure. The research by Slabbekoorn (1999) shows that the intensity of emotions decreases under the influence of the administration of testosterone, but that it increases under the influence of anti-androgens and the ('female') hormone oestrogen.

Research into hormonal influence inside the womb will probably provide more and more facts in the years to come. Research is being carried out by, among others, Buitelaar and his research group at the University of Nijmegen about the influence of the hormonal environment inside the womb on the child's behaviour, where especially testosterone and the stress hormone cortisol will be researched. The first results show that women produce hormones under the influence of stress, hormones that show up in the blood of the foetus. As a consequence the risk of behavioural problems increases (Delfos 1997, 2003; Huizink, De Medina, Mulder, Visser and Buitelaar 2002; Buitelaar, Huizink, Mulder, De Medina and Visser 2003; de Weerth, Van Hees and Buitelaar 2003; Huizink, Mulder and Buitelaar 2004). Paarlberg (1999) discovered that chronic stress in the first three months of pregnancy gives a greater risk of a baby whose weight at birth is too low. Research by van Os and Selten (1998) showed that the stress that pregnant women had experienced during the invasion of their country by the German army caused the children to have more chance of schizophrenia, especially when the stress occurred during the first trimester of the pregnancy, and for male embryos also during the second trimester.

In addition to the idea of predisposition formed by genes and the environment inside the womb, one may wonder to what extent learned behaviour through generations is part of predisposition. Jung (1999) states that these are stored in the *collective memory* as *archetypes*. Dawkins (1989) speaks in that case of *memes*, units that are passed on culturally; this is in contrast with *genes*, which are passed on physically.

The predisposition indicates the margins within which a child can develop itself. When we look at the development of the child and the problems that may occur, we will have to take that predisposition into consideration.

Respect for a child also means respect for the limits which the child's predisposition sets.

Environment

The second factor in the child's development is the environment; this includes a number of more or less *structural* influences, such as:

- The reaction of the environment to the *nature and the predisposition of the child*: it makes a difference whether a child is born a boy or a girl and it makes a difference whether a child is of white or non-white origin.

- The *nature and predisposition of the parents*: for the child's development it makes a difference whether it grows up with a psychiatrically disturbed parent or in a 'normal' family; teenage parents are less stable childrearers, especially during their child's puberty, than middle-aged parents.

- The *childrearing*: it makes quite a difference for the physical and mental development of a child if the child is being abused or neglected. Another example is the *childrearing technique*: a democratic style of childrearing has more chance of being successful in western countries.

- The *education*: teaching people how to read and write makes a difference to the way in which they experience the world; this is seen in the fact that emancipation of minority groups by means of education has far-reaching effects on their social functioning.

- The *socio-economic environment*: growing up in a deprived neighbourhood influences the development of the child's opportunities; growing up in an area where there is hunger carries risks that hardly exist in prosperous countries.

- The *cultural and religious group*: growing up as a Muslim differs from growing up as an atheist; growing up as a member of a minority group in a country has far-reaching effects, for example, on the development of one's own identity.

- The *historic-geographic circumstances*: it makes a difference whether the child grows up in the western world or in the Third World, in a war zone or in an area where there is peace.

> According to Willems (1998) we are still far from being a child-friendly society in the Netherlands; for example, in his thesis *Who Will Educate the Educators?* he states: 'Our attitude and efforts with respect to the most defenceless in our midst — tens of thousands of maltreated children, and especially the youngest of them who are physically abused, neglected and sexually abused by both parents ... — are still far from what can be expected from a *decent society*.' (p.1008)

In addition to structural environmental factors there are also *incidental* life events such as the birth of a little brother or sister; a removal; divorce of the parents; death of parents, brother or sister; disease or traumatic events.

For its development the child is largely dependent on his or her environment, especially when it is young. A child has rights, just like adults. Nevertheless the rights of the child have only been in existence for the last ten years or so. They were adopted unanimously by the General Meeting of the United Nations in New York on 20 November 1989. The *Convention on the Rights of the Child* has been ratified by almost all countries in the world, except Somalia and the United States of America, who have however signalled their intention to ratify by formally signing the Convention. The Convention contains 54 articles. The rights of the child include, among other things, the *right to care* (right to adequate nutritious food, right to education, right to health, right to engage in play); the *right to protection* (no child abuse, no war or violence, no sexual abuse); the *right to an own opinion* (right to express one's own opinion, right to own religion, right to own choice of friends, right to necessary information); the *right to extra care* (in the case of a mental or physical handicap, in the case of lack of family, when having fled from one's home, when having come into contact with the police and justice system).

The most important environmental factor is formed by the direct childrearers of the child. In his book *Who Will Educate the Educators?* Willems (1998) quotes the 'Ten prohibitions', the 'ten things you will never say to a child', which were published by Schaefer in *Psychological Reports* in 1997. They give a fair image of the way in which the child's childrearing can damage the way it *develops as a person*:

> Prohibition 1: Thou shalt not reject your child by saying, 'Nobody will be able to love you.'

> Prohibition 2: Thou shalt not denigrate your child by saying, 'You are so stupid!'

> Prohibition 3: Thou shalt not drive your child to perfectionism by saying, 'How come you only came second?'

> Prohibition 4: Thou shalt not curse your child by saying, 'You'll never get anywhere!'

> Prohibition 5: Thou shalt not negatively compare your child by saying, 'Why are you not more like your brother?'

> Prohibition 6: Thou shalt not make your child a scapegoat by saying, 'It is your fault that we are getting a divorce.'

> Prohibition 7: Thou shalt not embarrass your child by saying, 'Look how childishly John is acting.'

> Prohibition 8: Thou shalt not call your child names, 'Shithead! Cow! Asshole! Whore!'

> Prohibition 9: Thou shalt not physically threaten your child by saying, 'I'll beat you to a pulp!'

> Prohibition 10: Thou shalt not emotionally blackmail your child (make him feel guilty) by saying, 'How can you do that, after all I've done for you?'

Maturation

The third factor in the development of human beings is the maturation of the central nervous system (CNS). This is influenced by both other factors, predisposition and environment. The maturation of the CNS takes place during an important period after birth. The brain consists of the 'old' brain – the brainstem (cerebellum) – and the 'new' brain – the cerebral cortex. The 'old' brain is mature at birth. The baby initially functions mainly through this brain and the accompanying innate reflexes, such as the grab and suck reflex. It is mainly the cerebral cortex, the 'young' brain with its typical human functions, that has to develop further. *Maturation* is understood to mean the process of further maturation and further forming of the central nervous system. The brain and nerve tracts increase in size and mature into the functions they have to fulfil. Fischer and Rose (1994) show that the size of the child's head, which increases steadily from birth, increases to an extra degree during certain periods. These periods correspond to the periods of the jerky growth of the brain, as was observed by, among others, Plooij (1990, 1994) and van de Rijt and Plooij (1992, 1993). The growth of the brain does not concern so much the number of cells – it mainly concerns the forming of connections between cells. Cells die in order to make room for new connections.

> For a long time it was suspected that the left and right hemispheres of autistic people would differ strongly. The expectation was that the left hemisphere would be significantly less developed than the right hemisphere. Post-mortem research did not prove a clear difference in the size or weight of the hemispheres. With the new measuring techniques such as *MRI* (*Magnetic Resonance Imaging*), *PET-scan* (*Positron Emission Tomography*) and *MEG* (*Magneto-Electroencephalography*) it is now possible to map live brains. It is proven that the two hemispheres with autistic people differ significantly. The left hemisphere contains more cells than the right hemisphere, but significantly fewer connections compared to the right hemisphere. The left hemisphere is substantially underdeveloped, unmatured (Bauman 1996; Bauman and Kemper 1994).

The development of these connections continues for about 25 to 30 years after birth, while the number of brain cells in the same period is already decreasing (Gesell 1965; Tanner 1978; Virgilio 1986). New connections can be formed during the whole life, but the forming of the typical human functions will be completed after approximately 20 to 30 years. The increase of connections between cells takes place by means of forming branched extensions – *dendrite* – and *synaptic connections* giving rise to the functions of the brain cells, such as for example the language function. In order to make connections *neurotransmitters* are needed; these are the messenger substances of the brain, like *hormones* are for the rest of the body. Well-known neurotransmitters are dopamine, (nor)epinephrine, serotonin and acetylcholine. Important hormones are, for example, testosterone, progesterone, oestrogen, insulin and adrenlaline. Research like that of Timiras, Hudson and Segall (1984) show how important a good maturation is for the CNS. Undernourishment or unsuitable food can have consequences for the development of neurotransmitters and form a lifelong problem.

The integration and co-ordination of the brain increases after birth because of maturation including, among other things, the growth of the *corpus callosum*, the connection system inside the brain, which also connects both hemispheres. During maturation the nerve tracts that connect the brain with the rest of the body become thicker and therefore better insulated. In this way information can be passed on more purely, without interference and influence by other information. An example of the development of the brain is the spectacular growth of the corpus callosum after birth.

Ramaekers and Njiokiktjien (1991) indicate that between birth and the age of one year, the posterior part of the corpus callosum (the *splenium*) increases by 42 per cent, and again by 110 per cent between the years one and 28.

Van de Rijt and Plooij (1992) researched the growth of the brain after birth. This growth, which according to them happens in ten leaps during this first year and a half, leads to *development transitions*: sudden qualitative changes in skills and in the way in which the child experiences the world. Research by Plooij and van de Rijt has been criticised (van der Maas *et al.* 1998). The existence of brain leaps is not under discussion, but the question of whether there were more than the already known four steps is. The assumption that it would concern fixed periods in time was also criticised. Flexibility in growth and development is contrary to fixed periods.

The body in fact has two important 'telephone exchanges': the *corpus callosum* with the *hippocampus* for connections inside the brain; the *nerve tracts* for connections from and to the brain. The 'messenger substances' in the brain are the *neurotransmitters* that transfer messages which in the rest of the body is done by *hormones*. Some hormones can also function as neurotransmitters.

Various parts of the brain get their specific functions during the maturation. The growth of the brain can cause crying periods with the baby, due to uncertainty, and probably also the pain which may be involved. Children probably experience pain more strongly than adults. The body produces *endorphins* when there is pain, the body's own painkiller. As a result of the still inadequate development of the brain, the production of these endorphins in young children is probably limited and this may cause the experience of pain to be stronger.

The various parts of the brain develop into their specific functions during maturation. The brain starts to *lateralise*, that is to say to fulfil specific functions in its left and right sides. The right hemisphere will, in general, develop more strongly with boys and the left hemisphere more with girls compared to boys. This means that the difference between the two hemispheres is generally larger in boys than in girls. In the right hemisphere there are, among other things, the functions of spatial perception and abstraction, in the left hemisphere the functions of consciousness and language orientation. Because the language centres with girls are often localised in both hemispheres, there is a greater language availability with them. We will see later that the difference in language orientation plays a part with the form that conduct disorder takes with boys and with girls.

Apart from the normal maturation that progresses during the development of the brain, it is also possible that there is a *further maturation*. Recent research shows that the making of connections is a constant activity of the brain. The extent of this, and the speed with which it takes place during the first years, is significantly higher than later on. There are also functions which are formed during the early years and later cannot develop at all or otherwise cannot develop to a level as fluently as in the early years, such as the language function. Martens (1997) researched the process of further maturation with psychopaths. This process takes place between the ages of 30 and 35, according to Martens. Psychopaths show an immaturity of the brain, among other things, an increased theta-activity, that is to say slow brain waves, and a too low level of irritability (I will discuss this in more detail in Chapter 4). Martens prefers to speak of 'further maturation' instead of 'cure' in the case of psychopaths, because there has to be a neurological cause at the basis of the completely changed functioning of psychopaths who are 'cured'. He did not examine neurological elements such as the theta-activity. Future research will have to examine this further.

The night presumably plays an important role in the maturation of the brain. During the first years, but especially in the first year, a lot of sleeping time is *REM*-sleep, the *dream sleep*. The REM-sleep, named after the rapid eye movements behind the closed lids, is the state of sleep when one dreams. The younger the child, the more sleeping time is spent on dreaming. With *premature babies* this mounts up to 80 per cent of sleeping time. Modern theories about the dream sleep assume that the sleep is necessary to 'sweep' the brain 'clean', to untangle useless connections formed during the day (Stickgold *et al.* 2000). The dream sleep, REM-sleep, is therefore of essential importance for the functioning of the brain. The dream sleep is also necessary for the working of the memory. Sleep consists of a cycle of various stages – settling stage, deep sleep, REM-sleep, sleeping-through stage – which is repeated several times during the night. It is especially the REM-sleep during the fourth time that the cycle is run in one night which ensures that the short-term memory is 'cleaned up' and elements are transferred to the long-term memory (Stickgold *et al.* 2000). For the working of the long-term memory a long sleep where at least four sleeping cycles are gone through is therefore of great importance.

In view of the amount of dream sleep which the young child goes through, and the increase thereof in the case of *prematurity*, it is possible that dream sleep plays an important part in the maturation of the CNS. In that line of thinking it is therefore not surprising that many of the disorders in the maturation of the CNS (for example *pavor nocturnes – night terror, sleep walking, bedwetting* and *stereotypical movements* like head banging and rocking) occur during the night. The best remedy for an optimal maturation is probably getting through the night well and safe, having a good night's sleep. The environment can work by stimulating or restricting in that sense, enabling the child to sleep and dream optimally.

Maturation disorders

As shown above, the maturation of the CNS is of great importance for the child's development. The maturation of boys, in general, goes more slowly than that of girls (Rutter and Rutter 1993). In research by van Os and Selten (1998), which I mentioned before, concerning the chance of schizophrenia due to stress experienced by women during pregnancy, they indicate that the longer risk period for the male foetus has to do with his slower maturation. A lot of the problems we see in professional help for children are related to a deviant, disturbed or problematic maturation, which is not always expressed in exterior characteristics. Disorders in the maturation can be innocent, but have serious consequences. ADHD is an example of an overall disorder of the maturation of the central nervous system, and this disorder is often accompanied by lighter disturbances of that maturation.

When we examine the DSM-IV (American Psychiatric Association 1994) for the description of the cause of disorders, we see that with various diagnoses the maturation of the CNS is indicated as the cause. They can be classified under a common name: *maturation disorders* (Delfos 1996b). Table 2.1 states the disorders where the DSM-IV explicitly mentions a disorder of the maturation of the central nervous system.

Table 2.1 Maturation disorders
Primary enuresis (bedwetting)
Primary encopresis (soiling)
Restless legs
Involuntary muscle spasms
Tics
Dyspraxia (movement co-ordination disorder)
Teeth grinding
Sleep talking
Stuttering
Sleep walking
Sleeping with eyes open
Pavor nocturnes (night terror)
Stereotypical movements: head banging, rocking
Language development disorder

In addition to the explicitly mentioned disorders various conditions can be founded on a maturation problem – for example, the learning disorders *dyslexia* and *dysgraphia*. These disorders also occur often with children with ADHD, in addition to the symptoms described specifically with this maturation disorder, such as hyperactivity, impulsiveness and concentration disorder. With important disorders such as *autism* and schizophrenia a deviant maturation is thought of, in the sense of a limited maturation.

Interaction between predisposition and environment

The way in which a child can cope with his or her predisposition depends on the circumstances in which the child grows up. The way in which a child copes with the environment also depends on his or her predisposition. Also the way that people, who are part of that environment, treat the child plays a part. Then again the way people in the child's environment treat the child depends on their own predisposition and the circumstances of their own environment. There is a continuous interaction. An optimal environment means that the child gets enough food, care, safety, stimulation and space for *autonomy* (independence).

For centuries there has been discussion about the question of how important the part that predisposition or maturation plays on the one hand and the influence of the environment on the other. Answering this question is made more difficult by the fact that they are not static influences, but that it is a matter of a continuous interaction. The degree to which the predisposition is actualised depends on the environment. A child with a language disorder will in general be more bothered by his or her predisposition when it grows up in a language-poor environment. Such an environment gives little linguistic behaviour, asks little linguistic behaviour from the child and will stimulate the child less, causing the child to fall behind with regard to other children. With respect to problems in language development the conclusion of Felsenfeld (1994) is, from the extensive adoption research carried out in the state of Colorado in the USA, that the cause of the problems should mainly be looked for in the predisposition, and more precisely in genetic factors. Plomin (1994) makes clear that predisposition and environment closely interact. The influence of the environment can also be noticed at the level of the genes. A factor such as the way in which the childrearing by parents is experienced by a child proves to be directed by genes. Environment is not unrelated to predisposition. Environment influences the way in which the genetic material can express itself and the predisposition is an important factor that influences the environment. I recall Sandra Scarr (Scarr and McCartney 1993) who states that a child, proceeding from his or her predisposition, forms the environment.

Dunn and Plomin (1990) make clear that within the environment there are factors that play a part and that are not shared by the various children in a family – for example, the place in the family, an

A 'cry-baby' is hard to comfort and cries day and night. His parents will be exhausted after some time, no matter how happy they are with the small child. The baby will hardly see friendly, smiling faces around it and will only receive highly necessary attention. The peacefully sleeping child will usually find friendly smiling parents in the morning. The 'cry-baby' creates a difficult environment, the quiet baby a pleasant one.

illness with the child, their own friends – and which in addition to the genetic influences can have a significant influence on the differences which may arise between children. For example, within the same socio-economic situation a mother still treats her children very differently. There are for example large differences in the way that a boy or a girl is raised, or the first child and the late arrival.

In the environment there are shared and non-shared factors which influence the arising or not of differences between children from the same family.

No matter how difficult it is, I have already stated that an attempt to determine the influence of predisposition and environment is of essential importance for professional help. When the predisposition is the most important factor, then professional help should be aimed at teaching the child and his or her parents, and further environment, to cope with the predisposition. When the environment is the most important factor, professional help will be able to treat the influence of the environment or the consequences thereof.

Barbara Lloyd researched the effect of gender on the childrearing by parents. She discovered that girls are touched more often, are cuddled more often and treated more gently than boys. Her idea is that the gender differences are mainly formed by the difference in approach by parents to their male or female child (Duveen and Lloyd 1986).

The interaction between environment and predisposition can also be found in the continuous adjustment (*adaptation*) of the body to the environment. The inner household is not detached from the external environment. We can see that in the case of danger. Danger gets the body ready to experience a number of changes and that conjures up the emotion *fear*. The body is brought into a state of readiness, with the help of adrenergic hormones such as adrenlaline. This makes it possible to develop intense activity. I will discuss this in more detail in the next chapter.

No matter how difficult, with psychological problems it is of great importance to research whether it is a matter of problems controlled by predisposition – we call this a *disorder* – or of problems controlled by the environment, of which we say that it is a matter of an *impediment* that causes a *problem*.

Disorder versus impediment

A *disorder* finds its origin particularly from inside the body and directly influences the development functions. This influence can be exercised on one function in particular, when it concerns a limited disorder (for example, late toilet-training); or on the whole of co-operating functions, when it concerns an important disorder (for example, autism). I mean here 'psychological' or development functions, so for example 'reading' and not a physical function like 'seeing'. Handicaps are therefore excluded. In the case of a *handicap* it is a physical function that is disturbed, like walking or hearing. The boundaries are, however, not sharply defined. We speak, for example, of a mental handicap, when the child's predisposition causes a deviation in his or her complete cognitive functioning.

In the case of a disorder there is a direct relation between the cause and the effects. The chaotic functioning of a child with ADHD is, for example, directly related to the disorder, it is a characteristic thereof. In an optimal environment the child with a disorder will still show deviation from the normal development.

An *impediment* finds its origin mainly from the outside, not from the body itself, and does not affect the whole of the co-operating functions. It does not change the course of the development, but makes it run less smoothly. The natural development is, temporarily, taken off track. In the case of an impediment one could say that the effect on the behaviour and the possibilities are a by-product of the cause. There is no direct link between both. The result is not solely and directly determined by the cause. Various effects can result with regard to the cause. When a child starts wetting or soiling itself again after the birth of a little sister, then this is not *directly* related to experiencing this event; *indirectly* it may be caused by it. A different reaction than wetting or soiling itself again can take place, for example aggression or anxiety. A *psycho trauma* is an example of an impediment. Due to a traumatic event a child can lose newly acquired skills for a short time. This skill is not lost irrevocably, but the natural development thereof is temporarily hindered; there is a 'stoppage' and a delayed development.

An impediment can also come from within. This is the case with a disease or a condition, for example childhood illnesses. The condition does not affect the development of the functions themselves, but hinders their natural course, unless we are dealing with brain damage as a result of a condition. This can, for example, be the case with meningitis or with serious forms of epilepsy.

Making this distinction is of fundamental importance for providing professional help. A help strategy is only really effective if it takes the source of the behaviour into account. With a disorder the degree in which influence from outside is possible is limited, excluding medication and medical interventions. If one adopts an attitude in that case as if the behaviour is under control and is displayed on purpose, the help strategy will not prove to be effective. In the case of a disorder the help will only prove to be effective if it starts taking the disorder and its specific characteristics as a starting point. The change has to come from within, to be built up starting from the possibilities that are already there. In that case the functioning can sometimes be surmounted in such a way that the disorder hardly plays a part any more. In the case of an impediment the possibility of external influence is bigger. An impediment can lead to a disturbed development, but not to a disorder.

In the case of an impediment it is not the potentials, the possibilities, that are affected, but the realisation of them. In order to make this difference clear, the terminology that Vygotsky (1896–1934) developed is of good use. He called the

The possibilities of children with autism and from the autism spectrum to make contact are restricted by various factors. The most important one is their limited ability to interpret social interaction, proceeding from an insufficiently developed empathy. A second factor is that these children are preoccupied with the programmes they form in their own mind and which conjure up fear when they are not executed. A third factor with some children is the sharp sensory sensitivity, causing them to be hardly able to bear physical contact. With them there is a clear difference between wanting contact and enduring contact (Delfos 2004a).

entity of potentials, of possibilities of the child which are present without being able to be carried out independently, the *zone of proximal development*; the possibilities which the child can carry out independently, he calls the *zone of actual development*. In Vygotsky's (1978) terms this means, in the case of a disorder, that the zone of proximal development has been affected, namely the possibilities that are potentially present. In the case of an impediment it is the zone of actual development that is affected, namely the degree to which the potential is actually developed.

An example of an impediment is *attachment disorder*, where the possibility to attach is potentially present in the zone of proximal development, but cannot be realised due to the way of the child's growing up. In the DSM-IV (American Psychiatric Association 1994) these problems are called *reactive*: reacting to the environment. When the possibility to attach is potentially insufficiently present in the zone of proximal development due to a disorder, like with a *contact disorder* where there is an insufficient possibility to make contact, no real attachment will be developed even under optimal circumstances. In the case of a reactive attachment disruption it is possible to restore the attachment.

The characteristics of disorder versus impediment are put together in Table 2.2.

Table 2.2 Disorders and impediments: characteristics	
Disorder	*Impediment*
Most important source: predisposition and maturation	Most important source: environment
Direct relation between cause and effect	No direct relation between cause and effect
Influence on development functions and/or their co-operation	Influence on pace of development
Development can become abnormal	Development can be delayed
Affects the zone of proximal development	Affects the zone of actual development

When we look at psychiatric disorders, and by that I mean the problems controlled by predisposition, as a whole, then there often prove to be two elements, which form two common threads, as it were, right through all disorders. These are *resistance against change* and a *problematic empathic capacity* (Delfos 1996b). They cause a more ego-focused activity, an egocentric thinking. We can see that, for example, to an extreme extent with the *pervasive* development disorders, disorders of the general functioning, which continue from childhood into adulthood, such as *autism.*

The resistance against change is related, among other things, to the size of the corpus callosum and the differences in hemispheres. On average, a child with a smaller corpus callosum has difficulty in processing new stimuli and has trouble with changes that are offered or asked. The child with ADHD has, for example, the tendency to go into every new stimulus and to let go of the stimulus with which it was occupied, even though it is more attractive. The autistic child resists a change with regard to his internal plan, even when this would be a change for the better. Because of the difference in hemispheres, the left–right co-ordination can be more laborious and result in a *non-fluent motor system*, often a bit wooden. This fact can be used for the early observation of disorders. A non-fluent motor system can form an indication for predispositional problems (Hadders-Algra *et al.* 1997). The resistance against change can be translated into the physical sign of a *non-fluent motor system*.

The second thread with disorders forms the problematic empathic capacity. This is, among other things, related to the development of the left hemisphere and the ability to put oneself in someone else's place. In the next chapter I will describe the development of this in more detail. We will see this element again in the social sphere, in the difficulty with the association with peers. We can see this in an extreme form with the autistic child, who has a lot of difficulties in dealing with other people, to such an extent that we speak of a *contact disorder.* The second thread can therefore be translated into the psychological sign of *difficulty with contact with peers.*

For a while it was fashionable to use a diet against *colouring agents allergy* for the treatment of ADHD. The idea behind it was that the disorder ADHD could be caused by an allergy to colouring agents in certain foods. When children would take food without colouring agents, the ADHD, notably the hyperactivity, would disappear. This proved to be the case in the short term. Further research showed, however, that this also applies to other interventions and that also giving focused attention, diet or childrearing support is effective in controlling the hyperactivity, but does not lead to automised behaviour, so that the behaviour recurs after some time.

Food for the brain

In order to be able to grow and mature, food is necessary. Research shows that there is an interaction between mental functioning and nutrients. It was once thought that food only determined our physical health; now research shows us more and more that food is related to mental health. New research techniques teach us more precisely how that works. At the same time, however, there is a tendency to exaggerate the importance of this. In the coming years research will provide more information about the extent to which food can be used to fight and prevent illnesses, and following on from that to what extent it influences our psychological functioning.

An example of substances which are produced by the body itself is anabolic steroids. These are synthetic forms of testosterone, the sex hormone that is produced by the body. The fact that the use of anabolic steroids can lead to aggression explosions is therefore not surprising, because the amount of aggression is connected to the level of testosterone, as we will see in the next chapter.

For a long time we have known the solution of the use of medication for psychological disorders, the *psychopharmacology*. These are, however, nothing else but substances produced by human beings, which are developed by researching what happens in a human body and how substances from the outside could affect that. These could be substances which are a chemical translation of the substances made in the body, like anabolic steroids, the chemical form of testosterone. These could also be substances that link up to body-own substances with the intention of provoking a reaction or stopping the working of certain body-own substances.

The human being can influence his feelings by using his mind, and vice versa. There is a continuous interaction between thinking and feeling, which is possible through the production of substances in the body. A peaceful thought can be the signal for the body to 'produce' a 'sedative', like the substance *endorphin*, the body-own painkiller. A restless thought, like an anxious thought, starts 'arousal' and stimulates the production of a 'restless substance' such as the substance *adrenlaline*.

Research like that of Schagen van Leeuwen (1991) proves that the body in the case of pain and illness starts to produce endorphins after taking a *placebo*, a substance without chemical active ingredients. These endorphins are the substances which are formed by the body itself in order to fight pain, for example. For a long time it was not known how it was possible that taking a placebo could work in a curing manner; now we know that taking a pill apparently conjures up a *cognition*, a thought, causing a psychological sign to be given. In a manner of speaking: 'I take a pill, so I am really ill; something has to be done.' The body subsequently starts to produce active substances. The cure by means of a placebo is therefore not imagination; the thinking promotes the production of substances needed to fight the disease. Some people have a lower threshold for producing these necessary substances, but the placebo will be still be effective for them.

Medication can work in three cases: deficiency in producing certain substances (for example adding painkillers), lack of substances (like adding insulin with diabetes) or with an over-production of substances (like helping to break down substances in case of a depression).

Food influences the mental state and vice versa. A *psychosis*, where the experience of reality is disturbed, is in general preceded by long nights of waking and bad eating. During a psychotic period you see some people try to 'eat away the psychosis' and take large quantities of sugar or fat. Proceeding from the 'wisdom of the body' these people try to fight a problem that takes place in the body. By eating sugar or fat they try to add substances that are insufficiently present in the body to fight the psychosis, or, to put it differently, to fight the substances that the body produces by the upcoming psychosis.

Human development is influenced by many factors. Behaviour is influenced by the same amount of factors. The brain is the fundamental organ from where behaviour is directed. A deviation from the normal functioning of the brain can therefore have important consequences. The brain can deviate due to hereditary predisposition or be damaged during birth by an accident or because of certain illnesses. What are the differences between a deviation or damage of the brain and a disorder of the maturation of the brain?

Visible versus non-visible

Disrupted development on the basis of predisposition has usually something to do with a disruption in the functioning of the central nervous system in general and the brain in particular. The brain has to be mature, and more or less intact, in order to make normal functioning possible. From the brain there are various circumstances that can adversely influence the growth and development of the child: a *deviation*, *damage*, or a *disturbed maturation* of the brain.

In addition to directing and co-ordinating, keeping the level of consciousness is an important task of the brain. When large fluctuations arise here, one can end up with delusions. This can, among other things, be caused by contagious diseases, like meningitis or high fever. But smaller fluctuations can also have important consequences, as we will see with conduct disorders.

We tend to make a distinction between people 'with whom something is wrong, physically', and then this should actually be visible, and people 'with whom nothing is wrong', because nothing is visible, physically. When something is not visible, people tend to forget or deny that something is wrong. We easily forget, for example, that someone has a headache. Recognition of a non-visible disorder is often a big problem. We could say that a child with a non-visible disorder is doubly burdened – first, by the disorder itself and, second, by the fact that the child will be approached as if it does not have a disorder. When a disorder is not expressed by external characteristics, the behaviour will quickly be blamed on the childrearing or the environment; as though a physical influence would restrict itself to visible characteristics. Brain damage or deviations are usually visible in the external characteristics; to disorders like ADHD or conduct disorder this does not apply. The diagnosis is therefore often more difficult to make.

Differences in visibility have consequences for the way in which a child is approached. In order to clarify this, I have placed a number of differences and similarities between a deviation of the brain and a maturation disorder in Table 2.3.

Table 2.3 Differences and similarities between an important deviation of the brain and a maturation disorder	
Important brain deviation: Down's syndrome	*Important maturation disorder: ADHD*
Deviant appearance, deviant functioning	Normal appearance, normal functioning
Structural problem: for life	Can possibly, with a lot of effort, be restricted
Behaviour that cannot be directly confused with childrearing problems, for example tongue hanging out of the mouth	Behaviour that can be directly confused with childrearing problems, for example not responding when being talked to
Recognised as being difficult to raise, a heavy burden	Not immediately recognised as being difficult to raise; more likely interpreted as badly brought up
Often various visible handicaps	Often various non-visible handicaps

I have chosen a distinct comparison in order to make the essential points clear. I use an important deviation, *Down's syndrome*, and an important maturation disorder, *ADHD*. The hyperactive and impulsive child will often be seen as a badly brought up child. Down's syndrome will, however, never be attributed to bad childrearing.

The environment will respond differently to a child with a visible disorder that is expressed in physical characteristics than to a child with a non-visible disorder. The same goes for parents. When the diagnosis has not been made, parents will often desperately try to direct the child. As a result the negative interactions between parents and child increase. Parents often cry out desperately, 'We tried everything, nothing helps.'

The extent to which the environment can adjust to the predisposition also depends on the insight into the predisposition. Adjusting to problems is initially aimed at the directly visible and recognisable. With a *spastic* child the predisposition is expressed from the start, and the environment will be inclined to help the child with all daily activities. A predisposition for explosive aggression is not expressed in visible elements, and proceeding from that the environment will be less inclined to help the child and can hardly anticipate the behaviour. On the contrary, the child is more likely to receive punishment than help.

In our usual way of childrearing it is expected that a child, when it is ready for something, quickly masters a certain skill with our help. We stimulate the child, show it a few times and the child quickly performs the skill independently. Without knowing it, we have a kind of 'statistic' in our head on the basis of which we assess the behaviour of, for example, children. Part of these 'statistics' are probably

Stuttering is a problem of the maturation of the central nervous system. It is supposed to have something to do with the fact that the co-ordination of the muscles that control the vocal cords is too slow (Peters and Guitar 1991). The production of a sentence comes to a halt, even though the sentence has already been formulated correctly in the brain. Slowing down of the behaviour, like taking care of even breathing or talking slowly, slows down the process and contributes to the prevention or corrects the stuttering. When the maturation has been completed, the stuttering often continues, because by now it has become a habit for years on end and the child has never been able to develop a normal pattern of communication. This has consequences for the socio-emotional development. After completion of the maturation, a training aimed at promoting self-confidence and correct language production can be effective in correcting the stuttering. Stutterers have to learn a completely new form of communication.

innate, instinctive. Another part is formed on the basis of what we learn during our lifetime. These 'statistics' are also the reason why parents already feel at an early stage that their child is deviant, that something is wrong with the child, long before specialists are able to make the diagnosis of an autistic disorder. The child with an autistic disorder, for example, does not comply with a number of the statistics we have in our head and especially not those regarding social contact, reciprocation in contact or feeling what goes on in someone else's mind (Delfos 2004a). We therefore, if we want to help a child with an autistic disorder, have to let go of these statistics. The child with an autistic disorder will master certain skills only later in life or not at all. In addition it will also take longer to learn these skills when it is ready to learn them. So it is not only that the learning process is *delayed*, in certain areas, it also goes *more slowly*. Moreover, the child often does not get the help which is appropriate for his or her mental age and as a result the development is even more of a struggle. The child will be offered subjects which belong to his or her calendar age, causing the development to run the risk of becoming strongly deviant and strange. If we do not anticipate that, the child's development will be less optimal than possible and the child will be more strongly deviant.

In order to understand what physical and psychological processes play a part with conduct difficulties, we first need insight into the differences between men and women. We will see that the way that a conduct difficulty manifests itself is to an important degree dependent on the child's sex.

Summary

There are three different sources that can play a part with the arising of development disruptions: predisposition, environment and the maturation of the central nervous system. The first contains hereditariness and factors that play a part during pregnancy and birth. Environment includes a number of structural factors, like parenting style, and incidental factors such as traumatic events. The maturation of the central nervous system is influenced by predisposition and environment. This maturation takes place in part before birth, but also to an important extent after that. On the basis of these three factors a disorder or an impediment of the development can arise. In the case of a disorder the most important source for the behaviour is the predisposition or the maturation of the central nervous system. In the case of an impediment it is the environment that causes a delayed development. This distinction is important for professional help. When we are dealing with a disorder, professional help should be aimed more at teaching the child and the parents how to live with the predisposition. In the case of an impediment professional help can try to take away the impediment, so that the development can be continued.

In order to develop, food is necessary, for body and mind. The latter two are in fact inseparable and physical disruptions have psychological effects.

A disorder is not always visible physically and is therefore often misunderstood. A physical influence, however, often extends further than the visible characteristics.

3

Differences between Men and Women

Before I explain further what I mean by conduct disorders, it is necessary to consider some of the differences between men and women. With conduct difficulties, in particular conduct disorders, these differences are expressed more strongly in the manner in which the problems manifest themselves with girls and with boys. The gender is an essential conditional factor that determines the child's development to an important extent.

In this chapter the differences between men and women in general will be discussed. There are a number of main lines. The human being is infinitely varied and such a chapter can therefore not be anything else but generalising. I do not speak of the individual woman or the individual man, but about the 'average man' and the 'average woman'. In order to gain insight it is necessary to generalise; only then can larger connections be exposed.

In this chapter I will discuss the biological basis of a number of differences between men and women. It is not popular within western culture to employ this view – people are quick to speak of *biological determinism*, the idea that the human being is determined by his or her biological constitution. People sometimes ignore what the human being in fact knows himself and sees around him, namely that biological make-up influences behaviour substantially. The result thereof is that we try to *emancipate against the biological stream*, instead of *with the biological stream*. In the first case we try to eliminate the differences between men and women; in the second case we try to become aware of those

When we speak of the differences between men and women we tend to settle biological differences with one subject. The difference in spatial perception by men and women is swept away by naming women we know who do have mathematical perception and then explaining the statistical abundance of men due to a lack of emancipation of the woman. When, however, we consider various characteristics and their relation, within one person, we will usually see that that mathematical woman is also strongly inclined to develop guilt feelings and tends to look after other people. That means that the characteristics in relation with each other give a more feminine image. Within the human being as a whole there usually exists a 'female' versus a 'male' image.

differences and to use these in order to reach equivalence.

For a long time we have been explaining the differences between men and women in terms of *socialisation*: the way in which men and women are raised and are taught which role they are supposed to play in society; in particular the man-role or the woman-role. Naturally socialisation is an important factor. It is, however, not the socialisation that causes the differences. There are important differences that are predispositional and that go further than only the visible ones.

> Autism is a disorder that to a large degree influences behaviour; men have almost all forms of this disorder significantly more often than women. It has has now been established that autism is related to a chromosomal anomaly. *Rett's syndrome*, however, is almost exclusively found in women. *Muscular dystrophy* is a disease that only occurs in men. These are some examples to show that on a physical as well as on a psychological level there exist fundamental differences between men and women.

Perhaps it is wiser to think that socialisation maybe wants to link up to basic structures. Because of socialisation, the differences between men and women can be more strongly wrongly emphasised and talents may be ignored, but the differences nevertheless are evidence of fundamental conditions. In that case women get too few possibilities to develop their talents, while men hardly get any room to develop care duties. The emancipation of man and woman taught us that many differences are indeed confirmed by socialisation, but we are starting to realise more and more, also thanks to scientific research, that there are basic differences. The value judgements linked to differences between men and women have, together with the structural physical power of men, ensured and still ensure that the woman is considered less important than the man in many areas. Galjaard (1994) reminds us of the strong statement by UNICEF within this context:

> As long as food and education of girls takes second place after that of boys, as long as women eat the least and work the hardest, as long as the demand for birth control is only met by the abortionist, as long as most babies come into this world without help, that long will bearing children result in the death of one young woman per minute. (p.346)

Man or woman, *xy* or *xx*?

The sex, determined by the *xx*- or *xy*-chromosome pair, the female and the male chromosome pair respectively, causes important differences in development. Although at first sight the differences in outward appearance between men and women are apparent, it is not always clear at birth which sex the child is. In some cases the doctors have to take a decision about whether the child is a boy or a girl – a decision that may prove to be the wrong one or the less suitable one. This example shows that even the physical development is not always unambiguous. The differences in the psychological field are generally not that apparent and often cause a battle of the sexes. It remains difficult to approach differences between men and women open-mindedly and without value judgements; equivalence and equality are often mixed up. Unfortunately inequality is often experienced as an attack on equivalence. The female xx and the male xy-chromosome pair, however, carry the genetic information, which activates a range of both physical and psychological differences between men and women, and socialisation links up to that, not always rightly so.

The differences between men and women are already activated at the first signal of the xy-chromosome pair, a few weeks after the conception. When a y-chromosome is present a signal is given, some five weeks after the conception, to produce testosterone and start the development of the embryo into a man. The testes with the male embryo are developed and provide a large production of the androgenic hormone testosterone. In addition, the mother herself produces testosterone which ends up in the womb, so that there is a double flow of testosterone with male embryos.

Within the framework of behaviour of men and women there are three important influences exercised by the xy-chromosome pair via an increased production of testosterone during the growth in the womb. These three influences belong to what is called the *Geschwind hypotheses* (Geschwind and Galaburda 1984, 1987, 1995):

- a restraining influence on the immune system

- the inhibition of the development of the left hemisphere

- the testosterone level of the human being after birth.

This influence is mainly exercised on the male embryo by his own production of testosterone in the testes. The amount of testosterone that is produced in the ovaries of the female embryo is significantly lower than the amount produced in the testes of the male embryo. The production of testosterone by the mother is significantly lower than that of the male foetus.

In this chapter I will discuss a number of these differences which occur because of the xx or xy-chromosome pair. I will pay attention especially to the *self-knowledge of the body*, the *orientation on linguistic functioning* and the *action-readiness of the human being*.

One of the first effects of the signal by the xy-chromosome pair and the increase of the production of testosterone is the inhibition of the development of the *thymus gland*. This gland is the first building block of the *immune system*. We will see that this has important consequences for the differences between men and women.

The biological self

The thymus gland forms the 'biological self', according to, among others, Hamilton and Timmons (1990). In every human being there is a biological self present, containing the information of what is biological 'me/self' and 'not-me/non-self': the 'self-knowledge' of the body (Damasio 1999). Examination of whether a substance in the body is 'self' or 'non-self' is initially carried out by the thymus gland. It is on this organ that the restraining influence of testosterone on the development of the embryo's immune system inside the womb is exercised, as shown by research by Frey-Wettstein and Cradock (1970). Hamilton and Timmons (1990) state, as an important aspect of the restrained development of the immune system, that the recognition of the self and non-self by the biological self functions less well. The function of the biological self means, among other things, that the body recognises substances which are natural, belonging to the own body, and actively examines strange substances and, if necessary, fights them by means of the immune system. As a result of a less well functioning recognition by the thymus gland, by the biological self, the organism knows insufficiently whether a certain substance has to be fought or not. This is the principle of the immune system: fighting substances that are harmful to the organism, such as germs.

It is from a biological self that the human being has an inner wisdom of the body at their disposal, from where he or she can fight shortcomings in this body. A dramatic example of inner wisdom is mentioned by Wilkins, Fleischman and Howard (1940) (see also Gray 1999):

> A small boy had a great need for salt and did everything to obtain salt. The child licked the salt off crackers. No matter how well the parents tried to hide the salt, the child climbed, looked for and ate all the salt he could find. At the age of three-and-a-half the child was admitted to hospital and put on a diet of normal salt consumption. After seven days he died. The post-mortem proved that the child had an abnormality causing him to take salt externally, otherwise he would die; the lack of salt in the hospital was the cause of death. He had managed to stay alive by taking extra salt until he was admitted into hospital. The little boy had kept himself alive through his inner wisdom and against the so-called wisdom of the people around him. He died as a result of the so-called 'wisdom' of the people around him.

Another striking example of the wisdom of the body, which has been translated culturally and religiously through many generations, is the manner in which the yam harvest is consumed in parts of Africa, as described by Hamilton and Timmons (1990 p.6, paraphrased):

> The yams are harvested at the start of the rainy season, but not eaten until a religious ceremony at the end of the rainy season. This strict religious rule is also adhered to in times of scarcity. Members of some of the African tribes

go hungry, while there are plenty of yams in the sheds. The yam apparently has an element that combats sickle cell anaemia. This in itself is very desirable, but not in the rainy season because sickle cell anaemia protects against malaria, which is active in the rainy season. It is therefore wise to eat yams to combat sickle cell anaemia, but not during the rainy season, so that the sickle cell anaemia can be active in the protection against malaria. The religious tradition proves to be a translation of a physical condition under climatological circumstances.

These are two examples to illustrate the unconscious knowledge that is encoded in the body. I can give many more examples; the human being functions mainly through unconscious knowledge, some instinctive or reflexive. If all processes took place at a conscious level, life would not be possible, conscious processes being far slower than unconscious processes, like instinctive reactions.

Because the effect of the restraining influence by means of testosterone will manifest itself most strongly with the male embryo, we can, from this perspective, state that the biological self of men in general is less developed than that of women. The immune system shows important differences between men and women in line with this biological self.

The immune system

As a result of restraining the development of this system inside the womb, men in general will have a weaker immune system than women (Gomez 1991). Because the biological self functions less well, it is less well distinguished with men whether a certain substance is naturally produced by their own body or not and whether it is harmful. This distinction is necessary in order to take action, either to fight or not fight the substance. Should a substance not be recognised as harmful then the necessary antibodies will not be produced. The harmful substance, for example a germ, is not fought or not sufficiently fought. The result is that men are more often bothered by all sorts of diseases, like infections, than women, from feverish convulsion and diabetes to hereditary diseases (Zlotnik 1993). Women, on the other hand, suffer more from psychosomatic illnesses. As mentioned, Gomez (1991) states that men generally have a weaker immune system. In their blood and other biological liquids they have less immunoglobulin, a protein that plays a part in the defence of the body against alien substances. The immune system of women, however, works too well, as it were – their immune system is stronger than is actually necessary. This causes an 'overreaction'.

The under and overreaction starts from a matured immune system. There exists, however, also what we could call an 'immature immune system', which deals insufficiently with normal things like food processing. Later we will see that here there are also differences between men and women in the sense that with boys,

In laboratories where research into the immune system is carried out, female rats are preferred for research into new antibodies. They generally have a strong immune system and therefore produce more antibodies (Aarden 1997).

who in many aspects have a slower maturation than girls, it is often a matter of an immature immune system.

There are three ways to distinguish how the immune system dysfunctions (see Table 3.1). The first is: being less effective in combating diseases (*underreaction*); this is more likely to be the case with men. The second form is: an immune system that reacts too strongly (*overreaction*), which is more likely to be the case with women. These are the autoimmune diseases and allergies. The third form is: *immaturity* of the immune system.

Table 3.1 The different disturbed relations of the immune system	
Reactions of the immune system	*Resulting dysfunction*
Underreaction	Less effective fighting of diseases
	Susceptibility to diseases
	Susceptibility to infections
Overreaction	Allergies
	Autoimmune diseases
Immaturity	Atopic syndrome

Acting on a signal that a germ is present, the immune system takes care that a large number of antibodies are produced. The stronger the immune system, the more antibodies will be produced. Among these produced substances there may be, by coincidence, a substance that forms an antibody against a body's own cells. The result is that this substance starts to 'attack' its own cells. This is the case with autoimmune diseases, such as *rheumatoid arthritis*. It is therefore not surprising that women who have a stronger working immune system than men suffer significantly more often from these diseases: up to ten times as often than men.

In the case of allergies the organism reacts extremely strongly to substances that are quite harmless, nickel for example. The immune system recognises it as not naturally produced by the body, but takes the action to combat the substance too quickly and too strongly. With allergies the picture of differences between men and women is a bit more complicated than with the autoimmune diseases. Women in general have more allergies than men. Up to about the age of 12, however, boys have a few more allergies than girls. This concerns especially a specific group of allergies, the *atopic syndrome*, where hereditary predisposition causes the production of a specific kind of substances. It is then not so much an underreaction or an overreaction of the immune system, but a hereditary predisposition regarding a certain production of substances. Children usually outgrow these allergies. It is therefore maybe better to speak of a 'not completely adjusted' immune system than of an under or overreaction, which are more structural during life.

Just like the body as a whole, the immune system also has to mature after birth. Gesell and Ilg (1949) for example indicate that contagious diseases generally are more dangerous before the age of five than after that, as a consequence of the immunological immaturity. Following from the general slower maturation of boys in relation to that of girls, it is to be expected that with boys the immune system matures more slowly than with girls. When we see the atopic syndrome as the expression of an immature immune system, we expect this immune problem more with boys than with girls. The atopic syndrome includes *Chronic Non-Specific Lung Disease* (CNSLD) including *asthma, food allergies* such as *cow milk allergy* and the often accompanying *atopic* or *constitutional eczema*. With the atopic syndrome it proves indeed that during the first few years, the baby and pre-school time, boys are in the majority, but subsequently girls and women are in the majority. We may place this fact within the context of differences between men and women in expressing disorders. When women have a disorder that normally occurs more often with men, they have it on average in a more serious form. An autistic woman is generally more deeply autistic than a man (Delfos 2004a). Also, the atopic syndrome occurs significantly more often with boys than with girls (Zeiger and Heller 1995), but when a girl has it, on average she outgrows it less often than a boy does. After the age of 12 and during the course of life women are generally over-represented in the case of allergies.

Geschwind and Galaburda (1984, 1987) developed a hypothesis regarding the influence of testosterone on the development of the foetus in the womb. On the basis of the restraining influence of testosterone on the immune system and on the development of the left hemisphere they expect a connection between the male sex and a number of characteristics such as left-handedness, which points to a dominance of the right hemisphere. They expect that among left-handed people there are more men. This proves to be the case (de

The occurrence (frequency) of the atopic syndrome according to the CMR-Nijmegen (Continuous Morbidity Registration, Catholic University of Nijmegen) is in the case of young children higher with boys than with girls (CMR-Nijmegen 1997, 2000). In the case of atopic eczema, which is connected with food allergies, this changes within a very short period of time. In the period 1990–1994 between birth and the age of four, 60 per cent are boys and 40 per cent are girls; after this age the picture has changed, from the age of 5 to 14 it is only 38 per cent boys versus 62 per cent girls, and between the ages of 15 and 24, it is 30 per cent boys and 70 per cent girls respectively. With asthma, the change takes place a little later, from the age of 24. With boys the allergic reaction often disappears after some time. On the whole women suffer more often from asthma than men (Ruwaard, Gijsen and Verkleij 1993).

Graaf-Tiemersma 1995; Hellige 1993). We expect more extremely right-handed people among women; this is also supported by research (Tan and Tan 1997). Geschwind and his assistants expect that with men and with left-handed people dyslexia, stuttering, allergies, migraine and immune disorders occur significantly more often and that mathematical skills are more strongly developed, while the linguistic skills are less developed. This is called the Geschwind hypothesis.

Boys have dyslexia significantly more often than girls (de Graaf-Tiemersma 1995). In her research into the Geschwind hypothesis, which among other things predicts that there is a connection between dyslexia and allergies, de Graaf-Tiemersma (1994) discovers that girls are more often allergic than boys. This would not support the Geschwind hypothesis. I stated, however, that there are three kinds of immune problems. In the case of a restrained immune system we do not expect autoimmune diseases or allergies, but more likely a weaker ability to fight the diseases. Because with girls it was a matter of the overreaction of allergies, in my opinion the Geschwind hypothesis is actually supported by de Graaf-Tiemersma's research. Geschwind and Galaburda did not make a distinction within the immune disorders. Allergies, atopic syndrome, autoimmune diseases, all were expressions of a restrained immune system according to them. Autoimmune diseases and allergies are, however, expressions of an immune system that reacts too strongly, that takes action too quickly, and are not expressions of a restrained system. The fact that women often show the overreaction of allergy is connected to their stronger immune system. The fact that de Graaf-Tiemersma's research showed more girls with allergies is therefore not contradictory to the Geschwind hypothesis, but on the contrary supports it. Other outcomes of de Graaf-Tiemersma's research (1995) support the Geschwind hypothesis. Boys are more often left-handed than girls, boys are significantly more often dyslectic than girls, dyslectic children are twice as often left-handed as right-handed.

Geschwind expected on the basis of his hypothesis that with psychiatric disorders, like autism, more autoimmune diseases would occur. When we regard the three different kinds of immune reactions (Table 3.1), then we expect with psychiatric disorders an underreaction and maybe the atopic syndrome, but less the overreaction of allergy or an autoimmune disease. In their research regarding autism, van Gent, Heijnen and Treffers (1997) find that with autistic people there is a reduced working of the immune system.

> Van Gent, Heijnen and Treffers (1997) indicate that with autism it is a question of a reduced working of the immune system. This is shown by various researchers showing a lack of T-cell and NK-cell reaction (the 'killer cells' reacting to diseases) with autistic people. This is in accordance with what we would expect on the basis of the biopsychological model presented in this book. Autism can be regarded as the extreme end of the male continuum – Asperger (1944) expressed it this way – and with this disorder we therefore expect a reduced immune reaction, possibly the atopic syndrome, but less the allergies and autoimmune diseases.

The fact that the atopic syndrome is connected to psychopathological syndromes is confirmed by research by Dabkowska and Rybakowski (1997). They noticed an allergic reaction of the atopic type in almost half of the people with a depressive disorder (both bipolar and unipolar) as well as with people with schizophrenia. Here it is also proven that men show this more often than women.

Research by Flaton *et al.* (1997) showed that there is a connection between conduct difficulties and food sensitivity. Here it is also proven that boys show this more than girls. Their interpretation as to whether the conduct difficulties are caused by the food sensitivity does not seem to be thorough enough. From our model it follows that conduct difficulties and food sensitivity both arise from the same source, notably the influence of testosterone on the immune system and the brain, and not that they arise because of food sensitivity. The influence of testosterone seems to be the intermediating variable. They are both, in connection, predictable from the model. Mesman's research (2000) also shows that with children who have strong, structural externalising and internalising problems there have been many health complaints in their early years.

Perception of illness by women

The recognition by the biological self could play an important part in the way in which men and women deal with illnesses. A lot of research shows time and again that women consult their GP more often than men, while they are less vulnerable to illnesses and have a longer life expectancy.

Brezinka (1995) indicates that there are not only differences in the degree to which men and women consult their GP, but also how doctors respond. Women are more easily regarded as being plaintive than men. Gijsbers van Wijk, Huisman and Kolk (1999) state in their article regarding the occurrence of illnesses with men and women that it may be true that women report more illnesses than men, but that these are mainly less serious conditions. Their reports mainly concern complaints like headache and back pain, while men more often have serious life-threatening diseases. They state that the *symptom perception* of women is stronger than that of men. Reporting more often does not have to be a reflection of the occurrence of illnesses. According to them social factors play an important part here, like having more time to occupy themselves with physical signs as a result of lesser participation in the work force.

However, when we consider the biological self that seems to function better with women, then it is important to note that in addition to social factors a better recognition by the biological self with women could mean that deviations from that 'self' are spotted sooner. From this point of view it could well be that women report symptoms more often and go to their GP more quickly because due to recognition by their biological self at an early stage and with a larger range of

The average life expectancy of men is shorter than that of women. This is also determined by the higher death rate of boys at birth and during the first 14 years. The difference in life expectancy between men and women decreases with age (Delfos 1999b). The difference in life expectancy of a boy and a girl born in 1980 is 80.95 and 89.02 years respectively, a difference of 8.07 years (French statistics, INED in Meslé and Vallin 1996). A boy and a girl who are 20 years old in 1980 have a life expectancy of 82.48 and 90.18 years respectively. The difference has been reduced to 7.7 years. The life expectancy of a man and a woman who are 60 years old in 1980 is 86.86 and 91.73 respectively. The difference has by now been reduced to 4.87 years. A similar development can be seen when we speak of the life expectancy of people who were born for example in 1990, or are 20 or 60 years old in that year. The differences between men and women then go from 7.78, through 7.54 to 4.66 years difference in life expectancy. These are only two examples to illustrate that these differences are structural during life and from birth and even before that, because there are more miscarriages of boys than of girls and more stillborn boys than girls. (For these calculations I used the statistical data about the life expectancy of people in France from the eighteenth up to and including the twentieth century, because I had the INED's (1996) data made available to me by Meslé and Vallin.)

complaints than is the case with men, they experience that something is going on in their body. In addition, women are probably more sensitive to stress factors, causing psychosomatic complaints to occur more often with them. When we discuss the *anxiety model* later, this extra sensitivity will become clear (see also Appendix 1).

We can see this when men and women have to place their physical sensations. For women it will generally be clear where a physical sensation is located, men often have a vaguer image.

Biological self > psychological self > neural self

Following from the *biological self* is the *psychological self*. These two are in principle just as difficult to divide as body and mind. The dualism body–mind also does not apply here. It is therefore logical to assume that the 'biological self' and the 'psychological self' are interwoven.

Damasio (1994, 1999), who rejects the Cartesian dualism of division of body and mind, states that body and mind are one. His concept of a (biological) self as a *constant neural system of information processing* contains therefore both aspects, biological and psychological, as inseparable. The psychological self is, as far as he is concerned, connected to the biological self; together they form one structure, the *neural self*. Damasio (1999) speaks of a *core self* (the biological self) from which an *autobiographical self* develops.

In the example of the little boy who ate salt, we saw that the knowledge of the own body directs behaviour, even if this does not take place at a conscious level. It is an example of the transition of a biological principle to a psychological principle. The 'analysis' of the physical condition led with this boy to the behaviour of looking for and eating salt. The connection between body and mind becomes even clearer in the example of arousal, the physiological state of alertness. The production of adrenlaline can lead to the thoughts 'I am angry' or 'I am scared', even if it was not enticed by a social situation. Damasio (1994) states that the physical sensations form the basis for feelings and that these arise in that order. The fact is that feelings would not exist without the physical sensations. Body and mind are inextricably bound up with each other; a *psychological* self can therefore not exist without a *biological* self. More than that, this division is arbitrary and only serves to make information manageable and easier to discuss. The division being arbitrary has, according to Edelman (1991), led to many scientific errors. Body and mind cannot be separated. *thinking is material.*

According to Damasio (1994) the thymus gland can be regarded as a part of the complex biological self, that exists as a continuous active neural structure in the brain and is fed constantly by information from the organs: a neural system of information processing. The thymus gland as source of origin of the immune system and as 'examiner' of the selfness of cells could be regarded as the first building block of the biological–psychological–neural self. After having done its first task, the thymus gland shrivels up and is not important any more.

An example of the idea of the biological self as a constant neural system of information processing is the *body scheme* that Sacks (1984) describes. This body scheme, a 'map of the body', is constantly updated. Each body part has, or rather forms, an

> Experience shows us that men more often give a vague answer, with vague gestures, to the question of where the pain is, while women often can give precise information. In addition, it is also regarded that men are generally 'frightened of pain'. This is not right. They are not more frightened of pain, but experience more pain due to the fact that men generally produce less endorphins, the body's own pain-killers, than women. In order to be prepared for a possible birth, women are generally capable of a larger production of endorphins than men. Sensitivity to pain seems to be genetically set (Uhl, Sora and Wang 1999).

area in the brain. This area disappears when the body part is amputated or when the information cannot be transported to the brain because the sensory track has been cut. When the sensory track between hand and brain is cut, for example, there is no area of the hand in the body scheme of the brain, even though the hand exists in reality. The hand is then not experienced as one's own and a sense of alienation arises. A disorder of the body scheme goes together with fundamental estrangement and anxiety. The body scheme is a part of the co-ordinating neural self. The concepts of a continuously forming *total self* as neural structure can be traced back to Edelman (1991).

To what extent one has a clear image of the 'self' has important consequences for how one stands with respect to one's environment. The first building block for this is the *me–other differentiation.*

Me–other differentiation and empathy

We have already seen that the development of a biological self, and in line thereof we can say a psychological self, faces more problems with men than with women. That means that men in general have a less clear picture of their 'self' than women.

Developing a 'self' is inextricably bound with the development of a picture of the 'other'. One can develop a clear picture of what one is, by experiencing what one is not. Our behaviour becomes noticed by us by seeing other people's behaviour or by losing habits.

A less defined picture of the 'self' means that the image of the 'other' is also less clear. The process where the self, the 'me', becomes distinct from the 'other' is called the *me–other differentiation*, or also the *individuation process*. On the basis of what we observed about the neural self, we should expect that the me–other differentiation with men is less crystallised than with women.

> Not only as a child, but even as an adult, we are still restricted in our image of ourselves in relation to the other. Travelling makes us, for example, aware of the cultural determination of behaviour which beforehand we experienced as natural and universal. A different example is that we discover how often we use a certain finger only after we cannot use it for a while because of an accident.

Mahler (1968) made an extensive description of the individuation process. Initially the child is physically and mentally in a symbiotic state with the mother. Physically it cannot adequately distinguish 'me' and 'other'. This goes for many areas. The development of the senses, for example, makes it impossible in the beginning for a child to see depth or colour – the baby lives mainly in a 'smelling' world. But it is also psychologically connected to the mother. The young baby feels the frame of mind of his or her mother infallibly and responds to it. It seems to be 'telepathically' connected to the mother; this is how Sullivan (1953) describes the early childhood *symbiosis* with the mother.

If there is no or an inadequate me–other differentiation, then the 'other' will be seen too much as an extension of the 'self'. Thinking on the basis of an inadequate me–other differentiation will be more egocentric.

The me–other differentiation is a condition in order to reach an *empathic capacity*, the ability to put oneself in someone else's shoes. In order to be able to understand an 'other' there will have to be a realisation that the 'other' differs from the 'me'. We can see this in the development of children, when the partnership behaviour, the making of friends, only occurs after the completion of the *individuation period*, not sooner than the age of three. Bowlby (1988) states that during the development of attachment, where the child becomes attached to one or more persons, the child is not able to show *partnership behaviour* until the age of four. It strikes up friendships with other people like partners and does not see the other as an extension of itself any more. The child starts a relationship with an 'other' on the basis of a 'me'. The *egocentric thinking* makes room for *empathic thinking*.

The development of the 'me' has been discussed by various theoreticians. We then speak in general about the development of the 'ego'. One of the most important theoreticians in this field was Freud (1947), who saw the 'ego' as a development of the self from the subconscious, by means of a confrontation with reality. In relation to the restrictions brought on the child by reality, the 'ego' develops itself. Loevinger (1990) set up an extensive model of the development of the ego. This development, in nine stages, takes place as a result of a growing insight into the surrounding world.

When I discuss conduct disorders, it will be seen that the degree of me–other differentiation plays an important part with these disorders.

The me–other differentiation can suffer both from environmental factors and from predisposition factors. A mother who does not let her child go and implants her own thoughts and feelings in the child will impede the development of the me–other differentiation and the necessary self-reflection within the child. In the most serious case we speak of a *symbiotic relation* in which it seems that mother and child cannot function apart from each other. In that case there exists an anxious orientation towards the mother. Breaking up this relationship means that both run the risk of disintegrating, that is to say that their normal functioning falls apart, when they have to function apart from each other. If, however, we speak of an inadequate me–other differentiation proceeding from the predisposition, then this looks completely different. An inadequate me–other differentiation in principle is not accompanied by a strong, anxious orientation towards the mother. Such a child seems to function in a way that is more free from the environment. It is strongly egocentric.

In the event of an increase of the me–other differentiation a decrease of egocentricity takes

Loevinger (1990) developed a model with respect to ego development. She distinguishes nine *ego stages*, from E-1 to E-9, in which a progressing me–other differentiation can be seen:

- E-1: *Pre-social stage*: no socially oriented behaviour, rarely observed in humans

- E-2: *Impulsive stage*: follows own needs and wants wishes to be fulfilled immediately

- E-3: *Self-protecting stage*: understanding of rules, aimed at own interest and not wanting to be punished

- E-4: *Conformist stage*: own interest is identified with interest of others, for example a group

- E-5: *Self-conscious stage*: understanding of personal emotions and way of thinking, experiencing deviant behaviour in itself and others

- E-6: *Principle stage*: responsibility and tolerance in relation to own feelings and thoughts

- E-7: *Individual stage*: realisation of individual differences and acceptance of differences

- E-8: *Autonomous stage*: aimed at individual development and social responsibility

- E-9: *Integrative stage*: understanding and responsibility of the place of own individuality in the social order.

place. Following from this *empathy* becomes possible, that is being able to place oneself in someone else's position.

An inadequate me–other differentiation will therefore go together with a diminished ability to be empathic. Given the differences in me–other differentiation with men and women we can also expect a difference in empathy. Women are, generally, more empathic than men. It is a matter of both a difference in possibilities

Empathy is often confused with being sensitive. Someone who is not empathic is often unjustly regarded as a person without feelings. Empathy means that one is able to put oneself in someone else's place and can imagine the other person's feelings. This does not necessarily have to mean that one has those feelings oneself and sympathises. Empathy is most noticeable when it concerns sensing and feeling the feelings of someone that one does not know oneself. A lack of being able to sense what goes on in someone else's mind does not mean that one does not have any feeling oneself. It only means that the range of feelings are limited to those one knows and experiences oneself.

The empathic capacity is linked to caring behaviour and is associated with altruistic behaviour. The difference between men and women in this respect is deeply anchored in the evolution of the human being. Darwin (1872) was one of the first people who systematically studied empathy. His starting point was that empathy and emotional communication are necessary in order to *maintain social order*. Dawkins (1989) stated that altruistic behaviour of the mother was inspired by the certainty she has that the child carries her genes and her need to protect and take care of the carrier of these genes. The father is less certain that the child carries his genes. According to Dawkins' theory, based on Darwin's theory of the *selfish gene*, that focuses on genes maintaining themselves, the mother will be more altruistic than the father. Buck and Ginsburg (1997) state that there are both *selfish* and *social* genes. The latter stimulate social interaction and make empathic functioning possible, both from the most simple form of life up to and including the human being. I propose still another explanation for the difference in empathy between men and women, as will be seen further on.

and a difference in active orientation causing empathy to keep developing further in women than in men (Graham and Ickes 1997). This is not that surprising when we realise that the woman from her biological being, her duty in procreation, is geared to being able to put herself in someone else's place. In principle she can bring another being, a child, into the world. Men, however, are better than women at noticing signs of danger and anger (Eisenberg, Murphy and Shepard 1997). It is therefore better to speak of an *empathic spectrum* (Delfos 2004a, 2004b) where women are on average stronger in sensing what goes on in someone else's mind in general, but men are stronger in sensing signs of danger, anger and fear. Here we also see the original evolutionary role. The man, in order to protect the nest, had to observe signs of danger in particular. This difference in empathic capacity has consequences for the way in which men and women on average look for safety and confirmation. A woman is more likely to look for emotional confirmation in interpersonal contact, where she can personally put herself in the other person's place. A man is more likely to look for safety in his social status, because it is there that he observes danger. We will see that the difference in empathic capacity plays an important part with conduct disorders.

I already mentioned in Chapter 2 that one of the basic characteristics which we see all the time with psychiatric disorders is a *problematic empathic capacity*. With autism, the male end of the continuum of psychiatric disorders, we see that expressed in a serious form. These children live, also as adults, in a complete world of their own. Empathic functioning, in the sense of feeling what goes on in someone else's mind, seems to be foreign to them. On the other hand they are very sensitive to receiving negative signals, especially signs of stress with their mother (Delfos 2004a).

A number of factors influence the development of an empathic capacity on the basis of the ongoing me–other differentiation (Eisenberg, Murphy and Shepard 1997). There are a number of factors that influence the extent to which children can decipher other people's emotions. These are, apart from sex (women are better able to decipher and sense emotions with other people), age (but very young children are already able to decipher emotional signs), the complexity of the emotions, the way in which the emotion is communicated (verbal, non-verbal), the extent of the task component in what is asked of the child (for example to spontaneously name an emotion) and the accurateness of the person who is sending out the emotion. Intelligence is an important factor and can be employed as compensation when direct sensing is failing. Children are better able to read feelings of peers than of adults. The ability to empathise increases with age. Men are better able than women to assess signs of danger and anger.

There is increasingly more attention paid to the *social* or *emotional* intelligence. In addition to the usual intellectual skills, the degree to which a child or adult is socially intelligent is looked for. There is a worldwide effort to develop an *EQ* (Emotional intelligence Quotient) in addition to the *IQ* (Intelligence Quotient).

On the basis of experiences with autism a theory has been developed regarding empathic capacity, the Theory of Mind: TOM (Premack and Woodruff 1978). This theory assumes that every human being develops a theory about how other people think, feel and are. In order to be able to do that the child of course first has to understand that the other person has a 'mind', that they are thinking and feeling. On the basis of this theory the thoughts and feelings of others are deciphered and this forms the material for the empathic capacity. The assumption is that autistic people have an inadequate TOM.

Research into empathic capacity is still inadequate; many outcomes are contradictory. This is probably connected to the fact that children have to be able to express themselves verbally in order to explain how they assess an emotion of another person. Research into conversing with children, which is by the way still very young, shows that the outcome of research is strongly dependent on a number of factors. Conversing with children has characteristics that are linked to the age, depending on the verbal abilities of the child, but also depending on the extent to which the child knows the conversation frameworks and knows what is expected of him or her. The quality of the conversation increases significantly when children have it explained to them what the expectation and the intention of a conversation or a (psychological) examination is (Delfos 2000a).

Moral development

Empathy is an element that plays an important part in *moral development*. This development arises by virtue of the limits the child experiences when realising his or her own wishes. A moral development is therefore preceded by an individuation process. A developed moral sense needs a well developed me–other differentiation. Kohlberg (1969) made an extensive map of moral development. He partly based his work on the cognitive stages of Piaget (1972). Moral development takes place along two principles: *interest* and *conflict*. Children do not develop a moral sense because they are taught to, but because their interest is awakened. When the interest of a child in a moral subject is awakened, the child takes a standpoint. Subsequently it can be confused again by new information, causing it to come into conflict with the standpoints which were developed up to then. The child tries to solve the conflict in a way that is more complex than the solution method it had available up to then, so that the new solution can include the new information. Kohlberg (1969) states that initially the moral development is focused on obedience. The child is led by the authority of whom it is dependent on for the satisfaction of his or her needs. Then the child discovers, on the basis of an extension of his or her physical and social environment, that differences are possible and it focuses itself more on its own needs. The experience gained by the reaction of the environment teaches the child what a 'good child' is supposed to be. The child wants to meet this in order to prevent *withholding of love* and to obtain a positive self-image. In the next phase the child learns that there are not only norms at micro level, but that there are also norms in society, with which one is expected to abide. Depending on the possibilities, also in the intellectual field, the child, by now an adolescent, will develop higher values. The highest form is a stage of moral development which, according to Kohlberg (1969), few people reach. The human being then discovers values that exceed the individual and society.

Kohlberg (1969) marks a difference in moral development between reasoning and acting. The development is based on reasoning, which does not mean to say that the child or the adult will act accordingly. The human being is inclined to subject to an authority and will make his or her moral values and standards usually subordinate to what the authority demands from him or her.

Moral development depends on various factors: upbringing, culture, intellectual abilities, and gender. Like many other areas moral development also shows differences between men and women. Damon (1988) shows that these differences are already evident in boys and girls. He observes that research in that field shows that the boy is more focused on *competition and justice*, while the girl is more focused on *care for the other and co-operation*. This difference is in all probability connected to the differences in me–other differentiation and following from that the more egocentric or more empathic thinking. Moral thinking has to do with the way in which people assess good and bad, how they stand with respect to their fellow man and how they deal with that human being. Within this framework the difference in lying between men and women is also characteristic. Men are shown to tell

Kohlberg (1969) researched moral development by presenting people with moral dilemmas. An example is the 'dilemma of the medication'. This concerns the assessment of the moral meaning of the behaviour of a man who cannot afford a unique medicine that could save his dying wife and subsequently starts stealing. The question of whether the behaviour of the man is 'good' or not is then asked.

lies more often out of self-interest, women more out of the interest of the other (Vrij 1998).

Egocentricity and empathy form an area of tension. The orientation of girls on 'care for the other and co-operation' reflects their larger empathy; the orientation of boys on 'competition and justice' reflects their greater *action-readiness*. Later we will see that testosterone supports a greater action-readiness with men. Damon (1988) states that the differences in fact mean that girls in general have a moral development that is of a higher order than boys, when we apply Kohlberg's criteria. Care and co-operation are higher moral standards than justice and competition. The same difference is mentioned by Loevinger (1990).

Table 3.2 The effects of the influence of testosterone on the development of the thymus gland and the immune system

Man	Woman
Xy-chromosome pair > large production of testosterone in the testes > restrained development of thymus gland/biological self	*Xx*-chromosome pair > small production of testosterone in the ovaries > unrestrained development of thymus gland/biological self

Less developed neural self
 	
• weaker symptom perception
 	
• less strongly developed psychological self
 	
• weaker me–other differentiation
 	
  – weaker empathic capacity
 	
  – moral development oriented to justice and competition
	Strongly developed neural self
	
	• stronger symptom perception
	
	• strongly developed psychological self
	
	• strong me–other differentiation
	
	  – stronger empathic capacity
	
	  – moral development oriented to care for the other and co-operation

Less strong immune system • less effective fighting of illness • underreaction of immune system • fewer autoimmune diseases • fewer allergies	Strong immune system • more effective fighting of illness • overreaction of immune system • more autoimmune diseases • more allergies

Up to now I have discussed the differences between men and women that arise as a result of the first important influence exercised by the hormone testosterone, notably restraining the development of the thymus gland and following from that the immune system. In summary we can say that the effect of testosterone in restraining the thymus gland, considered to be the biological self, is stronger in men. And it follows from this that the psychological-neural self in men is less well developed than in women.

Recognising the self less causes an inferior illness perception and a less strongly developed me–other differentiation. Following from that again lies a diminished empathic capacity and a moral orientation on justice and competition. A restraint of the development of the thymus gland causes a reduced functioning of the immune system, causing diseases to be fought less effectively, but on the other hand there is less overreaction of the immune system as in autoimmune diseases and allergies. With women we see, in principle, the opposite pattern. By way of illustration I will place the conclusions regarding this subject in Table 3.2.

The second important effect of the increase of testosterone is the influence exercised on the central nervous system (CNS) in general and the left hemisphere in particular.

Testosterone and the central nervous system

In addition to the influence that the *y*-chromosome, by means of the increase of testosterone, exercises on the immune system, it also has a stimulating influence on the right hemisphere and a restraining influence on the development of the left hemisphere during the growth in the womb (de Lacoste, Horvath and Woodward 1991). With boys there is on average a more developed right hemisphere and a less developed left hemisphere. It should be noted here that the left hemisphere with the male *and* the female embryo matures later than the right hemisphere and that with boys this is exaggerated by their slower maturation in general. Development of the left hemisphere is caused by making connections from the right hemisphere. When this left hemisphere has not matured enough, it is not possible to make a proper connection with it. The brain *lateralises* during maturation; that means that various functions end up in the left or right hemisphere. Because the left hemisphere with boys develops later and less strongly, more functions that mature early will end up in the right hemisphere and less in the left one. The linguistic function with women is less lateralised than with men. With women the parts of the linguistic function can end up both right and left; with men the linguistic function is usually lateralised in the left hemisphere. Language is therefore more accessible for women (Harasty 2000).

For some functions the lateralisation is univocal; the motor system is one of them. The right hemisphere directs the left motor system and the left hemisphere the right motor system. Left-handedness is therefore an indication of the dominance of the right hemisphere. It is then a dominance of the motor area and specifically the motor area that directs the hand. This does not mean to say that all areas on the right hemisphere are dominant simultaneously. This makes research into the differences between the left and right hemisphere difficult, because most researches are, in principle, aimed at one element. When an element within the right hemisphere is dominant, that does not mean to say that the other areas in that hemisphere are also dominant. It is, however, the case that when a hemisphere is dominant in a motor area, there is more chance of more dominant elements in that hemisphere. That is why a lot of research is aimed at a combination of left-handedness and other elements. We expect from this difference in hemispheres between men and women that men are more often left-handed. Hellige (1993) states that left-handedness does indeed occur more often with men than with women and that this is connected to the influence of testosterone on the development of the right hemisphere of the foetus.

Testosterone causes a difference between men and women which plays an important role from the earliest beginning and exercises a big influence on their social functioning. We are now finding it more and more easy to accept that there are biological differences between men and women, but it still causes us trouble. The fact is that the differences have never been so small since the start of mankind's existence. When we look at the development of the human being in an evolutionary sense, we see that the characteristics that were important for the survival of the species become less and less important. There is no real bear on the road any more; no longer does food have to be acquired by hunting. The woman's task in the survival of the species has not changed fundamentally, except that her role has become a little less important and can be shared with others. Hrdy (1999) indicated that the human being is unique in employing other people for the upbringing of children. Fundamentally there are differences between men and women. The *emancipation* of women has contributed largely to reducing the differences. Still, differences remain that cannot be altered by emancipation. From an evolutionary point of view, differences between men and women are necessary. But similarities are also necessary from an evolutionary point of view (Delfos 2004b). The necessity for similarities delineates the room for emancipation.

The linguistic centres are located to an important extent in the left hemisphere. The linguistic functioning of the human is therefore supported by the left hemisphere. In the linguistic function there are important differences between men and women. Broca's area, a region of the brain where an important part of the linguistic functioning is located, and Wernicke's speech centre are in comparison larger with women than with men (Harasty *et al.* 1997). The ability to put thoughts and feelings into words is located in the left hemisphere. Hamilton and Timmons (1990) indicate that, as a result of the function of putting thoughts and feelings into words, various researchers regard the left hemisphere as the place where *consciousness* is located. Damasio (1999) indicates that the left hemisphere is responsible for typical human consciousness. From the brain stem comes the more general consciousness that animals share with humans. Brain surgery where the left hemisphere is taken away results in a more animal-like kind of consciousness. The left hemisphere is important for language capacity, among other functions. Human consciousness is characterised by the capacity to put feelings and thoughts into words, and therefore depends largely on the left hemisphere. The right hemisphere has knowledge regarding processes which are regulated by this hemisphere, but not about the possibility to be aware of this and to catch it in language. The ability to put thoughts and feelings into words is of great importance when directing behaviour, as we will see later when we will discuss the subject of *self-reflection*.

When men cannot put their feelings into words, women often make the, less empathic, mistake that they do not have those feelings. Being aware of feelings and subsequently putting them into words is, however, not the same as having those feelings.

The left hemisphere is in general more analytically and logically focused, which once more supports the analysing of thoughts and feelings.

The restraint of the development of the left hemisphere by testosterone therefore has consequences for the linguistic functioning and the extent to which the man is aware of his behaviour. Women will, in principle, be more linguistically oriented than men, that means to say in the emotional and social field, and will be more aware of their thoughts and feelings. We already see these differences occur with language development that in general is slower with boys (Rutter and Rutter 1993).

The more strongly developed right hemisphere is related to spatial and abstract thinking and to creativity. These possibilities will therefore in general be more developed with men than with women.

Testosterone: aggression and action-readiness

The higher production of testosterone has consequences for the development in the womb; it also has consequences for the testosterone level of the human being after birth. With men there is on average a more stable and higher level of testosterone than with women. The testosterone content of the blood plasma of men is on average almost nine times as high as it is with women (0.7μg% with men and only 0.08 μg% with women), stated by, among others, Bernards and Bouman (1993). On becoming older the testosterone level with men decreases, as was found by researchers like Dabbs and his assistants (Dabbs 1990, 1992a, 1993; Dabbs and Hopper 1990; Dabbs *et al.* 1991). There are also seasonal influences, but these are not as strong as the age effect. Kaplan (1990) states that by means of the biological clock, with men, the body measures the testosterone level every 90 minutes and when necessary it is added to. The testosterone level can, however, also be influenced by circumstances. Every person has a basic level of testosterone and this can become higher based on social stimuli. Stress or conflict, for example, can cause an increase of the production of testosterone, as is shown by research by Dabbs (1992b).

Testosterone regulates growth processes in the sense that it starts the production of the growth hormone. At birth the level of testosterone is high and after a few months goes down to approximately one fifth of the level at birth. Then around the age of four there is a temporary increase and subsequently beginning at the age of 11 to 13 the level of testosterone increases enormously up to about 800 per cent higher than in the pre-school period. This enables children in (pre-)puberty to grow; this often happens by means of a growth spurt (Donovan 1985). The peak of production of testosterone with men lies around the age of 20 and subsequently decreases to 50 per cent less at the age of 60 and older (Gomez 1991).

Hormone production does not only regulate physical processes, like growing or ovulation, but also psychological processes. In the case of danger, for example, the human being is brought into a state of increased alertness, *arousal* through the adrenergic hormones. This enables him or her to 'fight or flee', the *fight or flight response* (Selye 1956). Anxiety and aggression are related to this.

Testosterone plays a part for example in the sexual drive. In a biological sense the man, because of his higher testosterone level, is more strongly supported in his sex drive than the woman. Testosterone is also connected to aggression.

Researchers like van der Dennen (1992) showed that to humans, and also to animals, the fact applies that the higher the testosterone level, the more aggression is shown. Although a clear connection was found between the amount of testosterone in the blood and the amount of aggression, this relation is less clear during puberty, as is shown by researchers like Halpern *et al.* (1993a) and also by Constantino *et al.* (1993). The results from this period are not always univocal. Coe, Hayashi and Levine (1988) show a connection between aggression and the increase of testosterone during puberty. Slap *et al.* (1994) show that a higher level of testosterone with girls during puberty is related to a worse adjustment to social standards. A higher level of testosterone resulted in more conflicts with the environment. Archer's article (1994) shows, however, that the aggression shown in this period can be best explained by the combination of the testosterone level and social factors. The point here is the factors of the childrearing situation and socio-economic factors. The detachment process which occupies the adolescent forms a constant source of conflict between the youngster and his or her environment,

The relation aggression–sexuality–testosterone has already been made several times. An interesting example of this relation is provided by research that Biddulph (1998) mentions with respect to delinquency in youth. During the six months before their first sexual experience the chances that boys would be in contact with the police were many times higher than after that.

unconnected to the level of testosterone. On the other hand, the conflicts which in the world of the adolescent are common can raise the testosterone level.

The differences in aggression between boys and girls are already visible in their first play. Furbay and Wilke (1982) showed that differences can already be observed during the baby phase: girls more often choose soft and softly coloured cuddly toys, boys hard and strongly coloured ones. Kubey and Larson (1990) found that 80 per cent of the children between 9 and 15 years of age who play computer and video games are boys. This difference is probably related to the aggression in these games, which links up more with boys than with girls.

The differences in playing are probably, like all differences between men and women in general, not only socio-culturally determined, but are also related to the hormonal level. One of the indications for this is research by Berenbaum and Hines (1992), where the post-natal preference for boys' toys seems to be related to the level of testosterone. Another example is the research by Meyer-Bahlburg *et al.* (1988), where the level of the female hormone progesterone was connected to the decrease of rough play.

Boys are more often behind the computer playing games than girls are. These are often action games, where competition and aggression play an important part. The way in which boys and girls work with a game plays a large part. Boys behave more in a 'trial and error' way and start immediately: 'Click and go!' Girls on the other hand first try to understand the game and then start. By that time you have already lost a 'life' in an action game and you become demotivated. Computer manufacturers are still looking for games that are attractive to girls (Valkenburg 1997; van Gelder 1998).

The testosterone level is not only dependent on predisposition and gender specific factors. Testosterone production can also be influenced by certain activities. Conflicts may be a cause of the production of testosterone. Research by Archer (1991) shows that stressful activities like being involved in politics or acting are an important stimulator for the production of testosterone. In a more general sense researchers like Dabbs and his colleagues (Bernhardt *et al.* 1998; Dabbs 1992b; Dabbs, La Rue and Williams 1990) showed that the level of testosterone is not only related to aggression and sexuality, but also to dominance and to success in the exercise of the profession.

Aggression is often seen as a negative expression of behaviour. It is, however, behaviour that may be necessary to survive and that contains the action-readiness of the human in a less sharp form. Testosterone can therefore be seen as a hormone linked to action-readiness. It may therefore be called the *energetic* hormone, that directs behaviour. The high testosterone level with men means that they are in general more ready to act than women. With this term I do not mean that men are more active than women, or would work harder. UNICEF's quote stated earlier shows that women are particularly hard workers. What I mean is that there is an outwardly directed orientation, fed by ambition and initiative. The man is in general more ready to act in case of danger. The activity of the woman is more likely to be centred around the care of her family (Taylor *et al.* 2000). The actionreadiness of the man translates itself in a search for social status and is expressed in case of danger. A nice example of this is research mentioned by Galjaard (1994) which showed that female American scientists publish half as much as their male colleagues, without there being a connection with forming relationships or having children.

> A nice example of the relationship between testosterone and emotion is the research by Dabbs (1997) which proved that the level of testosterone in men was related to the width of their smile. Men with a low level of testosterone have a broader smile, look more friendly and are less dominant.

'No words, but action' is an expression that seems to link up better with men than with women; while the motto 'express your feelings' seems to be woman's own.

The anxiety model

The thirst for action also has consequences for the way in which men deal with danger and stress. There are various theories about stress. The founder is Hans Selye (1956), who linked stress to hormones. Building on Selye, Henry and Stephens (1977) developed a model of positive and negative stress and the accompanying hormones. In the case of negative stress adrenlaline would play an important part, with positive stress it would be cortisol. But now it is proven that cortisol works only in a later stage of stress and adrenlaline immediately at the beginning. In the brain the *hypothalamus* gives the signal to produce the hormones and in this way a chain of reactions is started in the body.

I suggest a model where anxiety, aggression (I mean here physical aggression) and depression are brought together in one hormonal model, which at the same time clarifies the differences between men and women with regard to anxiety, aggression and depression. This model is in part scientifically founded and in part started in order to research it. The model assumes that there is a relation between the hormones testosterone and adrenlaline, the emotion of anxiety, and the behaviours aggression and depression. The model has been reflected in Figure 3.1.

The relationship between testosterone and aggression has been researched amply and it has been proven that the more testosterone the more aggression, and that men have more aggression problems than women. With women who were in jail because of violent offences, there proved to be the same relation between aggression and testosterone (Dabbs and Hargrove 1997).

> Henry and Stephens (1977) start from a division of *positive* and *negative* stress. With positive stress more cortisol would be produced, with negative stress more adrenlaline. Van Doornen (1999) assumes a close co operation between both systems. Cortisol inhibits the working of adrenlaline.

The relationship between testosterone and anxiety has, as far as I know, hardly been researched. Indirectly there is a link via

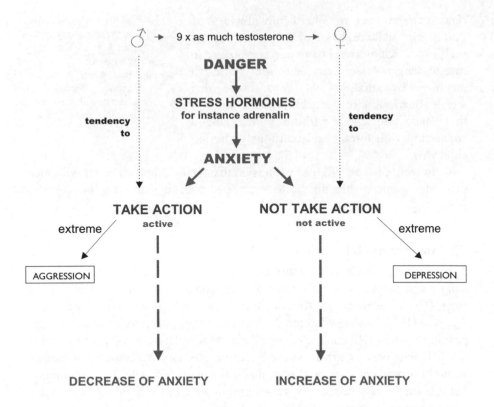

Figure 3.1 Anxiety Model (Source: Delfos 1997, 2003)

the relation between testosterone and cortisol. The hormone cortisol seems to reduce the degree of violence and aggression (Dabbs, Jurkovic and Frady 1991). Bergman and Brismar (1994) researched very violent men and showed that they had a higher testosterone level and a lower cortisol level. Scerbo and Kolko (1994) found a relation between a high testosterone level and the externalising problems of aggression and a high cortisol level and internalising anxiety problems. Steiger *et al.* (1991) researched the levels of testosterone and cortisol with depressive patients who had recovered. Testosterone proved to have increased and cortisol reduced. This information is fully in accordance with the anxiety model. Further research will, however, have to prove the validity of the model.

The starting point for the model is that humans respond to danger. The *amygdala* plays an important part in the detection of danger. The information enters the amygdala and it is 'decided' there what will be passed on because of its importance.

Detection of danger is not a conscious process. Danger can mean a physical threat, but also a negative thought. On the basis of danger the human being produces stress hormones, for example the adrenocorticotrophic hormone (ACTH) noradrenlaline, cortisol and the adrenergic hormone adrenlaline. This starts off a number of physical processes enabling the human to act. The heart rate is activated causing the blood to be pumped through the body more quickly and oxygen to be sent to the muscles quickly, in order to be able to fight and run, and to the head in order to stimulate the thinking. Breathing is stimulated in order to get more oxygen into the lungs. The pupils are dilated in order to receive more visual information. The body is put into a state of *arousal, alertness,* enabling the body to face the danger by the *fight or flight* response (Selye 1956).

In response to the production of these hormones the human being forms the emotions of excitement and anxiety (Damasio 1994). The intensity of the emotions depends on the amount of hormones produced, not on the danger. One person

> The importance of the amygdala for the detection of danger is visible when these are removed. The result is the Kluver-Bucy syndrome which is characterised by an abnormal lack of anxiety and aggression (Buck and Ginsburg 1997).

makes a lot of hormones in the case of a relatively small threat and will therefore experience a lot of anxiety. Another person produces few hormones in the case of a relatively large threat and as a result will experience less anxiety. The amount of hormones that are produced depends on a number of facts: the unconscious (amygdala) assessment of the danger, the conscious assessment of danger, the predisposition of the degree to which stress hormones are produced, the *habituation* to danger and the habituation to the production of hormones. Both the unconscious and the conscious assessment of danger determine the need to produce hormones.

After the triplet danger–hormones–anxiety there are two roads open. The human being can proceed to take action, act, or respond passively, not act. To act can be a physical activity, fight or flight, but every activity will reduce the anxiety, even pacing up and down, singing or vacuuming. The most effective action is the one that fights or solves the danger. To act can also be a constructive thought, especially when this copes with the danger. In the case of not-acting there will be an increase of anxiety and the risk that the thinking turns into fretting, that means to say forming destructive thoughts that mean danger and start off the production of stress hormones again.

Acting is behaviour and in fact consists of two elements. First, it must be able to be carried out; for this purpose the *adrenergic* hormones are necessary, notably adrenaline. Second, it has to be actually carried out; for that purpose *androgenic* hormones are needed, notably testosterone. Because men have on average nine times as much of the androgenic testosterone in their blood than women, men will tend to act when there is danger; women on the other hand will generally tend not to act. Because aggression can be seen as the most extreme form of acting in case of danger, it is not surprising that men have significantly more aggression problems. Men are not necessarily less scared, but are often more effective in solving the anxiety because of their tendency to act. Men are on average more aimed at solutions than women. Because men act, they experience less anxiety and for a shorter period of time. Women are less inclined to act and as a result they feel more anxiety and for a longer period of time. The most extreme form of not-acting is *depression*. Someone with a depression is listless and can hardly be motivated to do anything. Women have depression problems significantly more often than men.

The lack of balance between testosterone and adrenlaline can cause *aggression* when the testosterone level is higher, or depression when the adrenlaline level is higher. Taking action restores the balance, the *homeostasis*, between testosterone and adrenlaline. The stress hormone cortisol forms the connecting link in the anxiety model. Cortisol has, among other things, the function of allowing the level of adrenlaline to go down when it is too high (van Doornen 2000). When someone acts in the case of danger, the adrenlaline is transformed into another substance and the level of cortisol will not rise; it is logical therefore that the level of cortisol will be low in the case of aggression. If the person does not act, the adrenlaline level does not go down enough and the adrenlaline is removed from the body, first by trembling or sweating and then by the production of cortisol which ensures that the production of adrenlaline is restrained.

A typical example of the working of adrenlaline and depression is sleeping in. Especially when you are physically very tired, sleeping late is wonderful. When we get up at that moment, we feel fit and the day starts off pleasantly. When we turn over again, on the other hand, the situation is not that pleasant any more within a short time. Still a bit later you start to feel uncomfortable, the fretting starts and the mood can switch to a sombre one. This is in fact the characteristic of a foundation of depression on a small scale. The background is probably that when you have slept enough, the body produces adrenergic hormones in order to be able to take action. When you do not do that, the situation slowly turns around, the adrenergic substances are not actively converted and as a result there is a toxic amount of adrenlaline in the body in relation to the other hormones.

The fact that testosterone and activity are related is shown for example by research by Windle (1994). He discovered that a higher testosterone percentage was associated with higher activity and aggression. Higher behaviour inhibition on the other hand was related to more cortisol, more anxiety and depression.

When there is a lack of testosterone there is a surplus of adrenlaline. Too much adrenlaline in relation to the other substances is harmful to the body. The body tries to solve this surplus and a way to lose excess adrenlaline is to discharge it through sweat. This is what we see with *cold sweat*. When the adrenergic hormones, for example adrenlaline, are not converted into taking action it can become dangerous for the body. Depression or psychosomatic complaints could be the result. The consequences of the lack of balance between adrenlaline and testosterone can be found back in the range of psychosomatic complaints. These have been brought together in the psychosomatics model in Appendix 1.

When we speak of taking action, there is a difference in the nature of actions by men and women. Men have, under the influence of the hormone testosterone, the tendency to *act with regard to the danger* and more quickly come to physical activity. Women on the other hand have more the tendency to *act by looking for safety and help* in case of danger. Under the influence of the hormone oxytocin, mainly produced by women, women are more likely to look after the nest, the children or the household and talk to friends (Taylor *et al.* 2000).

When we take the consequences of this difference in taking action between men and women seriously, we will be able to understand better a number of problems between men and women. We can see this pattern (work versus talk) often arise when men and women are in stressful situations. The most painful one is maybe the loss of a child, probably the deepest mourning known by humankind. The chances of divorce prove to be very large in this situation (75%). The cause for the divorce is the drifting apart of men and women in the way they react to the pain of losing their child. Women blame men if they 'flee' into their work and do not talk about their child with them. The woman may not be able to see that the work is a strategy for the man to ease the pain of the loss, just as talking fulfils this function with the woman.

Men often tend to blame their wife for 'keeping on about it', and are blind to the importance of talking. Talking and action are two solutions for the problem, and not one. In fact they are the two pieces that together fit the puzzle. A similar pattern can be seen when a partner dies. Men who become widowers tend to focus themselves on their work and neglect their family; women tend to focus on their family and neglect their work (Worden 1996).

The difference in taking action between men and women in case of danger has been expressed in Figure 3.2.

In order to compensate for the lack of her physical action-readiness, the woman uses her verbal strength. The dominance of the right hemisphere of the brain at the expense of the linguistic left hemisphere among men and their tendency to take action due to the higher testosterone level will both contribute to men being in general less linguistically and more action-readiness focused than women. Research by the National Longitudinal Survey of Children and Youth (see Tremblay 1999) shows how this difference works out at the level of aggression. Physical aggression among boys of primary school age was at its peak at the age of four and reduced slightly until the age of 11. Boys were significantly more physically aggressive than girls. In the field of non-physical aggression, indirect aggression, the hurting of another person's feelings, the picture is reversed. Girls show more indirect aggression than boys, and this increases from the age of four to the age of 11, with a peak at ten. Meaningful within this framework is possibly the

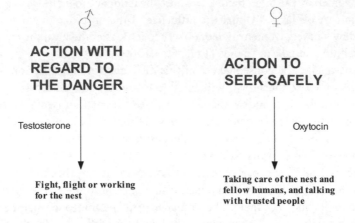

Figure 3.2 Fight or flight versus tend and befriend (Source: Delfos 1997, 2003)

fact that ten years is the age for girls at which the *adrenarche* takes place, the moment at which the maturation of the adrenal glands, the glands that play an important part in the hormonal production that is related, for example, to emotions, comes to a conclusion (Friedman, Charney and Deutsch 1995). Indirect aggression needs a greater me–other differentiation than physical aggression. In order to hurt someone's feelings, you have to be able to put yourself in someone else's position so that you know what is hurtful to the other person. Interesting within this framework is research by Dabbs and Hargrove (1997), which I have already mentioned; they discovered that there was a relation between the level of testosterone and aggression with women who had committed violent offences and were in jail as a result. The degree of violence was higher with women who had a higher level of testosterone. Also, their behaviour in jail was physically more aggressive and they were more ready to take action. Women with a lower level of testosterone were characterised as sneaky, gossiping more and sly.

   The difference in linguistic functioning can cause friction between partners of the opposite sex. When we enter the area of putting feelings into words, the difference in linguistic functioning between men and women is often experienced as being painful. Women focus strongly on this occupation and men seem to prefer to avoid it, although 'being less able to do so' would be more correct. Tannen's

(1990) sociolinguistic study about the difference in linguistic functioning provides an excellent insight into these differences.

Shown in Table 3.3 is the relationship between testosterone, action-readiness, aggression and anxiety.

In the next chapter when I look at conduct disorder, I will discuss a specific part of the central nervous system, notably the autonomic nerve system, where important differences between men and women direct the behaviour, the point being the response to stimuli. Men and women differ so much in that, that in its extreme form it can even explain the criminal differences between men and women.

> Tannen (1990) describes the differences in communication between men and women. Women feel criticised and patronised by men. Men, in turn, have the feeling that women complain and are not clear. She even calls these problems 'genderlect', in order to show that both sexes have their own 'dialect', from a world of their own in which they live. According to her there is a fundamental asymmetry in communication between men and women.

Table 3.3 Testosterone, aggression and anxiety		
More testosterone >	more action-readiness >	more aggression
Less testosterone >	more helplessness >	more anxiety

When we put the differences we have observed so far in a row, we can state that the male brain structure in general is more adjusted to spatial and abstract thinking, more creative, less linguistic, less logical and analytically thinking, more action-ready in case of danger, more in search of social status, less empathic and more egocentric. That is what boys and men in general are good at: expressing their inner emotions through behaviour, whether it is expressing love by having sex, reacting to danger by taking action, or dealing with a problem by giving smoke signals in the form of difficult behaviour. A boy lets us know, sometimes noisily, that something is going on. Proceeding from that we can expect in a culture like ours, where there is a certain 'unmasculisation' of the man in the sense of a strongly female-dominated code where men have to suppress their aggression, have to take on care duties, pose less as a leader and be less authoritarian, and are expected to talk more instead of acting, that there will be an increase in anxiety problems and depression with men.

I have already stated that the woman as a result of putting a new being into the world must in fact be empathic. Van der Dennen (1992) states that in all cultures, all through the ages, care for children is a task which is mainly, if not exclusively, carried out by women, even in the emancipated West. The man is originally more outwardly focused on obtaining means of existence for the family and the protection of the family. The fact that he is therefore more oriented towards action and less empathic follows from that. In order to protect there has to be the ability to be aggressive and this is hindered by the ability to imagine someone else's feelings. A case in point for this relation between aggression and empathy is the research published by Kaplan and Sadock (1995) with respect to empathy, where the aggression of men in general decreased when their victim showed signs of pain or torment. In this respect I speak of general lines, of averages. There are large individual differences. Apart from that the characteristics differ in the extent to which they can be influenced. Intellectual abilities can, for example, be strongly influenced by education; emotional abilities can on the other hand be less influenced or we may not yet know enough about how they can be influenced.

By way of illustration I will set out the conclusion regarding the influence of testosterone on the development of the brain and the level of testosterone after birth for men and women in Table 3.4.

Table 3.4 The influence of testosterone on the hemispheres and the level of testosterone after birth

Man	*Woman*
Restrained development of left hemisphere, stronger development of right hemisphere	Unrestrained development of left hemisphere, weaker development of right hemisphere
• not very focused on language	• strongly focused on language
• diminished ability to put thoughts and feelings into words	• strong ability to put thoughts and feelings into words
• more spatial, abstract and creative thinking	• less spatial, abstract and creative thinking
– more aggression	– less aggression
– less anxiety	– more anxiety
– more action-readiness, less helplessness	– less action-readiness, more helplessness

I have now paid attention to a general difference in brain functions between men and women. There exist also specific differences in brain structure that cause material differences between men and women. An important example is the corpus callosum.

The corpus callosum

Research has provided information concerning a specific part of the central nervous system where there are differences between men and women: the *corpus callosum*. Without knowing exactly why they occur and what part testosterone plays in it, researchers like Burke and Yeo (1994), Oka *et al.* (1999), Steinmetz *et al.* (1992, 1995), Habib *et al.* (1994) and Holloway *et al.* (1993) showed that there are differences between men and women in the size of their corpus callosum. The research outcomes were not always univocal until it became clear that this difference especially applies to the posterior part, the *splenium*. With women the corpus callosum is relatively larger than with men. Looking for the correct measuring techniques provided, however, a not always univocal picture (Constant and Ruther 1996). Dorion *et al.* (2000) showed that a smaller corpus callosum is related to a larger lateralisation of the brain. This part of the brain, together with the hippocampus, forms the connection centre within the brain, the connection with all areas of the brain and between the two hemispheres. The size of the corpus callosum is related to the number of 'connecting cables'. The conduct of various stimuli that enter the two hemispheres, for example auditive-hearing, tactile-feeling and visual-seeing, goes faster and more effectively with a larger corpus callosum.

These researchers also showed that the size of the corpus callosum decreases more quickly with men on becoming older than with women. The larger size of the corpus callosum with women means that the co-ordination of all sorts of information, of various stimuli that enter the brain, can go faster with them than with men.

The fact that we are able to draw such conclusions is partly due to refined measuring techniques becoming available. An important technical progress is the possibility of making the blood flow through the brain visible via the *PET-scan* (Positron Emission Tomography), *MRI* (Magnetic Resonance Imaging) and *MEG* (Magneto-Electroencephalography). These methods are harmless and can be carried out on a live brain. In this way we could for example measure the size of the corpus callosum, without needing an operation to do so. Normal and deviating behaviour patterns can be related to brain structures in this way. Research by, for example, Semrud-Clikeman *et al.* (1994), Hynd *et al.* (1991) and Giedd *et al.* (1994) proved that the corpus callosum with children with ADHD is smaller than that with children who do not have the disorder, although the outcomes are not always univocal (Overmeyer *et al.* 2000). Kayl *et al.* (2000) support the idea of a smaller corpus callosum with children with ADHD, in the sense that the degree to which the corpus callosum was smaller was related to the seriousness of the attention disorder. A smaller corpus callosum means that these

> The differences in size of the corpus callosum can be seen again in practice in the fact that men generally tend and are able to focus on one activity for a long time, while women can easily focus their attention on several activities at the same time and combine different tasks. It is thought that this corpus callosum is responsible for what Darwin called the female intuition: 'fast information processing' leads to 'fast knowledge'.

children have more difficulty in processing the stimuli that reach them. They are easily distracted by a new stimulus that reaches them and can hardly combine that one with the stimulus which they were processing or weigh the priorities between stimuli. Their attention turns naturally to the new stimulus. For many of these children this means that they function better in a stimulus-free environment. What we could already read from the behaviour of these easily distracted children is now supported by knowledge about the structure of their brain. The fact that autistic children have problems with processing stimuli is also supported by research that shows that also with autistic people, the corpus callosum is smaller than on average (Piven *et al.* 1997).

Self-reflection

On the basis of, among other things, the above-mentioned elements, the neural self, the left hemisphere with its language focus and its consciousness of processes, the empathy and the corpus callosum, a difference in *self-reflection* can be assumed between men and women. Self-reflection means researching the self, especially the behaviour and motives behind it. Although self-reflection can be seen as an essential part of human existence, this activity has not been developed to the same extent with everybody. With various disorders it is even proven that there is no or an inadequate self-reflection, as with autism. Self-reflection requires a good me–other differentiation. In order to be able to think about yourself, to self-reflect, it is necessary to regard your own 'me' as such and for that reason it has to be clearly separated from the 'other'. Self-reflection is an opinion about yourself and for that it is necessary to take distance from the self. Self-reflection happens on the basis of a self-image and is also the continuous source of correction of that self-image.

Self-reflection first needs a recognition of the self, knowledge about the self, a developed me–other differentiation, and a good linguistic functioning. Self-reflection is linguistic behaviour, without it having to be expressed in spoken language. It is mainly, as Piaget (1972) and Vygotsky (1978) called it, *inner speech, egocentric language.*

A less developed neural self, which is usually the case with men, will impede the process of self-reflection. Self-reflection exists by the grace of speech or at least inner speech. Putting thoughts and feelings into words is an activity that is located in the left hemisphere, a hemisphere which is less developed with men. In addition to these elements the corpus callosum also plays an important part. In order to be able to think about oneself and to be able to feel what goes on inside oneself, it is necessary to make connections between various parts that play a role with self-reflection: facts, emotions and memories. The corpus callosum as 'connection centre' within the brain promotes making these connections.

The differences in development, of the left hemisphere, corpus callosum and neural self, stimulates women to practise self-reflection. With women it is also the case that, due to their *menstruation cycle*, they are, as it were, 'trained' in examining their physical and mental state. The menstruation cycle can cause important fluctuations in the frame of mind. This frame of mind can be very positive around the ovulation and depressive or aggressive just before the menstruation. Synchronous to the hormonal menstrual cycle runs an emotional cycle that influences the frame of mind of women (Delfos 1993). Kaplan and Sadock (1988) mention that conduct disorders and psychiatric disorder can fluctuate as a result of these hormonal fluctuations with women. Because the functioning of the woman is subject to these fluctuations she will often end up in a particular frame of mind and wonder what is going on. She is as it were 'called up' from her body to find out what is going on, just to find out that the frame of mind is related to the menstruation cycle.

People need to examine their frame of mind in order to give an explanation for their physical sensations. The human being cannot cope with being in a frame of mind that he or she cannot explain. The experiments by Schachter and Singer (1962) showed this in an ingenious manner. They gave their test subjects either the correct information or incorrect information about the physical sensations they would undergo as a result of an injection. Those who were correctly informed about the physical sensations were not or were hardly influenced by events in their environment. Those who were given the wrong information contributed their physical processes to events in that environment. That way they had a satisfying explanation for the state of arousal, alertness, in which they found themselves as a result of the injection. The realisation of what was happening in their body made them less dependent on their environment.

When we speak of deeds, response to danger and spatial thinking, we can say that men seem to have an advantage; when we speak of verbally expressing and examining a frame of mind,

Research by Schachter and Singer (1962) was intended to examine the *cognitions*, thoughts, of people that are connected to alertness (arousal). They injected their test subjects with epinephrine (adrenaline). This causes the body to change into a state of alertness and excitement: increased heart rate, dilated pupils, sweating and the like. These general physiological changes take place both with negative and positive emotions. Subsequently some of the test subjects were given the correct information about the physical reactions to be expected. Others were given the wrong information. They were told that they were injected with a substance that would enable them to see black–white contrasts more clearly. They were not told about heart rate or the other physical reactions. The test subjects were then, individually, brought into a waiting room, where someone else was waiting. This person was, without the test subject knowing this, an assistant to the research and showed happy and playful behaviour or, on the contrary, angry, irritable behaviour. Results showed that the persons who were correctly informed about their physical state were not or were hardly affected by the behaviour of the person who was in the waiting room with them. The people who were wrongly informed were strongly affected. They were happy or irritated, in accordance with the other person's behaviour. Lack of clarity about the physical state makes one dependent on stimuli in the environment and causes physical sensations to be contributed to events in the environment.

self-reflection and empathy, women seem to have an advantage. We then mean initially the pace at which these processes of self-reflection and placing oneself in someone else's place happen. With women these processes on average go faster and are at a more conscious level.

The differences in predisposition between men and women are not restricted to differences arising from the constitution of the human being. Differences are also influenced by the *socialisation* of boys and girls. The differences have consequences for functioning in society. No matter what disorder we discuss, it will have different consequences when it concerns a boy than when it concerns a girl. The consequences of a disorder are always measured against the social functioning. What we already knew for centuries, but seemed to forget during the 1960s and 1970s, is that men and women are different and are treated differently. A male child will meet a different future from his predisposition than a female child. Socialisation will often emphasise these differences.

Summary

Differences between men and women are not restricted to what is visible. Physically there are exterior and interior differences, for example an essential difference in brain structure. These differences already start in the womb with the xx or xy-chromosome pair. The male xy-chromosome pair takes care of an increase in the production of the hormone testosterone. A high testosterone level causes inhibition of the linguistic left hemisphere, a stimulation of the right hemisphere, a diminished working of the immune system and a higher testosterone level after birth. This results in women being in general more linguistic and empathic, able to fight diseases more strongly and being less ready to act in case of danger. They suffer from anxiety and depression more often. Men on the other hand think in general more spatially, are more creative, are ready to act in case of danger, are less linguistic, less able to put thoughts and feelings into words and physically more aggressive. The moral development also shows differences. Women more often employ moral values that reflect the care for another person and co-operation; men are more likely to employ thoughts of justice and competition as a moral standard. Being oriented towards language and the ability to put feelings and thoughts into words causes women in general to be more skilled in self-reflection than men. With these differences in mind we have to emancipate with the biological flow instead of against it if we want to give people optimal scope to develop. Although socialisation is often seen as the most important source of differences, these probably link up, too strongly, to fundamental differences that already exist. A socialisation encouraging tough and assertive behaviour with boys links up with the tendency for action-readiness as a result of the influence of testosterone. The socialisation of the girl to care for others links up with her empathic capacity.

4

Conduct Difficulties

The Conduct Disorder

In general 'conduct disorders' (before I break this down according to predisposition, maturation and environment, I will use the term as it appears in the DSM-IV (American Psychiatric Association 1994) and ICD-10 (World Health Organization 1992) and place it between quotation marks in order to indicate that the term has not yet been crystallised) are understood to mean only those behaviours where the child comes into conflict with his or her environment: the aggressive form. The DSM-IV characterises these problems as:

> A repetitive and persistent pattern of behavior in which the basic rights of others or major age-appropriate societal norms or rules are violated. (American Psychiatric Association 1994, p.85)

The DSM-IV states 15 behaviours, divided into four subjects, of which three or more have to occur, and at least one for longer than six months, in order for us to speak of a 'conduct disorder':

Aggression to people and animals

1. The person often bullies, threatens or intimidates others.

2. The person often initiates physical fights.

3. The person has used a 'weapon' that can cause serious physical harm to others (for example a club, rock, broken bottle, knife, firearm).

4. The person has been physically cruel to people.

5. The person has been physically cruel to animals.

6. The person has stolen while confronting a victim (for example has knocked someone down from behind, snatched a bag, used extortion or armed robbery).

7. The person has forced someone into sexual activity.

Destruction of property

8. The person has deliberately engaged in fire setting with the intent to cause serious damage.

9. The person has deliberately destroyed other people's property (other than by fire setting).

Deceitfulness or theft

10. The person has broken into someone's house, building or car.

11. The person often lies to obtain goods or favours from other people or to avoid obligations (for example swindling).

12. The person has stolen items without confronting the victim (for example shop-lifting without breaking in, forgery).

Serious violations of rules

13. The person often stays out late at night despite parental prohibitions (before the age of 13).

14. The person has run away from home overnight at least twice while living in parental home (or once without returning for a lengthy period).

15. The person is often truant from school (before the age of 13).

(American Psychiatric Association 2000)

The DSM-IV distinguishes two kinds of 'conduct disorder': one that starts during childhood, with at least one of the aforementioned 15 criteria already occurring before the age of ten; and the kind that starts during adolescence, with none of the aforementioned criteria occurring before the age of ten.

Van Acker (1995) aptly points out that in view of the diversity of behaviours, there is the impression that the criteria have been set by the DSM-IV without a clear understanding about what 'conduct disorder' means and what it is based on.

The ICD-10 (World Health Organization 1992) on the other hand does not state any criteria which the 'conduct disorder' should meet. It is enough for them to indicate various behaviours and to give a classification of the circumstances within which a 'conduct disorder' can exist. Hyperactivity and aggression in a group are excluded. The ICD-10 distinguishes four defined categories:

- *'Conduct disorder' confined to family context*: dissocial (antisocial) or aggressive behaviour that is, almost exclusively, confined to members of the household to which the child belongs.

- *Unsocialised 'conduct disorder'*: combination of pervasive dissocial and aggressive behaviour with a general 'abnormality' in peer relationships.

- *Socialised 'conduct disorder'*: pervasive dissocial and aggressive behaviour where the individual is well integrated into a peer group.

- *Oppositional defiant disorder (ODD)*: with children, younger than nine or ten years, blatantly provocative, disobedient behaviour without serious dissocial or aggressive behaviour.

(World Health Organization 1992)

With this the ICD-10 does more justice to the large variety of sources of origin of conduct difficulties than the DSM-IV, and the conduct *problem* is already partly distinguished from the conduct *disorder*, because a distinction is made between the nature and the context of the conduct.

The diagnosis 'oppositional defiant disorder' is meant as a possible precursor of the 'conduct disorder', which is more serious. ODD has the following symptoms, of which four have to be apparent in order for it to be ODD:

1. having outbursts of anger which occur without any cause

2. continually fighting with adults

3. being deliberately disobedient

4. always blaming other people

5. being ready to explode (in a short and intense way)

6. being often angry and annoyed

7. often taking revenge.

Both the ICD-10 and the DSM-IV do not place the aggressive, outwardly directed form next to the opposite form as Achenbach (1978) did. The ICD-10 does, however, state *mixed 'disorders' of behaviour and emotions*, where in addition to aggression and dissocial behaviour, anxiety and depression also occur; they also mention the *depressive 'conduct disorder'*, characterised by a clear depressive mood as a child.

Based on factor analysis of the behaviour of 1500 boys in the Pittsburgh Youth Study, Loeber (1998) distinguishes three areas of problem behaviours, representative of various types of developmental retardedness:

1. *Conflicts with authorities*: these reflect a weak bond with parents and teachers and an increased, and often early, tendency for independence.

2. *Open problem behaviours*: these often have to do with the inability of children to solve social problems in a non-aggressive manner.

3. *Secret problem behaviours*: these are expressions of a lack of honesty and a lack of respect for the possessions of others. Secret problem behaviours (notably theft) show a lack of readiness and skills to obtain goods or to earn money in a socially acceptable way.

Loeber drew up a model of development paths for these three areas of problem behaviour.

I believe that the *externalising*, outwardly directed, aggressive problem also has its opposite. This is what Achenbach called the *internalising*, inwardly directed, problem where anxiety is at the centre. These children and youngsters suffer from extreme shyness and feelings of depression, and are strongly inhibited in their social functioning. Both groups of behaviours are classified by Achenbach (1978) under 'conduct disorders'; modern views often follow this classification, because one of the most important tests for behaviour assessment is based on this classification. Achenbach developed the 'CBCL, Child Behavior Checklist', in which a large range of behaviours has been assembled.

Externalising and internalising

In order to do justice to the various sources of origin, I made a distinction in the first chapter between a *disorder* and a *problem*, which both have an externalising and an internalising form.

Boys usually show the *externalising*, aggressive form; girls mostly the *internalising*, anxious form (Verhulst and Akkerhuis 1986). Although there are, of course, exceptions, we shall for the sake of convenience from now on speak of 'he' in the case of the externalising form and of 'she' in the case of the internalising form.

With regard to social functioning, the aggressive or the anxious form make an important difference. Aggression is mostly experienced as more troublesome than anxiety. From a social point of view this means that boys are often experienced as troublesome for their environment and girls mostly as troublesome for themselves.

The reason that the externalising, aggressive form occurs more often with boys has, among other things, a biological cause. With boys the level of the hormone testosterone is higher; this means that it is more likely that there is a higher degree of (physical) aggression. Their aggression is conjured up more easily because of their genetic disposition. On the other hand, tough, aggressive behaviour is also promoted because of *socialisation*, where this behaviour is stimulated more with boys than with girls.

The internalising form is characterised by withdrawn, anxious behaviour with regard to other people. The child does not adopt an active attitude towards the environment, and adjusts itself badly. Research carried out by Verhulst *et al.* (1990) and that of Bates and Bayles (1987), among others, shows that the tendency not to adjust during early childhood can predict internalising behaviour problems later.

The child with the externalising form shows *acting-out* behaviour. This child lacks self-control and adopts an active attitude towards the environment, causing it to be in conflict with that environment regularly. The child can arouse rejection and irritation. As a result children with the externalising form have an increased risk of *abuse* and at the same time their externalising behaviour is possibly a reaction to the abuse.

Internalising behaviour can cause denial, lack of understanding, lack of patience and concern. Children with an internalising behaviour problem are more at risk of their problem not being recognised and as a result are more at risk of *neglect*.

Children possess a limited repertoire of behaviours, therefore also a limited repertoire of difficult behaviour. There can therefore be various causes behind a behaviour. A striking example of this is the aggressive behaviour of two young children at bedtime, as shown below. On the face of it, it seems to be the same behaviour, but different causes are at the base of it and as a result different treatments are required.

> A little boy of almost seven years old and his little sister of five are living in a treatment house and both show excessive aggressive behaviour when they have to go to bed at night. During the day the boy is, however, calm and cautious, while the girl is very busy and has unbridled energy. Although their history is partly the same, and they both have been exposed to aggressive example behaviour from their parents, their aggression arose from different sources. On further inquiry the boy proves to be afraid of the night. He tries to postpone going to sleep in the frightening dark by provoking conflicts with the group leaders. The girl, however, is not ready to sleep yet in the evening and her busyness turns to aggression when she is forced to be quiet and go to sleep. The help for the boy consists of giving him a cuddly toy which guides him through the night, Brave Bear, his big protector. For the girl a little rhyme is made that she has to repeat to herself all the time. This way a 'buffer' is created for her between busyness and movement, and

sleeping. By practising the rhyme, the state of increased activity is cut down from the brain, while her body starts to rest. Both interventions proved effective because each of them linked up to the difference of the problems of the children.

Conduct difficulties, externalising or internalising, can, to a greater or lesser extent, be present from childhood onwards, or arise at a later age. They can have a biological cause, occur as a result of a specific event such as a trauma or be connected to a specific development phase such as puberty. Conduct difficulties can also be connected with a style of upbringing or with socio-economic factors.

In her research Mesman (2000) shows that there is a clear relation between conduct difficulties during childhood and frequent illness during the first year. This applied to persistent, structural problems. This connection proved to exist both with the externalising problems and the internalising problems. Mesman states that this is a strong indication of a constitutional component with these problems. Predisposition would play an important role, unless it has to be assumed that the environmental factors would play a determining role during the first three years. The conduct difficulties are probably not so strong and not so structural when the environmental factors play the most important role. In the case of problems due to predisposition we can, moreover, state that environmental factors play a part if they are not already there. A child with a conduct disorder has a less favourable effect on his or her environment and demands more of the upbringing qualities of the parents.

I have already stated that it is of the utmost importance for the treatment to determine whether it is a question of a *disorder* directed from within or of a *problem* directed from outside. With a disorder, you have to learn how to live with it, whereas a problem may be resolved. The group of children with conduct difficulties will be further categorised into children with mainly constitutional (predispositional) problems and children who mainly react to the environment and function according to their life history.

A conduct *problem* is mainly reactive, and a conduct *disorder* is mainly predispositional. Here we come across the distinction that I stated in Chapter 2: *disorder* versus *impediment*. The conduct *problem* occurs as a result of what I in Chapter 2 called an impediment: circumstances arising from the environment of the child.

In this chapter we shall concern ourselves chiefly with the *predispositional* problem, the *disorder* (see Table 4.1).

Table 4.1 Conduct difficulties: externalising and internalising, controlled by predisposition		
	Externalising	*Internalising*
Controlled by predisposition	Externalising conduct *disorder* or aggressive *disorder*	Internalising conduct *disorder* or anxiety *disorder*

I will compare the conduct *disorder* to the conduct *problem* in the next chapter, in order to make a more detailed definition. The conduct *problem* is summed up in Table 4.2.

Table 4.2 Conduct difficulties: externalising and internalising, controlled by the environment		
	Externalising	*Internalising*
Controlled by the environment	Externalising conduct *problem* or aggressive *problem*	Internalising conduct *problem* or anxiety *problem*

At first sight there seem to be quite a few similarities between the conduct *disorder* and the conduct *problem*. In both cases the externalising form of lying and stealing occurs frequently, as we will see; in both cases anxiety and avoidance play a part in the internalising form.

It is correct that the *externalising* and the *internalising* form are named under the same concept of 'conduct disorders' (conduct difficulties) in literature. We will see that they are both connected to the same subject coming from predisposition, which manifests itself in opposite ways. For example, testosterone plays a part in both cases: in the case of the externalising, aggressive disorder a high level of testosterone plays a part; with the internalising, anxiety disorder on the other hand, a low level of testosterone plays a part. We can regard the aggression and anxiety disorders, controlled by predisposition, as two poles of the same continuum. When the characteristics of these two forms are compared to each other, it defines in an extreme form, as it were, the general differences between men and women, as we saw in the previous chapter.

The conduct disorder

The constitutional component, the predisposition, dominates the conduct *disorder*, both in the aggressive and in the anxious form. This means that the number of children affected by it is very small. Problems due to predisposition always occur less frequently than problems due to the environment. Within the group of children with conduct difficulties it will only be a small percentage who show the behaviour as a consequence of his or her predisposition; the larger part will show the behaviour with the environment as the main source of influence. The longitudinal research shows that with the aggressive form it is the group that emerges as the 'hard core' which shows delinquent behaviour during their childhood until adulthood, consisting of 4 to 5 per cent (Moffit 1993). Although this number of chronic delinquents is small, they are, during their youth, responsible for more than half of all juvenile crimes (Loeber 1998).

When we look at the seriousness of the problems, the *disorder* is usually the more serious form. In the case of the externalising, aggressive disorder we find antisocial personality disorder, the psychopathic personality structure and the criminal. In the case of the internalising, anxiety disorder, we find people with *GAD* (*Generalised Anxiety Disorder*), *agoraphobia*, *social phobia* and anxiety and stress ending in an endogenous *depression*.

I stated that two elements can be found as a common thread with disorders: *resistance against change* and *problematic empathic capacity*. These two elements can also be found with the conduct disorder.

Thomas and Chess (1977) classified children according to their temperament and found three forms: the baby with a *difficult temperament*, with an *easy temperament* and the *slow starters*. Resistance against change is an important element of the baby with a difficult temperament. New stimuli are not received well by these babies; initially they react with shock or rejection. This can be seen in their motor system. Research into the motor system of babies shows that the baby has in principle a 'dancing', rather supple motor system. When the motor system is more wooden and nervy, this can be a possible indication of a disorder. This gives a first sign making early recognition of problems possible, as is shown in research by Hadders-Algra *et al.* (1997). Research by Hadders-Algra and Groothuis (1999) shows for example that a strongly deviant, stiff, wooden motor system is associated with serious brain abnormalities. A less strongly deviant motor system is associated with less serious neurological deviations such as ADHD and aggressive behaviour.

Children with a difficult temperament have trouble with new situations and cry regularly, unlike children with an easy temperament who respond inquisitively and positively to new stimuli. This difference in temper is seen as a risk factor for their development. The difficult temperament is often the precursor of conduct disorders with children during their youth, as is noted by Kaplan and Sadock (1995). I have already mentioned the research by Verhulst *et al.* (1990) and that of

Bates and Bayles (1987) that determined that the internalising conduct disorder is in conjunction with the tendency not to adjust during childhood. This tendency can be seen as a consequence of a resistance against change, in view of the fact that adjustment means change.

In addition to the structure of the brain there are two important physical processes which play a part with conduct disorders and which are correlated. Those are hormone production, in particular testosterone, adrenlaline and cortisol, and the working of the central nervous system, in particular the autonomic nervous system. These two physical processes have, among other things, as I indicated in the previous chapter, influence on the degree of *me–other differentiation, egocentricity, empathy, self-reflection, moral development, aggression,* and, as we will see later, the *level of consciousness* and the *sensitivity to stimuli.* In the effect of these physical processes, the conduct disorder distinguishes itself from the conduct problem and the externalising form from the internalising form. These physical processes and brain structures form the building stones of the model of conduct *disorders,* which I present in this chapter.

In the previous chapter we saw that the *xy*-chromosome pair starts off with a different development of the embryo than the *xx*-chromosome pair. Table 4.3 contains the elements discussed within that framework.

The importance of the *y*-chromosome is often emphasised by the outcome of research regarding the deviation where there is an extra *y*-chromosome: the *xyy*-variant. With boys who have this deviation more than half of them appear to show learning disorders, and with 58 per cent there proves to be a conviction with regard to 'petty crime'; this in contrast with the control group where only 3 per cent had been convicted (Rose, Lewontin and Kamin 1985). Galjaard (1994) states that it is impossible to maintain that an extra *y*-chromosome has no effect at all on psychological characteristics and behaviour, even though it is not always the case that an extra *y*-chromosome leads to aggression and violent crimes. Raine (1993) indicates that there is a connection between the *xyy*-variant and petty crime. He argues that this chromosome variant is actually associated with delinquency, but that there are other chromosomes which play a part, and that as a result the picture is not immediately clear when it is only based on that chromosome. We can see in this deviation of the *y*-chromosome that there is a link with externalising problems.

Raine (1993) states that it emerges every time from research that delinquents and criminals have a relatively lower IQ. This is in particular caused by a weaker performance on the verbal side. This points, according to Raine, to an inadequat working of the left hemisphere and inferior linguistic comprehension. Research b Njiokiktjien and Verschoor (1998) supports this idea. They examined childr with verbal and non-verbal *learning disorders,* who had a low verbal or a l performal IQ respectively. They discovered that a low performal IQ is in princ associated with dysfunction of the right hemisphere. With children, a low v

IQ seems to be connected with a dysfunction of the left hemisphere. In the previous chapter I stated that a diminished functioning of the left hemisphere is connected with, among other things, an inadequate me–other differentiation and a less strongly developed moral thinking.

As far as other parts of the brain are concerned, Raine (1997) reports that the frontal lobe of the brain in people with criminal behaviour shows deviations, notably orbitofrontal deviations. In their research Raine *et al.* (2000) state that they think that for the first time they have found scientific proof of the dysfunction of the *prefrontal cortex* with antisocial and psychopathic problems. This area of the

---

Table 4.3 The influence of the male *xy*-chromosome pair via an increase of the production of testosterone

Inhibition of the development of the immune system and as a consequence a diminished recognition of the *biological self*. In line we observe:

- an inadequate forming of the *(psychological) self*
- a diminished *me–other differentiation*, and in line thereof
- a diminished *empathic capacity*
- a *moral development* aimed more at competing than at co-operating.

Inhibition of the development of the *left hemisphere* and as a consequence:

- less focus on *linguistic functioning*
- a lesser ability *to put feelings and thoughts into words*
- diminished *self-reflection*.

Stronger development of the *right hemisphere* and as a consequence:

- more *spatial thinking*
- more *abstract thinking*
- more *creativity*.

Higher testosterone level after birth and as a consequence:

- more biological support of *sexuality*
- more tendency to *act* instead of to *talk*
- more *action-readiness* in case of danger
- more *aggression*.

brain plays a part in the low *arousal* and conscience problems which are characteristic of antisocial personality disorders and psychopaths. Little is known yet about the corpus callosum with antisocial personality disorders, but this part of the brain appears to have a role, according to Raine (1993). The left hemisphere also plays a part. There is asymmetry in hemispheres; that is to say, a more strongly developed right hemisphere in relation to the left hemisphere. In the case of sex delinquents it appears that the temporal lobe is functioning in a deviating manner.

The power of testosterone

It is particularly the working of the hormone testosterone that means that with conduct disorder the characteristics for boys and girls are divisible and seem to be each other's opposites. The high testosterone level with men increases the chance of aggression; the lower level of testosterone with women increases the chance of anxiety. Both the aggression and the anxiety from the conduct disorder are not linked to a situation but have a general nature. We therefore speak of *generalised aggression* in the case of the externalising conduct disorder and of *generalised anxiety* in the case of the internalising conduct disorder. With the generalised aggression, the *frustration tolerance* is low – everything seems to be a reason to become aggressive. With the generalised anxiety the *anxiety tolerance* is low – everything seems to inspire anxiety. The risk of developing anxiety problems such as *separation anxiety, fear of failure, homesickness* and *phobias,* and also *depression,* is high.

We have already seen that the fact that aggression disorders occur more often with boys and men and anxiety disorders more often with girls and women in the first instance has a biological cause. Research by Verhulst and Akkerhuis (1986) confirms earlier research in this field, which proves that the *externalising,* aggressive conduct difficulties occur more with boys and the *internalising,* anxious form more with girls. The great differences in violence between men and women cannot only be explained by pointing at the *socialisation process.* Research by, for example, Moffit (1990, 1993) among adopted children shows how important the biological, neuropsychological make-up of antisocial behaviour is. Research by van den Oord (1993), for example, shows that externalising, outwardly directed, aggressive problems can for 63 per cent be attributed to the factor of hereditariness.

Raine (1993) states that twin research proves that more than half of the monozygotic twins correspond in criminality (51.5%), while the figure is one fifth for dizygotic twins (20.6%).

Our starting point is that in the case of the *externalising* conduct disorder there was a greater than average influence of testosterone during the embryonic development and after, and that in the case of the conduct disorder in the *internalising* form there was a lower than average influence of testosterone. In the following paragraphs I will state the differences between the externalising and internalising conduct *disorder.* There are quite a few and so for clarification purposes I will put the characteristics next to each other in Table 4.4 towards the end of this chapter.

Starting from the anxiety model described in Chapter 3, we can, in view of the importance of aggression with the externalising conduct disorder, expect a higher than average testosterone level and we can also expect that with the anxiety disorders it will be a matter of a lower than average level.

I have already indicated in the previous chapter that research shows that the degree of aggression is in conjunction with an increased production of testosterone. Research by Granger *et al.* (1994) shows that the testosterone level of boys with externalising conduct disorders is higher than average. The higher testosterone level in this research only applied to boys who showed aggressive and delinquent behaviour, but who did not suffer from depression or anxiety disorder. This research supports the anxiety model which shows that depression and anxiety do not seem to go together with the action-readiness which is promoted by testosterone.

Anxiety disorders have not been directly connected to testosterone, because the relationship between testosterone and anxiety has, as far as I know, hardly been researched. In general the line which emerges from research into aggression is as follows: the more testosterone, the more aggression (Banks and Dabbs 1996; Coe, Hayashi and Levine 1988; Dabbs 1997; Dabbs and Hargrove 1997; Dabbs and Hopper 1990; Scerbo and Kolko 1994, 1995; Slap *et al.* 1994; van der Dennen 1992). Research sometimes shows that this relation is not always linear (Albert, Walsh and Jonik 1993), for example during puberty, when various sources of conflict exist (Archer 1994; Constantino *et al.* 1993; Gray, Jackson and McKinlay 1991; Halpern *et al.* 1993a, 1993b). Research further shows: the less testosterone, the more cortisol, although this connection is also not always unequivocal. Bergman and Brismar (1994) researched extremely violent men and showed that they had a higher testosterone level and a lower cortisol level. Research by Dabbs, Jurkovic and Frady (1991) shows that cortisol influences the relationship between testosterone and behaviour. Cortisol reduces the violence of the offence. Alcohol seems to interact with cortisol, states Raine (1993), because with extremely violent alcoholics there is a high level of cortisol. Antisocial personality disorders, in general, have lower levels of cortisol. People with antisocial personality disorders generally use significantly more alcohol than other people. Violent alcoholics, however, have a higher level of cortisol which remains high for a long time after abstinence from alcohol (Raine 1993). McBurnett *et al.* (2000) showed a low cortisol level, and especially a narrow range, that means a small variation in the level of cortisol over time, in the case of serious and structural aggressive male adolescents and adults.

Cortisol has the role of a mediator and no direct role in aggression. This fits in with the anxiety model which is based, among other things, on the working of the sympathetic system (see p.99) which comes into action in response to danger. It fits because cortisol is not directly controlled by the sympathetic system. The research regarding cortisol, a connecting link in the anxiety model, indicates in general: the more cortisol, the more internalising problems; the less cortisol, the more aggression. Scerbo and Kolko (1994) discovered a connection between high testosterone level and externalising aggression and high cortisol level and internalising problems. In his research among 4462 veterans Windle (1994) discovered that a higher level of activity was associated with higher testosterone level, more alcohol and more aggression, more substance abuse, and an antisocial personality disorder. Higher conduct inhibition on the contrary was connected with more cortisol, less social support, more *GAD* (*Generalised Anxiety Disorder*) and the depressive disorder. In their handbook on psychiatric disorders, Kaplan and Sadock (1995) state that with depressive people there is a raised cortisol level. In their research into Americans who were taken hostage in Iran, Rahe *et al.* (1990) discovered that cortisol was linked with sadness and anxiety.

Various researches indicate that depression with female adolescents seems to be connected more with the hormonal situation than with events in their life and their self-image (Angold *et al.* 1999; Silberg *et al.* 1999). Depression goes together with a significantly raised cortisol level (Jiang, Wang and Lin 2000). I would like to recall the research discussed in the previous chapter in which Steiger *et al.* (1991) examined the levels of testosterone and cortisol with depressive patients who had recovered. Testosterone proved to be raised and cortisol reduced, as can be predicted from the anxiety model.

Research regarding the hormone cortisol supports the connection of high level testosterone with aggression and low level testosterone with anxiety and depression, as described in the anxiety model in Chapter 3.

A different indirect connection between testosterone and anxiety becomes apparent through the research of Pine, Cohen and Brooks (1996) who discovered that the height of adults was related to the level of anxiety in their childhood. Girls who were very anxious proved to be on average five centimetres smaller than their peers. When we consider that testosterone is a stimulator of the growth hormone (Merimee *et al.* 1991), the lower height of very anxious girls makes clear that anxiety is connected with a lower level of the growth hormone and also a lower level of testosterone.

Although a direct connection between a low testosterone level and anxiety, as far as I have seen, does not seem to have been researched, there is however every reason, as we can see in the stated research, which for example suggests cortisol as a link, to make a direct connection between a low testosterone level and a high anxiety level and depression following on from that

There is an overwhelming amount of research which indicates in general the connection between testosterone and aggression problems. Through cortisol the connection is made between lower testosterone and anxiety. There is therefore a growing amount of research that supports the idea of a biological basis for aggression and anxiety problems. I mean here serious forms of both anxiety and aggression which stand in the way of normal functioning. I would like to point out that prevalence is not high. Crimes are commited by a fairly small number of people, but they affect many.

Because many differences between the externalising and the internalising conduct disorder are stated in this chapter, I will continue to put the characteristics of each disorder next to each other, in anticipation of the table towards the end of this chapter.

Main points

EXTERNALISING CONDUCT DISORDER	INTERNALISING CONDUCT DISORDER
* mainly boys	* mainly girls
* high testosterone level	* low testosterone level
* low cortisol level	* high cortisol level
* generalised aggression	* generalised anxiety
* low anxiety	* high anxiety

Me–other differentiation

The male structure of a less adequate self-recognition by the biological-psychological self and a higher testosterone level gives rise to the expectation that with children with an externalising, aggressive disorder the *me–other differentiation* will be inadequate. According to Matthijs (1990) it is indeed the case that an inadequate me–other differentiation is characteristic for children with an externalising conduct disorder. In diagnostics this concept can also be found in terms such as a 'weak ego' or 'insufficiently developed super-ego'.

We can observe very early on how the me–other differentiation is proceeding. A case in point is for example the behaviour of a young child in front of the television:

> A small boy aged one and a half was very fond of a television programme especially intended for the very young. He was fascinated by a scene that he particularly enjoyed and looked behind him to see whether his parents were also enjoying it. As soon as he saw that they were in the room and also watching, he continued his activity, smiling contently.

In this scene the child proves to possess a certain me–other differentiation. The child can imagine, while he is engrossed in the television programme, that his parents are not in the room and that if they are, they are not enjoying watching it. He experiences the other people, his parents, as individual identities which undertake individual actions, for example not being in the room, not watching television or not enjoying it, more or less apart from himself.

A child with an inadequate me–other differentiation seems not to realise what is going on around him. He does not pay a lot of attention to what other people are doing. Only when they frustrate his wishes does he seem to become aware of the other person.

We have already seen that an inadequate me–other differentiation is connected to a number of subjects, such as *egocentricity, little empathy* and *a moral development aimed at justice and competition*. The differences we observe between men and women can also be seen, to an intensified degree, in conduct disorders. The differences there are, however, are more extreme.

Main point

EXTERNALISING CONDUCT DISORDER   INTERNALISING CONDUCT DISORDER

  * limited me–other differentiation   * strong me–other differentiation

Egocentricity and empathy

When there is an inadequate me–other differentiation, the child will think that the world evolves around him, around his 'me'. In that case the childish *egocentrism* is not sufficiently conquered. From this point the child, the youngster and later the adult experiences the people around him as subjects in his world, as an extension of himself. He can use them *instrumentally*, like an instrument for the satisfaction of his own needs. There is little reciprocity.

As a result of the inadequate me–other differentiation the representations, the ways in which the child experiences itself and others, of the child with (externalising) conduct disorder are deviant. According to Matthijs (1990) others are seen in relation to, and as a function of, himself. Boys with an externalising conduct disorder tend to be a one-sided, superficial and action-aimed image of other people. They think more in terms of the function that the other person can have for them. Because of a lack of insight and sympathy, children with an externalising conduct disorder do not respect the other person enough as a total person. Their behaviour towards other people can therefore be very instrumental or manipulative. The child with a conduct disorder can be intimidating regarding other people, and for example force sexual behaviour.

According to the theory of ego development by Loevinger (1990), we can expect that these children are mainly in Egocentric Stage Two (impulsive) and Three (self-protecting) (see Chapter 3).

The attitude towards other people stands in the way of striking up friendships. The child with an externalising conduct disorder can be found in the ICD-10 (World Health Organization 1992) in the 'unsocialised conduct disorder', which is characterised by dissocial and aggressive behaviour and a general disorder in being able to deal with peers. In his research into bullying of children van der Meer (1993) reports that notorious bullies have little *empathic capacity* and that the chances of them becoming criminals are four times higher than with children who do not bully. It is probable that among these children there is a higher number of children with an externalising conduct disorder.

The instrumental use that a child with an externalising conduct disorder often makes of people around it is possible because he is not good at putting himself in someone else's position and has little idea of the damage that he may cause the other person. The blow that he delivers another is not experienced by himself as bad. He feels that the other person should be able to take the blow, be 'tough'. The lack of empathy causes aggressive people to interpret signals by others incorrectly and they are more likely to attribute aggressive intentions to other people as they themselves have been.

The me–other differentiation is a condition for empathy. Friendship is necessary for the development thereof, Sullivan (1953) observed. Through a friend you learn how to place yourself in the world of another person. As a result of its often instrumental use of others, the child with an externalising conduct disorder will have trouble striking up friendships. The development of the empathic capacity is hindered further by this. When a child cannot deal with peers very well, it may point to a *lack of empathic capacity*. Research by Verhulst (1986) shows that from the extensive questionnaire 'CBCL, Child Behavior Checklist', with which a large number of behaviours and characteristics are researched, 'problematic relationships with peers' is the most important predictor of future problems.

Children with an externalising, aggressive conduct disorder are characterised by more aggression, a weak me–other differentiation, strong egocentrism and little empathy. The opposite of this, a strong me–other differentiation, can be found at the other side of the continuum, with anxiety disorders.

Following a strong me–other differentiation is a strong *empathic tendency*. The child is always busy with other people and has the tendency to efface itself. This seems like *altruistic* behaviour, but is in fact behaviour that works to avert anxiety and in that sense serves someone's own interest. The child wants to please other people in order to prevent them turning against her – in fact an egoistical aim, not egocentric, for the child is aware of the individuality, the desires and the needs of the other person. We cannot, however, speak of egoism because the behaviour is not aimed at the satisfaction of the child's own needs *at the cost* of the other person. In Loevinger's (1990) terms these children are probably mainly in the fifth stage, self-consciousness (see Chapter 3).

Children with an anxiety disorder are permanently busy putting themselves in the other person's place. Because of that they tend to show great consideration for the other person, causing them to lose track of their own interest. We could say that such a child lacks assertiveness.

Main points

EXTERNALISING CONDUCT DISORDER	INTERNALISING CONDUCT DISORDER
* egocentric	* 'altruistic'
* less empathic	* strongly empathic
* assertive	* less assertive

Moral development

When we look at the *moral development* of children with a conduct disorder, we again see a difference between the externalising and the internalising form. The aggressive, externalising form will often go hand in hand with a moral development which is strongly aimed at justice and competition. The anxious internalising form will go hand in hand with what Freud (1947) would call a super-ego that is too strong: a moral development which is out of proportion and which quickly and frequently arouses *feelings of guilt* with the child. The child with an anxiety disorder is focused too much on what the other person thinks and expects of her.

The focus on justice, combined with egocentrism and a diminished empathic capacity, ensures that the child with the externalising conduct disorder often feels that it is snubbed and slighted. These children cannot depict the motivation that another person has for his or her behaviour. They see each event mainly from their own perspective. Because they are not good at putting themselves into someone else's place, they do not understand that someone else's behaviour is caused by their own behaviour. As a result they have trouble understanding their own role in an event. At school they often have the idea that the teacher always has it in for them and is treating them unjustly.

Because they usually have a relatively normal intelligence and do not show any apparent or visible disorders, while their behaviour is very problematic, these children often end up in special schools where most of the school population are boys. An inadequate me–other differentiation also means that the difference between 'mine' and 'thine' will be developed less strongly. This is because 'mine' and 'thine' is connected with a realisation of 'me' and the 'other'. Based on this and in combination with the lack of empathy, the child with the externalising conduct disorder is more likely to go out stealing and feels less guilty about that than the child who has no conduct disorder. The *functioning of the conscience* with children with an externalising conduct disorder is inadequate. Stealing will not become a conscious deed before the individuation period, at the earliest from the age of three. Loeber (1998) states six years as the youngest age at which *serious* criminal behaviour occurs. Stealing means that you are aware of the other person, of the fact that something is owned by another person and that taking that possession is not desired by the other person. For a child who has an inadequate me–other differentiation it will be the case that if it sees something lying somewhere, it will regard that as something that can be taken: 'finders, keepers'.

Raine (1993) states that aggressive children are morally not further developed than the *preconventional stage*, which Kohlberg situates up to about the age of ten and which is mainly oriented to obedience, punishment and a focus on pleasure.

The child with the internalising conduct disorder will not be so quick to go out stealing but on the contrary will be more likely not to be assertive enough with regard to her possessions. Because of feelings of guilt and fear she will be withheld from doing something which may harm the other person.

Main points

EXTERNALISING CONDUCT DISORDER

* limited moral development, and focused on justice and competition

* inadequately developed sense of 'mine' and 'thine'

INTERNALISING CONDUCT DISORDER

* strong moral sense, focused on co-operation and care for the other person

* strong sense of 'mine' and 'thine'

The ability to self-reflect

In the previous chapter I observed that there is a difference between men and women in the ability to *self-reflect*. This applies even more to children with a conduct disorder. Children with an externalising conduct disorder have difficulty with self-reflection. The difficulty that these children have with this is shown in the answers which they give to certain questions. Characteristic responses to questions like 'Why did you do this?' or 'What goes through your mind when you do those kinds of things?' are 'Dunno' or with the familiar shrugging of the shoulders, 'Because'. What is often considered to be an easy answer proves, however, to be a correct reflection of inadequate self-reflection. The child is not very good at recognising feelings and putting them into words – activities which are mainly situated in the left hemisphere of the brain, the hemisphere of which the development is inhibited as a result of the flow of testosterone in the womb.

Researchers such as Matthijs (1990) show that the boy with an externalising conduct disorder has an image of himself and of others in terms of activity, of acts. Questions like 'What did you do?' will be easier for him to answer than 'Why did you do that?'.

The opposite of the inadequate self-reflection of the child with the externalising conduct disorder can be found in the constant process of self-reflection of the child with an internalising conduct disorder. From an excess of empathy the child with this disorder is as it were constantly wondering what other people think of her or of something that she has to form an opinion about. There is unremitting self-reflection, which is excessive. The child with an anxiety disorder is constantly busy thinking about itself: 'Why am I so scared? Will they think that I'm stupid for saying that? Can they see that I don't have any friends?'

A striking example of excessive self-reflection, linked to a strong feeling of guilt, can be seen in the remarks of the young woman with an internalising conduct disorder:

> An adolescent could still feel uncomfortable even at an adult age about an event which took place in the third year of primary school, when during a school trip she had been 'difficult' about choosing a souvenir. She had the feeling that the teacher would think of her as being very stupid and greedy if she insisted on having that one particular object, as it was a little bit more expensive than the other one. The idea that this school teacher would have judged her negatively, she still found extremely unpleasant, even when she had passed the age of 20.

An important effect of the inadequate me–other differentiation and the inadequate self-reflection that follows from it is that the child is not well able to assess its own role. Starting from a normal intelligence the child with an externalising conduct disorder is not well able to assess his own role in an event. He will, in the case of a conflict, find it easy to accuse another person of starting it, and to consider the role of the other person in an offence as more important than his own role. Although this is often considered as passing the buck, it is more a lack of understanding. We have already seen that it is difficult for the child to see his own role, because in order to do that it is necessary to place oneself in someone else's position and to imagine how his own behaviour comes across to the other person and what behaviour it can stimulate. In particular, putting oneself in someone else's shoes is what is lacking with the child who has an aggressive disorder. The result is that the behaviour of the other person is experienced as the first behaviour in the chain, as if nothing has preceded it.

The other person, who is seen in terms of action with regard to the child itself, will be quickly judged as the instigator of the evil. The onlookers do see the chain of behaviour and blame the child with the externalising conduct disorder for his behaviour. The result is that the child feels snubbed and treated unjustly and goes into conflict with the other person.

Self-reflection provides the opportunity of adjusting one's own behaviour, based on analysis of that behaviour. For children with an externalising conduct disorder adjusting their own behaviour is therefore a problem. These children will act more as a continuation of their impulses. They therefore end up in situations in which they wonder how they ended up there.

The question is about the extent to which self-reflection can be learned. Self-reflection would, however, help these children and youngsters to adjust their behaviour better and in a more desirable direction.

Children with an internalising conduct disorder are often well able to analyse behaviour. Their ability to put things in perspective, however, is small, causing them to be weighed down under the assessment of the meaning of their behaviour, as is shown above in the example of the souvenir. They will constantly adjust their behaviour in an attempt to please the other person. The extent to which children with an internalising conduct disorder adjust their behaviour restricts them in their social functioning. They adjust their behaviour too often to accommodate the other person, at their own expense. They lack the assertiveness to advance themselves.

The boy with the externalising conduct disorder will have trouble *distinguishing his own role*; the girl with the internalising conduct disorder will generally have trouble *putting her own role into perspective*. The boy with an externalising disorder will feel that he has little grip on the events; in the case of an internalising disorder the child will have the feeling that she is always causing problems. Very soon the child with an internalising conduct disorder will regard her own role as disproportionately important and be weighed down under a feeling of guilt.

Main points

EXTERNALISING CONDUCT DISORDER	INTERNALISING CONDUCT DISORDER
* weak self-reflection	* strong self-reflection
* few possibilities of adjusting own behaviour	* strong tendency to adjust own behaviour
* not well able to assess own role	* not well able to put own role into perspective
* feeling of being treated unjustly	* feelings of guilt

The autonomic nervous system

Various researchers indicate that in the case of the externalising conduct disorder there is a decreased responsiveness of the *autonomic nervous system* (Martens 1997; Raine 1993). The autonomic nervous system forms the connection via the nerve tracts between the organs and the brain. It is one of the two 'connection centres' of the body, the other one is the corpus callosum with the hippocampus which takes care of the connections inside the brain. The autonomic nervous system consists of the *sympathetic* and *parasympathetic* systems. The two systems keep each other in balance. The sympathetic system is activated by, among other things, 'danger' or 'necessity to act'. The heartbeat, for example, increases via sympathetic working and decreases via parasympathetic working. If the sympathetic system is not activated, the parasympathetic system comes into action. Reactivity of the autonomic nervous system therefore means an increased response of the sympathetic system. During the day there is a continuous change of sympathetic and parasympathetic activity. During the night it is mainly the parasympathetic system which is active. A decreased activity of the autonomic nervous system means that the sympathetic system is activated less quickly. The sympathetic activity causes an increase of the sensitivity of the senses (hearing, seeing, smelling, tasting, feeling). With a diminished sympathetic functioning, sensory perceptions filter through less strongly and less quickly.

Research shows that in the case of an antisocial personality disorder there is a lower arousal (Martens 1997; Raine 1993). The heartbeat on average is lower, especially with youngsters who have this disorder. As far as brain activity is concerned research seems to show that in brain activity there is more theta-activity, slow waves. These waves occur more during sleep and are associated with parasympathetic functioning. Because of that these youngsters seem to be looking for sensation stimuli to increase their brain activity and with that their consciousness. In addition, their concentration function does not seem to be optimal (Raine 1993; Raine *et al.* 2000).

Lahey *et al.* (1987) state in their articles that children with an aggressive conduct disorder show a decreased reaction to various degrees of responsiveness of the autonomic nervous system: heartbeat when in state of rest, skin conductivity, epinephrine level and serotonin level. Raine and his assistants Venables and Williams (Raine and Venables 1984; Raine, Venables and Williams 1990a, 1990b, 1995) investigated the reactivity of the autonomic nervous system with criminal youngsters who remained criminal when older and youngsters who stopped being criminals after their youth. They discovered that those who only showed delinquent behaviour during their puberty had a higher activity of the autonomic nervous system than those who remained criminals and had already shown antisocial behaviour before their puberty. A diminished activity was, among other things, expressed by a diminished rate of heartbeat. The youngsters who remained criminal showed a less than average reactivity, while the youngsters who stopped later and did not show any more criminal behaviour showed a more than average reactivity. Those who were structurally criminal had an 'underarousal': a diminished reaction to danger, a *diminished alertness*. Raine therefore calls the increased reactivity of the autonomic nervous system a factor that protects against criminality (Raine *et al.* 1995). Research with a *polygraph*, a *lie detector*, a machine that measures the sweat reaction, breathing or rate of heartbeat, manages to register some tension with psychopaths, even though their reaction is low (Vrij 1998).

In accordance with the diminished reactivity of the autonomic nervous system Kaplan and Sadock (1995) indicate that children with an externalising conduct disorder score lower on various degrees of sympathetic activity. Children with an externalising conduct disorder have, based on a diminished responsiveness or reactivity of the autonomic nervous system, a lower stimuli sensitivity. This results in these children experiencing less fear, feeling pain less quickly and not being so sensitive to danger. Their nervous system goes, as it were, too easily into 'standby', a state of little alertness.

In the case of the internalising conduct disorder we would expect that there is an increased responsiveness of the autonomic nervous system. This proves indeed to be the case. Kaplan and Sadock (1995) indicate that with anxiety disorders there is an increased or excessive responsiveness of the sympathetic nervous system.

In the case of the externalising conduct disorder it can be said that there is dominance of the parasympathetic system; and with the internalising conduct disorder dominance of the sympathetic system. Boys with an externalising conduct disorder can therefore come across as being very quiet, contrary to, for example, children with ADHD who are hyperactive. It often is the case that the child with an externalising conduct disorder, who commits arson, plays truant, runs away and does all sorts of serious things, is in general also friendly and quiet. The people around them are often surprised that this quiet child can show such seriously antisocial behaviour, or that the friendly, quiet neighbour has committed such serious crimes. The two 'different children' seem contradictory.

Kaplan and Sadock (1995) indicate that with people who have anxiety disorders the sympathetic system has a strong reaction to stimuli and that this reaction lasts for a long time. These people show a slow habituation to repetition of these stimuli; the effect hardly decreases. The sympathetic system is activated, among other things, by danger and puts one on 'standby'. A slow habituation of the sympathetic system to stimuli means that this person is able to stay alert longer. A slow habituation goes together with an increased responsiveness of the autonomic nervous system. When there is a diminished activity of this system the body will no longer stay alert. A fast habituation of the autonomic nervous system goes with diminished activity.

Therefore, when a child with an externalising conduct disorder receives a negative remark, it will quickly get used to this stimuli and soon be indifferent to it. A child with an internalising conduct disorder will, however, slowly get used to such a remark and the effect will therefore influence it for longer.

The increased reactivity of the autonomic nervous system with the internalising conduct disorder causes a large production of adrenergic substances. When the sympathetic system is active without there being a real 'necessity to act', these substances are nevertheless produced. The adrenergic substances cause a feeling of anxiety and in order to give it a place, the person forms *cognitions*, thoughts, which correspond to the anxiety, and makes them fret. Schachter (1968) showed that people have a need to place physical perceptions, and to put a 'label' on them. The cognitions in their turn can conjure up anxiety and in this way the generalised feeling of anxiety is caused, which is characteristic of the child with an internalising conduct disorder.

Main points

EXTERNALISING CONDUCT DISORDER

* diminished responsiveness of the autonomic nervous system

* diminished sensitivity of stimuli of all senses: hearing, seeing, smelling, tasting, feeling

* not very alert

* slow heartbeat

* quick habituation to negative stimulus

INTERNALISING CONDUCT DISORDER

* increased responsiveness of the autonomic nervous system

* strong sensitivity of all senses: hearing, seeing, smelling, tasting, feeling

* over-alert

* fast heartbeat

* slow habituation to negative stimulus

Lowered consciousness

Connected with the responsiveness of the autonomic nervous system is the *degree of consciousness*. Because of a diminished activity of the sympathetic system the child with an externalising conduct disorder can end up in a state of low alertness, of lowered consciousness. As a result there are strong fluctuations of alertness. The autonomic nervous system of the child with an externalising conduct disorder goes into 'standby' mode too often and not in accordance with the situation – a state of under-alertness. It seems as if nothing gets through to the child, and parents who are in conflict with the child often have the tendency to raise their voice and to start screaming because of a feeling of pure powerlessness. The parents start to utter stronger, powerful statements in an attempt to get through to the child. The child undergoing this, contrary to what is often thought by the adult, does not think about what is being said, but waits until the parent's anger has passed. What parents often interpret as indifference is in fact a waiting attitude. We can see that when we look at the child's body language. The child is waiting and has no reactive or fighting attitude. It often keeps its hands in its lap or lets them hang alongside the body and remains motionless until the parent ends the situation. This attitude can easily conjure up aggression with the parent and the situation may end with a physical act, like a slap. Although the child is not consciously thinking about what he is hearing and does not respond, he is not deaf. Everything that is being said, he can hear and store. Children prove later that they are more troubled about what has been said against them than about the physical violence they endured. Although it usually does not show in their rather expressionless face during the fire and brimstone sermon, these children are really deeply hurt and damaged by the hurting words.

One of the results of a strongly fluctuating consciousness is the fluctuation of the intelligence. Intelligence is not a stable fact. Although we have the tendency to see it as such, experience teaches us that intelligence fluctuates with our physical and mental condition. In a situation of increased responsiveness, of 'arousal', one can be at the top of one's thinking and have access to the creative flow (Csikszentmihalyi 1996). In the case of alertness we see for example an optimally working short-term memory. The fluctuations in consciousness cause the child with an externalising conduct disorder to be unable to have the possibilities of his own intelligence always optimally available. We can see this clearly at the moment when the parents shout out desperately, 'What were you thinking of when you were doing that?' or, 'Do you have sawdust in your head instead of brains?' Such angry and hurtful statements come from their amazement about their child's behaviour. Compared to their experience with the child in other situations, they are surprised when it shows this kind of behaviour. A child with a brain deficiency, such as *Down's syndrome*, will not encounter such an outburst from its parents, who know that the thinking ability of this child is limited. Especially with children where the intelligence is fluctuating, the parents will not understand how their child has reached this delinquent behaviour. The child itself also does not understand it. An example of this can be found in the child with conduct disorder who can answer the question as to what he did, but cannot explain why:

> A boy with a conduct disorder was asked how he would describe himself. He had great difficulty in answering. He saw himself as a boy who did stupid things and did not know why. When he tried very hard he managed not to do anything wrong, but he did not know why.

In this example we see the impasse in which parents and children can end up. They notice that when the boy tries really hard, he manages not to 'get into trouble'. This puts enormous pressure on the child. A different child would, however, achieve the same without any effort. The reason why 'doing your very best' works is that this puts the intended and the to-be-avoided behaviour 'in front in the memory' – consciousness remains high, the child is alert. The child runs a smaller chance of showing antisocial behaviour when it is in an alert state.

Contrary to what is often thought, the child is in fact motivated of its own accord to behave well and will be able to do so as long as the consciousness is aimed at that. This state is, however, not structural and therefore the child will lapse into undesired behaviour. Lack of possibilities for self-reflection ensures that the child is largely dependent on his impulses and on the environment.

These children have the feeling that everything happens to them, without them being able to influence it very much. Their *locus of control* is strongly externally situated. This concept, coming from Rotter (1966), indicates what ideas the person has with regard to the relation between his or her behaviour and the consequences thereof. It concerns a 'centre of control', 'mastering your Self'. The location of the locus of control shows where the person places the control, the power of events, the control over the situation. It is important for the child's development where he places his locus of control. When the locus of control is internal, situated within himself, the child has the feeling that he is able to influence the circumstances. If the locus of control is external, outside himself, then he will feel strongly dependent on coincidence and circumstances. The child in the first case, with internal locus of control, has a feeling of power; the child in the second case, with external locus of control, will experience a feeling of powerlessness. The child or the adult with an externally situated locus of control has the feeling that everything happens to him or her. When a child always places the locus of control externally, *learned helplessness* can arise (Seligman 1975). This means that the child has the idea that it cannot help itself and is structurally dependent on other people. Where the child places the locus of control strongly depends on upbringing, and ethnic and cultural descent. The location of the locus of control proves to be strongly influenced by the environment, especially by upbringing and culture.

For the child with an aggression disorder the locus of control will mostly be situated outside itself. The child will have the feeling that things happen to him. Because his self-reflection is limited he will also not have the feeling that he can change much about himself. The promise 'I will never do it again' reflects more their own hope than a conclusion based on insight. Willingness to change behaviour and aiming for it greatly differ. However, the child does not come across like that. From his egocentric acting he is more likely to come across as someone who does what he wants and who has control. The child can even come across as terrorising and authoritarian. His acting is, however, not based on an egoistic assessment of the effect that his behaviour will have on others, but on a *social egocentrism*, a natural lack of ability to take other people into account. His motto is often that each person has to look after himself. That is what he does. He can hardly imagine that anyone else could not do that and therefore does not take that into account. An externally situated locus of control is therefore not the same as exercising control. Janssens, de Veer and Janssens (1991) researched the connection between the parents' location of the locus of control and the upbringing behaviour. They observed that an externally located locus of control of parents was connected with more authoritarian behaviour and that this was especially the case with parents with children who showed strongly externalising or strongly internalising behaviour.

In the way of thinking of our model, a more externally situated locus of control of parents with regard to the upbringing is to be expected sooner in the case of strongly externalising or strongly internalising behaviour of their children. The strength of the behaviour is a sign that the behaviour is possibly more directed by predisposition and can as such be influenced to a lesser degree. Strongly externalising or internalising behaviour can therefore be an indication of predisposition problems rather than environment problems and as a result can be influenced less. The fact that parents of these children would have a more externally situated locus of control with regard to the upbringing is in accordance with our model.

When parents and children are aware that fluctuations in consciousness and intelligence can occur, then this will make it easier for them to handle the problems. I will discuss this later in the chapter about the treatment of the externalising conduct disorder.

A state of diminished consciousness can involve serious risks. Not being alert enough means that a person can be in danger without being prepared for it. Children with an externalising conduct disorder can therefore intentionally look for danger, as a kind of 'correction' from the brain.

> A little boy with a conduct disorder crossed the road together with other children. They crossed the road dangerously, right in front of cyclists. One shocked child said, 'We must be careful and pay attention.' The child with the conduct disorder said, 'No, because I *always* do things a little danger-ously.'

Research by Quay (1965) shows that there is a connection between low autonomic reactivity and looking for danger and antisocial behaviour.

Looking for danger therefore has a function. The most exciting antisocial behaviours are things such as *stealing*, and especially *arson*. Fire appeals to primal feelings of fear in humans. By looking for danger, the child can, from a state of diminished consciousness, end up in a state of increased consciousness. Arson seems pre-eminently suitable as a subject for danger-seeking. Such behaviour can arise from a state of diminished consciousness up to and including a strongly lowered consciousness. The latter is the case with a *twilight state* which goes with a lack of sense of reality. Just how typical this behaviour is can be told by the father of a boy with an externalising conduct disorder:

> I don't know. Every time when there is fire on the table, for example matches, his eyes start to shine. He has it with nothing else and has always had it. He then *has* to play with the fire. He would love to throw methylated spirits over it. When I tell him he is allowed to do so, that he can mess about with it in the ashtray, it seems like it is all over. When he is allowed to do it, apparently all the fun is gone.

What this father observes is the decrease of danger, after he has allowed the child to play with fire. It is not the arson itself that interests the child so much, but the danger involved. Arson is rare, but Gomez (1991) observes that 84 per cent of arsonists are boys.

Looking for excitement and danger by the child with an externalising conduct disorder can be seen as a problematic form of 'wisdom of the body'. The body registers a level of consciousness which is too low and starts looking for possibilities to increase this, for a possibility of activating the sympathetic system. Danger is the most direct possibility. The often observed fact that children with a diminished reactivity of the autonomic nervous system seem to be looking for danger can be explained by this line of thinking.

A state of diminished consciousness can especially be provoked by two situations. The first is a *monotonous* situation, for example cognitive work which requires concentration, situations which require little movement, but are perceived as mainly boring. The second risky situation is that of *psychological isolation* – the child cutting itself off from others when it is hurt. Cutting oneself off mentally generates a state of lower consciousness and poses a risk for the child with externalising conduct disorder. Starting from a state of a level of consciousness which is too low, the child can subsequently start looking for danger. A negative approach can cause these children to withdraw into a lower state of consciousness, thus increasing the risk that they will 'get into trouble'.

Children with an externalising conduct disorder are often helped by structure, which gives them something to hold on to in their day-to-day functioning. It fills in the time and prevents boredom if it is interesting enough. Structure, combined with a positive approach, is favourable and has a preventative effect.

What is striking with these children is that they are actually looking for protection. They want help with the handicap which they experience without being aware of it. A striking example of this need for protection is the question asked by a teacher to the therapist of a youngster with an externalising conduct disorder:

A youngster said to his teacher, 'Sir, when I go for my apprenticeship, don't put me near a cash register, because I will empty it out.' The teacher wondered whether he should listen to the child and protect him against himself or whether he should give the child the confidence that with such an insight he would not rob the cash register.

Such an example clarifies that the reaction of the environment must be adjusted to the underlying problem. If we deal with a child with a conduct *disorder*, then we must listen to what the child is saying. The child knows that he sometimes loses control and can do things which he himself does not want and which he cannot predict, or prevent. Giving him the protection he asks for is then the right answer. A child with a conduct *problem*, on the other hand, requires an opposite approach. In the said example the boy was listened to and he had a perfect apprenticeship for eight months, where he had no contact with money. But when some visitors from abroad left behind a small suitcase, he took the suitcase and this immediately meant the end of his apprenticeship. Protection can never be watertight and the problem remains. In the chapter concerning externalising conduct disorder this will be discussed in more detail.

Contrary to the diminished responsivity with the externalising disorder, with the internalising conduct disorder it is a matter of an increased responsivity, an increased consciousness, 'being on your guard' all the time. These children are not looking for danger, but, on the contrary, avoiding it. The degree to which they observe danger is disproportionately high. Danger is not only experienced in physically threatening situations, but also, and especially, in social situations. They seem to hear and see everything. Each sound in the house seems to be picked up and each look intercepted. Unlike the child with an externalising conduct disorder, with this child the stimuli are passed on to the brain much more quickly, through the autonomic nervous system, and the stimuli are processed much quicker there. This does not mean, by the way, that processing of the stimuli is also more quickly converted into action. The fact that this disorder occurs more often on the female side is not surprising when we realise that, in general, the sensitivity to stimuli is higher in women. Velle (1992) states in his article that women are more sensitive than men to stimuli from all senses. They receive the stimuli of hearing, feeling, smelling and tasting more strongly than men. As far as 'seeing' is concerned the situation is a bit more complex. 'Seeing nearby' is parasympathetic and 'seeing far' is sympathetic; there are therefore differences in the various kinds of 'seeing'. It is, however, the case that women receive visual stimuli considerably more quickly than men. Women show an increased responsiveness with regard to all senses than men do; that does not mean to say that they also show a quicker reaction to the stimulus, because that is action, and, on average, the male is quicker to act. We can therefore see the differences in responsiveness of the autonomic nervous system with the conduct disorder again alongside the normal differences between men and women.

Within this framework it is interesting to mention recent research which looks at the processing of sensory stimuli of children with dyslexia. This disorder occurs much more often with boys than with girls and often goes together with a different maturation disorder such as, for example, ADHD. Children with dyslexia have often more than average problems with the processing of sensory information, both visual (Cornelissen *et al.* 1998) and auditory (McAnally and Stein 1997).

Children and youngsters with an anxiety disorder feel continuously threatened and try to resist that threat by way of *avoiding.* We find the same kind of behaviour with *phobic anxiety,* and theoreticians have proved that this avoidance behaviour ensures that the anxiety remains. A realistic testing of reality is lacking and as a result the subject of the anxiety cannot be brought back to seeing things in proportion. With children with an internalising conduct disorder it is a matter of generalised anxiety; the anxiety is not restricted to a specific situation or a specific subject. Social situations, however, conjure up excessive anxiety. The child shows the characteristics of a *social phobia.* A specific element of this can be found again with *selective mutism,* where the child is extremely shy and, although it has command of language, refuses to speak to people other than those familiar to her, usually the mother.

In addition to *phobic behaviour* it is possible that *compulsive disorders* arise. Frith (2003) says that *repetitive behaviour* and *stereotyped behaviour* with autistic people increase in situations that conjure up anxiety. *Obsessions* conjure up anxiety and *compulsive actions* try to combat anxiety, which becomes understandable in light of the anxiety model.

Generalised anxiety can be translated by children into *psychosomatic complaints.* In general these children have many physical complaints.

Children with an internalising conduct disorder can end up in social isolation by avoiding social situations. We can see this isolation arise in a different way with the child with an externalising conduct disorder because their lack of empathy hinders the formation of friendships. They are usually also not part of a group.

> The police were concerned about a boy who had been diagnosed as having an externalising conduct disorder. He was involved in a lot of burglaries. That was, however, not the greatest concern the police had. They were seriously concerned about the atypical picture, that this boy did these burglaries all on his own and not, as is common with delinquent adolescents, as part of a group.

The element of lack of friendship with the externalising child can be found back in the ICD-10 (World Health Organization 1992). A distinction is made here between 'conduct disorders' in *socialised* and in *unsocialised* form. This distinction refers to the ability of forming friendships with peers. This ability shows the

me–other differentiation and the empathy which is followed by striking up friendships.

Main points

EXTERNALISING CONDUCT DISORDER	INTERNALISING CONDUCT DISORDER
* diminished consciousness	* increased consciousness
* not seeing danger	* seeing danger everywhere
* looking for danger	* avoiding danger
* social isolation because of lack of empathy	* social isolation because of the avoidance of social situations
* few psychosomatic complaints	* psychosomatic complaints

Hormones during puberty

An increase in externalising behaviour can occur during puberty as a result of
hormonal changes in addition to family conflicts which are linked to the request
for autonomy of the adolescent. The changes, the increase of testosterone among
other things, are a biological breeding ground for conduct difficulties, which can
also arise with children who do not have a conduct disorder. They incite the adolescent to more action-readiness and increased sexual interest. The growth of the
intellectual possibilities during this phase, together with the increase of
action-readiness as a result of the increase of testosterone, means that adolescence
is characterised by big deeds, risky behaviour and fighting on the barricades for
big ideals.

  Puberty is in fact one of the most healthy stages of life, physically. Youngsters
usually do not die due to illnesses during this period. Causes of deaths are mainly
accidents, violence or suicide. Puberty is also the time when the child will detach
itself from its parents. We have already seen (Chapter 3) that the conflicts which
may accompany this, due to the increase of testosterone, influence the degree of
aggression which occurs during this period.

  When the hormonal flow during puberty comes together with *risk factors* for
the development, the chances of conduct difficulties increase. I will return to this
subject in the next chapter, when I discuss conduct *problems*.

  The effect of the hormonal changes with the externalising conduct disorder is
different from the effect with the internalising conduct disorder. The behaviour of
the child with an externalising conduct disorder will be amplified and an increase
of aggression is possible. As a result the problems around the adolescent will
increase. The flow of testosterone during puberty can, however, have a favourable
effect on youngsters with an internalising conduct disorder. The anxious

behaviour of the child with an internalising conduct disorder may diminish; the flow of testosterone increases the action-readiness, reducing the helplessness and anxiety. Lack of balance between the hormones can, however, also become so big that the anxiety disorder ends in a depression. I will come back to that in the next section.

With adolescents there exists fluctuations of the hormone levels. This is even stronger in women because the menstruation cycle also causes fluctuations of various hormones. I have already mentioned that this cycle can cause particular frames of mind. Within this framework it is intriguing that research by Dalton (1961) proved that almost half of the women who were sentenced for an offence committed the offence in the four days before and after menstruation. Later studies support this result (Fishbein 1992).

Depression

In the Introduction I mentioned briefly that in the case of depression a division between predisposition and environment is possible. Someone who has a tendency for depression may possibly end up in a depression caused by just a small, sometimes unimportant, event, or, as is more likely, may end up in a depression after a long period of anxiety. The reverse is also possible: someone who hardly has a tendency for depression may end up in a depression because of a serious cause. With this description it becomes clear that the origin and the course of depression for the *endogenous*, genetic depression is different from the origin and course of the *exogenous* depression, where the environment plays an important role. In addition, the possibility of immaturation of the hormone production, for example, can be significant with children. (See Table 1.2 in Chapter 1 which shows the two sources for depression.)

Depression can occur in various degrees; the DSM-IV (American Psychiatric Association 1994) speaks of the *major depression* and the *dysthymic disorder*, and in addition the (remainder) category *depressive disorder not otherwise specified*. With the *adjustment disorders* is also stated the *adjustment disorders with depressed mood*. As yet there is no specific description of depression with children and adolescents. The DSM-IV does indicate that the manifestation of depression with children can be different than with adults. Somatic complaints, irritability and social withdrawal is found more often with children than with adolescents and adults. Irritability as an expression of depression with children becomes clear in the anxiety model. Notwithstanding a basic feeling of anxiety, the child when younger may be still on the acting side, but as the child grows older a shift towards the non-acting side can arise and the depression becomes clearer. The psychosomatic consequences connected to these problems will become clear from the psychosomatic scheme in Appendix 1.

Depressive children are more often irritable, while we tend to think of depression causing listlessness, slowness, lack of activity – the picture we see with adults. That is the reason why it took so long to recognise depression within children. The first systematic description of depression within children was the *anaclitic depression* which Spitz (1945, 1965) observed with children who did receive physical care, but no emotional contact. A number of these children (15%) ended up in a depression and died. Anna Freud and Burlingham (1974) described the same phenomenon with war orphans. Nevertheless, the idea of depression within children moved into the background again. With the concept of *masked depression* the concept of depression within children came into the picture again in the 1960s and 1970s. Depression would be hidden underneath different problems, for example conduct problems. The ideas about depression have in the meantime developed so much that we do not speak of 'masked depression' any more, but of a different manifestation of depression within children. De Wit (2000) talks of the *being-a-child factor*; that means to say, the immaturation of the child causes depression to occur and to have a different manifestation. Depression with a baby manifests itself in listless crying and protesting behaviour; with pre-schoolers and children at primary school in sadness, irritability, agitation or anxiety. With the adolescent it is more often a case of dull sorrow and irritability, and finally with adults listlessness and a dull and empty feeling dominate.

In these descriptions we see that when activity diminishes, listlessness comes more and more into the foreground. Starting from the anxiety model we could say that depression is preceded by a period of anxiety, of stress. Depending on the predisposition, sometimes a short period of stress is enough to cause a depression. This is the case when the processing of the stress hormones, the adrenergous substances, is insufficient and the anxiety is not or not enough converted into action or when so much is produced that it cannot be converted by means of action. The image of energy loss and listlessness then presents itself early. When it is still possible to fight the anxiety and activity takes place, the image of irritability, agitation and anxiety will emerge more quickly. Children who from their predisposition have trouble with coping with the balance between adrenergous and androgenous hormones, or who have matured insufficiently to maintain the balance, will show this active, irritable image in cases of anxiety and stress.

It is therefore not surprising, proceeding from the anxiety model, that in the case of depression within children there is an extraordinary amount of co-morbidity (the simultaneous occurrence of various disorders) with other disorders, such as *anxiety disorders, ADHD* and *conduct problems*. The most important disorders here are anxiety disorders. Co-morbidity is 90 per cent with adults and 95 per cent with children (Reichart and Duyx 1998). Anxiety disorders and depression resemble each other in various respects, for example in the cognitions which play a role, especially cognitions of low self-esteem. As a difference between both of them de Wit (2000) indicates that in the case of anxiety there is a feeling of threat and that the person assesses that he or she will not be able to cope with the threat; with depression there has been a loss and the person is giving up. In terms of the anxiety model this means that with anxiety it is a lack of action, an inability to act, and with depression not being able to act at all because the substances have met in a toxic relation.

According to the model there is a risk that, after some time, the 'irritable, anxious' depression changes into the listless symptoms. In most cases the depression with children proves to occur after the other disorders, namely the anxiety disorders, according to the AACAP (1998). According to the model this points more to a transitionary phase from anxiety to depression than to a real co-morbidity. An exception is the depression which goes together with substance abuse; there the abuse is, on average, preceded by four and a half years of depression. Substance abuse could in that case possibly be used as 'self-medication' for the depression. With adults it seems that the depression does not necessarily have to be preceded by an anxiety disorder. Birmaher *et al.* (1996), however, indicate that 60 to 70 per cent of depressed adults in the year preceding a depressive episode have gone through one or more seriously stressful events and, in particular, experiences of loss. In that case it is not a question of an anxiety disorder which preceded the depression, but of an anxious, very stressful situation. It is possible that for the rest of the group of depressive disorders there is no clear stressor which conjures up the depression, but a lengthy pattern of a vague anxiety which converts into a depression. It is interesting within this framework to mention that there is a link, and an active reciprocal communication, between the autonomic nervous system and the immune system. Stress influences the working of the immune system. With depression there proves to be a reduced working of the immune system (Dunn 1995). The reason for that is that cortisol, which is at a high level with depression, has a suppressing role towards the immune system (van Gent *et al.* 1997).

Fully in our line of thinking Garber (1984), Birmaher *et al.* (1996) and the AACAP (1998) indicate that depression during adolescence does indeed take the form of the endogenous, biologically tinted depression. Depression increases enormously during adolescence and it applies to a higher degree to girls than to boys (Cyranowski *et al.* 2000; Hankin and Abramson 1999). This is generally attributed to the hormonal changes during puberty (Warren and Brooks-Gunn 1989). Proceeding from the model I can state that, although testosterone increases during this period and more action-readiness is possible, there are various factors that work against this. First, in order to explain the difference in prevalence of depression with boys and girls, the testosterone which is produced by girls during adolescence, for example in connection with the menstruation cycle, has to be transferred for an important part into oestrogen. Second, the flow of testosterone is not stable during puberty but has large fluctuations. Finally, there are many sources of conflict and stress as a result of detachment from the parents. We have already seen that during puberty the relation between aggression and testosterone, which in general is linear, shows a fluctuating picture.

Little research has been done into sex differences in the manifestation of depression. Boys, however, seem to externalise more and girls internalise more. Research is, however, too limited to reach any conclusions. In line with all other problems it is, however, to be expected that this difference in externalising and internalising will occur.

Plomin and Rutter (1998) state that the same genetic vulnerability seems to be the basis of anxiety and depression and are of the opinion that research in the coming years will prove this. In line with my model I think the same and suspect a genetic predisposition for a specific ratio of adrenergous and androgenous hormones.

As far as the classification into *endogenous* or *exogenous* is concerned we can say that when it is a matter of a long-term build-up of irritability and anxiety leading to depression, the *predisposition factor* could possibly play a dominant part. When there is a decrease of symptoms on becoming older, *maturation* possibly plays a part; finally, when there is a sudden demonstrable start with a clear stressor it is more a question of an *environment factor*.

Psychopathy

Within the framework of the externalising conduct disorder it is relevant to discuss the antisocial personality disorder, the psychopathic personality and criminality. The aggression disorder during youth bears the risk of developing an antisocial personality disorder, psychopathy and criminality. The relation between these problems and those during youth lies in the volume and gravity of the externalising conduct. The pre-schooler will not be a criminal, but researchers like Raine are convinced that with the adult psychopath the core was already present in the child. That core is given in the structure of the CNS, especially the hemispheres, notably the left hemisphere, the alertness of the brain and the low response of the autonomic nervous system. Martens (1997) indicates that the psychopath has in fact an immature CNS and that curing means that continuing *maturation* takes place. The most important cause for the continuing maturation proves to be having a meaningful, intimate relationship. The aggressive component of the psychopathic personality structure is less strong. The aggression is much more situated in time and less omnipresent. This makes one suspect that the hormonal structure has undergone some maturation, but that the development of the left hemisphere, for example, has not (yet).

The psychopathic structure can be considered as an especially serious form of the externalising conduct disorder, where the aspects occur to a serious extent. We then think for example of a very limited me–other differentiation and a very low response to danger. When continuing maturation is possible through a meaningful relationship with an adult, then it is feasible that preventive help can be offered to further stimulate the parts of the brain involved and help them to mature. What is needed for that will be considered in more detail in Chapter 9, when I will discuss the treatment of the externalising conduct disorder.

Predisposition *and* environment

Adrian Raine is one of the most important researchers in the field of criminology. He is of the opinion that there are grounds to believe that criminality is a disorder. He bases this supposition on the criteria used in the DSM for disorders and the abundance of research which offers biological support for this idea (Raine 1993, 1997).

Raine indicates that research carried out up to now does not yet have a solid basis for the *genetic* basis of psychopathy, but expects that more refined research will show this in the coming years. I mentioned earlier that when women have a disorder, which normally occurs more often with men, they have it, on average, in a more serious form. We can see that again in the case of serious crimes. It appears that the genetic basis is stronger with women than with men. When we take as a starting point that a genetic basis is more difficult to change than problems which are controlled by the environment, we therefore speak of more serious problems unconnected to the nature of the crime. Criminals, says Raine, are handicapped by many biological and social factors.

Apart from genetic and biological factors with the antisocial personality disorder and criminal personality, brain damage due to accidents and injuries are also thought to be a factor in developing antisocial personality disorders. Rosenbaum's research (1991) shows that in 92 per cent of the cases prior to a husband's aggression towards a wife a head injury had taken place. Interpreting that kind of research is, however, not that easy. It does not mean that aggression is a result of the head injury, because the chance of aggression is associated to a risky life with a larger frequency of accidents. In that case the head injury would not be the cause of the abuse of the woman, but both could arise from an aggressive way of living.

Externalising conduct can be caused by both biological and social factors. In 1973 Scott (1973) made the shocking discovery that although only 1 per cent of the babies in England had a stepfather, 53 per cent of the babies who suffered abuse resulting in death proved to have been killed by their stepfather. The size of the family is related to criminality. Children are more at risk in large families (Raine

1993). The question is how important the influence of peers is. Harris (1998) thinks that this is an important factor in the forming of the personality of children, without specifically referring to the antisocial personality disorder. According to Raine the influence of peers can best be considered as a way in which delinquency is expressed, but not as a causal source.

When there is a conduct disorder, the child will most definitely also have conduct problems, as I stated earlier. The first reason is that with a problematic predisposition the chances are greater that the same or related problems are present in the environment. The best predictor of later criminal behaviour is parental criminal behaviour. It is not clear whether this is due to a genetic influence, family circumstances or a weak upbringing. Of the environment variables, little supervision at home proves to be one of the better predictors of criminal behaviour (Raine 1993). The second reason is that the child comes into conflict with his environment because of his behaviour and can develop conduct problems proceeding from that. A desperate parent who shouts hurtful things upsets the self-image of the child and this increases the chance of externalising conduct.

Also let us not forget that the externalising conduct disorder occurs only infrequently; the conduct problems which I will discuss in the next chapter occur much more frequently.

Based on his sound scientific research Raine (1993) pleads in his book for us to have respect for the predisposition of human beings and in the case of a criminal person not be too quick to think that he can control his behaviour:

> It is argued that while criminal behaviour is often viewed as volitional in nature, free will is better conceptualized as a dimension than as a dichotomy and that there are strong social and biological pressures beyond the individual's control, which to some degree at least, strongly shape that person's antisocial behaviour; consequently, such offenders can be viewed in part as not being entirely responsible for their actions. (p.320)

A lot of research is aimed at aggressive and criminal behaviour. The internalising problems are often underexposed. Maybe that is understandable because society is more troubled by aggressive and criminal behaviour. But the internalising problem can also be caused both by predispositional and biological factors and by environmental factors. The same predisposition that occurs in the child can, for example, be active in the socially anxious mother. For the child this means that, in addition to the disorder, there are conduct problems, because the mother's behaviour will hinder the child, who already does not easily enter into social behaviour, even further.

Antisocial behaviour and socially anxious behaviour

Children with an externalising conduct disorder show a number of characterising *antisocial behaviours*: stealing, lying, aggression, arson. They show egocentrism in social contacts and therefore want to determine everything themselves. These children often show criminal behaviour later. Because of their inadequate me–other differentiation and limited moral development they run the risk of showing psychopathic behaviour at a later age.

The children with internalising conduct disorders suffer from *socially anxious behaviour* and can, when adults, suffer from serious anxiety problems such as *panic attacks*.

In order to make a clearer division between the nature of the antisocial and socially anxious behaviours with a conduct *disorder* and a conduct *problem*, I will discuss these behaviours in a separate chapter (Chapter 7), after I have compared the conduct disorder with the conduct problem.

Outline of characteristics of the externalising and internalising conduct disorder

To close off, I will summarise in Table 4.4 the most important differences between the externalising and the internalising conduct *disorder*. I mean those behaviours where predisposition plays an important part. In the course of the following chapters I will continue to try to explain the diagnostic criteria of the various conduct difficulties and ADHD.

By means of a number of tables I will put the various criteria next to each other, in order to provide handles for diagnostics and treatment. I will start with the externalising and internalising conduct disorder. The aspects of the disorder are grouped according to biological systems. This is a simplification in the sense that in fact the systems co-operate and various aspects are supported by more systems. Using this classification I chose to classify the aspect in the most important system, me–other differentistion for example has been inserted under the heading 'weak recognition biological self.'

Using these characteristics we can reach a further definition of conduct *disorders*.

The *externalising conduct disorder* can be defined as follows:

> A general pattern which has been developing since early childhood of an inadequate me–other differentiation, little empathic capacity and an inadequate ability to put thoughts and feelings into words. There is a diminished responsiveness of the autonomic nervous system, making it possible for the child to reach a state of diminished consciousness. In order to leave this state, the child may start looking for danger by, for example, committing arson or going out to steal. A poor empathic capacity causes the child not to

be good at striking up friendships. The child suffers from generalised aggression and can emotionally explode in all sorts of situations which conjure up feelings of frustration. The child has shown a consistent pattern of antisocial behaviour since earliest childhood. This behaviour is not limited to a certain situation or a certain period such as puberty.

The *internalising conduct disorder* can be described as follows:

There is continuous anxious and shy behaviour in social situations, which increases with the unfamiliarity of the situations. The child tends to avoid these situations and in this way maintains the anxiety. There is an increased responsiveness of the autonomic nervous system, causing the child to seem to hear and see everything. The behaviour has existed since early childhood and is structural, not linked to one or a number of specific situations – the child has not started to show this behaviour after experiencing a trauma. The me–other differentiation has been strongly developed, causing the child to be strongly empathic and not very egocentric. There is, however, a lack of assertiveness. The child is continuously busy with self-reflection and with its self-image. Within the generalised anxiety the child shows the characteristics of a social phobia. Although the child is good at putting itself in someone else's place, it will still often be afraid to play with others and will choose the familiar and reliable. The child has shown, since its earliest childhood, a consistent pattern of socially anxious behaviour.

Summary

Based on the differences in predisposition which normally occur between men and women, I made clear how conduct disorders proceeding from the predisposition can, in principle, lead to aggressive disorders with boys and, in principle, lead to anxious disorders with girls. With the conduct disorder I make a distinction between the externalising and the internalising conduct disorder: the externalising, outwardly directed, aggressive form mainly occurs with boys; the internalising, inwardly directed, anxious form mainly occurs with girls. These two forms are each other's opposites in a number of fundamental areas: the me–other differentiation, the degree to which feelings can be put into words, the ability to self-reflect, aggression, anxiety, egocentrism, empathy, moral development and the degree of alertness of the autonomic nervous system.

Depression follows in principle from anxiety and stress. Depression can also be controlled by predisposition (or maturation) or more by the environment. This can be noticed in the nature and the course of the depression.

Regarding psychopathy, criminality and the antisocial personality disorder it has been shown that these are the externalising conduct disorder in a serious form.

With regard to criminality and psychopathy there are strong indications that these relate to a genetic disorder.

Table 4.4 The characteristics of the conduct disorder: aggressive and anxious form

Conduct disorder: externalising, aggressive form	*Conduct disorder: internalising, anxious form*
Mainly boys	Mainly girls
High testosterone level	Low testosterone level
Low cortisol level	High cortisol level
• generalised aggression	• generalised anxiety
• little fear, assertive	• anxious, not very assertive
• few psychosomatic complaints	• psychosomatic complaints
• antisocial behaviour	• socially anxious behaviour
Diminished responsiveness of the autonomic nervous system	Increased responsiveness of the autonomic nervous system
• diminished sensitivity to stimuli of all senses: hearing, seeing, smelling, tasting, feeling	• strong sensitivity to stimuli of all senses: hearing, seeing, smelling, tasting, feeling
• not very alert	• over-alert
• low heartbeat	• high heartbeat
• quick habituation to negative stimulus	• slow habituation to negative stimulus
• important fluctuations in consciousness	• increased consciousness
• what is said penetrates with difficulty	• avoidance behaviour, avoiding danger
• looking for danger as self-medication for diminished consciousness	
• risk with monotonous activities and being offended	
Inhibited development of left hemisphere	Strongly developed left hemisphere
• not very language oriented	• strongly language oriented
• difficult putting thoughts and feelings into words	• good at putting thoughts and feelings into words
• little self-reflection	• continuous self-reflection
• little capability of self-directing behaviour	• constant urge of self-directing behaviour

Continued on next page

Table 4.4 continued

Conduct disorder: externalising, aggressive form	Conduct disorder: internalising, anxious form
Weak recognition of biological self	Strong recognition of biological self
• limited me–other differentiation	• strong me–other differentiation
• egocentric	• altruistic
• not very empathetic	• empathic
• limited moral development aimed at justice and competition	• strong moral sense, aimed at care for others and co-operation
• less developed realisation of mine and thine	• strongly developed realisation of mine and thine
• norm-exceeding behaviour according to own needs	• little risk of norm-exceeding behaviour
• poor ability to assess own role	• poor ability to put own role into perspective
• antisocial behaviour	• need of contact with others, linked to anxiety, need of bosom friend
• little need of playing with others	
• feeling of being treated unfairly	• feelings of guilt
• social isolation as result of having trouble striking up friendships	• social isolation as a result of avoiding social situations
Risk of conduct problems because of conflicts with the environment	Risk of conduct problems because of not adjusting and limited experience with social situations

5

Conduct Difficulties

The Conduct Problem

Having discussed the conduct *disorder*, I will now proceed to the conduct *problem*. The problematic behaviour we see with the child who has a conduct *disorder* can partly be found with the child who has a conduct *problem*. The physical processes I mentioned with the child who has the conduct disorder, however, do not play such an important role with the child who has a conduct problem – the environmental factor is of more importance. Although a number of behaviours seem the same on the surface, there are clear differences. The frequency with which conduct problems occur is significantly greater than that of the conduct disorder.

Sources of conduct problems

The child who has a conduct *disorder* experiences the world around it differently from the child who has a conduct *problem*. In the case of a conduct disorder the child has a more or less steady, fairly undifferentiated, view of the world. With the externalising form the child will have the feeling that problems happen to him and that he has little grip on that. The child with the internalising form will usually have the feeling that the things that happen to her are her fault. The child who has conduct problems will, however, have a more differentiated view of the world. It will experience various parts of his or her world as problematic, for example home or ballet class, and other parts as non-problematic. In the *ICD-10* (World Health Organization 1992) this is expressed, for example, in the category '*conduct disorder' confined to family context.*

One of the most obvious differences is that the conduct disorder manifests itself from early childhood onwards, while the conduct problem in most cases does not occur until later, as a response to certain circumstances or during certain phases of development such as puberty. It is, however, possible that conduct *problems* have existed since earliest childhood, but that means that the environment factor has played a part since earliest childhood. This is, for example, the case with *educational impotence* of the parents, the inability of parents to offer the child a proper upbringing.

In the case of conduct problems the behaviour is mainly *controlled by the environment* and *situation bound*. The *DSM-IV* (American Psychiatric Association 1992) pays attention to this aspect by stating two kinds: the conduct 'disorder' which starts in childhood and the one which starts in adolescence. So we see the classic diagnostic measures, *DSM-IV* and *ICD-10*, both observing isolated aspects from the group of conduct difficulties without reaching an overall picture.

We can name four important sources which can cause conduct problems:

1. *The childrearing situation and its socio-cultural context:* this concerns both the factors within the child, the family, and the socio-economic situation and the cultural circumstances of the family.

2. *Puberty:* this concerns a meeting of the hormonal flow on the one hand and conflicts as a result of the process of breaking away from the parents on the other.

3. *Trauma:* undergoing a traumatic experience, especially when this cannot be shared.

4. *Divorce or separation:* changing family situation and possible new partners.

The childrearing situation and its socio-cultural context

I mentioned in Chapter 2 the structural and incidental factors in the environment which can influence the child's development. These could be a source for the arising of conduct problems. One of the important factors in causing conduct problems is a childrearing situation where children are *neglected, abused* or *sexually abused*. But also incidental factors like the birth of a new baby or the family moving home can cause conduct problems.

Research into the development of the child previously only consisted of looking at factors that have a negative influence; nowadays we look at *risk factors* that increase the chances of problems in the child's development and at *protecting factors* that

The extent to which the extended family plays a part in the child's upbringing is mainly determined by culture. In western culture, being brought up by the grandparents has become unusual; with immigrants from Asian and African countries, however, this is very common. Depending on the culture this can be the grandparents on the mother's side, for example in Surinam culture, or from the father's side, for example within the Turkish culture. In western countries, being brought up by the grandparents is more often associated with the socio-economic situation instead of the cultural values. When women *and* men take part in the labour process and child care does not keep up with that, being looked after by grandparents becomes more common.

decrease those chances. The *risk factor model* developed by Greenberg *et al.* (1990) indicates four *risk domains*:

1.   biological factors with the child

2.   family variables

3.   parenthood practices

4.   attachment relations during the first years of life.

Risk and protecting factors can lie within the child, the family or in the socio-cultural environment of the child. In addition to the risk factors that are within the child, the most important source of risk factors is the childrearing situation. Important for the start of research into protecting and risk factors was the research into the positive development of children under strenuous circumstances. Rutter (1979) discovered that in the early interaction between mother and child a pattern is developed of reaction to *stress*. The baby experiences stress, which is then expressed in crying, for example. This crying is already a way of dealing with stress. By crying the child can learn to mobilise help. In response to the reaction which the child gets to his or her crying, it will learn how to deal with stress. The child learns that its activity either helps or does not help to remove the source of the stress. In this way it can become *resilient* and cope with stress, or, on the contrary, can become very *sensitive* to stress: *steeling* and *sensitisation* respectively. When the child learns to arm itself, this can become an important protecting factor. Another example of the research into protecting factors is that of Robins, West and Herjanic(1975). They observed that black children, coming from a broken home with a low social status, showed less truancy when they were raised by their grandparents. The care by the grandparents proved to be a protective factor for the child's developent.

A term that is closely connected to resilience is the *locus of control* (Rotter 1966). The location of the locus of control can play a part as a protecting or indeed a risk factor. With an internal location the child will have more possibilities of taking protective measures

With children of alcoholic parents the influence of the environment on the location of the *locus of control* can be seen clearly. In the case of the eldest child this is often situated internally. This is connected to the fact that with alcoholics there is often an externally situated locus of control (Ude 1977). The child of alcoholic parents is generally strongly *parentified*: the child takes over the role of the parent to an important degree. The second child, on the other hand, has placed his locus of control more externally. For an important part it is raised and looked after by the eldest child. With this second child a 'learned helplessness' arises (Seligman 1975). When the eldest child leaves home, the location of the locus of control of the second child will shift towards an internally positioned locus of control. He or she is now 'forced' to be responsible for the course of affairs, because the alcoholic parents are not sufficiently able to do that themselves. For an eldest child from such a family a foster care placement is often very difficult. It cannot easily let the role of 'adult' go, because that has been his or her *survival strategy*, and it has difficulty conforming to the child-role which is required by the foster home.

itself; in the opposite case it will be more dependent on the part played by the environment.

This proves that it is not possible to make a link between one specific risk factor and conduct problems with children. It is, however, the case that a combination of factors will increase the risks of conduct problems by four. This is called the *multiple risk model*. It is also the case that a factor can be a risk in one case and protection in the other.

A striking example of a factor which in the one case can be protective and in the other a risk is the research by de Vries (1984) into survival of babies in famine-struck East Africa. The frequent crying by babies, which is a characteristic of a 'difficult temperament', is seen as a risk factor. In East Africa it was proved that the 'difficult' babies, who cried a lot, survived more often than the 'easy' babies. The difficult temperament in this case ensured survival, while in other cases it is a risk factor in the upbringing of the child.

Child factors

Within the child, *temperament, intelligence* and physical and mental *health* are important factors that influence the development. The child's temperament can play a part in the forming of relations with the family members. A child with a difficult temperament sets high demands on the availability and educational qualities of his or her parents and will evoke negative interactions more often. To maintain a positive interaction with the child is much more difficult on that ground. Janssens and van As (1994) observe that, in families with children with an externalising conduct, the *affective relation between parents and child* leaves something to be desired and children have *little faith in their parents*. A child with a *disorder*, autism for example, will demand more from the educational qualities of parents and can seriously affect the balance between resources and burden of the parents. *Diseases* as well, especially life-threatening ones, greatly influence the developmental possibilities of the child and the way in which the environment responds to the child. A child with a *handicap* will be greatly influenced in its development, depending on the seriousness and the extent of the handicap. Because *intelligence* is an important factor in the degree to which humans can have a grip on the surrounding world and to an important degree determines his or her social possibilities, the intelligence of a child plays an important role in its development. There are other child factors that play a role, for example the child's *skin colour* determines the identity and the way in which the child grows up, especially if there is a difference between his or her skin colour and that of the people around it.

Family factors

Within the family the *childrearing style*, the *relation pattern* and the *stability* of the family are seen as important factors.

There are various childrearing styles. The style can, for example, be child-oriented, neglecting, indulgent, democratic or authoritarian. Research by, for example, Conger and Petersen (1984) shows that the democratic style of childrearing seems to link best to the period of puberty. Which style is protective or a risk factor can, however, not be determined univocally, because this also depends on the context within which the family is functioning. An *authoritarian childrearing* can work as being protective in one culture and be a risk in another. Children who grow up within two cultures with conflicting styles of childrearing therefore run a greater risk.

We can see conflicting styles of childrearing with immigrants. What is seen as, and functions as, a protective factor in one culture is suddenly considered an authoritarian childrearing style in the country where the immigrant lives and works and is considered a risk factor.

Neglect, physical abuse and *sexual abuse* are extremely important risk factors from an educational and affective point of view. In the case of neglect, the child will develop a structural and deep-rooted negative self-image. It will build a world model where there is no care and togetherness, where one has to fight to survive. The moral values will hardly be given a chance to develop and the qualities and talents of these children will not easily be discovered and stimulated. In the case of physical abuse, the child will learn that aggression is a solution to problems. This also applies when the child is not abused itself but witnesses abuse of a mother by a father or vice versa. In the abused child, aggression will be piled up which cannot be sufficiently expressed to the abuser and will as a consequence come out when the child gets into a powerful position with regard to a powerless person. We can see the first signs of this with children who are structurally aggressive and are bullies at school. These are often children who have been abused themselves. The second important risk situation is when this child itself grows up and is confronted with the helplessness of the baby. To his or her amazement the grown-up child can be overwhelmed by a desire to hurt the child, despite he or she wanting the opposite, because they know from their own childhood how disastrous abuse is. A parent who has been abused before should be prepared for this wave of emotions, so that he or she recognises it and it does not do harm to their self-image, making them think, 'I'm a bad parent'. It should be recognised as the consequence of earlier abuse: 'I'm a parent who has been abused as a child and is overwhelmed by old emotions that are not adapted to the present situation.' The effects of sexual abuse of a child, especially when this was committed by an upbringer, can be serious and penetrate deeply into adulthood, even if the nature of the abuse did not go very far sexually. The child will definitely develop feelings of guilt. I will discuss this further later with the subject 'trauma'. The effects of sexual abuse often cannot be differentiated from the effects of physical abuse, because the two forms of abuse often exist in the same upbringing situation (Delfos 2001b).

A proper *attachment* with the child, a concept originating from Bowlby's (1984) range of thoughts, works protectively and proves to be an important factor in the child's development. Warm relationships within the family also protect.

Marital problems and divorce, on the other hand, are risk factors. Research carried out by Rutter (1978) showed that if there was one warm relationship with the child within the family, this would work as a protective factor, even when the other relationships in the family were disturbed.

A child develops *attachment* based on the relationships around it. The child comes into the world vulnerable and unprotected. In order to be protected, it has to develop an *attachment system*. By means of *attachment behaviour* it tries to keep the parent near it, so that it gets help when needed. Baby's first behaviour to attract the parent's attention is crying. The second attachment behaviour is the smile. When a baby smiles, the parent feels love and the desire to stay with the baby; the goal of keeping the parent near is being achieved this way. Other attachment behaviour is babbling, grabbing, sucking and following. Bowlby (1984) states that *attachment behaviour* develops according to certain lines. During the first weeks babies are not yet able to follow objects with their eyes, but they are already able to have social contact. They cry, babble and smile. This behaviour is not specific – they smile at every face. Between approximately three and six months babies restrict their *social reactive* behaviour to a number of family members and carers and they develop a clear preference for one person. By six months they have determined a number of trusted people and one person as central figure, and show *exclusive attachment*. They then show *fear of strangers*. From six months onwards babies are becoming more and more mobile and their behaviour is actively aimed at keeping the *attachment figure* near. They keep an eye on the parent. With any sign that might mean that the parent may go away, the baby will show that he or she wishes to follow the parent.

What it is all about for the child is in fact the *availability* of the parent in times of need. The baby attaches itself to different people. In this way an *attachment network* arises. The mother normally plays the lead part, but also fathers and, for example, day-nursery leaders have a role. In order to have a good attachment network, quality and continuity are essential rather than quantity. Forming such a network is necessary in order to help the child to cope with short-term separations from the attachment figure. The attachment is dependent on the way in which the parent responds to the signals of the baby. The attachment research, of which Ainsworth and her colleagues (Ainsworth and Bell 1970; Ainsworth *et al.* 1978) laid the basis, shows four types of attachment, all connected to a certain style of childrearing (see Table 5.1).

The principle of attachment as availability becomes clear when a pre-schooler is playing. When the mother is sitting on the couch, not doing anything, the child will play on. When the mother picks up a book, the child will often ask for the parent's attention. It feels that the availability decreases when the mother is reading a book. The same goes for the telephone. The child can be playing quietly, but when the mother is on the phone, it will start to be noisy and make the telephone conversation impossible.

Table 5.1 Style of childrearing and attachment type	
Style of childrearing	*Attachment type*
A. Consistent-responsive	Secure
B. Consistent-not responsive	Insecure: anxious-avoiding
C. Inconsistent-responsive	Insecure: anxious-averting
D. Varying-responsive	Insecure: disorganised, averting/avoiding

Mutual attachment takes place through interaction between baby and carers. When the mother responds systematically (*consistently*) warmly to the wishes of the baby (*responsive*), that is to say a *consistent-responsive* style of childrearing, then the baby will be *securely attached* at the age of one. It likes to have his or her mother nearby, but can examine a situation on its own. Securely attached children perform better in the pre-school period and later than other children. They have a higher *frustration tolerance*, more self-appreciation, are less anxious and socially more competent. Mothers who always ignore the signals of their baby (*consistent-not responsive* style of childrearing) leave the baby in isolation. When the parent responds warmly, but only when it feels like it (*inconsistent*) and not so much at the baby's indication, the baby will tend towards *over-attachment* and *anxious-averting* behaviour. An example of this is the parent who goes to play with the baby because he himself or she herself has the need, while the baby wants to go to sleep.

Children in this situation do not know when their mother will respond; they are unsure about that and are helpless when left alone. The most *insecure attachment*, the *disorganised attachment*, arises especially as a result of traumatic events, for example when because of the loss of a parent the attachment process is interrupted for a shorter or longer period, or with children from parents with a psychiatric disorder and parents who are addicted to drugs. Intergenerational research (IJzendoorn 1994) shows that a *disorganised attachment* can lead to preoccupation with, and anger towards, the parents. *Avoiding attached* adults have a tendency to idealise their parents.

Anticipating the baby's needs also means accepting that the baby needs rest and does not want any contact. A clear example is the baby's behaviour when it has contact with the parent. The baby likes this and finds it exciting and his or her heart rate increases as a result. In order to let the heart rate go down again, the baby will look away now and again. A parent who forces her baby to have contact at such a moment, because she otherwise feels rejected, ensures that the baby become restless and starts to avoid contact (Field 1987).

Important factors that play a role with conduct problems are affective and educational neglect. As a result of this neglect the child can suffer *attachment disruptions*. The child then develops an *insecure attachment* because the parents or carers do not respond adequately to his or her needs. We can find that in the child's behaviour when it adopts a *rejecting* or *averting* attitude in relationships. When a child undergoes attachment disruptions in earliest childhood, he or she runs the risk of a *school phobia*. A school phobia, contrary to what the name suggests, is generally not a phobia of going to school, but is a fear of leaving the trusted house and the attachment figure. There are indications that *agoraphobia*, fear of open places, is developed following from attachment disruptions or a school phobia.

Despite the importance which the childrearing has according to many researchers, there are also indications that make one think otherwise. Mathijssen's research (1998) shows that family functioning has little influence on the course of problem behaviour. Her research showed that problem behaviour, independent of help or family factors, is fairly stable through the years.

Socio-cultural context of the family

Within the socio-cultural context of the family, the most important factors are the *socio-economic status*, the *social network* around the family, the *school* and the *cultural group*. A low socio-economic status is a risk factor; social isolation of the family and lack of a social network, growing up in a large family, living in bad accommodation and living in old parts of big cities are also threatening factors. In the previous chapter I mentioned Raine (1993), who indicates that children from large families run more risk of having conduct problems; the question is, however, what the underlying factor is.

A 'favourable' school is considered to be a protective factor. After the family, the school is the second most important childrearing climate for the child. This childrearing climate consists of teachers and fellow pupils. There is a lot of competition at school and conflicts can therefore easily occur.

There is a distinction between *teasing* and *bullying*. Bullying is hostile behaviour towards an innocent and helpless victim, when and because the actual source of frustration is not present, or cannot be attacked for whatever reason. The most important source is usually the situation at home. Bullying can start to increase when there is a strong emphasis on school performances. In this way failure or success at school can become an important stress factor and lead to big frustrations. Bullying can, due to its discriminatory and aggressive working, be a release for some children for the tension caused by stress at school. Teasing is incidental; bullying on the other hand is systematic. Teasing supposes equivalence; bullying is based on a difference in power, causing the child not to be able to defend itself. In the case of bullying there is psychological and possibly also physical damage. This bullying is done especially by classmates, in particular boys.

> Initially boys want to test their position in the group physically. They want to know who is the strongest of the class. When that is clear, there is some more peace for all the boys. Often they can resign themselves amazingly well to the 'pecking order' which has been determined. A new boy in the class means that it has to be redetermined who is the boss physically (Biddulph 1999).

Bullying and being bullied by fellow pupils can be seen as a risk factor for the development process. Children who have been bullied in their youth can suffer the effects for the rest of their lives and it can even lead to suicide. The self-image of the bullied child is fundamentally affected and fear of the surrounding world is promoted. It affects one of the most healing powers which the child possesses: hope. Painful situations can be faced by means of hope of improvement or hope that it will not happen again.

Whether a child grows up in a *cultural group* which is in the majority in the area or in a minority group has effects on the development of its own *identity*. An immigrant child will develop part of his or her identity as being different, whereas in the country of origin the same child would not experience itself as different. When appearances start playing a role, the confusion becomes even greater. A non-white boy in the Netherlands will be quickly looked at suspiciously in a shop or in the street, even if this is his country of origin. People will tighten their grip on their purse and steal a look at the boy. In a country where that skin colour dominates, this will not happen to him. The Korean adopted child who may be seen in western countries as a 'closed' child with 'silent mouth and looking eyes' is considered as a perfectly normal child in the country of origin.

When clear characteristics can be read from the appearance, the child also has to deal with prejudices, positive or negative, which go with the external characteristics.

General

Humour can be mentioned as a general protective factor. With the help of humour a stressful situation can be put into perspective. It is also a way in which people can feel connected. This applies both to the child, the family and to the socio-cultural environment of the child.

In Table 5.2 I give the various factors which can be seen as protective or risky. I base this on Groenendaal *et al.* (1987) and Goudena *et al.* (1988). I will add the sex of the child to the factors stated by these authors. A boy has a greater chance of dying young (even miscarriages are more often boys than girls and the same goes for still-born babies), more chance of diseases, of psychiatric disorders and of having to attend special education.

Table 5.2 The factors which play a part either as risk or protection in development	
Child Factors	*Characteristic*
Sex	Male risky, female protective
Prematurity	Risky
Health	Good health protective, bad health risky
Temperament	Difficult temperament risky, easy temperament protective
Intelligence	The lower, the more risk
Psychological condition	The better the condition the more protective
Family factors	*Characteristic*
Reaction pattern to stress	'Steeling' protective, 'sensitisation' risky
Location of locus of control	External risky, internal protective
Adopted or foster child	Risky
Problems of parents	The more serious the problem the more risk
Style of childrearing	Style of childrearing can be protective or risky
Style of attachment	Secure attachment protective, insecure attachment risky
Relation pattern of the family	Warm relations protective, cold relations risky
Stability of the family	Stable protective, unstable risky
Health of parents and other family members	Healthy protective, serious diseases risky
Psychological condition of parents	The better the condition the more protective
Care by extended family	Protective

Table 5.2 continued

Socio-cultural context	Characteristic
Socio-economic situation of the family	The lower the situation the more risk
Culture difference	The bigger the difference the more risk
School	Warm climate protective
Bullying by peers	Risky

General	Characteristic
Humour	Protective

In order to conclude the subject of 'the childrearing situation and its socio-cultural context' I will state the 12 conditions for the development of the child mentioned by Bartels and Heiner (1994):

1. adequate care
2. physically safe environment
3. continuity and stability
4. interest in the child
5. respect
6. security
7. supportive, flexible structure
8. safety
9. sufficient adequate examples
10. education
11. contact with peers
12. knowledge and contact with own past.

Puberty

The second source that may cause conduct problems is puberty. During puberty there are two elements that play a part together with conduct difficulties. There is a question of increase of the hormone testosterone, and at the same time the *breaking-away process*, which the youngster goes through with regard to his or her parents, ensures that conflicts can arise between the youngster and his or her environment.

The breaking-away process which youngsters go through during puberty is often painful for them and also for their parents. It is often even more painful for the parents than for the child. Freud called this aspect of parenthood the most difficult experience in the life of human beings. From birth a process of *individuation* takes place which reaches its completion during puberty. Josselson (1980) mapped the phases of individuation during puberty (see Table 5.3).

Table 5.3 The phases of individuation according to Josselson (1980)	
Differentiation	Early adolescence, 12–14 years, emphasise difference from parents
Execution	14–16 years, tries out, thinks that he/she can do anything, listens more to friends, sees no danger
Approach	Mid-adolescence, fear of breaking away completely makes them return to base
Confirmation	End of adolescence, feeling of own identity

First the child detaches from the mother, then it starts to direct itself towards peers and forms a *social identity* – the picture that the youngster has of how others see him or her (Delfos 1999b), based on the behaviour of others, especially peers. During puberty the individuation progresses. In the first phase, the *differentiation*, the youngster will especially emphasise the difference between him or herself and the parents. In the eyes of adults it often concerns details and mainly external characteristics. For the youngsters, however, it is an important step to lay down his or her individuality. Subsequently the phase of *execution* follows which is especially difficult for parents, when it becomes clear how little their opinion is taken notice of. During puberty many parents will hear themselves say to their child, 'This is not a hotel, you only come here to eat and drink!' This statement expresses the hurt of the parent who experiences that peers (seem to) take first place. It is also a dangerous phase in the sense that the youngster often lacks knowledge and experience, but feels the action-readiness of testosterone within them and from that a great urge to experiment. It is the phase when youngsters who have never showed any signs of delinquent behaviour may come into contact with the police. After the youngster has detached from his or her parents and experiences a sense of insecurity as a consequence, the youngster will subsequently try to *come closer* again. Parents who felt hurt during the previous phase will sometimes have trouble allowing the conciliation without feeling 'used'. Finally the individuation process is completed by a *confirmation*, where the youngster develops its own identity.

During puberty there is an inner search and the youngster discovers his own *psychological identity*. Marcia (1980) distinguishes various forms of identity (see Table 5.4).

Table 5.4 Forms of identity according to Marcia (1980)	
Formed identity	The adolescent has undergone a crisis and has developed political and ideological ideas independent from the parents.
Identity diffusion	The adolescent may or may not have undergone a crisis, but there is no connection with profession, politics and the like.
Moratorium	The adolescent is in a crisis.
Foreclosure	The adolescent is not going through a crisis, but has political and ideological ideas which strongly match those of the parents. There are no changes in the ideas held from childhood; these ideas are adhered to rather rigidly.

Marcia found differences between girls and boys in the form of the identity which was adopted. A healthy development with girls often went together with the forms *formed identity* and *foreclosure*. With boys a healthy development often went together with a *formed identity* or a *moratorium*. According to Meeuws (1993) this means that for girls it is not exploration which is a healthy principle but choice or bonding.

Youngsters and their parents can have serious conflicts and a *generation gap* may occur. There are, however, indications that this gap is not as great as is often thought. The differences of opinion between parents and youngsters are often not about basic matters; youngsters often hold the same values as their parents (Bowerman and Kinch 1969). Only a minority of families have serious conflicts (Rutter *et al.* 1976). When other adults fall into the trap of an alliance with the youngster against the parents, they are not doing them a favour. This method has the opposite effect because he or she attacks the loyalty which children have towards their parents (Boszornemyi-Nagy and Spark 1973).

Knowing and understanding one's own origins plays an important part when forming an identity. In this period we see adolescents who do not know their biological parents start looking for them. Meerum Terwogt (2001) speaks in that case of *origin unrest*. Foster and adoptive parents are often concerned about whether their tie with their foster or adopted child will be seen as more important than the biological tie. According to Meerum Terwogt and Reijnders (1993) more than 80 per cent of the youngsters who met their biological parents satisfied their curiosity after one meeting and contact with this parent ended. Research carried out by Koomen, Hoeksma and Meerum Terwogt (1998) showed that three factors have a positive effect on a feeling of being well informed about the genetic father: to have met the father, death as reason for the father's absence and being informed at an early age about the existence of the genetic father. Meeting the father proved to be the most important factor and resulted in better social functioning and more satisfaction with social contacts. The reason for the father's absence proved to be the second most important factor which influences personal functioning. Not so much contact with the father but knowledge of who the father is and why he did not raise the child prove to be important for the development of the child's identity.

Puberty as we know it in western countries does not occur in all cultures. Whether there is a period of puberty and how long this lasts depends on the degree to which the physically grown-up man or woman is expected to take on adult tasks. The difference in time between being physically adult and fulfilling social adult tasks marks out puberty. This period is becoming longer and longer in the West, because youngsters attend school for longer and longer periods. In the case of a fluent transition from biological adulthood to fulfilling the role of adult, puberty does not have to take place at all.

The breaking-away process does not have to be dramatic. No matter how different parents and children seem to be during puberty, children quickly prove to follow the norms and behaviour of their parents. Parents and carers have to accept that a child will look for his or her limits. This is necessary in order for him or her to function independently. It is as it were a second *obstinate phase*. During the first obstinate phase, between approximately the age of two and four, the child shows its environment that it is a person with its own wishes and feelings – translated into 'no' uttered almost as a reflex, whether it is relevant or not. During puberty the youngster does this by making clear that his or her standards and values would be different from those of its parents. It is a time of reckless behaviour, of increased risk of accidents and suicide, but also of big ideals. Testosterone supports this increase in action-readiness in a physical sense, causing boys to run more risk during this period than girls. Of the small amount of youngsters between 14 and 24 who die, 70 per cent are boys and 30 per cent girls (Delfos 1996a).

Kapteyn (1985) speaks of the *moral aggression* which can come from the adolescent. He or she enforces their opinions and proclaims them fiercely. An adolescent is proud of the intellectual abilities he or she possesses in this period and wants to show that. An adolescent does not like to be told how things are. They want to find out for themselves and subsequently have the need to tell everybody about their insights. A parent or carer who does not recognise this can easily come into conflict with the adolescent.

The *democratic childrearing*, where there is room for consultation and attention for the development of the individual with regard to the (family) group, seems to connect the best with puberty, that is at least in the ego-aimed culture of the West. Democratic childrearing is, however, contrary to the family-aimed cultures, as we often find with immigrant families in western countries. The youngster can deal better with the consultation culture of the democratic childrearing, because it links up to his or her need for equality and the desire to be approached as an adult. This does not alter the fact that the youngster needs limits. Parents, however, often do not realise that the youngster does want to have reasonable limits set but does not want to thank the parent for setting these limits – this happens only after they have become adults. That means that the youngster objects to the limit, but usually accepts it. The most difficult aspect of this is that the youngster protests almost as if the protest is a reflex, and this reaction is what the parents remember. If they would look at the behaviour of the youngster afterwards, they would see that most of the time the youngster meets the parents' standards.

Traumas

Serious, traumatic events leave traces in a person's life. The younger the child is when it experiences a traumatic event, the more all-embracing and lengthy the consequences are, and these will take on a pervasive character. We can speak of a *PTE – Pervasive Traumatic Experience* (Delfos 2001a). The traumatic experience may have a pervasive effect on the child. That means to say that it affects all developing tasks (intellectual, socio-emotional, physical and motor development) and that it starts in early childhood and goes on into adulthood. The child and the youngster can show behaviour that deviates from their usual behaviour. The child can have a relapse in its skills. A child who was already toilet-trained can start wetting its bed again in the case of a traumatic or problematic event, such as a traffic accident or the birth of a brother or sister. The child can also start to show conduct problems. A docile child may suddenly become cheeky. The degree to which a child shows conduct difficulties is, in addition to predisposition, not only dependent on the seriousness of the trauma, but is also and mainly dependent on the degree to which the child has been able to share the trauma and has been comforted. Here it is important whether the trauma has caused a breach between child and parents.

An important event is therefore the loss of a parent. When a parent dies, the child suddenly ends up in an insecure world and it needs several years of mourning to give this loss a place. Worden (1996) indicates that the child is strongly dependent on its parents for coping with mourning. In addition to his or her own loss, the child will also be strongly influenced by that of his nearest and dearest, who also lost a well-loved person. The reaction of the remaining parent again is strongly dependent on the quality of the marital relationship prior to the death (Silverman 1989). The younger the child, the more dependent on the parent. In order to live on, the child needs care, protection and contact. It does not only need food in order to survive and be protected against dangers, but it also needs emotional contact. The extent of the meaning of emotional contact for the child has for example been made clear in research by Spitz (1945, 1965) and by Anna Freud and Burlingham (1974), who discovered that children could die when, although receiving proper physical care, they had to go without emotional contact. The same had already become clear from research that the German emperor Ferdinand II had carried out in the thirteenth century with the aim of finding out with what language children were born. The research, probably the first in the field of nature/nurture, led to nothing because the fact that the babies were only cared for and had no emotional contact led to their death (Stone and Church 1973).

Worden (1996) showed that there are various reactions to the death of a parent. Children who had lost a parent were ill more often and had more anxieties. After two years their self-confidence had decreased seriously in general, and they had more accidents. School results, however, did not go down spectacularly during the first two years after the death. In general the loss of a mother has more consequences for the daily life of the child than the death of the father. A father has the tendency to focus himself on his work in order to cope with his wife's death, causing the daily routine for the child to be seriously disrupted. Mothers tend to stop working and focus more on the family (see also Chapter 3 for the explanation of the behaviour of men and women in bereavement).

Out of *loyalty* (Boszornemyi-Nagy and Spark 1973) towards the remaining parent and other family members, the child will quickly hide its grief from the adults around him, especially from the ones which the child is dependent on. It does not want to add its own grief to that of the remaining parent and wants to make this one strong again as soon as possible so that normal life can be resumed again and the child can rely again on this parent. In this way a child can keep its own grief inside and remain silent. Worden (1996) states that most children who lose a parent are afraid of losing the other parent as well.

Because the young child's thinking is strongly egocentric it will be inclined to give events in its life a meaning which is connected to its own person. Coincidence is a concept that, especially younger, children cannot comprehend. Their world has a strongly intentional character. This means that when a traumatic event takes place, this will be linked to the own person. In this way the young child can place the death of a parent in a framework of guilt. Children who have lost a parent prove to be less supported at school than children who are involved in a divorce. Children feel a lot of shame about the death of their parent, which affects their self-image. They are even often bullied by their peers about their grief (Worden 1996). In the case of loss of a loved one it is therefore not only the fact itself that plays a part, but also the circumstances under which the mourning process has to take place. These circumstances are often more difficult for children than for adults and their appeal for help is often less univocal.

For dealing with traumas the degree to which the person understands the meaning of what has happened is important. With children we can in this respect speak of progress in understanding concepts around the age of seven. Also in other aspects an intellectual and emotional turn takes place around the age of seven. At the age of seven we can therefore speak of a *hinge age* (Delfos 1999a). This can also be found in the origin of a new image in the gene pattern (Fulker, Cherry and Cardon 1993). As far as the realisation of death is concerned, this means that the child up to about the age of seven experiences death as a long, reversible absence (like a journey or sleeping); after that time it starts to understand the irreversibility of it (Boszormenyi-Nagy 1948; Speece and Brent 1984; Steiner 1965).

> A seven-year-old girl had experienced the violent death of her mother. She had been present at the cremation and was aware of the fact that her mother had died. Three quarters of a year later she asked at length about the cremation. At that moment she realised the irreversibility of death: 'So my mother will never come back.'

From the age of around five children are actively busy with understanding death. When a loved one has died, people are often afraid to talk about death with young children. They are afraid that the child will not understand it and will have problems with it, especially if the death was caused in a traumatic manner. There is also the question of asking young children to come to funerals. In view of the way in which their thinking is developing, it is to be recommended that very young children be involved in a funeral and are told the truth about death. Children who are younger than seven years old and therefore do not yet realise the irreversibility of death will be able to deal with someone's death in two stages: first as a *long-term* absence and as soon as they are ready as a *permanent* absence. The child first experiences the long absence of the deceased and after some time, sometimes years, the child realises that the deceased is not coming back. Young children often deal with difficult messages relatively easily because their thinking process makes this gradual coping possible.

Research into French writers who lost a parent during early childhood suggests that this age phase is crucial with this group (Delfos 1999a). Bowlby (1990), who wrote a biography about Darwin, states that Darwin lost his mother when he was eight years old. He is of the opinion that this loss was the basis of the physical complaints and anxieties which troubled Darwin all his life. He makes this plausible by noting that Darwin repeatedly denied the death of his mother, after his sister forbade him to talk about their mother any more.

A poignant example of a breach with the parent, without the parent dying, is the one that occurs as a result of *sexual abuse* within the family. Sexual abuse by the father or stepfather, for example, results in the child suddenly having to do without a father role. In one blow the child has lost the father as a father figure and has become a 'partner' of the father, unable any longer to turn to him for safety and help. Sexual abuse outside the family can also cause trauma. This applies to extreme sexual behaviour, and also the behaviour which is most common with sexual abuse: touching and stroking, 'fondling' (Delfos, 2003).

> Guilt feelings with traumatic events have a function. A traumatic event is serious and often happens to a person without he or she being able to influence it. This causes a fear of repetition. Guilt feelings can work as a weapon against the threatening feeling that the traumatic event can happen again. Guilt means that there is some control over the situation, control which could ensure that next time the event will be avoided. This is probably the reason that guilt feelings are so persistent and even go against all logic.

Sexual abuse does not only have consequences for the sexual behaviour of the child as a youngster or adult; it affects the self-image and is a source of serious guilt feelings. The development as a whole is restricted and unbalanced growth can arise. Many of the effects are not obvious and often cannot even be traced back directly to the abuse. Only in the sexual field is the recognition easier. Sexually abused children have a greater chance of showing sexually provoking or prudish behaviour. Sexual abuse affects the development of intimacy and has different effects at different ages (Delfos, 2003).

I have already mentioned child abuse as an important risk factor in the development of children. Willems (1998) indicates that the definition of child abuse is not easy to determine. The definition used by the Dutch Office for Child Abuse is:

> Child abuse is any form of physical and/or emotional violence or neglect which happens to children, not by chance or accident, but by the agency or neglect of parents or other carers, and where mental and/or physical damage or deviations arise or can arise. (Quoted in Willems 1998, p.495)

The figures that are known only show the 'tip of the iceberg'. Child abuse is the most important or second most important cause of death with babies. This applies to all countries from the Netherlands to the USA. As far as sexual abuse is concerned it is proven that girls are over-represented as victims (three times as many girls as boys). It is estimated that between 7 and 10 per cent of girls between birth and the age of 16 have been sexually abused.

Apart from these forms of traumas for children, many situations can be traumatising. The death of a classmate, a traffic accident or placement in care are examples of situations which can be traumatising for children. Not every situation is traumatising or equally traumatising for every child. Children can develop an anxiety disorder as a response to a trauma, the *acute stress disorder*. This is the case when the reaction to the trauma takes longer than two days but less than four weeks. A child can develop a *PTSD* (*Post Traumatic Stress Disorder*) because of a traumatic experience, especially when this is an existential threat. This is the case when the disorder is still present more than four weeks after the traumatic event (see the *DSM-IV,* American Psychiatric Association 1994). The reaction to a traumatic event includes intense fear, horror or helplessness. With children the reaction often takes the form of irritability and excited, chaotic behaviour.

> The reaction to a traumatic event and depression with children can take the form of irritability. We see here the analogy with the state of overstrain in adults. The nervous system is frayed and cannot process new stimuli. One of the first signs of overstrain is that sounds are not endured well. The overstrained person tries to avoid stimuli. With children it is possible that the immaturation of the nervous system plays a part. Their immature nerves cannot process the amount of stimuli and as a result they become irritable.

A traumatic event may be relived in a dream, nightmare, or play. The experienced trauma is not always easily recognised in the content of children's nightmares.

A general reaction to a trauma is avoiding the elements which can be associated with the traumatic event and which conjure up fear. There is a decreased interest for activities and people, a numbing of general reactivity and feelings of detachment. There is a higher arousal, in the sense of *sleeping disorders, hyperactivity* or *temper tantrums*. There can be partial *amnesia*, loss of memory, regarding the trauma. The chances of this, however, are very small with children. Before the age of seven the working of the memory is, however, such that it is not easy to recall and remember. The elements are not stored under a linguistic label, but for example under a smell or a colour. Recalling then, for example, is more likely to take place through a smell than through an active searching of the memory, via linguistic subjects. This fact has already caused a lot of confusion. Freud (1947) was of the opinion that the painful memories from early childhood were suppressed. Schachtel (1973) suggested, brilliantly, that pleasant memories are also hardly available and that the memory function in early childhood works differently. The unreliability of the memory has given rise to an interesting scientific discussion which showed that the memory is treacherous and can easily be 'talked into' something that did not happen.

Guilt feelings are characteristic for PTSD, for example because a person is a survivor or has the feeling that they did not help enough.

The nature of the reaction to a psycho trauma depends on the age of the child. Pynoos (1990) indicates that pre-schoolers often have trouble with the ability to put things into words, which means that they have a cognitive disorder, and in addition also suffer from *separation anxiety*. School children often react aggressively, or are inhibited or have psychosomatic complaints. Adolescents often want to become independent from their parents, or on the contrary dependent again.

With the reaction to a trauma predisposition and socialisation again both play a part. Boys will be more inclined to react aggressively, in a way that is directed outwardly: *externalising*; girls will more often react in a withdrawn, anxious way: *internalising.*

Divorce

A fourth source that can influence the starting of conduct difficulties is divorce or separation. Although divorce occurs much more often than it used to and we have probably learned better how to deal with this, it is in general a serious problem for children.

A new balance has to be found after a divorce. There may or may not be an arrangement concerning parental access for the parent with whom the children do not live, or the children may be brought up in co-parenthood, which means that they spend half their time with the one parent and the other half with the other parent. Noorlander (2000) indicates that in 40 per cent of divorces the relation with one parent is broken off after one year. When parents living together without being married break up their relationship, the situation is even more unfavourable. As time goes on, the problems with the arrangement concerning parental access do not seem to decrease, but rather increase.

After a divorce children are at risk of having to take over the role of the absent parent. This causes what Boszornemyi-Nagy (Boszornemyi-Nagy and Spark 1973) calls 'parentification'. Children have the tendency to adjust more and more to the wishes of the parents because consciously or not they hope that the divorce can be undone or that in any case they do not cause any more conflicts.

In order to find a new balance after a divorce, children depend on adults. Children who, for a long period of time, have been involved in a divorce have difficulty in building up a clear image of their parents. Their image of the parents is limited to a man or woman who lives in disagreement with his or her environment. When the parents' problems are so large, the chance is smaller that the child's problem will be discussed. Full of their own problems the parent can fall short in caring for and paying attention to the child. The child's feeling of security is affected by this. The child's *social optimism* and the *courage to live* can be seriously damaged by a divorce. Analogous to the reaction to a trauma, boys generally react more aggressively to a divorce, being demanding and action-ready, while girls are more sad and inwardly directed. Here as well we see an externalising reaction with boys and an internalising reaction with girls.

Meesters and Singendonk (1994) describe the consequences of a divorce for children and adolescents in a developmental psychological perspective. The general course of a divorce consists of three stages: the *crisis stage*, which has as its climax the actual separating of the parents; the *transitional stage*, where new living conditions are experimented with; and the *stage of renewed stability*, where the family recovers a new balance and in this way offers safety again. After two to three years most parents and children have adjusted themselves to the new situation, according to Meesters and Singendonk (1994). Children need help with dealing with the divorce of their parents, that means to say learning to live with it (Delfos 2000b).

An important phase in accepting the divorce is the acceptance of the mother's or father's new partner. Children can start to show conduct problems when this acceptance does not pass off well. It is therefore important that the step-parent bears in mind the fact that the child did not choose the divorce, nor the new partner. The child, out of loyalty and because of dependency on the parent, cannot but seem to accept the new partner and is often already happy when his or her parent feels happier. After some time this will avenge itself and the child can oppose the new partner or the parent who chose the partner. Papernow (1993) mentions three stages in forming a new step-family. The process of becoming a new family takes about seven years, according to her, of which the first phase of about four years is the longest. The first phase is the one where the new family runs mainly via the biological parents, the step-parent being an outsider. The second phase is the one where restructuring of the step-relations takes place; the fight between insiders and outsiders decreases. Subsequently the relations in the third phase become more regular and more reliable; the step-parent becomes an 'intimate outsider'. From that moment on the family starts to create a history as a family. It is striking that the step-parent still remains an outsider. The biological lines remain the most important. Step-parenthood proves to be a risk factor for the development of children; within this framework I have already mentioned research by Scott (1973) about the high percentage of step-babies among the babies which are killed.

Wallerstein and Blakeslee (1989) stated various tasks which the child has to undertake in the case of divorce:

1. Accepting the reality of the break-up of the marriage. Learning to live with reality instead of having fantasies about loss and being abandoned.

2. Breaking away from the conflicts and the loss of parents and picking up the normal course of events again.

3. Solving grief and going through a mourning process.

4. Solving anger and self-reproach (we call this *depersonalising* from the divorce). Children blame themselves, or blame their father or mother. It is, however, difficult for the child to oppose the parent who takes care of him or her.

5. Accepting the permanence of the divorce. When the parents remain single and themselves hope for reunification, it will be difficult for the children to accept the definiteness of the divorce. Although it is nice for the children when the parents still have a good contact after the divorce, it has the disadvantage that it maintains hope.

6. Forming of realistic, hope-carrying relationships of their own.

A seventh task could be added: *finding one's own right to exist.* Breaking the relationship of the parents unsettles the child's existential right. Something similar applies when one of the parents discovers that he or she is homosexual. Discovering and especially recognising homosexuality during a heterosexual marriage affects the marriage's right to exist and, with that, that of the child. It is necessary to pay attention to that and to offer the child the possibility to regain his or her right to exist. Psychoanalyst Dolto (1985) does this by advising parents to talk 'normally' about their divorce and subsequently say that the marriage did not fail because the child was born out of it. This way the child regains its right to exist in one statement. Research into children coping with divorce shows time and again that coping goes better when an open conversation about the divorce has taken place. A bad conversation seems to be better than no conversation.

Research regarding the effects of divorce on children show that the short-term effects with children are considerable. In the case of the death of a parent it seems that the effects are postponed. Lack of confidence increases during the first two years. A child whose parent has died becomes more isolated than one from a divorced family. The child experiences more shame in talking about the death and is more often bullied by peers (Worden 1996).

For children who lose their parents, the experience generally has little effect on their school performance during the first year, which is different from children experiencing their parents' divorce. Especially in the first two years after the divorce, the school performance of children often seriously deteriorates. After some time the effects seem to decrease and the confidence of the child also increases. After two years there is usually some stability in the new family structure. The effects of divorce decrease, although they are still noticeable for 15 years after the divorce has taken place (van der Valk 2004). But the effects of the loss of a parent increase with the years (Worden 1996).

> To many adults' amazement children who have lost a parent are bullied at school for that reason. We rather expect support for the child, which by the way also happens, but in general each child is also bullied. The shame of children who have lost a parent is great, greater than with divorce. The reason that children are bullied lies probably in the fact that the loss of a parent is also a shock to peers. The certainty that your parents will stay alive has been affected by that. For children who are used to externalising their problems there is a chance that they will take their problems out on the child whose parent has died by bullying that child.

I have now described the characteristics of conduct problems and the circumstances in which they occur. I have still to describe the ADHD disorder, of which conduct difficulties seem to be a part, as they often occur together. Subsequently I will dedicate a chapter to the differences between behaviour which belongs to a conduct *disorder* and behaviour which belongs to conduct *problems*. In this way the difference between the conduct disorder and the conduct problem are explained in more detail regarding their consequences for behaviours.

Summary

The circumstances in which conduct problems may occur have been described. Some differences between the conduct disorder and the conduct problem have been made clear. Although some behaviours seem to be the same on the surface, there are still differences between both forms of conduct difficulties. The most striking is that the conduct disorder already manifests itself from early childhood and the conduct problem usually occurs later, sometimes not until adolescence. The most important source of influence with conduct problems is the environment and this can be divided into four factors: childrearing and socio-cultural context, puberty, trauma and divorce or separation. In the childrearing, in a wide sense, risk and protective factors can be distinguished. The detachment process that the adolescent goes through with regard to its parents can cause conduct problems during puberty; also conduct problems can be caused by the hormonal flux of testosterone during this period. Traumas may cause conduct problems, especially when the trauma affects the tie between child and parents. Divorce is a process which not only the parents but also the children have to go through. Difficult divorce proceedings can cause serious conduct problems with the child or the youngster and often have a detrimental effect on school performance.

6

The Attention Deficit-Hyperactivity Disorder, ADHD

The diagnosis *Attention Deficit-Hyperactivity Disorder*, or *ADHD*, is the successor of *MBD*, *Minimal Brain Damage*. With *MBD* it was assumed that there was a light, hardly (or not) demonstrable, damage of the brain during birth due to a lack of oxygen. Nowadays, it is generally assumed that a different cause lies at the bottom of these often active, restless children, a disorder of the *brain function*. Important here is, among other things, the transference of a neurotransmitter in the brain, *dopamine*. There are more brain functions which play a part with ADHD, like the *corpus callosum* and the *frontal brain*. Children with ADHD can grow out of their disorder, but that does not apply to every child. Research found convincing indications for a delayed maturation, but until recently this could not be established sufficiently (Barkley 1995). Research by Rubia *et al.* (2000), with the help of fMRI (functional Magnetic Resonance Imaging), confirms the delayed maturation hypothesis. Also, in general growth it seems that there is delayed maturation, in the sense that children with ADHD are smaller on average, but they usually catch up at the end of adolescence (Spencer, Biederman and Wilens 1998). Taylor (1994) indicates that children with ADHD have a number of developmental problems, for example language development disorder, delayed motor development and a low birth weight.

We therefore reserve the term ADHD for the problems which are based on a *maturation of the central nervous system*. The problems are not new. The highly active, not concentrated, impulsive children have been allocated various diagnoses and various causes in the course of time. At the beginning of the twentieth century these children's behaviour was allocated to a brain disorder which was the result of Spanish flu (Gunning 2001). Weiss and Hechtman (1993) indicated that 3 to 4 per cent of primary school children have to contend with ADHD. Among them there are three times as many boys as girls and half of them still suffer from the disorder during adulthood and adolescence.

A number of the symptoms of ADHD, notably *hyperactivity* and *concentration disorders*, can also occur as a result of other factors such as a traumatic experience, being bullied or parents getting divorced. Because it is of great importance for the treatment to make a distinction with regard to the origin of the behaviour, for example when we want to use medication, I will use the term *hyperactivity* for the environment variant. See Table 1.3 in the Introduction.

Characteristics of ADHD

ADHD encompasses three areas of attention: *attention deficit*, which means *concentration disorders*, *hyperactivity* and *impulsivity*. There are three forms of ADHD: the form which mainly shows hyperactivity and impulsivity; the form which mainly shows attention deficit; and the *combination form*, where all three elements are present.

Children with ADHD have trouble combining the stimuli which reach them. They are distracted by each new stimulus and are inclined to direct themselves to the new stimulus and to interrupt the activity which they were engaged in. This fault in the stimuli processing causes a limitation of their ability to adjust their behaviour. The child follows the stimulus which occurs and acts on impulse. The lack of stimuli processing indicates a problem in the functioning of the corpus callosum, the 'connection centre' of the brain. I have already mentioned research by Hynd *et al.* (1991), Semrud-Clikeman *et al.* (1994) and Giedd *et al.* (1994) which showed that the corpus callosum of children with ADHD is smaller than average, but that this picture is not always univocal. Here we see a fundamentally different problem than with the *conduct disorder*. One of the 'connection centres' of the body plays an important part both with the conduct disorder and ADHD. With ADHD it is the corpus callosum, the connection centre within the brain. With the conduct disorder it is the *autonomic nervous system*, the connection centre between organs and the brain. While we see with ADHD that the stimuli are badly combined, we see with the conduct disorder that the stimuli do not get through properly as a result of the diminished reactivity of the autonomic nervous system.

This increased reactivity to stimuli and the tendency to respond quickly and not plan for the long term is translated into the characteristic *impulsivity*. Impulsivity proves to be an important element for development at school. Research into this aspect has been given shape long ago in the 'candy reward test'. This simple test proves to have excellent predictability value regarding school success. Four-year-old children are presented with the question of whether they would like to have one candy now or two later. Children who opt for two later, in general, prove to have a more successful school career. Impulsive children find it difficult to postpone a reward. They are therefore expected not to score well on the 'candy reward test'. Rapport *et al.* (1986) presented a similar test to children with ADHD and also to children who do not suffer from this. It now concerned a reward for doing a number of mathematical sums. The children with ADHD more often chose to solve a few sums and receive a small reward immediately than to do more sums and receive a bigger reward later. Campbell *et al.* (1992) researched impulsivity with pre-schoolers. When varying the waiting times for eating a cookie, hyperactive children more often made an impulsive choice than children who were not hyperactive. According to the development scheme of *ego-stage* by Loevinger (1990) the child with ADHD will hardly outgrow stage E-2 (that is, the *Impulsive stage* in which a child will follow its own needs and will want wishes to be granted immediately).

In the case of ADHD, hyperactivity cannot be seen separately from impulsivity because of the processing of stimuli; they always occur together. When this is not the case, and the hyperactivity stands on its own, it is not ADHD.

Another area in the brain where there are problems with processing stimuli with the child with ADHD is the prefrontal area in the brain (Castellanos *et al.* 1996; Njiokiktjien and Verschoor 1998; Rubia *et al.* 1999, 2000). This area is connected with concentration. *Concentration disorders* point out that this area does not function sufficiently and is not developed enough and possibly that the connections from the corpus callosum to this prefrontal area of the brain are disrupted. Children with ADHD often have concentration disorders. However, we also see this symptom with other problems, such as a traumatic reaction, or at specific moments such as the excitement of anticipating a Christmas party in the case of young children, or an exam in the case of adolescents.

ADHD has various forms, in which the three elements hyperactivity, impulsivity and attention deficit play a part.

1. ADHD, Attention Deficit-Hyperactivity Disorder, combination form hyperactivity-impulsivity-attention deficit

Most children with ADHD fall under the combination form category and suffer from the three characteristics together. Children with ADHD combination form have a chaotic behaviour style. They are extremely active, impulsive and have difficulty with concentrating. Their restlessness is uncontrolled, because there is something wrong with their 'steersmanship'. Transferring information into actions does not run correctly. Absorbing and processing signals and subsequently taking a decision is still apparent with these children in general. However, when they have to transfer a decision into an action, that is where they often make a mistake. It is as though one is driving a car and goes straight for a parked car. One desperately turns the wheel, which proves to be loose, and in this way, despite all the efforts made, one still smashes into the parked car. The next example illustrates the confusion caused by an action that is not tuned in to the thinking process:

A boy with ADHD is busy playing a computer game with complete abandon. He wants to have a break. With this programme it is possible to have a break by pressing the letter 'p'. So he says, completely correctly, 'Pause is "p"' but he presses 'Esc'. The key 'Esc', however, closes down the programme, after which it has to be restarted. Although he made the right decision in his head, the action he took was not in line with it.

With approximately one third of children *hyperactivity* is apparent from the baby stage onwards. These are often the babies with what Thomas and Chess (1977) call a *difficult temperament*. A second group gets noticed at their playgroup or in kindergarten because of their active and aggressive behaviour, because they cannot manage the requirements set by a group. Finally, there are the children who start showing problems in the first year of primary school, when learning becomes important in the sense of learning to read, write and do arithmetic. These children have learning difficulties and *fear of failure*, and as the requirements become higher, the problems increase. Making the diagnosis ADHD when a child is a baby and up to and including pre-schooler age is difficult because hyperactivity is a normal part of young children's development.

This disorder demands a lot from parents, often the impossible, and the child slips through their fingers. It cannot concentrate on contact for a long period of time and the parents therefore often feel rejected. When the child 'goes mad', cannot stop screaming and kicking, it gives the parents the feeling that 'the child has got a screw loose'. A child with ADHD can be very impatient. The short-term memory of the hyperactive child is restricted. The child is forgetful and therefore easily forgets that it is not allowed to do something. When the child concentrates on the activity, it does better, but it is precisely that level of concentration which is difficult to maintain.

Parents of children with ADHD observe that the child functions better when it tries hard. The parent will therefore be quick to say that it should try harder. The parent does not realise that the child has to make an effort to do this when others can do it naturally. It is even harder when the child does its best, because there is a limit to its capacity to do its best with one subject and other subjects also ask for its attention. When the child does not do its best any more, the behaviour is usually not yet automised, as it may be with other children. The child subsequently slips back into its old behaviour.

The memory is sensitive to the nature of an event. According to Bower (1981), events at which the emotional charge meshes with the emotional experience of the person at that moment, *emotional congruity*, are remembered relatively well. This applies particularly to positive experiences. In general these are better remembered than negative ones. Babies younger than two months can remember things, especially pleasant things (Rovee-Collier and Fagan 1976; Sullivan 1982). When the short-term memory works in a limited way, this will be noticed more strongly with the child with ADHD than with the average child.

ADHD arises from a combination of factors, especially where the genetic predisposition which passes on the *maturation disorder* plays a big part. That is why many parents, often fathers, recognise the active behaviour of their hyperactive child from their own childhood. Twin research proves that with 79 per cent of identical twins, when it has been established that one has ADHD, the other one has it as well; with dizygotic twins the match is 32 per cent (Barkley 1995). Barkley takes the position that the inadequate *behaviour inhibition* (the system where the behaviour is inhibited) is the core of ADHD. The prefrontal brain plays an important role with behaviour inhibition. Baird, Stevenson and Williams (2000) indicate that in the case of ADHD there is indeed an inadequate inhibition system, and that the attention function is connected with the bad co-ordination between the neural language circuits.

> A child with ADHD is told regularly that he can remember things if he finds them nice and important. This seems to confirm the unwillingness of the child. It is, however, the way that the memory works that pleasant things are remembered better, especially when this takes place under pleasant circumstances.

In addition to the maturation factor of which the pace is predispositional, the environment plays an important part in optimising the maturation or not.

A hyperactive child isolates the family socially. Wels, Jansen and Penders (1994) and Jansen and Wels (1998) researched the possibility of *video home training* for the improvement of communication between parent and child. The behaviour of the child with ADHD could hardly be changed, but the understanding by the parents of the active behaviour of their child became greater. Also the experienced difficulty of their child decreased and the feeling of responding adequately as childrearer increased.

A large number of hyperactive children become calmer during puberty, but keep their insecurities and tensions. During that period they often suffer from depressive moods. These children often have an inner restlessness well into adulthood, which for a part of them will never stop. Seventy to 80 per cent of the children still have ADHD during their puberty, according to Buitelaar (1993).

The criteria for the diagnosis ADHD combination form are, according to the *DSM-IV*, having at least six symptoms of attention deficit and at least six symptoms of hyperactivity-impulsivity. The list of symptoms will follow after the two other forms of ADHD.

2. AD(H)D, Attention Deficit Disorder, attention deficit

With AD(H)D *attention deficit*, also called ADD, the child does not come across as being active and chaotic. This disorder is generally only visible with tasks that require concentration. For the diagnosis ADHD attention deficit, there have to be at least six symptoms of attention deficit and fewer than six of hyperactivity-impulsivity.

Starting from the idea of a reduced functioning of the corpus callosum it is probable that the connections from the corpus callosum with the various parts of the brain function well, with the exception of the connection with the prefrontal lobe, where concentration is located. The concentration of the child with ADHD deviates from the concentration disorder of a child with limited intellectual powers. With the child with ADHD the concentration problems are there from the beginning of a task and are an issue continuously. The child will therefore come across as being active. With a child with limited intellectual powers the concentration runs out, as it were, and the child is subsequently more likely to be tired than active.

3. ADHD, Attention Deficit-Hyperactivity Disorder, hyperactivity-impulsivity

In the case of the form ADHD *hyperactivity-impulsivity* the child is able to concentrate on tasks. It is, however, extremely active and chaotic. In structured situations, where concentration is necessary, the child is often calm and the hyperactivity and impulsivity are less obvious. This often applies to the school situation. In that case teachers do not recognise the child's behaviour that the parents talk about. It applies to the diagnosis ADHD hyperactivty-impulsivity that at least six symptoms of hyperactivity-impulsivity are present and fewer than six symptoms of attention deficit.

List of symptoms of ADHD according to the *DSM-IV* (American Psychiatric Association 1994)

Attention deficit

1. often fails to pay close attention to details or makes careless mistakes in school work, work or other activities

2. often has difficulty sustaining attention in tasks or play activities

3. often does not seem to listen when spoken to directly

4. often does not follow through on instructions and fails to finish school work, chores or work duties (not the result of oppositional behaviour or of incapacity to understand instructions)

5. often has difficulty organising tasks and activities

6. often avoids or dislikes tasks that require sustained mental effort (like school or house work)

7. often loses things necessary for tasks or activities (for example, toys, homework, pencils, books or tools)

8. is often easily distracted by extraneous stimuli

9. is often forgetful in daily activities.

Hyperactivity-impulsivity

HYPERACTIVITY

1. often fidgets with hands or feet or squirms in seat

2. often leaves seat in classroom or in other situations when expected to remain seated

3. often runs about or climbs excessively in situations in which it is inappropriate (with adolescents or adults this can be restricted to feelings of restlessness and agitation)

4. often has difficulty playing or engaging in leisure activities quietly

5. is often 'on the go' or acts as if 'driven by a motor'

6. often talks excessively

IMPULSIVITY

7. often blurts out answer before questions have been completed

8. often has difficulty awaiting own turn

9. often interrupts or intrudes on others (for example suddenly intervenes in conversations or games).

(American Psychiatric Association 2000)

Scholte and van der Ploeg (1998) developed the AVL (ADHD questionnaire) which is based on the *DSM-IV* list of symptoms and gives an image of the totality of the criteria of ADHD based on the DSM-IV with due importance given to each criterion as compared to the others.

Hyperactivity

I have already stated that some symptoms of ADHD also occur with other problems, in particular *hyperactivity* and *concentration disorders*. We can see these occurring in situations where there is anxiety and tension, especially when this is long-term. Hyperactivity is a form of behaviour in which children, especially boys, express their problems. This hyperactivity is not necessarily linked to impulsivity and can possibly go together with concentration disorders. In Chapter 8 I will describe in more detail how this distinction can be made. Hyperactivity is one of the externalising behaviours. We can therefore expect hyperactivity in situations where children are exposed to problems or stress for a shorter or longer period of time. It is possible that children have been diagnosed as having ADHD when they do not have this disorder, but have a problem which they express in troublesome, hyperactive behaviour.

But hyperactivity can play a part even without a problem at the basis of this. Children nowadays are raised in a high-speed lifestyle. The speed of images, for example, that children process looking at television and computers is much faster than it used to be. We can see that in the busy video clips on television. The music programme *The Old Grey Whistle Test*, which now seems very slow, was busy and noisy for the parents of that generation. The pace of images is now, however, significantly faster. Designers of computer games have to make ever faster games because the youth of today become bored when the pace is too slow. The pace with which young children have to brush their teeth, get dressed, have breakfast and go to day-care is much faster today with their two working parents than in the generations before them.

In addition, hyperactivity is also linked to developmental stages. Around the ages of three to four years children are more active, sexual and aggressive (Raine 2002).

Proceeding from the anxiety model which I presented in Chapter 3, it is to be expected that the hyperactivity of children is based on adrenergic hormonal activities and that the active behaviour forms an outlet for anxiety. When we talk about hyperactivity as a result of tensions, there is temporal hormonal activity. With ADHD it is probable that here there are structurally hormonal problems, in the sense of a still immature hormonal level. I have already mentioned the high co-morbidity of ADHD with anxiety disorders and depression (see Chapter 4).

Learning disorders

ADHD is a disorder of the maturation of the central nervous system: a delayed maturation. A delayed maturation means that the child possibly, after some time, will grow out of it; this is contrary to the effects of a deviant brain structure, which are structural and play a part for the rest of their lives. It can also be the case that the maturation remains limited and goes on into adulthood. When the child grows out of it, this means that the specific problems are over. The disorder has, however, often brought with it socio-emotional consequences, which can keep on exercising their influence. A child with a delayed maturation, causing it not to become toilet-trained until late, can be damaged in his or her self-image. It can therefore be afraid to go to stay with someone and can still be troubled by these additional consequences, long after the *toilet-training problems* have stopped. The maturation disorder can, however, also mean a limited maturation, where the maturation does go on for some time, but is finally not fully completed. Some of the specific problems will then still remain. We can see that with adults who still struggle with ADHD.

Because ADHD is a disorder of the maturation of the central nervous system, we often see *co-morbidity*, the prevalence of various problems at the same time, with other *maturation disorders*, which I mentioned in Chapter 2 in Table 2.1. These are *primary enuresis* (bedwetting), *primary encopresis* (soiling), *restless legs, involuntary spasms, tics, dyspraxia* (co-ordination disorder), *tooth grinding, sleep talking, sleep walking, sleeping with eyes open, pavor nocturnes* (night terror), *stereotypical movements* (such as head banging and rocking), *language development disorder* and *stuttering.*

One of the most often occurring co-morbid problems is delayed toilet-training, both *encopresis,* soiling, and *enuresis,* bedwetting. The delayed maturation causes a late command of the sphincter and the bladder sphincter. ADHD children often show learning disorders which are connected with a disrupted maturation of the central nervous system: *dyslexia* (30% of children with ADHD), *mathematics disorder* and *dysgraphia* (writing disorder). These learning disorders occur, just like the other maturation disorders, predominantly (75%) with boys (de Graaf-Tiemersma 1995).

Dyslexia is characterised by serious reading and spelling problems, which are persistent and hardly respond to the didactical measures and remedial efforts which are usual in education. The automation of word identification (reading) and/or typeface forming (spelling) does not develop, or develops very inadequately or very laboriously (Health Council 1997). This disorder often goes together with left-handedness, which indicates dominance of the right hemisphere. Dyslexic people often have slight *speech disorders,* stuttering among other things, which also occurs more often with boys than with girls.

With dyslexia various factors can play a part: problems in distinguishing sounds; problems in distinguishing visual stimuli; problems with the integration of visual elements; difficulties with integrating auditive elements; and difficulty with transferring visual and auditive elements into sounds.

With a *mathematics disorder* it is a matter of a weakly developed logical thinking, a lack of insight into numbers and inadequate mastering of mathematical techniques. We have to be attentive to the fact that here it concerns a disorder of *organising* and not only a disorder of mathematics itself.

In order to be able to write, a command of the fine motor system and a good eye–hand co-ordination is necessary. A disorder of this is called *dys(ortho)graphia.* This disorder is characterised by a writing pattern with a difficult-to-read, chaotic image. The writing takes a lot of time and is a struggle, without really becoming regular (Hamstra-Bletz and de Bie 1985). When writing in print, the readability improves. With people who have dysgraphia the programming does not work properly. This disorder exists with 10 per cent of the children.

Conduct problems with the child with ADHD

The child who has ADHD regularly comes into conflict with his environment because of his impulsivity and hyperactivity. Because the child hardly responds to what his parents say, they often think that the child does not listen to them. Also the child with ADHD often stays busy when talking with his parents. One can even say that he usually concentrates better when he keeps moving. Parents often feel rejected by the child because the contact is so fleeting. As a consequence of the many problems in daily contact, which arise due to the chaotic behaviour of the child, he often gets into conflict with his parents and teachers. Parents can become desperate because of the child's response where nothing seems to sink in. They can become angry and treat the child badly. Hyperactive children run the risk of being physically abused and usually get too little positive attention. The parents tend only to give negative attention: 'Stop that! Careful not to throw that table over! Did your bike break down yet again?' As a result the child can show *conduct problems*. He can adopt a negative attitude towards parents and childrearers.

In order to teach behaviour, positive attention is needed. Parents are, however, often so happy when the child is calm for a minute that they do not give him any attention, apart from negative attention. In addition, the parents get a feeling of guilt because they keep on punishing him. They often receive a lot of criticism from their environment. As the child shows behaviour which suggests a bad upbringing, people are quick to shake their finger at the parents.

Hyperactive youngsters run more risk of going off the rails and starting to use drugs. After having heard all through their childhood 'sit still', the 'joint' provides 'cool, relaxed' behaviour. They use drugs as a form of 'self-medication'. In Chapter 12, where I will discuss the treatment of ADHD, I will come back to the nature and meaning of this 'self-medication'.

Not seldom will children with ADHD show criminal behaviour during puberty. This behaviour is not the same as that of the child with the externalising conduct disorder, whose criminality is prompted by his own needs. The child who starts having conduct problems due to ADHD can start showing criminal behaviour as a response to his environment. When the ties with his environment become worse, the chances of going off the rails increase. There are differences between the conduct *disorder* and ADHD. There is co-morbidity with ADHD and conduct *problems* are possible and even probable, both internalising and externalising. But also, although less frequent, a combination is possible between ADHD and an externalising conduct *disorder*. In that case there are, in addition to ADHD, also the specific characteristics of the child with the externalising conduct disorder, such as an inadequate me–other differentiation. Co-morbidity between ADHD and the internalising conduct *disorder* is also possible.

Externalising conduct disorder and ADHD

The co-morbidity between ADHD and the externalising conduct disorder is particularly problematic. The frequency is not that great, but the problems are all the more. In order to comprehend both ADHD and the externalising conduct disorder better, it is useful to compare them. When we put ADHD next to the externalising conduct disorder, we see that in both cases there is a disorder of the functioning of the central nervous system. With ADHD there is a maturation disorder and many of the children with ADHD will suffer less from it when they are adults or can even outgrow it, depending on whether it concerns a delayed or restricted maturation. In the case of the conduct disorder there is inhibited development of the left hemisphere and a reduced responsiveness of the autonomic nervous system. These characteristics are structural and the child does not outgrow them. He can learn to live with them. These children are at risk of developing into *psychopathic* adults. To both disorders it applies that the child comes into conflict with its environment. As a result these children can also develop conduct problems with both disorders.

The child with ADHD does not have to have an inadequate *me–other differentiation*; his *moral development* therefore does not have to be problematic. He should, starting from a normal empathic capacity, be able to make friends. He has, however, due to his hyperactivity and impulsivity, difficulty with playing with his peers. The peers will often perceive him as a disruption to their game. As a result the child's feelings will often be hurt. Because of his normal need of social contact he will keep trying to make contact with people.

The child with the externalising conduct disorder will find it hard to make friendships due to an absence of *empathy*. Because of his *egocentrism* he will tend to play the boss and only use others for his own benefit. He will therefore have few friends, and when playing with them he will quickly feel frustrated and may become aggressive. He will be more likely to be frustrated than to have his feelings hurt when associating with peers. He will therefore avoid children whom he cannot exercise control over. The child with a conduct disorder will play little with others and is more aimed at using the other in order to satisfy his own needs.

> A child with ADHD has problems dealing with his *peers*. Because of his chaotic behaviour he is not calm enough to play with his peers, who subsequently reject him. With the example of a girl with ADHD this had taken such proportions that she had become afraid of other children. She had been rejected so many times that she wanted to avoid that. She developed phobic behaviour and avoided her peers. If she saw a few children whom she did not know in the street, she would walk around the block. She showed the avoidance behaviour of people who suffer from phobias.

The child with ADHD is bad at processing the many *stimuli* that reach him, and as a result he will often feel restless or anxious. He will experience this anxiety less as long as he carries on activities which, as it were, form an antidote against the *anxiety*. Anxiety, but also depression, is maintained by not-acting and avoiding. Anxiety is experienced when there is a large production of adrenergic hormones.

The hormones enable the organism to take action. When action is being taken, these hormones are 'transferred' and the anxiety decreases. In the case of not-acting these substances are not transferred and a 'poisoning' takes place which leads to an increase of anxiety and depression possibly following from that. The hyperactivity of the ADHD child leads to decrease of anxiety. When becoming an adult the hyperactivity is controlled because by now it has been learned that this behaviour is undesirable. It is therefore not surprising that adults with ADHD (*ADHD-A* refers to an ADHD adult) often suffer from *GAD*, a *Generalised Anxiety Disorder*, characterised by a lot of fretting. They also often suffer from *obsessive-compulsive disorders* (OCD). Shekim *et al.* (1990) found that more than half of the people with ADHD-A they examined suffered from GAD. Adults have learned to control their activity in order to have fewer conflicts with their environment. This decrease in activity could well be the cause of the increase in anxiety. We saw in Chapter 3 that anxiety can exist on the basis of a lack of taking action. This would mean that children with ADHD are very anxious, but that this is more difficult to see during their childhood because of the hyperactivity they develop. We can already see the increase of anxiety and depression during puberty. Many ADHD youngsters suffer from alternately depressive and anxious feelings. This is even clearer when they become adults. I have to point out that in that case I speak of ADHD as a maturation disorder and not about hyperactivity based on anxiety, which may be overcome in the course of their development.

Children with ADHD are not necessarily *aggressive*. Aggression can arise as a result of the problems that their functioning causes with their environment. Because of the flow of testosterone during puberty, the child with the conduct disorder will show more aggression. With children who have ADHD this is not the case, because they are not naturally aggressive. The aggression does not naturally increase during puberty; on the contrary, they can become anxious and depressed during this period.

I have already mentioned that with adults who have ADHD, decrease of activity can go together with an increase in anxiety. Following from that the depression, which we often see during puberty with children who have ADHD, can arise. Their need of social contact and their failure to have this with their peers will, especially during puberty when this is so prominent, be an important breeding ground for depression.

Although a child with ADHD may show more often than average *norm exceeding behaviour*, it is not the case that the child necessarily comes across as being immoral. He has feelings of guilt and is anxious about what has happened. The norm exceeding behaviour is more likely to arise as a response to the problems which the child experiences in his functioning with others and the aggression he experiences with that. The child with the externalising conduct disorder will on the other hand come across as being immoral because he will not experience the norm exceeding behaviour as exceeding someone else's boundaries, but instead is likely to experience it as a concession to his own needs, as being his right.

When parents talk to a child with a conduct disorder, they often have the feeling that the child is in a different world, absent, that what they say does not sink in with him. When the other person is talking, the child sits or stands still, has a 'wait and see' attitude, and has a somewhat faraway look. As with children with a serious contact disorder, the eyes temporarily have no 'depth'. With the child with ADHD the picture in general is different. Also with this child the parents have the feeling that nothing sinks in, but the behaviour is different. While the parents are talking, the children tend to continue with their activity. They do not show the parents that they are listening. Such children listen only fleetingly due to their problem of processing stimuli. It regularly happens that a parent notices that what he or she has said did not make a lasting impression and is already forgotten. This is connected with the inadequate short-term memory. With the child with an externalising conduct disorder the problem is not that the stimulus does not make a lasting impression, but that the stimulus does not sink in properly due to the diminished *responsiveness of the autonomic nervous system.*

In Table 6.1 the differences between an externalising conduct disorder and ADHD are reflected. I chose the combination form of ADHD here because this occurs the most and all three elements are represented therein.

The elements that play a part with ADHD and with the externalising conduct disorder starting from the central nervous system do not overlap and are not conflicting. With ADHD the maturation of the central nervous system, including the corpus callosum and the prefrontal brain, and possibly an immaturation of the hormonal structure play a part; with the externalising conduct disorder there is a restrained development of the left hemisphere and a diminished responsiveness of the autonomic nervous system. Because the elements do not overlap, co-morbidity of ADHD and the externalising conduct disorder is possible. We are then not only dealing with a child with hyperactivity, impulsivity and a concentration disorder, but also with an inadequate me–other differentiation and an inadequate moral development. If a child has co-morbidity of ADHD and the externalising conduct disorder this means that the elements that mainly belong to a normally developed left hemisphere of the brain *(situation-bound aggression; norm exceeding behaviour as an outlet for problems; normal empathic capacity; normal me–other differentiation, therefore normal moral development; need to play with others; ability to assess own role; ability to self-reflect)* are omitted and replaced by how these aspects function with the externalising conduct disorder. The prognosis for these children is very negative.

Also the internalising, anxiety, conduct disorder is not in conflict with the disorder ADHD as far as the central nervous system is concerned. Co-morbidity with this conduct difficulty also occurs.

Table 6.1 The differences between the externalising conduct disorder and ADHD	
Externalising conduct disorder	*ADHD, combination form*
Mainly boys	Mainly boys
High level of testosterone	Immaturity of central nervous system
Low level of cortisol	– smaller corpus callosum
– generalised aggression	– stimuli are not processed well
– little anxiety, assertive	– restlessness, impulsivity
– few psychosomatic complaints	– diminished working of prefrontal brain
– antisocial behaviour	
Diminished responsiveness of the autonomic nervous system	– inadequate concentration
	– trouble with forming an impression of what is being said
– diminished sensitivity to stimuli of all senses: hearing, seeing, smelling, tasting, feeling	Possible immaturity of hormonal structure
– not very alert	– generalised anxiety
– low heart rate	– hyperactivity
– situation-bound aggression	– norm exceeding behaviour as an outlet for problems
– quick habituation to negative stimulus	Risk of unmatured development of left hemisphere of brain
– important fluctuations in consciousness	
– difficulty with comprehending what is being said	– chance of dyslexia
	– chance of learning disorders
– looking for danger as self-medication for diminished consciousness	Normal me–other differentiation (if co-morbidity with externalising *disorder* a limited me–other differentiation)
– risk of engaging in problematic behaviour in monotonous situations	– normal moral development
	– need to play with others
– risk of engaging in problematic behaviour when being offended	– normally able to assess own role
– normal self-reflection	Chance of addiction as self-medication in order to become calm

Continued on next page

Table 6.1 continued

Externalising conduct disorder	ADHD, combination form
Inhibited development of left hemisphere of brain	
– not very language oriented	
– difficulty putting thoughts and feelings into words	
– inadequate self-reflection	
– little capability of self-directing behaviour	
Limited recognition of biological self	
– limited me–other differentiation	
– egocentric	
– not very empathic	
– limited moral development, aimed at justice and competition	
– norm exceeding behaviour according to own needs	
– less developed realisation of mine and thine	
– poor ability to assess own role	
– antisocial behaviour	
– feeling of being treated unfairly	
– little need of playing with others	
– social isolation as result of having trouble striking up friendships	
Risk of conduct problems because of conflicts with the environment	Chance of conduct problems due to conflicts with the environment

I have now discussed the sources for the development of conduct difficulties and ADHD. I will now, in order to close off, discuss typical behaviours, the *antisocial and socially anxious behaviours*. These occur both with the conduct disorder and the conduct problem and ADHD. I will make here, where possible, a distinction with regard to the nature and occurrence of these behaviours with the various conduct difficulties: conduct *disorders* and conduct *problems*.

Summary

I restrict the use of the term ADHD, Attention Deficit-Hyperactivity Disorder, to the disorder of the maturation of the central nervous system. When it is a question of the symptom hyperactivity, and it is controlled by the environment, I speak of hyperactivity. Children with ADHD have trouble with processing all stimuli that reach them. Their smaller corpus callosum is the physical translation of this problem. Their underdeveloped prefrontal brain plays a part with their concentration disorder. Because it is a maturation disorder, often more maturation problems occur with these children: among other things, toilet-training disorders and learning disorders. ADHD can include three elements: impulsivity, attention deficit and hyperactivity. The combination form occurs most frequently and is characterised by active, chaotic and not concentrated behaviour. Children with ADHD often get into conflict with their environment because of their behaviour. In this way conduct problems can arise. In addition, a small number of the children also suffer from an externalising conduct disorder. The children with a co-morbidity of ADHD and the externalising conduct disorder have a negative prognosis and a high chance of criminal behaviour when they become adults. Hyperactivity can be age-bound, caused by environmental factors such as traumas or physical abuse, or connected with the pace of life expected of children.

7

Typical Behaviours

Now that I have discussed the various conduct difficulties and ADHD and stated their characteristics, I will go on to discuss behaviours. Conduct difficulties cause a great deal of confusion in their diagnosis and treatment; this is because there are a limited number of behaviours where the behaviour itself does not show the cause of the behaviour. If you want to make a correct diagnosis and, following on from that, decide on the right treatment then you will have to know the source of the behaviour. Many behaviours occur with various conduct difficulties. Many of the behaviours also occur with people who do not have conduct difficulties and these behaviours, such as lying or shyness, are a normal part of human functioning.

I will try to discuss the various behaviours which are connected to conduct difficulties in the light of their occurrence with a conduct *disorder* or a conduct *problem*. In addition I will discuss the core behaviours of ADHD. For the characteristics of the various conduct difficulties and ADHD please refer to the summaries of Chapters 4 and 5, Table 4.4 (regarding conduct disorder), Table 6.1 (regarding externalising conduct disorder compared with ADHD) and Table 1.1 (regarding conduct difficulties in general). The same rules apply to co-morbidity as to the separate behaviours. That is to say that in the case of, for example, co-morbidity of an internalising conduct disorder and an internalising conduct problem there will be both generalised fear (as part of the disorder) and situational anxiety (as part of the problem).

I will discuss the various behaviours in order to show, as far as possible, how these manifest themselves in the disorder form or in the problem form. With every behaviour the characteristic of the behaviour as it occurs with the various conduct difficulties has been placed in a framework. The externalising behaviours are categorised under 'antisocial behaviour' and the internalising behaviours under 'socially anxious behaviour'.

Antisocial behaviour

The antisocial behaviours have an important role with the child with an externalising conduct problem. There are two kinds of antisocial behaviour: *aggression* and *dishonesty*. *Aggression* can be directed against people, animals and objects. *Vandalism* and *arson* are also classified under aggression. *Dishonesty* comprises *lying, stealing* and *cheating*.

Aggression

Aggression can take the form of deliberately hurting another person. The hurting can be physical, committing physical violence, or it can be in a psychological sense, like bullying or threatening. Children with an externalising conduct disorder often have ill-developed *empathy*. In addition, they themselves do not feel pain or fear as strongly as others as a consequence of the diminished responsiveness of the *autonomic nervous system*. Because of these two characteristics they have difficulty in realising that another person does experience that pain. The protests and crying of others can surprise them and come across as unnecessary and therefore irritate them. This may result in them tending to experiment with hurting other people. The experimental stage of young children who take animals to bits as a form of scientific investigation remains, as it were, with them. They often find it almost pleasant to hurt another person. Through this pain they try to understand the experience of the other. In order to avert the accusation that what they do is bad they often laugh it off. Animal abuse occurs regularly with these children and it can be a sign of serious psychopathic problems.

Olweus (1977, 1978) states that when children are very aggressive at the age of eight, the chances are that they will also be so at the age of 30. The environment can amplify or confine the child's behaviour. Although children who are not aggressive will hardly be influenced by aggressive television programmes, the amount of aggression in aggressive children will be increased by such programmes (Groebel 1998). The same applies to computer games (Delfos 1994b, 2003 Provenzo 1991; Wiegman 1995). The physical and psychological arousal conjured up by these films and games can easily lead to aggressive expressions with these children (van der Voort and Valkenburg 1994). Heusmann (1998) states that aggressive behaviour at a later age is connected to watching aggressive television programmes during childhood. The aggressive expressions will not always be imitation behaviour; the aggression will usually be expressed in a less direct manner. Seeing a man being stabbed in a film will not immediately lead to a stabbing; however, the chance of a boy kicking his sister when passing will be greater.

The aggression of the child with a conduct disorder will be distinct from early on; the aggression is often unexpectedly violent in relation to the cause. Aggression can arise as a reaction to a frustration. The *frustration tolerance* of these children is very low. The aggression of the child with a conduct problem will possibly have come into existence later and is more situation bound. This aggression is more likely to be directed at people than at objects.

A striking example is often the aggression against peers and siblings. The child with the conduct disorder will also show aggression often in relation to these people, because he has genetically less possibilities for empathy and is therefore less able to play with others and make friends. The child with a conduct problem will more often direct his aggression towards adults and outsiders. He will more often have friends and not often direct his aggression towards them. The adults are often the source of the aggression because of their style of childrearing, a trauma that they cause, their divorce or separation or because the child has to detach itself during puberty. It is therefore logical that the aggression is directed towards them.

These two forms of aggression have a different nature from the aggression shown by the child with a disorder within the autism spectrum. These children have a basic problem with putting themselves in someone else's place, more so than with the child with an externalising conduct disorder, and have a great resistance to change. Their aggression is often fed by two sources. The first is the thwarting of their plan. Their plan is a way of keeping the frightening situations in the world under control. Deviating from their plan, no matter how good this deviation could be with regard to content, conjures up fear which initially will be expressed by 'going on and on' and 'terrorising', and subsequently can take on aggressive shapes (Delfos 2004a). These early stages are not explicitly present with the child with the externalising conduct disorder. The second source of aggression is the seriously inadequate empathic capacity. This can cause children with a disorder within the autism spectrum to feel unjustly treated because they think that the other person has bad intentions. The child assumes that the other person knows everything that he or she is thinking and feeling, so when it does not get what it needs, it thinks that the other person is causing that on purpose. With the externalising child this does not happen structurally, but mainly when it gets into conflict with the environment and it is accused of something.

Extra attention has to be paid to *alcohol*-related aggression. Aggression which occurs, for example, at football matches is almost completely caused by alcohol and takes place in groups. This aggression is mainly related to youngsters and, more specifically, boys. Both youngsters with conduct disorders and conduct problems can show this behaviour. It is, however, more likely to be expected with youngsters with conduct problems because functioning in a group is difficult for the boy with the conduct disorder. However, youngsters who do not have problems can, when influenced by alcohol and group pressure, show conduct that is in fact out of character for them. The aggression that takes place within this context is, however, less a sign of conduct difficulties. Only when it also takes place outside that situation is it a more serious problem, no matter how serious the football aggression may be on its own.

The *aggression* of the child with the conduct disorder will be a common thread during its life – a *generalised aggression*; the aggression of the child with a conduct problem is more likely to be restricted to certain situations – *situation-bound aggression*.

Vandalism

Vandalism, damaging or destroying other people's property, has increased enormously within western society in recent years. Respect for objects is formed through internalisation of the parents' standards.

When parents neglect their children emotionally, but attach a lot of value to material matters, objects can become a symbol for a lack of affection, according to psychoanalytic theory. As a result these objects can become a target for their children. Subsequently vandalism can spread to the environment. Public buildings can symbolise power, coldness and authority. Damaging buildings can be an expression of resisting authority. The chance of this behaviour is greater during puberty when the authority of the parent is being questioned, especially when there are authority conflicts between parents and child.

Another form of damaging a building is defacing it with paint. With *graffiti*, especially the *tag*, the name by which the graffiti artist makes himself known and recognised, the youngster can break with anonymity and experience power. It is therefore pre-eminently an expression of feelings experienced during puberty. To classify this under aggression is in fact not correct, because it is not so much an expression of aggression as a case of 'making oneself known'. The nature of the graffiti can therefore also be aesthetically pleasing. It is not for nothing that there are exhibitions of works of graffiti.

Vandalism is usually a passing form of expression during puberty. This behaviour will therefore generally occur less often with children with a conduct disorder and is more likely to be an expression of a conduct problem, specifically during puberty.

Arson

Arson is connected with an inadequate *impulse control* and goes, according to psychoanalytic theories, hand in hand with a fierce aggression against the parents. Initially it takes place near the parental home; only later will it occur further away from home. These youngsters often endanger themselves. It is a question of an unconscious aggression and the youngster seems to have a need for punishment.

Arson is exciting and in this way can be a release for instinctive impulses and wishes for omnipotence.

Starting from our model, arson can play a part with looking for danger in a state of diminished consciousness. The aspect of danger can be a possibility for the child with an externalising conduct disorder to increase the consciousness level. From there arson is a sign that there may be a serious problem. In that case this behaviour is a common thread during youth, from playing with fire as a child to arson as a youngster. Arson may also occur with the child with a conduct problem, but will not often be found as a common thread. It will also occur in the context of problematic situations, as direct aggression against the person and the situation which has damaged or hurt the feelings of the child, or in the context of playing with others. In the case of the youngster with a conduct disorder it is a need for flames and fire and enjoyment. With the youngster with a conduct problem it will more likely take on the aggressive form.

With the child with a conduct disorder *arson* may serve as an attempt to increase the consciousness level. Arson will be more likely to occur with children with a conduct disorder and be a common thread during their youth than with children with a conduct problem.

Lying

Lying is a form of externalising behaviour that occurs often. Although the general moral code prescribes that lying is unacceptable, it is tolerated socially and some-times even preferred if it occurs as 'a white lie'. People who are easy to get on with and popular lie more often than people who are not socially skilled (Vrij 1998). There are large individual differences in the nature, way and amount of lies people tell. In particular non-verbal signs of lying are in general badly interpreted (Vrij 1998). There exist nevertheless various forms of lying, and these can be distin-guished in aim and nature and can be placed as such in the framework of a disorder or a problem.

Fantasy and lying are sometimes very close. A young child does not always make a clear distinction between fantasy and reality. In addition, it does not find it necessary to let the adult know whether something is fantasised or not, because of the idea that the 'almighty' adult knows everything (Delfos 2000a). The child can be carried away by his or her fantasy without finding it necessary to communicate to the adult that it has moved from reality to fantasy. Lack of knowledge of the world also causes the child not to know so well what is reality and what is fantasy. This does not mean to say that the child itself is not aware that it is fantasising.

For the older child and the adult, fantasising can serve as having wishes come true. It can serve as an outlet for low self-esteem and as an antidote against constant *hurt.* A child who is constantly hurt by his parents may fantasise that they are not his parents, that his parents will meet a terrible end or that they are possessed by an evil spirit. After some time adults expect children not to communicate by means of fantasy any more, but by means of reality, and will call 'fantasy' 'lying' as if it is the same as consciously choosing to speak untruths.

When you play intensively with children, you will have experienced that the child gets its wires crossed when the adult seems to get completely absorbed in the game. For a moment the child is not sure any more whether the adult is aware that it is a game and not reality. The child quickly brings him or her back to reality by saying, 'It isn't real you know, it's only pretend.'

Children with externalising conduct problems lie frequently. This form of lying is, however, strongly related to fantasy and is often a form of a wish coming true. The lie serves to create a situation for itself in which an offence did not take place.

A serious form of fantasising which lasts into adulthood is the *pseudologia phantastica*, where there is an almost compulsive need to fantasise in the form of spreading lies.

In order to make a distinction between the form of lying which mainly occurs with the conduct *disorder* and the form we mainly find with the conduct *problem*, I will discuss the various forms of lying. Lying can be subdivided based on the aims of the lie:

- *Telling lies as a result of inadequate differentiation of fantasy and reality.* We see this especially with young children who, without any problems, can have various conflicting truths existing next to each other in their not fully integrated brain, and treat reality and fantasy as equal.

- *Lying in order to create a different reality.* The main aim of this form of lying is not so much to give the listener a certain image of the situation; the lie serves to create a different reality for the speaker himself, in which the unpleasant event did not take place. You will see children repeat these lies against all logic and proof. Adults often try to convince children that they have to admit to lying because the proof to the contrary is there already. The child, however, continues to imagine a different world. The fear of punishment does not seem to be the most important motive, causing communication problems. The listener receives the lie as directed actively against him or her and feels fooled by the child. The adult subsequently tries to wage a battle in order to get the truth out, while the child is busy keeping the truth away. There is no real communication; there is no active reciprocity in the contact. It is this form of lying that we see mainly with the child with the conduct *disorder*. The child itself wishes that the offence, about which it is lying, had not been committed by it and creates for itself, through the listener, a situation in which that offence did not take place.

- *Lying to fill a gap in the memory.* This form of lying is usually done unconsciously. The working of the memory makes it possible to elevate elements to memory which in reality never happened. We can already see this with the unlikely differences between witnesses' statements when describing a certain event. The memory is not a static, definite entity, but is constantly updated. Unconscious untruths are a natural part of the brain, according to Loftus and Ketcham (1994).

- *Lying as a reflex to spare the self-image.* This form of lying is as it were an automatically employed denial. This automatism can be so strong that it even occurs when there is no accusation. The child already says that it did not do something even when it has not been accused of doing so. We can see this form for example in certain phases of a *foster care placement.* When the foster child starts to take root in the foster home, it reaches a phase in which it starts to believe that it belongs in the foster home and will be able to stay there. The foster child will then often unconsciously start to explore the limits of acceptance of the foster parents. It will start to show all kinds of difficult behaviour (most frequent are lying and stealing) and will constantly deny doing anything. For the child itself it is generally a complete mystery why it shows this behaviour and this affects its self-image. Because of its behaviour the spectre of the child being removed from the family comes nearer. The child subsequently lies in order to spare its self-image and to try to turn the tide.

- *Lying in order to reach an egoistical aim (egoistical or delinquent lying).* With this form of lying the activity is aimed at the listener. The intention is to call up a certain image of the situation with the listener. The child is actively engaged to see whether the listener will 'buy' the story. If that does not happen then he or she will quickly bring forward new arguments. There exists between the child and the listener an active, although problematic, communication. This form of lying will mainly occur with the child with a conduct *problem.*

- *Lying in order to spare the other person.* This is the case with a 'white lie'. Socially it is particularly common to lie in order to prevent the truth hurting someone else. In view of the lack of empathic capacity this form will be less frequent with the child with the conduct disorder. He will even come across as 'honest through and through'.

- *Lying by withholding the truth.* In English we know the 'black lie' and the 'white lie', for lying and withholding the truth respectively.

Withholding the truth implies an active deed; this can be done both on good grounds and to serve a manipulative aim. This 'white lie' means withholding the truth and is based on a manipulation which will be advantageous to the silent person at the expense of the other.

In the case of frequent lying it is not wise to have 'did'/'did not' conversations. An accusation is not uttered if it is the first time that the child is lying. There have always been events prior to this happening which have affected the other person's trust. When a child has lied before, then the child knows that someone does not trust him any more; that is the consequence of lying and that can be explained to the child. The approach to the child should depend on the form of lying. There is no point in trying to force the child, who lies because of a need to create a different reality, to admit his lie. It is better to link up to his feeling that he rather wished it had never happened and together look for solutions to prevent it happening again in the future. In the case of egoistical or delinquent lying it is necessary to confront the child with the truth and the consequences of his behaviour, so that the child learns to recognise his limits. Egoistical lying occurs a lot during puberty because the interests of the parent and child are often conflicting and the adolescent wants to get his own way. Other issues with lying are the important factors of fear of punishment and damaging the self-image.

Lying in order to create a different reality frequently occurs with young children and children with a conduct disorder. They lie against all logic and proof. There is little reciprocity in the communication. Delinquent lying in order to reach an egoistical aim often occurs with children with a conduct problem. They actively oppose, through communication, discovery of the truth.

Stealing

Stealing is one of the most common problem behaviours. The fact that it occurs so frequently with the child with the externalising conduct *disorder* is connected to the inadequate development of the recognition of 'mine and thine' and its egocentrism. This egocentrism and its lack of empathy causes the child to think that taking other people's property is not really a problem. Although the child, when growing older, knows in his mind that it is a problem, he will not really feel it as such, unless he has experienced something similar and consequently starts to understand the loss. Stealing can also occur with the child with the externalising conduct *problem*. Earlier I mentioned the example of the foster child who in a certain stage of the rooting process in the family can start to steal. Stealing can also be a means of making friends and gaining appreciation of peers, and as such can occur at the end of primary school and the start of secondary school. According to psychoanalytical theory, stealing can be a *neurotic* disorder and arise when children are struggling with *guilt feelings* about forbidden impulses or fantasies. Stealing can then be a means of provoking punishment.

With the child with the conduct *disorder* stealing is, however, particularly a fulfilment of its own needs, and it is not hindered by judgements about 'mine and thine' and feelings of guilt. It can therefore, on its own, proceed to burglary. Children with conduct problems do this more often together with others. Stealing can also serve to increase the consciousness level because it includes the risk of being caught. Because it is prohibited, the activity becomes 'dangerous'.

Stealing occurs with the child with the conduct disorder from its earliest childhood. On becoming older it will often take on the form of burglary. These burglaries are usually carried out alone by the child with the conduct disorder. When children with a conduct problem steal, they will often do this together with their peers.

Socially anxious behaviour

People seem to have fewer problems in explaining socially anxious behaviour, like shyness and anxiety, than they have in explaining antisocial behaviour. This is possibly connected to the fact that these behaviours, much more than the antisocial behaviours, can be found in the normal behaviour repertoire and are accepted. Socially anxious behaviours are more likely to conjure up feelings of understanding while antisocial behaviour, which may also be an expression of problems, provokes a negative reaction. In addition, the socially anxious behaviours are often expressed physically whereas the antisocial ones are not. The best known physical expression is blushing. Following on from an increased activity of the autonomic nervous system as a response to danger, there is an increase in the rush of blood, which can be seen on the exposed body parts, especially in the case of a person with white skin. In the West that usually means the face and neck. *Blushing* seems to be dependent on exposure and is determined by culture. When it is usual that the upper part of the body is exposed then the entire upper part of the body will be seen to blush. This blushing 'betrays' the child, its social anxiety becoming literally and figuratively bare. With the child with the externalising conduct disorder the antisocial behaviour is not expressed in noticeable physical signs. His diminished reactivity of the autonomic nervous system, causing a diminished reaction to danger, will lead less quickly to blushing. On the contrary, his reactions are less strong than people usually expect. 'He can lie until he's blue in the face' is what people say to express how incredible they find it that the antisocial behaviour is not accompanied by shame expressed physically by blushing, casting the eyes down, a tremble in the voice, looking away or tics in the face.

Before I discuss the socially anxious behaviours I want to make clear why antisocial behaviours with the child with an internalising conduct problem do not or hardly ever occur. Characteristic for this child is that she tries to avoid danger. As a result she will usually not show antisocial behaviours so easily. She will want to avoid at all times the danger, the shame and the feelings of guilt which she would experience if she committed arson. For the child with the internalising conduct difficulties, stealing is unlikely to be an option because it does not fit in with the *moral development* of this child and the extent to which *guilt feelings* can be conjured up. The child with the internalising conduct disorder will be less inclined to lie, especially when it serves an egoistical aim. Lying is morally objectionable to her, and following on from the strong moral development the child will want to avoid this. From the fear of being bad and being judged negatively by others with regard to itself as a person, the child with the internalising conduct disorder is likely to be afraid of telling lies. Lying and even the suspicion of dishonesty will cause strong fears and feelings of guilt. The child with the internalising conduct problem will, however, have fewer problems with lying. This child can lie in order to conceal the subject of the conduct problem, for example a trauma, and will generally employ less strict moral norms.

Children with an internalising conduct problem will be less inclined to show aggressive behaviour. Their fear is likely to make them avoid the contact, and fear of repercussions is more likely to cause them to adjust their behaviour towards the aggressor (*identification with the aggressor*) than to cause them to adopt aggressive behaviour.

Shyness

Everybody is shy now and again, especially when confronted with new social situations. In itself this emotion, with its hesitant behaviour, is functional. It makes people more cautious and attentive, something which is necessary in order to assess what kind of behaviour is adequate in new situations. This behaviour is definitely not gender-specific: men as well as women can be shy, although the extent to which it occurs with men and women and the way it is expressed will probably differ. Shyness is a reaction to an unsafe situation, to danger. The greater action-readiness of the man is less compatible with shyness, and together with socialisation this means that the man will be more likely to make his presence felt and to solve or mask his shyness by taking action. The woman's tendency, based on genetic predisposition and socialisation, will be to adopt a more reserved attitude. Women will therefore in general be shy more often and for a longer period than men. Shyness is characteristic for internalising conduct difficulties. With internalising conduct difficulties shyness is frequent and does not only occur in *new* situations, but also in unusual situations, unexpected situations and social situations outside the context of the family. With the child with an internalising conduct *disorder* this will be strongly *generalised* behaviour. With the child with an internalising conduct *problem* this will mainly be restricted to a few specific situations which are linked to his or her problem, for example situations connected to a trauma.

The child with the internalising conduct disorder will be generally *shy* in social situations. The child will therefore come across altogether as being shy. The child with the conduct problem will not so much come across as being shy, but will adopt a reserved, shy attitude in certain situations.

Avoidance

One of the most characteristic solutions of the child with an internalising conduct disorder is to avoid situations which conjure up anxiety. A situation causing anxiety could be a birthday party or a thought. Avoidance mainly concerns unknown and unfamiliar social situations which require social interaction. Because anxiety can spread and attach itself to innocent subjects, unreal anxieties can develop. The original subject of anxiety can in the end not be recognised any more; the behaviour then takes on *phobic* characteristics. Both *single* and *complex* phobias can be developed.

A child with an internalising conduct disorder will try to *avoid* social situations, including familiar ones. The avoidance behaviour is generalised. The child with the conduct problem will avoid certain situations and not avoid others.

Withdrawal

Even socially familiar situations can conjure up anxiety in the child with the internalising conduct disorder. A birthday is such a situation. No matter how familiar, the child will often have trouble concealing its uneasiness. Initially it will withdraw by being silent; second, it will try to conceal its uneasiness by means of an activity. Pouring coffee is used as a flight from the anxious situation. From the anxiety model this means 'taking action' and this will lead to a reduction in the anxiety. Because it is not a specific action intended to fight the danger, the anxiety will easily surface again. The child feels anxious, has the idea that everyone is looking at how she pours the coffee, and subsequently acts clumsily. In this way a self-fulfilling prophecy arises. Finally, the child will, as far as possible, want to withdraw physically from the situation.

The child with the internalising conduct disorder will tend to *withdraw* from social situations. This behaviour will be less general for the child with the internalising conduct problem, but will be more connected to specific situations which have to do with the child's problematic area.

Hyperactivity

Hyperactivity is busy, over-active, restless behaviour. It can occur with ADHD and when the child is in a problematic situation, physically or emotionally. It occurs significantly more often with boys.

The hyperactivity which is a symptom of ADHD does not occur without impulsivity. It is characterised by a continuous unrest which occurs in a generalised way in all situations. The unrest diminishes when the activity is specifically repressed, and when the child concentrates on an activity, or changes between exciting activities and small physical movements, or is in structured situations or stimuli-free situations. It increases in situations of pressure, excitement, not being allowed to move, unstructured situations and stimuli-rich situations. Hyperactivity is a common thread in the life of a child with ADHD. With the child with conduct problems, hyperactivity is more situation bound and will decrease in situations when the child feels safe, whether this situation is structured or unstructured, stimuli-rich or stimuli-free. Hyperactivity will also be less strong and not form a common thread during life unless the factor causing the problems has been present since earliest childhood. Making a distinction between hyperactivity as a symptom of ADHD and hyperactivity as an expression of problems will in that case be more difficult and depend more on other factors, for example the occurrence of impulsivity.

Hyperactivity as part of ADHD is generalised, already present in early childhood and exists in safe and unsafe situations. It then occurs together with impulsivity and increases in stimuli-rich and unstructured situations. Hyperactivity as an expression of problems is more likely to be situation bound and disappear when the child is in a safe situation.

Impulsivity

Impulsivity has among other things to do with being able to postpone the satisfaction of a need. It consists of a combination of three elements. The first is being overwhelmed by an oncoming stimulus, for example the need to ask something. The second element is being unable to plan, not to see when the best moment is to satisfy the need, for example asking a question. The third element is to experience oneself as completely central at that moment, not to imagine what the satisfaction of the need means to the other, for example what the other person is doing at that moment. Impulsivity is a characteristic of the young child, because it is unable to process stimuli, to plan and to oversee what his or her behaviour means to someone else. To a child with ADHD it means that the limited processing of stimuli causes the child to proceed from one stimulus to the other, because processing two stimuli at the same time gives problems. The child tends to comply with the stimulus that occurs and does not take as a criterion whether something has high priority. That which presents itself gains the attention. The previous stimulus will be dropped, often unfinished. That means that the child can drop an activity even while it is enjoying it. This is fundamentally different behaviour from the egoistical behaviour of someone who does what he wants. Basically, humans are not free from impulsivity but thinking of another person should direct our own activity and maybe stop or influence it. When a child mainly tries to get its own way, we are not dealing with impulsive behaviour. Impulsive behaviour arises not as a result of a volitional act – it is not chosen because of its content – but as a result of how a situation develops and a stimulus arises. The stimulus can come from outside, but also from within, and needs which can arise inside oneself can lead to impulsive behaviour. Impulsive behaviour is the opposite of thought-out behaviour, because the behaviour is directed by an impulse and not steered in a direction by thoughts.

In the event of conduct problems impulsivity is not necessarily present. The child with the internalising conduct disorder will not be subject to impulsivity, because of her constant self-reflection. And she will not surrender to an impulsive stimulus because of this same self-reflection. With the externalising disorder and the conduct problem impulsivity will exist without having a structural character.

Impulsivity is a symptom of ADHD. It occurs with everyone to a lesser or greater degree and with the young child it is normal behaviour. With the child with ADHD it has a structural nature and does not pass when that would be expected because of its age. Impulsivity is not a structural part of conduct difficulties, but can occur especially following on from an aggressive indifference to other people.

Concentration disorder

Concentration is focusing all the attention on a subject. Other subjects therefore have to be pushed into the background. In order to achieve this, it must be possible to use the connections in the brain effectively. Certain paths have to be taken and others excluded temporarily. This does not work adequately in the case of ADHD. A characteristic of *concentration disorder* is, among other things, difficulty in keeping the level of attention up whether something one is doing is fun or not. Concentration can be influenced greatly. There are different ways in which concentration can be disturbed. It can come from within or from an outside source. Some people are able to concentrate without a problem under the most difficult circumstances. You can perform an Indian dance around them and they will keep on doing their work unperturbed. Others need optimal circumstances in order to carry out their work well. It is also not the case that everyone always concentrates at the same level. When you 'have a lot on your mind' it is difficult to concentrate. Having many worries means that there are many subjects in the brain which have to be 'kept an eye on' and be pushed aside. The brain is busy with that subject, and a different activity can only win when it is clearly more important or more fun and control over the painful subject is subdued. One of the solutions is to direct the concentration to a different subject causing the attention to be caught and to keep the inner problems more easily under control. Concentration problems are not structural and generalised. When a child has problems, for example because of the parents' divorce, it can have direct consequences for the level of concentration. In addition to sleeping disorders, concentration disorders are common in the case of children's traumatic experiences. The degree of concentration is also sensitive to the subject. Computer games almost naturally ensure concentration; boring, monotonous work on the other hand asks a lot of the ability to concentrate. Also a person's physical condition influences the ability to concentrate. When you are ill, it is more difficult to concentrate. The body, and therefore also the mind, is then very busy with the recovery process and there is little space for other subjects.

Intelligence is in some way connected to concentration. Children with lower intelligence often have trouble concentrating, but that is completely different from the concentration disorder of a child who has ADHD. A child with lower intelligence dedicates itself to a difficult task and becomes tired because of the effort. After some time, you can see that the level of concentration decreases and tiredness increases. The energy, and with that the concentration, 'runs out'. The problem with concentration which is allied to a child with lower intelligence occurs therefore after some period of time and has not been there from the beginning. With highly intelligent children you often see a great ability to concentrate. They are often able to concentrate for long periods and have a lot of energy. For some children this means that they become overactive.

Concentration disorder can be an ADHD symptom. With a child who has ADHD the stimulus processing in the brain is not optimal and the lack of concentration is immediately present when a task is started. Distraction is great. The concentration does not only become less from the inside but is disturbed from the outside when a new stimulus occurs. What makes it difficult for the child concerned is that this applies to every stimulus, but works much more strongly when it concerns one which is pleasant. This makes it seem that the child is lazy and only does what it likes and for the rest cannot be bothered. When you look at a child who has ADHD you will soon see that it is not unwillingness on the part of the child. Moreover the fierce unrest which the child experiences makes it even more difficult to concentrate.

Boys generally have much more difficulty than girls concentrating on school matters. Also normal boys, without ADHD, need to move around a lot – more so than girls. Consequently tasks which require little movement are more difficult to perform.

Concentration disorder can be a symptom of ADHD. In that case it is structural and is connected to being easily distracted and hyperactive. The *concentration problem* is generalised and has been there since earliest childhood, because the children's brains have to keep the 'problem area' under control. The concentration problem is not structural and is often directed to a different subject to divert it from the painful subject.

Concentration is very sensitive to the subject, situation, physical state and gender.

As I have now discussed the behaviours, Part 1, The Model, has been concluded. Part 2 is aimed at providing help and opens with a chapter on diagnostics, for which the material has been provided in the previous chapters.

Summary

Children's behaviour does not in general tell what the source of the behaviour is. In order to apply the appropriate form of help it is, however, important to know from where the behaviour arises. Although it does not always show at first sight, there are differences between behaviours that arise from a conduct disorder and behaviours that arise from conduct problems. With the externalising form (disorder and problem) we speak of antisocial behaviour; with the internalising form we speak of socially anxious behaviour. The behaviours with disorder and problem differ in nature and in frequency of occurrence. With a disorder there is a generalised occurrence of the behaviours; with a problem the behaviour is mainly shown in specific situations. ADHD has its own behaviour problems in the form of hyperactivity, impulsivity and concentration disorder.

Part 2
Professional Help

8

Diagnostics

In the previous chapters the characteristics of the externalising and internalising conduct problems were discussed next to those of ADHD. On the basis of the model we can make a distinction between disorders which are mainly predispositional and problems which are mainly controlled by the environment. In this way we can distinguish between the various groups who, based on their disturbing behaviour, are often heaped together. I have already emphasised the necessity of this distinction in order to decide on an adequate treatment which is adjusted to the specific problems. This requires, however, accurate diagnostics. Now, this has not always been developed to such a degree that this is possible. In order to provide as many handles as possible I will state the common and new diagnostic instruments, complemented by the criteria stated in the previous chapters. For the purpose of diagnostics I, in the course of this chapter, provide lists of questions to use in determining the problem:

- Questions in order to diagnose an externalising conduct disorder or conduct problem.

- Questions in order to find the possible causes of behaviour problems.

- Questions in order to diagnose an internalising conduct disorder or conduct problem.

- Questions in order to diagnose ADHD.

Here we will keep Vygotsky's (1993) plea for diagnostics in mind, diagnostics which in line with Gesell (1965) are not general, but cover specific areas: motor functioning, linguistic functioning, adjusted behaviour and social behaviour.

Within the framework of diagnostics and treatment I will initially always consider whether the behaviour stems from a *disorder* or *problem*, whereas earlier, in Part 1, I used the division between externalising and internalising as the first line of approach. I compare the externalising disorder with the externalising problem and the internalising disorder with the internalising problem. The reason for this is that for the professional helper the difference between externalising and internalising is clear in general. The difference between anxious and aggressive or shy and assertive hardly ever leads to confusion. Less clear, however, is whether the behaviour is a matter of a disorder or a problem; namely whether the aggression and anxiety comes from within or is conjured up by the environment. This latter distinction is, however, important in daily practice in connection with the treatment to be applied.

Externalising conduct disorder versus externalising conduct problem

The difference between a conduct *disorder* and a conduct *problem* is easy to distinguish when the environment is less problematic. There are, however, hardly any situations without risk factors in the environment; see also Table 5.2 in Chapter 5. It is therefore often difficult to recognise whether behaviour is the result of a disorder or of an impediment.

I will repeat the definition I gave in Chapter 4 of an externalising conduct disorder:

> A general pattern which has been developing since early childhood of an inadequate me–other differentiation, little empathic capacity and an inadequate ability to put thoughts and feelings into words. There is a diminished responsiveness of the autonomic nervous system, making it possible for the child to reach a state of diminished consciousness. In order to leave this state, the child may start looking for danger by, for example, committing arson or going out to steal. A poor empathic capacity causes the child not to be good at striking up friendships. The child suffers from generalised aggression and can emotionally explode in all sorts of situations which conjure up feelings of frustration. The child has shown a consistent pattern of antisocial behaviour since earliest childhood. This behaviour is not limited to a certain situation or a certain period such as puberty.

Because the conduct disorder is predispositional and there is an inadequate me–other differentiation, the conduct disorder will have been there from earliest childhood. Research by Tolan (1998), based on the development paths of Loeber, shows that starting with externalising behaviour at an early age is an actual predictor of serious violence at a later age. With the conduct problem there is no inadequate me–other differentiation; at the most there is egoistic behaviour. The problematic behaviour will, in principle, not have been there since earliest childhood. It is true that neglect can cause problems from an early age onwards, but it will, for example, not fundamentally hinder the me–other differentiation.

When we are dealing with problems which have not been present from earliest childhood, then we are probably not dealing with a conduct disorder but with a conduct problem. We can see this in the further description of the criteria in the *DSM-IV* (American Psychiatric Association 1994). The *conduct disorder* can be *restricted to groups, solitary aggressive* or *not differentiated*, where the behaviour takes place both alone and together with others. Starting from the model I outlined in Part 1, it may be clear that in the case of the conduct *disorder* there can be no group form. First, because the behaviour has been there since the beginning, even before the child started functioning in groups. Second, the inadequate empathic capacity will lead less to friendships and the youngster with a conduct disorder will not often be a member of a group. The group form will play a part mainly during a certain developmental phase, puberty. This means that this form is more likely to be a conduct problem than a conduct disorder. Although the predisposition, which makes the hormonal flow possible during puberty, forms a ground on which the behaviour becomes possible, it is the environment factor which dominates. With the conduct disorder we will be able to observe the behaviour in all situations, alone or in a group. The form which belongs to the conduct disorder is not differentiated.

An essential characteristic of the (externalising) conduct disorder is the inadequate me–other differentiation. When the terms 'an inadequate self-image', 'little ego development' or 'an underdeveloped super-ego' are used with regard to the child, then these are indications of an inadequate me–other differentiation. The diagnostic instruments that research these characteristics, mainly projective tests, can therefore be employed to research this criterion. On the basis of the inadequate me–other differentiation the child has little empathic capacity and is strongly egocentric. We do not yet have specific diagnostic instruments at our disposal with which the degree of egocentrism can be measured.

The child with a conduct disorder will tend to see others as an extension of itself. In the game and in projection tests the child will show to what extent the other is seen as an 'instrument' for the purpose of its own game and for the satisfaction of its own needs. Also the degree of empathy can be examined in this way. I want to point out again that the empathic capacity of the child with a conduct disorder is inadequate.

In order to research how serious the conduct difficulties are and what their nature is, psychological tests like the *CBCL-Child Behavior*

Piaget carried out experimental research into how egocentrism can be measured with a child. In an experiment he let a child sit at a small table. Before him or her was a small pile of sand, on the other side of the table sat a doll with a smaller pile before it and on yet another side of the table there was nobody but there was a small pile of sand. Piaget (1972) asked the child which pile was in front of the doll. Up to a certain age the child stated the pile it had in front of itself, and only after the child stopped thinking in a strongly egocentric way was it able to state the correct pile.

Checklist are useful. In addition there are instruments that relate to the childrearing situation, like the *FRT-Family Relations Test*.

Because the child with an (externalising) conduct disorder tends to regard other people as an instrument for the satisfaction of his own needs, he will often want to play the boss. Peers will not always appreciate this. These children often have little need to play with others. They are not so focused on the other, but much more on themselves, and get little pleasure from doing things with other people and from the contact itself. Information about interaction with peers is therefore an important contribution to the diagnosis.

The child with an externalising conduct disorder has an inadequate moral sense. His or her moral standards will mainly be dominated by punishment and reward. Moral dilemmas will be judged by the child to the extent that they provide punishment or reward.

If the child shows antisocial behaviour, but has enough me–other differentiation to think empathically and put himself in someone else's place and he does not see the other as an extension of himself, then it is more likely that we are dealing with a conduct *problem*. What is striking about the child with a conduct disorder is his aggression. This form of behaviour with the child with the conduct disorder generally differs from this form of behaviour with the child with the conduct problem. The aggression of the child with the conduct disorder can be conjured up by any source of frustration. The common thread is the frustration which the child experiences. The aggression of the child with the conduct problem is more likely to be conjured up by specific persons and institutions in its environment. I have already noted this difference between *generalised aggression* and *situation-bound aggression*.

The child with the externalising conduct disorder shows a diminished reactivity of the autonomic nervous system. It will therefore experience fear or pain less quickly, and can behave recklessly and even look for danger as a form of 'self-medication'. As far as physiological measures are concerned it should in principle be possible to research the testosterone level and the responsiveness of the autonomic nervous system, but there are no norms in existence yet against which the child could be tested.

Measuring consciousness fluctuations and the presence of theta-activity is in principle possible by brain research via an *EEG*, the *electroencephalogram*. In general no attention is paid to this with an EEG, because strong consciousness fluctuations that could point to deviations of the brain like epilepsy are looked at. It could, however, be employed as a diagnostic instrument. To what extent it can be decisive depends on the development of diagnostics and research into conduct disorders.

> A 15-year-old boy, who was already treated successfully for three years based on a diagnosis of externalising conduct *disorder*, accidentally had a bad fall. He was admitted to hospital for observation. In connection with

possible brain damage an EEG was performed; it showed that the fall did not damage him, but that he did suffer from consciousness fluctuations. In this way it accidentally came to light that he indeed suffered from consciousness fluctuations, as could be expected from the diagnosis externalising conduct disorder.

A remarkable characteristic of the child with a conduct disorder is its inadequate self-reflection. It will answer 'what' questions more easily than 'why' questions or questions about feelings. Linguistic expression of thoughts and feelings are restricted by the inhibited development of the left hemisphere, as we have already seen. These children will therefore have difficulty with talking to other people about what goes on inside their minds. When they are confronted with their deeds, they will be quick to drop out emotionally. They close themselves off and can even get into a state of diminished consciousness, as a result of which it seems that their eyes see nothing. The look does not make contact, is directed inwards and not at the other person. The eyes have no depth at that moment. The experienced diagnostician will recognise the milky haze that will pass over the eyes.

> The parents of a boy with a conduct disorder wanted to know what went on inside his mind when they were ranting and raving at him. They asked the therapist to help them with that. To ask for feelings was problematic. To questions like 'What is going on in your mind?' or 'What are you thinking when your parents rant and rave at you?' the boy kept looking friendly, but said nothing. To the question 'What do you do then?' the answer came immediately, 'Wait.' And that is exactly what one sees: a waiting body where no emotions can be observed. The emotional reaction comes much later. A question about a reaction is much easier to answer than a question about emotion.

A child with conduct problems is active in communicating with other persons. I have already mentioned that with lying you can observe differences between a child with a conduct disorder and a child with a conduct problem. A child with a conduct disorder will mainly lie to create a different reality and will in addition try to stick to it despite proof to the contrary. The child with the conduct problems is more likely to take action to find out whether it can manipulate the other person. When it notices that the other person does not follow the story, it will put new arguments forward. The older the child, the more these two forms will grow towards each other. The child with the conduct disorder will, as it becomes older, learn how to manipulate to get his or her way.

To conclude I will list the questions which apply to the diagnosis of the externalising conduct disorder or the externalising conduct problem.

Questions in order to diagnose an externalising conduct disorder or conduct problem

1. Do the criteria of the *DSM-IV* or the *ICD-10* apply?

2. Has the behaviour been there since earliest childhood?

3. Is there inadequate me–other differentiation?

4. Is the child capable of empathising?

5. Does the child need to play with other children?

6. Is the child capable of self-reflection?

7. Does the child have little fear and pain during its activities?

8. Is the child structurally aggressive or situation-bound aggressive?

9. Does the child have a low frustration tolerance?

10. Are there strong consciousness fluctuations?

11. In what way does the child lie?

12. Are there circumstances that could explain the child's behaviour?

A positive answer to Question 1 does not yet make a distinction between problems controlled by predisposition or by the environment. A positive answer to Question 2 is an indication for an externalising conduct *disorder*, unless environmental factors, which can explain the behaviour, have played a part since earliest childhood. A positive answer to Question 3, that means to say that the child has an inadequate me–other differentiation, is an important indication for an externalising disorder, but can also be an indication for a contact disorder. An inadequate me–other differentiation is not the same as having consideration for other people. When someone has a good me–other differentiation, it is possible that they will not have consideration for other people because of their upbringing or circumstances. What it is about, and Question 4 is connected with that, is whether a person is able to make a difference between himself and other people, whether he realises that another person has totally different thoughts and emotions. When a child or youngster naturally assumes that another person is just like him, then the me–other differentiation is probably inadequate. In order to be empathic it is necessary for him to be able to put himself in someone else's place. He has to be able to imagine what goes on in someone else's mind, even if it concerns thoughts and feelings which he does not have or does not know. Question 5 is concerned with whether the child enjoys playing with others for the contact itself, or whether playing with others is only desired when he needs the other for his own game, when the other is more an instrument than a source of contact. In the case of instrumentally having contact with others, this is an indication of an externalising conduct disorder or contact disorder.

As far as self-reflection is concerned, the child with an externalising conduct disorder is handicapped, despite possibly having normal intelligence. He will have difficulty in putting thoughts and feelings into words and will have trouble recognising the motivation behind his behaviour and putting this into words. This also means that he will have trouble properly assessing his own role in an event. With Question 7 we reach the area of the autonomic nervous system. When the child has a low reaction to danger and pain, his heart does not beat faster, he does not blush easily, does not sweat during exciting situations, does not find situations which other children and youngsters find exciting that exciting and looks for danger, like committing arson – this is an important indication for an externalising conduct disorder. The other way around it is an important indication for a conduct problem. As far as aggression (Question 8) is concerned it can be said that the externalising child is often generalised aggressive. That means to say that it can become aggressive in a large variety of situations and that aggression can be conjured up easily. This can be directed both to adults, peers and to animals or objects. A frustration is already enough for it to express itself aggressively. In the case of the child with a conduct problem the aggression is usually more situation bound, being directed towards certain persons, a sex or certain situations, or, for example, occurring only under certain circumstances, for example under the influence of alcohol. The frustration tolerance (Question 9) of the child with an externalising conduct disorder is low: he will quickly feel frustrated by something that does not go his way. In order to diagnose the externalising conduct disorder it is essential to establish whether there are consciousness fluctuations (Question 10). Here it is not a matter of large fluctuations as we sometimes see with the epileptic child, but of small fluctuations. The child seems to be in a mist, the eyes have no 'depth'. Question 11 concerns the form of lying. The child with the externalising conduct disorder is more likely to lie in order to create a different reality, sustain denial against all logic and in his lying be not very contact oriented. It seems more like an automatism than a passionate attempt to lead someone up the garden path.

When there are conduct problems this means that there have to be circumstances which can explain the child's behaviour (Question 12). I have already stated four sources: upbringing, trauma, puberty and divorce. It should be noted that the conduct problem must have started chronologically after the arrival of the environmental factor or have become significantly worse. If this is not the case, then this is a sign that it is maybe not so much the environmental factor which plays a part, but the predisposition of the child. The question about the beginning of the problems is therefore stated first in the next list of questions, questions used in order to find a conduct problem.

Questions in order to find the possible causes of behaviour problems

1. Is there a moment at which the problematic behaviour started?

2. In what situations does the behaviour take place?

3. In what situations does the behaviour not take place?

4. Is it known whether the child underwent a traumatic experience?

5. Did the child go through a divorce/separation of his or her parents?

6. How can you describe the childrearing qualities of the parents?

7. How is the relationship between the child and its parents?

8. How is the attachment of the child?

9. To what extent is the child autonomous?

10. Is the behaviour limited to the period of puberty?

11. What is the childrearing style of the family?

12. Do the other children in the family show signs of problems?

Because behaviour problems are generally situation bound, Question 2 is aimed at the situations in which the behaviour takes place. When we deal with a child we tend to look mainly at the problematic side and wonder less about the situations in which the behaviour does not take place (Question 3). Nevertheless, here lies information about how the behaviour is bound to the situation and the nature of the source. The characteristics of the situations that play a part in which the behaviour *does* take place and the characteristics of the situations in which the behaviour *does not* take place tell us what triggers the behaviour. For example, when the problems only take place at home, or only with a certain teacher at school. Questions 4, 5 and 6 are intended to establish the source of the behaviour. When looking for a trauma, chronology is important. When a clear difference in behaviour can be observed, then this is an important indication for a trauma (Question 4). A divorce/separation (Question 5) has strong effects especially in the year prior to the divorce, and by that I mean the physical separation of the parents and not the legal date, and the two years thereafter. In general it diminishes after that period. A child who shows behaviour problems within that period, and not or hardly before that, will probably express the problems with the divorce/separation through that behaviour. What is very and structurally important is how the childrearing qualities of the parents can be described (Question 6). Here we should think of the 12 conditions stated by Bartels and Heiner (1994) (see Chapter 5). The relationship with the parents (Question 7) is an important source of security, but also of stress, for children. Research by NIPO-TNS (2004) reveals that 68 per cent of the children in the Netherlands suffer from stress. The factor that contributes most to children's stress is 'parents', the second, 'homework'. Moreover, this relationship is of great importance for the providing of help to children with conduct problems. Questions 8 and 9 are aimed at two important consequences of inadequate childrearing during early childhood. In order to form relations, for making contact, attachment is important; for independent functioning the extent to which the parents stimulated the child in its autonomy is important. The latter is, among other things, an important ground for puberty where detachment from the parents and independence are central. During puberty conduct problems often arise which were not there before and which will not be there afterwards. This is what Question 10 refers to, namely whether the behaviour is restricted to puberty, in which case we can place it as bound to age and it is less worrisome. A condition for this is that puberty has started and the first visible sign for this is growth, especially when a growth spurt has taken place. The childrearing style (Question 11) gives information about how the child is given opportunities to develop, but also whether the child is in a situation where the childrearing style at home is in conflict with that of the surrounding people. In this way the child can come into conflict with his or her parents and the environment at the same time and consequently 'fall between two stools'. When a problem is more predispositional than controlled by environment factors, then this can often be seen in the difference that parents and children experience between that child and the other children in the family (Question 12).

Internalising conduct disorder versus internalising conduct problem

The characteristics of an internalising conduct disorder are the opposite of the externalising conduct disorder.

In Chapter 4 I defined the internalising conduct disorder as follows:

> There is continuous anxious and shy behaviour in social situations, which increases with the unfamiliarity of the situations. The child tends to avoid these situations and in this way maintains the anxiety. There is an increased responsiveness of the autonomic nervous system, causing the child to seem to hear and see everything. The behaviour has existed since early childhood and is structural, not linked to one or a number of specific situations – the child has not started to show this behaviour after experiencing a trauma. The me–other differentiation has been strongly developed, causing the child to be strongly empathic and not very egocentric. There is, however, a lack of assertiveness. The child is continuously busy with self-reflection and with its self-image. Within the generalised anxiety the child shows the characteristics of a social phobia. Although the child is good at putting itself in someone else's place, it will still often be afraid to play with others and will

choose the familiar and reliable. The child has shown, since its earliest childhood, a consistent pattern of socially anxious behaviour.

The child with an internalising *problem* shows, on the surface, the characteristics stated above, but then in specific situations. It is a reaction to the environment. It will be anxious in certain situations and not stick up for itself well. It will tend to avoid these situations but it will not be hindered in its total functioning. The child does not come across as being phobic. Because there is not an amplified responsiveness of the autonomic nervous system the child will not structurally react anxiously and alertly. Also the excessive self-reflection of the child with an internalising conduct disorder cannot be found with this child. It will probably have less difficulty in having contact with peers.

With the child with an internalising conduct disorder we speak of *generalised anxiety* and *generalised shyness*; with the child with an internalising conduct problem we speak of *situation-bound* anxiety and shyness.

In order to make a diagnosis the instruments that examine the extent of anxiety and conduct problems can be used, for example the CBCL.

Here it also applies that a general image arises that does not make a distinction as to whether the behaviour is controlled more by predisposition than by environment.

Because the *DSM-IV* (American Psychiatric Association 1994) does not make a distinction between the externalising or internalising conduct disorder and only discusses the externalising form, there are no criteria for the internalising conduct disorder available. The DSM does have criteria for anxiety problems like the *GAD*, the *Generalised Anxiety Disorder*, or the *social phobia*; these are however not specifically geared to the child and developmental disorders. The *ICD-10* (World Health Organization 1992) does state two forms in which the internalising problem occurs: the *mixed form conduct disorder and emotional disorder* and the *depressive conduct disorder*.

Just as with the externalising problem, the physiological measures of a low testosterone level and the increased reactivity of the autonomic nervous system cannot be tested for the individual child. The diagnostics of the EEG do not apply to these children as they do with the externalising conduct disorder, because these children do not suffer from diminished consciousness. At the most you could state, for example, that they show fewer theta-waves, the brain rhythm belonging to the state of rest, but also for this there are no standards available.

Just as with the externalising conduct problems, I conclude this section with a list of questions to use in order to diagnose the internalising problems.

Questions in order to diagnose an internalising conduct disorder or conduct problem

1.   Is the child's anxiety generalised or situation bound?

2.   Is the child's shyness generalised or situation bound?

3.   Has the behaviour been there since earliest childhood?

4.   Is there a strong me–other differentiation?

5.   Is the child strongly empathic?

6.   Does the child suffer from lack of assertiveness?

7.   Is the child constantly busy with self-reflection?

8.   Does the child show avoidance behaviour?

9.   Is the child excessively alert; does it seem to be on guard all the time?

10.   Does the child adjust easily?

11.   How is the child's moral sense?

12.   Are there circumstances that could explain the child's behaviour?

Just as with the aggressive disorder, it is the case for the anxiety disorder that the first indication of the predisposition factor is whether the child's anxiety is generalised (indication for a disorder) or whether the anxiety is more situation bound (indication for a problem). The same goes for Question 2 about shyness. Again the case is that when it is a matter of predisposition, this has in principle been present since earliest childhood (Question 3). In the case of an internalising conduct disorder the me–other differentiation is too strong (Question 4) and the child is too empathic (Question 5).

Empathy drives the child strongly towards social adjustment, which is unfavourable for the child in certain situations. The child is then not very assertive (Question 6) and will not easily stick up for itself. Out of fear of not coming across well with others, the child will constantly wonder how it will come across to other people and go through constant self-reflection (Question 7). The child will examine her motives for her behaviour and consider how she can steer her behaviour in order to satisfy the other (even more). She will have difficulty with putting her own role in perspective in these situations. Because the child experiences social situations as being very threatening, is insecure about whether she will come across well and whether she will do and say things right, this child will want to avoid these situations (Question 8). In the case of an internalising conduct problem the child will want to avoid specific situations and not others. The child with an internalising disorder experiences the world as being very dangerous and is therefore excessively alert and seems to be on her guard all the time (Question 9). Because the child with an internalising conduct disorder cannot face many situations, it does not easily adjust to the environment (Question 10). The child with an internalising problem on the other hand will often rebel against specific situations and not adjust. Within those situations lies the information about what the source of the problem is. The expectation of the child is that she will feel anxious or uneasy in those situations or even have to go through unpleasant things which she has already been through. A child with an internalising disorder has an overdeveloped moral sense (Question 11) – overdeveloped in the sense that the child uses standards which are not average and which impede her normal functioning. She needs as it were to use the high standards in order to prevent her from doing something that she could be reproached for. In the case of there being an internalising problem and not a disorder, this means that the behaviour arises from an environment source. In that case there must be circumstances (Question 12) which explain the child's behaviour.

ADHD, Attention Deficit-Hyperactivity Disorder, versus hyperactivity

When we look at the five problem areas (externalising conduct disorder and problem, internalising conduct disorder and problem and ADHD), we can say that the diagnostics for ADHD have been developed the most. At the same time the usual diagnostics are rather limited. Many diagnosticians restrict themselves more or less to the criteria stated in the *DSM-IV* (American Psychiatric Association 1994). On the basis of the characteristics of ADHD, also compared to other conduct difficulties, it is possible to refine the diagnostics and to obtain more certainty about the image. Below I list questions to use in order to diagnose ADHD.

Questions in order to diagnose ADHD

1. Do the criteria of the *DSM-IV* apply?

2. Are there neurological indications for immaturity or hyperkinesis?

3. Are there other maturation disorders?

4. Are there learning disorders?

5. Did the problems start in early childhood: as a baby, as a pre-schooler or in the first year of primary school?

6. Are there family members who have ADHD?

7. Does the child adjust easily?

8. Does the child have a good me–other differentiation?

9. Is the child able to self-reflect?

10. Does the child have a need to play with other children?

11. Does the child remain active during a conversation? (This question is useful if the element of hyperactivity applies.)

12. Are there circumstances that explain the child's behaviour?

The *DSM-IV* has a symptom list for the three aspects that play a part with ADHD: hyperactivity, impulsivity and attention deficit (Question 1). On the basis of this list of symptoms we can formulate a diagnosis, although it would be wiser to speak of a hypothesis which can be researched further. Because it concerns strongly subjective criteria here and experience with the problems plays a part, the following questions are intended to test the diagnosis more sharply and to support it. Neurological examination is also possible in order to underpin the diagnosis (Question 2). The most appropriate people to do this are the psychiatrist, paediatrician and neurologist. The degree of maturation of the motor apparatus can be measured neurologically and signs of *hypokinesis*, too little movement, or *hyperkinesis*, overactivity, can be diagnosed. Although it appears that the corpus callosum of children with ADHD is smaller than average and the prefrontal brain is underdeveloped, we do not yet have standardisation at our disposal, enabling us to find individual abnormalities, as is possible with, for example, IQ.

The diagnosis of ADHD without hyperactivity and impulsivity is often hard to make. We tend to imagine a chaotic child when we think of ADHD; this is, however, not the case with the form AD(H)D-attention deficit. A second difficulty is that the child with ADHD without inadequate attention function seems to function well in structured situations like a school. In that case the behaviour of the child is not recognised at school and people are quick to point, unjustly, at the childrearing by the parents as the cause of the behaviour.

To support the diagnosis of ADHD we can check whether there are other symptoms of a delayed maturation (Question 3). These symptoms do not necessarily have to be present but are an extra indication when they do occur. A number of areas that we can pay attention to can be distinguished. The first is the child's *temperament* as a baby. When the child cried a lot as a baby, this is possibly an indication for problems with the maturation of the brain. The second question is whether the child showed any *sleeping disorders*, because many maturation disorders occur during the night and maturation takes place for an important part during the night. The third area is the development of *toilet-training*. Late toilet-training can be a sign of late maturation. When the child is toilet-trained at night and not in the daytime, then it is not a maturation problem but more a behaviour problem. If it is a case of delayed maturation of the bladder muscles then this plays a role at least at night. Finally, there is the area of the learning disorders where indications for delayed maturation can be found: *dyslexia, mathematics disorder* and *writing disorder* or *dysgraphia* (Question 4). The diagnostics of dyslexia has been well mapped, for example thanks to the work of people like Dumont (1990, 1994), and is still being researched. As far as the writing disorder is concerned, Hamstra-Bletz and de Bie (1985) mapped the specific way of writing of children with a writing disorder. Table 2.1 showing maturation disorders can be found in Chapter 2.

Because children with ADHD are expected to be normally intelligent, an intelligence test will in principle not offer anything to hold on to for the diagnosis of ADHD.

ADHD, as a disorder of the maturation of the central nervous system, is already present from earliest childhood, but is not always clearly noticeable. I have already stated that there are three phases when the disorder becomes apparent, depending on the requirements set by the development tasks to the child: as a baby, as a pre-schooler and in the first year of primary school (Question 5). When it is not possible to point at one of these moments based on the *anamnesis*, case history, then the diagnosis ADHD is not plausible.

The behaviour of the child with ADHD is structural, systematic. If the child is hyperactive, then this will show in all 'free' situations. If the child has attention deficit this will become noticeable in all tasks that require concentration. If the child is impulsive, then it will always want to give into its wishes and new stimuli that occur. When the child only shows certain behaviours in specific situations, then it might be a conduct problem instead of ADHD. A child with ADHD-hyperactivity-impulsivity, without attention deficit, will generally function well at school. The structured situation ensures that the child does not attract attention by chaotic and active behaviour, except in free situations like the schoolyard and at home.

Because there are strong indications that ADHD is hereditary (Question 6) and seems to be easy to inherit, it is probable that there are family members who also have or had ADHD. It mainly occurs with boys. It is therefore useful when diagnosing to find out whether it occurs within the family. When it occurs with a family member, for example the father, the extent that he has controlled it is a possible indication for the pace of maturation of the son. The chances are that the child will show the same pace of maturation. This is an indication for the prognosis.

Because of their disturbing behaviour children with ADHD are easily confused with children with externalising conduct problems. When describing the various problems I stated similarities and differences (see Table 6.1 in Chapter 6). With the diagnostic outline, however, we start from a child who only has the disorder ADHD, although in many cases it goes together with one of the forms of conduct difficulties. Although he keeps on starting a new activity because of his impulsivity-hyperactivity, the child with ADHD has difficulty in adjusting to situations (Question 7) and is more likely to make his own plan than do what someone else asks.

The child with ADHD does not, in principle, have a strongly underdeveloped me-other differentiation (Question 8), unless there is co-morbidity with a disorder where that is the case. They will also not come across as unscrupulous. As a result of a reasonably developed me–other differentiation, the child will be able to self-reflect (Question 9) and he will understand his part in an event pretty well. This also means that he suffers because of the fact that his insights and possibilities to direct his behaviour are not synchronised.

Children with ADHD do generally show anxiety and are weighed down with conflicts with the environment. Despite the many conflicts that the child experiences and the rejection by peers, the child with ADHD will need to play with others (Question 10). Not thinking egocentrically and having a reasonable empathic capacity ensures that the child needs to be with other people. Other children, however, often see the impulsive, hyperactive peer as someone who disturbs their play. When the child is hyperactive, it will be even more troubled by it when a situation is exciting or when he is required to sit still for a long period of time, for example during a conversation (Question 11).

Finally, when the diagnosis ADHD does not apply, there must be factors in the child's environment that lead to the problem behaviour (Question 12). When the questions stated above do not lead to ADHD, but there is hyperactivity, then this is an indication for hyperactivity as a way of expressing underlying problems.

Co-morbidity

Although the various conduct problems and ADHD are described separately, there is the possibility of co-morbidity, the occurrence at the same time of various disorders or problems. When discussing ADHD I stated that, as a result of the frustrations which the child meets with his environment, conduct problems can arise. This co-morbidity often occurs in the group of children with ADHD, and applies both to internalising and to externalising *problems*. Because the child with ADHD shows difficult behaviour for the environment, he will often get into conflict with the environment and on those grounds develop behaviour problems. This means that children who have ADHD almost always exhibit problematic behaviour that is not directly caused by their predisposition in addition to the behaviour that is. Moreover, ADHD and the externalising conduct disorder do not exclude each other. With these two disorders some areas of the central nervous system are involved which are partly different and partly the same, but are not working in opposite directions. This means that co-morbidity of ADHD and the externalising conduct disorder is possible. This will, however, occur less frequently. The same goes for ADHD and the internalising conduct disorder. The latter will seldom occur and if it does then it will do so more with girls than with boys.

The characteristics of conduct *disorders* in internalising and externalising forms exclude each other. They cannot therefore occur at the same time. If there is a combination of externalising and internalising characteristics in the behaviour then we are dealing with *conduct problems*.

In order to make the right diagnosis it is important to diagnose all problems separately. In this way everything can be mapped correctly. When a child with ADHD has indications for an inadequate me–other differentiation, then it is necessary to examine the diagnostic criteria of the externalising conduct disorder alongside the finding of ADHD.

Because the child with ADHD has, in principle, a normal me–other differentiation, an inadequate me–other differentiation is an indication of different problems or co-morbidity with a different disorder. These could be the conduct disorder or a contact disorder like *PDD-NOS (Pervasive Developmental Disorder – Not Otherwise Specified)*.

Anxiety and depression

Externalising conduct can hide anxiety and depression. Irritable behaviour in children can be an indication that anxiety or depression is present. Because the co-morbidity of depression with children with conduct disorders, conduct problems and ADHD is rather high, this element must always be included in the research. The question then is whether there is a depressive mood underneath the conduct difficulties with the child with self-criticising cognitions. The criteria used in the *DSM-IV* (American Psychiatric Association 1994) for depression are not so suitable for children. There are questionnaires which examine depression with children in particular; for example, *CDI – Children's Depression Inventory* (Kovacs and Timbremont 1992).

The criteria set by Weinberg *et al.* (1973) can still be used to examine depression with children:

1. dysphoric mood

2. ideas which lower self-esteem

3. aggressive behaviour (agitation)

4. sleeping disorders

5. change in school performance

6. reduced socialisation

7. change in school attitude

8. somatic complaints

9. loss of energy

10. unusual change in appetite and/or weight.

These subjects have to play a part for more than one month (de Wit 2000).

In the following chapters the nature of the treatment of the various problems will be at the forefront. I divide this according to type of problems: externalising conduct disorder, internalising conduct disorder, externalising or internalising conduct problems and ADHD.

Summary

In order to provide adequate help, proper diagnostics are of the utmost importance. The difference between externalising or internalising behaviour is obvious, in principle. Even for the layman it is generally easy to make a distinction between aggressive and anxious behaviour. For diagnostics it is mainly important whether behaviours arise from a disorder or are caused by the environment. In order to find this out, I set up a number of questions for the five different areas. The first are 12 questions in order to make clear whether the externalising behaviours are caused by a disorder or a problem. I then did the same for the internalising problem: 12 questions to find out whether the behaviours arise from a disorder or a problem. I then formulated 12 questions in order to diagnose ADHD. Finally, I discussed the fact that depression of children can lie underneath this problem.

9

The Treatment of an Externalising Conduct Disorder

I will now look at the various conduct difficulties and ADHD and their treatment possibilities. I start with the *externalising conduct disorder*. I have already stated that there is a substantial difference in treatment when we are dealing with a predispositional disorder or with a problem that is mainly controlled by the environment. In the first case what has to be done first of all is to teach the child and its environment to learn to live with the disorder. We have to keep in mind here that the child got his or her predisposition from its parents and family and therefore there is a greater chance that one of the parents or other family members more or less have the same predisposition. Moreover, it is often the case that when a certain disorder is present in a family, there is a greater chance of other disorders and also certain abnormalities or diseases. Research by Spee-van der Wekke, Meulmeester and Radder (1998) shows that children who receive special education are considerably more often ill than children who receive regular education. Such a family network is strongly burdened. Not only does the child have to learn to cope with the predisposition and the parents with the predisposition of the child, but it is possible that the parent also has to learn how to cope with their own predisposition and aggravating family circumstances. Professional help often lays emphasis on the child and its parents, while the family network mostly takes a back seat. The contextual approach (Boszornemyi-Nagy and Spark 1973) and the Family Group Conference (Hudson *et al.* 1996) are examples of a wider perspective.

With the externalising disorder the emphasis should also lie on 'learning to cope with the disorder'. This means that we must aim at 'learning to live with it' and not expect that we can take the problems away completely. When parents and children know the characteristics of the disorder, they will be better able to deal with it. When they know that a child with an externalising disorder has consciousness fluctuations and that he does not always have his intelligence at the ready, his parents will find it easier to respond to him.

The externalising conduct *disorder* occurs much less frequently than the externalising conduct *problem*. The treatment described will therefore only apply to a limited number of the children with externalising conduct difficulties.

Moffit (1993) reports that with a relatively small group of children, about 4 to 5 per cent of the population, the antisocial behaviour starts during childhood and grows into serious conduct difficulties. This small group later accounts for a disproportionate number of delinquency-related problems, estimated at half of the offences committed by youngsters. This unfavourable prognosis applies mainly to aggressive crimes. We suspect that with these children it is a matter of problems controlled by predisposition and with the larger group of children it is mainly problems controlled by the environment.

Children with a disorder often show behaviour that is difficult to direct. Parents often cry desperately, 'We've tried everything, nothing helps.' Bringing up a child by 'trying everything' can, however, also mean confirming the undesired behaviour. A non-systematic way of rewarding, sometimes yes, sometimes no, is a *variable reinforcement scheme.*

Theoreticians discovered that this scheme leads to reinforcing the behaviour. In addition to looking desperately for a successful strategy, this manner of childrearing threatens to reinforce the undesired behaviour – more strongly than via a scheme where there is always reward or always punishment. Parents, however, do not reach this way of childrearing for no reason. The fact that something is predispositional makes it difficult to alter the behaviour, especially through the usual childrearing strategies; punishment or reward do not work, or have an adverse effect in the sense that child and parents only feel bad and desperate because of it. Parents subsequently keep looking through various methods for possibilities of changing the behaviour. It would suit the professional helper in these cases therefore to show some modesty and not to raise any false hopes with the parents and the child, because the parents have already tried so much themselves.

Treatment areas

Although the child often shows difficult behaviour, and it sometimes seems that the child 'chooses' this behaviour, the child with a disorder in fact wants to be protected. It wants to be helped not to end up with those kind of problems which his or her predisposition gives cause for. We can see this at the moment when the child experiences that there is understanding for his powerlessness. When the child notices that his parents believe that he would also like his behaviour to stop, it gives this child a feeling of security. The behaviour does not stand between the child and his parents – at that moment parents and child become *allies* with respect to the behaviour and they are no longer *opponents*. The child will therefore be much more open to help from the parents. The child feels 'unguiltied' and will feel safer with advice received from his parents because he is better understood. A child who does not feel understood will not be inclined to follow advice given by others. As long as the child has the feeling that it is not being understood it will more easily resist its parents, and also others, and the behaviour will be reinforced. He will feel that the advice is based on the wrong ideas, without him being able to put this into words as such. It would even be unwise to follow advice from someone who does not understand what is going on. Van Acker (1995) formulates the alliance as follows: *solidarity is the best weapon against destructive and maladjusted behaviour.*

Throughout the text I will give examples of interventions which illustrate the theory. The first example is a remark made by a parent to a child, with the purpose of forming an alliance:

> I know that you would also like it to be that you didn't do those things. You yourself also find it unpleasant. I would like to help you to make sure that it will not happen again so quickly.

In order to direct the treatment of the child with an externalising conduct disorder I will list the characteristics again:

- mainly boys
- high level of testosterone
- low level of cortisol
  - generalised aggression
  - little anxiety, assertive
  - few psychosomatic complaints
  - antisocial behaviour
- diminished responsiveness of the autonomic nervous system
  - diminished sensitivity to stimuli of all senses: hearing, seeing, smelling, tasting, feeling
  - not very alert
  - low heart rate
  - quick habituation to negative stimulus
  - significant fluctuations in consciousness
  - difficulty in comprehending what is being said

- — looking for danger as self-medication for diminished consciousness
- — risk with monotonous occupation and feelings being hurt
- inhibited development of left hemisphere
  - — not very language oriented
  - — difficulty putting thoughts and feelings into words
  - — inadequate self-reflection
  - — little capability for self-directing behaviour
- less recognition of biological self
  - — limited me–other differentiation
  - — egocentric
  - — less empathic
  - — limited moral development, aimed at justice and competition
  - — norm exceeding behaviour according to own needs
  - — less developed realisation of mine and thine
  - — poor ability to assess own role
  - — antisocial behaviour
  - — feeling of being treated unfairly
  - — little need of playing with others
  - — social isolation as a result of having trouble striking up friendships
- risk of conduct problems because of conflicts with the environment.

Medication?

Although there are physical aspects (level of testosterone, level of cortisol, diminished responsiveness of the autonomic nervous system, fluctuating consciousness, increased theta-activity in the brain) it is still hardly possible to treat the disorder by means of medication. First, this disorder is not clear enough and a specialised treatment does not (yet) exist. Second, the medicinal treatment would have to be extremely drastic. Testosterone and the autonomic nervous system are elements that play an overall part in the body. Influence, which, through medication, has to be exercised on both these elements, will therefore go further than the intended behaviour itself. The autonomic nervous system can be brought into a state of alertness via the sympathetic system; amphetamines can, for example, accomplish this, but the child would be in a continuous state of unrest because of that, which is not desired. Testosterone is a basic hormone that has many functions. If it were possible to neutralise testosterone, and there are chemical substances that can block the working of testosterone, then also many positive, essential and constructive functions would be affected. We then think, for example, of drastic interventions, like castration and chemical castration, which will be carried out with sex offenders. Although they sometimes ask for it themselves, because they cannot control the sexual mist which continuously washes over them, such an intervention will have far-reaching consequences for the functioning of the person and is therefore not desired. A state of complete apathy could arise, for example. With children we also have the problem that their development is still in progress and may be damaged by such interventions.

Furthermore, such interventions by means of medication (in any case for the moment) cannot bring change to aspects like the restricted me–other differentiation, the inadequate linguistic functioning or the inadequate empathy. For this an extra maturation or further maturation would be necessary. Medication that speeds up the maturation or delays it does not (yet) exist.

There are psychopharmacologic drugs that are used for specific areas, like the controlling of aggression, especially explosive aggression: Dipiperon®, Melleril®, Tegretol® (Dorelijers and Schornagel 1996). Buitelaar (2000b) examined the working of Risperdone® with serious aggression; apart from the side effects it seems to provide help with pushing back serious aggression. Antipsychotic drugs, like Haldol, can work on aggression as it occurs with serious conduct disorders. This in itself is not surprising when we realise that the strong fluctuations of the consciousness can make the child mist over and be in danger of losing contact with reality, as is the case with psychoses. In the case of conduct difficulties, especially when these occur together with concentration disorders, often Ritalin® is used. Ritalin® does not only affect concentration, but also aggression. The dosages that control aggression, however, are generally higher than those which are necessary for concentration disorders. This also means more chances of side effects. Medication can in case of co-morbidity of ADHD and conduct disorders make the problems manageable. I will discuss this further in Chapter 12 when I take a closer look at the treatment of ADHD.

A few important disadvantages of psychopharmacologic drugs are that they have side effects, the substance works on more areas than the specific problem area, that they do not solve the problem structurally, the behaviour starts again when the medication is ended, and that they are addictive – more and more is needed in order to have the same effect. There are different opinions about the use of psychopharmacologic drugs. Some think that Ritalin® is necessary for children with ADHD like insulin is for diabetics; others, especially in the Netherlands, are a lot more careful with administering this medication. Ritalin® has an almost identical effect on the brain as cocaine (Braams 1999). It is therefore not surprising that Ritalin® is increasingly being used as a substitute for cocaine, and this has once again made it clear how dangerous medication can be. Besides, research into the effects of treatment of psychiatric disorders have made it clear that the most effective treatment is not just medication; there also has to be therapy: 'pills and talks'.

Medication is not an unambiguous working solution. In providing help to children with an externalising conduct disorder we also use psychological knowledge on the areas which are problematic, both brain functions and behaviours, and try to deal with them with psychological and educational solutions.

Me–other differentiation, empathy and self-reflection

The first and basic problem area with the conduct disorder is the inadequate *me–other differentiation*. Providing help to children with an externalising conduct disorder will initially mean stimulating the me–other differentiation. This help should not lean too much on language, given that these children do not function well linguistically. By this I do not mean that they do not have a thorough command of the language of their country; in principle they have no problems with that. These children usually have a normal intelligence, although it is disharmonious on the verbal side (Raine 1993), and they can therefore become literate and use their language normally. I mean the problem of putting thoughts and feelings into words, connected with the development of the left hemisphere which in these children is restrained. We should therefore not stimulate the me–other differentiation with these children so much by using language or by means of conversations. The me–other differentiation, which one supposes the child has, can be developed more strongly by means of play, sports and by putting thoughts and feelings into words for the benefit of and on behalf of the child. It is necessary that the child, by means of specifically formulating in terms of 'me' and 'other', learns more about the consequences of his behaviour for other people.

The way that this stimulating takes place does of course depend on the age. With young children there are many play situations, where, even in ordinary daily life, the me–other differentiation can be worked on:

> A set-up of soldiers is made in the sandpit. Two sides. From the start the child makes it clear that his side is the boss. He determines who does what and who will win. Going along with the child increases his enjoyment of

the game. Opposing him will ensure that he becomes frustrated and wants to break off the game or get into conflict with his playmate. When, after going along with this, it is put into words that it is nice for the child to win, but that it is also nice for the other person to win, this stimulates the me–other thinking in the child.

Following on from the me–other differentiation, making the difference between 'me' and 'the other', lies the empathic capacity, placing oneself in someone else's place and sensing his or her feelings. This is another area in which the child will have to be stimulated – for example, by putting into words what goes on in someone else's mind and with the help of questions letting the child 'guess' what goes on in someone else's mind. A programme like that of Steerneman (1997) is intended to enforce *social cognitions*. It is not aimed at teaching *social skills*, but at mainly stimulating a me–other differentiation and putting oneself in someone else's place. Social skills can only be developed based on *social insight*. With a lack of insight only 'tricks' can be taught, which can be used in certain situations and which are often not generalised to other situations, because the insight in *social interaction* fails. When applying social cognitions training, it proves to be that when the social cognitions increase, so do the social skills (Steerneman 1998).

Children with an externalising conduct disorder will have to be helped with the way in which they treat other people. Interaction with peers is important for the development of a social identity (Delfos 1999b). Enjoying contact is not natural for these children. Because of the way they treat children they are often treated unpleasantly by peers, and peers are afraid of them. On that basis they learn to be averse to interaction with peers instead of enjoying it. It is therefore important to provide help with respect to this interaction.

There is a risk that the child, who tends to use the other as an extension of himself, will use these 'lessons' to manipulate others better. The thing is therefore to find a balance between teaching the child how to interact with others and giving the child the means with which it can learn better how to manipulate the other. A suitable border area is making use of the positive characteristics of the child himself. With this the child will learn that others can enjoy playing with him and enjoyment of the game increases the chances that the other will want to play with him again.

> You are very good at building castles in the sandpit. John loves that. He is very good at making tunnels and you need those for the bunkers that you make. This way you can help each other and you can enjoy what you are both good at. You will see that if John is also allowed to do what he likes, he will come and play with you more often.

It is important to explain to the child what friendship means and how you can work on it. Parents often explain that to their child in the beginning. Usually a short explanation is enough to achieve the desired effect.

> In their childrearing period parents practise empathy with young children in order to teach them how to control their aggression towards others. 'How would you like it if you were pinched?' 'It hurts you when you get hit, doesn't it? Well, the same goes for Martin.'

> A mother explains to a young child when he kicks another child that he should not kick, that it hurts the other child, just as it hurts him when he is kicked. The same happens with respect to pinching or biting. And with a few examples the situation becomes clear to the child: you should not hurt someone else; it hurts him as it does you.

With children with an externalising conduct disorder more explanation will be necessary, and also when they become older. The child will only be able to make the abstraction based on several examples.

Practising putting yourself in someone else's place is important. Sullivan (1953) stated that developing a close friendship opens people up to other people's feelings. Because a friend lets you enter someone else's world, friendship is of the utmost importance in order to develop empathy. Because the child with an externalising conduct disorder lacks the ability to make friendships easily, he is doubly handicapped in developing empathy. Offering and guiding contacts with peers is therefore of the utmost importance. In order to map the level of the child's development regarding friendships, the classification of friendships which Selman (1981) designed can be used. In Table 9.1 you will find an adapted version of this. Learning how to develop friendships is very important for the later forming of relationships. A lack of this during childhood can therefore have far-reaching, life-long consequences. I would also like to recall that the further maturation with psychopaths mainly took place when there was a meaningful, lasting and intimate relationship (Martens 1997). What is probably the case here is that the intimate relationship is a daily training in how people are and what effect your behaviour has on them. In such relationships you often see a certain pattern. With not very empathic men you often see the supplementation in the relationship by a strongly empathic but unstable woman. The woman 'guides' the man to understand the emotions of others. Her empathy, however, often goes together with an instability and a lack of common sense which the man in his turn brings into the relationship.

The child with an externalising conduct disorder has in fact an early-childlike perception of what goes on in someone else's mind. That means to say that it makes little distinction between what he himself is thinking and what the other is thinking. The early-childlike *egocentrism* ensures that a child thinks that what goes on in someone else's mind is the same as what goes on in the mind of the child itself. He also thinks that adults are fully aware of what goes on in his mind. You can see that effect in a funny way when children (and it also happens to adults) start to speak right in the middle of an internal dialogue: 'And I really think that is so mean of Eric!' The listener does not know what preceded that statement and asks, 'Who is Eric and what did he do?'

During childrearing the child is often stimulated to wonder what is going on in someone else's mind at negative moments: 'Do you really think that William likes to be hit?' The motivation to put himself in someone else's place will, however, be greater with positive events: 'What do you think Daddy thinks about you having built a road for your cars?'

Expressing emotions is an important area of attention. Pre-schoolers are generally prepared to draw their emotions. This form easily links up to the world of the child who does not like to communicate linguistically about his thoughts and feelings. Creative expressions make the child more aware of his own emotions. The child might be asked, 'That piglet is very angry; which colour do you want to use so that you can see that he is angry? Would you like to draw a shy figure?'

Table 9.1 Development of friendships, based on Selman		
Kind of friendship	*Period*	*Nature of friendship*
Playmate	Pre-school period	A friend is someone who lives nearby and who you happen to play with.
One-sided help	Early school period	A friend is someone who you know better than others and who knows what you like and dislike; a friend is important because he does the things you want done.
Sporty co-operation	Later school period	In this friendship there is more awareness of reciprocity in relations and more desire to adjust to mutual wishes; it is not long term, fights can easily break off the friendship.
Intimate reciprocally sharing relations	Late childhood, early adolescence	This relationship is closer and there is awareness of continuity; the friendship is not pursued mainly in order not to become bored but as an opportunity for intimacy; conflicts do not necessarily break off relations.

Children with an externalising conduct disorder often get into trouble in social situations. Their lack of empathic capacity hinders them in assessing such situations. Their orientation to instrumental use of others can bring them into conflict with their social environment. That is why these children, more than the average child, need to learn about social situations. They draw benefit from adults putting social situations into words for them.

Playing a sport, especially in a team, often offers these children information about social interaction in a well-organised and unambiguous way. However, they often have trouble with functioning in a team, causing them to fall out of the team and lose their motivation for sports. Playing a sport which needs less team spirit is therefore initially more suitable.

With older youngsters social skills training programmes like those of Gordon (Bakker-Brouwer and van Wieringen-Kemps 1991) and Goldstein (Goldstein 1973; van der Zee, van der Molen and van der Beek 1989) can help with their socio-emotional functioning. Goldstein aimed specifically at people from lower socio-economic classes in order to teach them social skills. The training programme proved to be very suitable for children and youngsters who, because of their intellectual skills, functioned inadequately socially. The Goldstein training is more aimed at *social coping* than at *social functioning*. Following from that it is less suitable for children with an externalising conduct disorder who have a normal intelligence.

Working on the me–other differentiation is, although not expressly, a natural part of these training programmes. It is often touching to see how tough adolescents enjoy such a training. They are often happy to learn how proper social interaction works, because this gives them the opportunity to prevent themselves from keeping on getting into trouble and being rejected. No matter how antisocial a child with an externalising conduct disorder seems, he still wants to belong somewhere and yet becomes more and more isolated due to his socially unsuitable behaviour. The youngster with a disorder wants to be protected and such a training offers protection through knowledge and skills. Most social skills training programmes, however, start from an empathic capacity. That is why they are often not tuned in to the child with an inadequate empathic capacity like the child with an externalising conduct disorder and also with a contact disorder. Especially for these groups social skills training programmes prove to be necessary but do not show great results. The training programmes mainly have effect on children, often girls, who do have sufficient empathic capacity but are not assertive enough. Prins (1998) indicates that social skills training programmes have more effect with children with internalising problems than with children with externalising problems. Eppink, Bok and Taris (1998) plead for a good social skills training for immigrants. This would not have to be an adjustment to the dominant culture but an opportunity to even out the barriers which they meet socially.

An important step in the development of the me–other differentiation, and progressing *individuation*, is practising *self-reflection*. This activity is difficult for children with an externalising conduct disorder. They tend less to examine their motives and feelings, and the diminished capacity of the left hemisphere makes it difficult for them to put their thoughts and feelings into words. It is necessary that these children practise their capacity to self-reflect. Here it is also important that the child feels understood. We might say to a child:

> It seems as if you don't feel like telling what you're thinking. I know that you want to, but cannot. Shall I help you by saying what I think you are thinking about? Shall I guess? Then you have to say whether I am right.

With young children self-reflection can be stimulated by telling a story about an animal. It makes projection possible, after which their own motives and feelings can be asked for (Delfos 2000a). It is important for children to know what the adult's motives are in asking for feelings and opinions. More than with other children *meta communication*, communicating about the communication, is necessary because the child with an externalising conduct disorder is not sufficiently aware about what goes on in the other person's mind and needs more information about it. We might say:

> You find it awkward that I want to know what goes on in your mind, don't you, but I can help you much better if I know it. Then I will not make such silly mistakes, because I will understand better what is going on.

Instead of a battle between the adult and the child, where the behaviour of the child comes between him and the adult, the whole thing then shifts to: *Help me to help you*. This attitude is constructive and will appeal more to the child than a hostile attitude. At the same time the adult has to realise that the child is not so much oriented to linguistic functioning and will also not be motivated to do this for a long time. Very short interventions are more likely to be successful than longer ones. The motivation of the child can be maintained with short conversations, especially when the child notices that the interventions work. In Chapter 4 I indicated that discussing events and actions by children with an externalising conduct disorder works much better than asking for motives and feelings.

In addition to actively stimulating self-reflection, by asking the child questions, it is necessary to teach the child self-reflection as a possible way to direct behaviour. Self-reflection has not much intrinsic value for the child with an externalising conduct disorder. Only after he learns that, through self-reflection, he can have control over the events in his life in a positive way will he self-reflect more often. This does not take away the fact that it will not be easy for him.

> I sit here talking to you in order to find out what you want. I cannot see that by looking at the tip of your nose. When I find out what it is, we can go on.

It would therefore be very nice if you could manage to think a bit more about those things; in that way you can make sure more often that something happens which you find pleasant. At the moment you are actually always waiting for what might happen.

A general consequence of an inadequate me–other differentiation is that the child does not have enough *ego-strength* to function well socially. Offering someone who can serve as an extra *ego-help* is of the utmost importance. Often people from the community centre and the sports club are very suitable for that. Because the moral development of these children is inadequate, such an ego-help can also act as an example of positive model behaviour. Moral development proves to be strongly dependent on model behaviour, as is shown by Bandura (1965).

Stimulating the me–other differentiation, the self-reflection and the empathic capacity will possibly cause a further maturation of the brain (Martens 1997), because there are areas that are stimulated which were underdeveloped. Offering ego-help is very important within this framework. The further maturation observed by Martens was for a significant part caused by a meaningful, intimate relationship. This acted as ego-help. For children and youngsters it is important that they learn that it is good to use certain people as a standard for their behaviour, as someone who you can get advice and help from – a mentor. It is important to teach these children to select and maintain relationships with such persons.

The necessity of structure

One of the big risks for children with an externalising conduct disorder is that they become criminals and in serious cases have a psychopathic structure. Their moral development is inadequate and their own wishes and impulses are at the centre. Following from the further individuation the child will have to be helped to develop a moral sense that is based on equivalence of people and not on the child being the centre and the others subordinates, more or less serving to satisfy his needs. When we talk about youngsters, another issue is that sexual impulses can pose a problem when they are expressed and satisfied in an egocentric manner. The other is then sexually used and possibly abused. Education about sexuality and sexual abuse is therefore of great importance with these children, and has to take place during childhood in order to try to prevent sexual derailment. With sex education I do not only mean the technical side but in particular the perception of it.

Attention has to be paid to impulse control, notably in the field of aggression. Because of egocentrism and a low *frustration tolerance* the aggression can become a significant problem when growing up. The child attaches too little value to the consequences of his behaviour towards another, and when he becomes frustrated he can easily take it out on the other person. An extra problem is that his behaviour worsens when there are fluctuations in his consciousness and dangerous situations which conjure up aggression.

Children with an externalising conduct disorder can be troubled by significant fluctuations in consciousness. Earlier, I named two important factors that could cause these fluctuations in consciousness: *monotonous situations* and *closing off as a result of feelings being hurt*. It is important that children with these problems learn to live with them and that they, and their environment, learn to act preventatively so that they do not get into serious problems.

Structure is a possibility to limit consciousness fluctuations. Structure offers something to hold on to and fills the time. Structure also means clarity about the limits set for the child. Because the child does not always feel the other person's limit, it is even more important to set a limit, so that he learns that his wishes and impulses have a realistic limit. Not setting limits for these children means that they run the risk of thinking that the behaviour is allowed, or at least not so problematic. The moral development is then damaged. Respect for a child does not mean that everything is tolerated, but that undesired behaviour is observed and condemned, without condemning the child itself. Making a difference between behaviour and person is, especially with these children, particularly important.

These children often function better due to the support of structure in the school situation than in a free situation. In the classroom their behaviour is reasonably manageable and can be discussed reasonably well in a one-to-one situation. In the schoolyard and around the school, there is often antisocial behaviour. At a school for children who have serious upbringing problems, there is a lot of fighting in the schoolyard and sometimes there are knives. In home situations it is also difficult, because offering a strict structure is contrary to normal family life. Besides, the structure can be too tight, causing the child to have the need to let off steam during the free situation at home.

Structure is, however, only accepted by the child on the basis of bonding, as Hart de Ruyter (1968), the founder of Therapeutic Family Care, has already emphasised. A cold, strict structure will be more likely to incite opposition than give rest. However, the child, and also the adult, can experience structure as security.

When there is no or not enough structure in the home situation, it may be necessary to offer the child a residential setting. In the case of conduct disorders when the child cannot be handled at home any more, a residential treatment often has more success than a (foster) family upbringing. Part of the treatment must be warmth, structure and tolerance. The continuous, and often surveyable, structure of the residential setting can offer the child something to hold on to. We see the same with some criminals who feel better when in jail. They like the structure and clarity in jail, despite being robbed of their freedom, because they feel protected against themselves.

Most children prefer to live with their own parents and will keep on wishing that they lived at home during the placement in the residential setting. The child realises that antisocial behaviour will drastically reduce his chances of living at home again. This wish functions as a common thread in the memory and as such works as a constant in the level of consciousness. As long as the child has the idea that the home placement can become reality, an increased level of consciousness can protect him against antisocial behaviour. It is not a real state of rest that arises then; the child is in fact always in a more or less alert state of increased reactivity of the autonomic nervous system. As I have already said, Raine, Venables and Williams (1995) regard an increased reactivity of the autonomic nervous system as a protective factor against criminality.

> The mother of a boy with a conduct disorder said that the children's home had never observed that he had committed arson during his placement. After coming back home this behaviour started again after a short time. The mother accused the home of inattention. 'They just did not pay attention, otherwise they would have noticed, he always does it' was her comment. It is more likely that the child, during the admittance to the residential setting, had fewer fluctuations in his consciousness, due to his alertness from wanting to go home and also due to the structure, as a result of which the need for the danger-seeking behaviour of arson could be temporarily omitted.

The opposite effect can also occur. Boszornemyi-Nagy (Boszornemyi-Nagy and Spark 1973) observes that the *loyalty* of children to their parents can have the effect that children keep showing the unwanted behaviour in a children's home. The stronger the conflict between group leaders and parents, and the more negative the group leaders are towards the parents, the greater the chances that the child will continue the negative behaviour it showed at home. Out of loyalty to his or her parents the child, without realising this consciously, does not want to give the parents the feeling that they did not do it right and that the group leaders can bring them up better than they did. Naturally this only applies if the direction of the behaviour is more dependent on the environment than on the predisposition or the maturation.

In the case of a conduct disorder it is also often a matter of parents failing to give their child enough attention. This may be related to the personality of the parents themselves. A child with a conduct disorder possibly has family members who suffer from the same problems and have entered into partner relationships on emotionally inadequate grounds. Research like that of Lahey *et al.* (1987) shows time and again that antisocial behaviour occurs in families. A father with a certain hereditary defect will be not very empathic and probably have chosen a wife who is also empathically not so strong. With this they are at risk, because of their own powerlessness, of giving their child too little attention. These parents can sometimes object too strongly against the treatment of their child, because according to them 'it would not help anyway'. Intuitively and from the experience of their own youth they feel that when the treatment is aimed at the lack of attention that they give to their child, the help will not be very effective. They sense the predisposition of their child. Their inadequate self-reflection and inadequate communication skills, however, mean that they cannot put that into words effectively. It is therefore important to approach the parents respectfully, although that is always necessary, and to show some modesty as a professional helper, because the parents have an expertise which can be used for the benefit of the help given to the child or youngster. The professional helper needs to employ their own empathic capacities to understand the parents and to help them to put their own expertise into words.

Behavioural therapeutic techniques

Help given to children with antisocial behaviour has to be oriented towards rewarding the desired behaviour, to avoid strict punishment and to help the child to make friends. A child with a conduct disorder will particularly have trouble with *inhibition* (controlling, restraining) of behaviour, at moments when there is a diminished level of consciousness. According to Gray (1987) the *inhibition system* (system to control behaviour) does not work well with these children and punishment will have little effect. Modern research by means of MRI teaches us that the prefrontal brain plays an important part there and with that supports earlier theories. People such as Barkley (1995) regard an inadequate inhibition system as the most important cause of ADHD. Because punishment is aimed at controlling the behaviour and not at stimulating desired behaviour, children with an externalising conduct disorder will profit more from help that is directed at amplifying certain behaviour than from solutions which are aimed at controlling the behaviour. This applies even more when they have ended up in some kind of 'mist' that leads to danger-seeking behaviour. Preventing this 'mist' is important and can be best realised by giving the child structure, including emotional structure, which it can hold on to. This (emotional) structure can be contained in an object.

> A boy with a conduct disorder kept 'running away' from the children's home. You could not really call it running away. After bad situations he would time and again suddenly find himself in a situation which could be called running away, without him actively trying to run away or having thought about it. This always happened in some kind of 'mist'. Because the situation had by then got out of hand, he had difficulty with coming back again. More time passed and sometimes the police were called in to bring him back to the children's home. This behaviour started to occur more and more frequently, sometimes three times a week. He was given an 'anti-running-away necklace'. This necklace was a bond between him and

his helpers. It was put into words for the child that the necklace symbolised his need to not run away and reminded him that others just like him knew that he actually did not want to run away. He wore the necklace day and night and the 'running away' did not happen any more.

All through the ages theoreticians of various backgrounds have emphasised that punishment has no positive effect on the development – the undesired behaviour will at the most stop temporarily. It can be desired and necessary to stop the behaviour temporarily, but this is something different from unlearning that behaviour, although the latter is still often the intention. Punishment does definitely not lead to learning new desired behaviour. Hard disciplinary measures of parents can even promote aggressive behaviour in children; this applies to a larger degree to boys than to girls (Deater-Deckard and Dodge 1997).

One of the forms of punishment is hitting. Researches into hitting are not always univocal. Hitting can promote aggression, and proves to be the case mainly in western culture. In Afro-American cultures, however, where hitting is more common, there is not more aggression amongst ten-year-olds at school, according to Deater-Deckard and Dodge (1997). The researchers' explanation is that hitting in this culture is not associated with not being loved and because of this does not so much call up aggression.

The theoreticians showed convincingly that new behaviour can only be taught by *reinforcing* the behaviour, for example by rewarding. In order to teach new behaviour, repeatedly rewarding the desired behaviour is necessary. Subsequently it will be enforced when an unpredictable pattern of rewarding is applied, a *variable reinforcement schema* (Bandura 1974; Skinner 1974). Locke (Gay 1964) mentioned that the most important form of rewarding the child is 'flattering' it, what we now call giving reinforcement or providing self-confidence. Behaviour is unlearned by *extinction*, extinguishing behaviour by neglecting it. Not only reward but also disapproval of behaviour works as a reinforcer. So if one wishes to accomplish a change in behaviour, the undesired behaviour should not so much be punished, but the desired behaviour should be reinforced and the undesired neglected. A difficult task may cause the child or the youngster to show strongly undesired behaviour. It is nevertheless good to realise that the new behaviour is not learned by punishing the child.

In professional help in residential settings, working with the *competence model* (Slot and Spanjaard 1999) is on the rise. This is based on theoretical principles. The starting point is that children and youngsters have skills and competences which can be employed as forces, and that with regard to specific tasks they do not have certain skills and that these have to be learned and developed. This model can be employed for youngsters with conduct disorders. The problem here is, just as with the social skills training programmes, that an underlying predisposition is assumed which is necessary to develop the skills. Should this model be used with youngsters who do not have this potential through predisposition, it may well be frustrating and discouraging for the youngster and the helper to employ the model, especially because generalising the behaviour to a situation where the model is not used is difficult with these children and youngsters. The competence model will therefore have more effect with children with conduct *problems*. In Chapter 11 the treatment of conduct problems will be discussed and I will go into the competence model in more detail.

The child with conduct disorders can benefit from so-called *behaviour contracts*, a specific application of behaviour therapeutic principles. With a behaviour contract, the child and parents bind themselves to positive behaviour and the behaviour can be redirected by mutual agreement. Such a contract is drawn up together with the child and has the character of mutuality. The nature of the behaviour and the reward is clearly defined. The behaviour contract always has to be drawn up in positive terms and contain behaviour that can be reinforced. In order to amplify the behaviour and 'to keep it in the memory', to speak in computer terms, it is useful to keep renewing the kind of reward. The desired behaviour can be divided into parts which through a process of *shaping* can gradually be built into complex behaviour. In Appendix 2 is an example of such a behaviour contract.

A behaviour contract is initially meant to amplify the motivation for positive behaviour. In view of the fact that the motivation for the desired behaviour is, in principle, not absent with the child with the externalising conduct disorder, not too much should be expected from a behaviour contract with these children. In general the child is prepared and able to show the desired behaviour. The problem arises when, due to a diminished level of consciousness, undesired behaviour takes place. Negative behaviour is less suitable to include in behaviour contracts.

With behaviour contracts it is sensible to build in the process of *shaping*. Rewarding sub-behaviours in order to build up to the target behaviour is, however, not suitable for the child with the externalising conduct disorder. This disorder usually concerns behaviour that has to be avoided, instead of behaviour that has to be rewarded. Later I will discuss the possibilities of behaviour contracts in more detail, considering where they can be more effective, that is with conduct *problems*.

If one wants to restrict the negative behaviour, one should mainly be aimed at preventing the behaviour and so preventing the state in which the child shows the behaviour, notably monotonous situations and situations where the child feels offended or hurt.

Help given to these children in fact contains five elements: dealing with the disorder; stimulating the development in order to stimulate further maturation; prevention; structure; and learning. In order to let the help and the protection be effective, it is necessary that the child knows what is wrong. It is essential that the child too knows that it can get in a kind of 'mist', when it is capable of doing things which will later surprise it. The child will then be able to protect itself more actively. The risk lies mainly in monotonous situations, of which boredom is a good example.

> A boy with a conduct disorder had been placed back home again after a few years. It had been explained to him that he ran more risk of 'getting into trouble' if he was bored. 'Try to prevent becoming bored; as far as I'm concerned you can go for a bike ride around the block' was the advice given. After a few months at home his mother enthusiastically said, 'He never gets bored. If he doesn't know what to do, he takes the bike and goes bicycling in the neighbourhood.' He had, following from feeling understood, taken the advice literally. With a boy who had done extremely bad things, it was impressive to see how desperately he tried not to get into trouble.

Psychiatric or educational residential help?

When the upbringing of a child with an externalising conduct disorder takes place at home, *educational support* for the parents will be urgently desired. This is because the problems are so serious, and because the family itself is often not so strong in the educational field. When the problems are observed at an early stage and the parents are not naturally blamed, it is possible to work together on promoting the development of the child and to restrict the chances of criminality. Here it is of the utmost importance that the parents are perceived and treated as full allies and not as second-class citizens. The same applies to the child. Only on the basis of mutual respect is help possible which has effect in the long term. Also it must be possible to provide help for a longer period of time, because the parents and the child must be helped to keep steering the development of the child and later the youngster in the right direction.

Although growing up at home with the parents is usually the most suitable situation for the child, there may be circumstances when this is not, or is temporarily not, possible. In particular the seriousness of the problems and the predisposition problems which usually also feature in the child's environment may mean that a home childrearing is not possible during the child's entire youth. The question is then about the form of residential help that these children need: psychiatric or educational.

What form of residential help should be given to children with an externalising conduct disorder is not easy to decide. Initially, psychiatric help is indicated due to the clear predisposition component. Nevertheless, the psychiatric institution will usually refer to a remedial educational setting, because of the socially problematic behaviour. With this behaviour it is often thought that the educational impotence of the parents is the cause of the behaviour and the predisposition of the child is ignored. Various theories stimulate this way of thinking, for example the psychoanalytic theory or the theory about attachment, which take as a starting point that an insecure attachment can be the cause of forming a psychopathic personality structure (Bowlby 1984).

Following from that a remedial educational setting instead of a psychiatric setting is thought of to give a renewed upbringing. I observed earlier that antisocial behaviour can easily be a cause for interpretation in educational instead of psychiatric terms. With adults we see a similar way of thinking in the providing of help. There are, apart from the schizophrenic and autistic men, often more women in psychiatric institutions who suffer from anxiety and depression problems. The men with aggression disorders and a criminal tendency are mainly found in prisons, where they are punished for their behaviour. Only a small percentage get treatment in the form of detention in a hospital. The men are punished for their predisposition, unlike the women, who receive help for their problems.

A remedial educational setting is aimed at educational problems. Therefore, in principle, a form of re-education is worked on. In a psychiatric setting the emphasis lies on a seriously disrupted or deviant development due to predisposition or traumatic circumstances. One tries to help the child to learn to live with its predisposition or one treats the consequences of a trauma or disrupted development. Following from this perspective a psychiatric setting would seem more appropriate. This setting is, however, less aimed at influencing the behaviour in an educational sense, and will therefore, as I have already said, often refer the child with an externalising conduct disorder to a remedial educational setting. In a remedial educational setting childrearing and structure are at the forefront. Children with an externalising conduct disorder therefore often function, temporarily, rather well in such a setting. It is important that this structure is offered on a basis of warmth, so that the structure is also accepted. It still has important disadvantages. The focus on educational problems and not on predisposition can mean that the actual cause of the behaviour does not become visible. This applies even more when the group leaders have the idea that they can do things 'better' than the parents. The result is that, as soon as the structure is removed and the child leaves the home, the problems will start again. A remedial educational treatment will only make sense with a child with an externalising conduct disorder when the treatment home takes the child's predisposition as the starting point and teaches the child to learn how to cope with his predisposition in co-operation with his parents and family. When the child is taught that his parents did not raise him that well and that he will now be raised better, he will lose out on the necessary protection because of this wrong analysis. When it is explained to a child what the role of his predisposition is and that he needs, among other things, a different structure in order not to get into trouble, this will offer protection. When the child leaves the home, he is then more likely to look for structure instead of having the idea that 'the upbringing has been restored' and everything is 'hunky dory'. For the problems are not over, just as the problem is not taken away with medication.

> After a period when he had been in a lot of trouble, the behaviour of boy with a conduct disorder suddenly improved. He was asked what he did now in order to prevent himself from getting into trouble again. 'I make sure that I always have something to do, so that I don't get bored,' he answered.

The limitation of the residential setting is also that it is temporary; the child will come of age and go his own way. He will then, if this is at all possible, go back to his family. If they have not learnt how to deal with the problems, the youngster runs the risk of getting stuck and showing serious antisocial behaviour. Co-operation between the parents and family and the staff at the residential home is therefore of the utmost importance.

In view of the aforementioned limitations of both the psychiatric and the remedial educational setting for the treatment of this disorder, it is gratifying that ever more institutions make room for a remedial educational department within their setting. When in these settings both aspects, predisposition and education, actually get attention, and the child with the externalising conduct disorder has a better chance of being helped.

Who does what in professional help?

The help given to a child with an externalising conduct disorder contains various aspects. When medication is opted for, the psychiatrist is the right person. Although GPs can also prescribe medication, it is not advisable to put the psychiatric-psychological problems in the hands of a GP only. Medication *alone* can never, and particularly not structurally, remedy the problems. For the help given to the child with an externalising conduct disorder it is of the utmost importance at what age the help is started. The younger the child is when the problems are observed, the better one can work in a preventative manner. With early observation we then initially think of the me–other differentiation, aggression control and learning to put feelings and thoughts into words. Collot d'Escury-Koenings (1998) emphasises the importance of paying attention as early as possible to the socio-emotional development, even with pre-schoolers. With the slightly older child, from the age of four, one can think about developing friendships, learning partnership behaviour and practising self-reflection.

When we think of me–other differentiation and naming feelings and thoughts, we are in the area of the parents' responsibility (especially as parents form important influences on children of this age). Some psychological characteristics can already be observed at a young age, for example at health centres, but the me–other differentiation does not (yet) form a part of this. If observation does take place, however, childrearing support could help parents to stimulate their child. At a later stage primary schools could help to develop partnership behaviour and self-reflection. In order to help the parents to provide structure to their child and to prevent them trying out all kinds of methods, educational help can be offered through, for example, social work. Techniques like *video home training, Families First, Intensive Home Support* and *Family Group* will prove to be less effective with the child with an externalising conduct disorder and are better employed with the child with the conduct problem and his environment. I will come back to these techniques in Chapter 11.

In the help given to the child with the conduct disorder, learning how to cope with the predisposition of the child should be at the forefront. When the parents are trapped in educational impotence, the extent to which the parents are capable of learning and changing will have to be looked at. Help has to link up to the possibilities of the parents and not be aimed at emphasising their mistakes.

To the therapeutic techniques it also applies that the therapy forms aimed at individuals will have more effect than the ones which are aimed at groups or families, without wanting to neglect the help given to the family as a whole. The help given to the family will have to take place more as a general childrearing support. For the child itself (play) therapeutic help could be offered, where the attention is focused on the underdeveloped areas of the child. The psychotherapist can help the child to cope with his predisposition and in that way teach him to prevent problematic situations. In play therapy the therapist, both with the help of the therapeutic relation and by means of the language of play, can communicate about social interaction (Hellendoorn 1998).

A treatment which is mainly focused on the strengthening of self-image and confidence can have a contrary effect in the sense that the child with the externalising conduct disorder already perceives itself as very central and the other person too much as its extension. A stronger self-image could amplify this effect; Baumeister (1997) therefore sees more benefit in ego-strengthening.

When the upbringing can no longer be given at home, a remedial educational setting will be more beneficial, on the condition that the starting point is the predisposition of the child and not the educational impotence of the parents. In this setting, in addition to the treatment given by the home, psychotherapy will be necessary. Offering structure, linked to warmth, can give the child and his parents a guideline to prevent problems in the future.

When the development and insight of the child are started, a social skills training can be employed in order to develop specific skills.

To conclude, the treatment aspects of the externalising conduct disorder are given in Table 9.2.

Table 9.2 The treatment aspects of the externalising conduct disorder
Coping with the disorder
Medication, if necessary
Stimulation of the me–other differentiation
Practising empathy
Stimulating putting thoughts and feelings into words
Stimulating moral development
Teaching interaction with peers
Preventing a state of diminished consciousness
Combating aggression
Structure based on bonding
Offering ego-help
Social skills training.

Summary

To summarise I can say that a child with an externalising conduct disorder benefits from learning how to cope with his disorder by stimulating the me–other differentiation, by developing social cognitions, by paying attention to prevention of diminished consciousness (among other things, by a different structure), by learning to interact with peers and by learning social skills. With an early diagnosis of the problems, the me–other differentiation, the empathic capacity and the self-reflection can be stimulated. Medication will in general offer little relief other than for the purpose of aggression control. Psychotherapy combined with childrearing support can offer the child protection against problems it does not want itself. The help should have a psychiatric-psychological and socio-educational nature.

10

The Treatment of an Internalising Conduct Disorder

The frequency of the internalising conduct *disorder* just as with the externalising form is not that high. This disorder occurs much less often than the internalising conduct *problem*. It is a disorder and that means initially that the child and its parents have to learn to live with it. The treatment should not be aimed at 'solving' the problem, but at teaching the child and its environment how to deal with the disorder.

Children with an internalising conduct disorder are often difficult to motivate. Although they do not show antisocial behaviour, they are maladjusted in the sense that they often cannot meet the social requirements set for them. Their problem is not so much protesting but more avoiding. Because they avoid social situations the contact with peers is more difficult. The child needs a lot of support in order to enter into social situations. The child with the internalising conduct disorder lacks assertiveness and can profit from assertiveness training.

Treatment areas

Before going into the treatment of the internalising conduct disorder I shall list all the characteristics of this disorder:

- mainly girls
- low testosterone level
- high cortisol level
    - generalised anxiety
    - anxious, not very assertive
    - psychosomatic complaints
    - socially anxious behaviour

- increased responsiveness of the autonomic nervous system
  - strong stimulus sensitivity of all senses: hearing, seeing, smelling, tasting, feeling
  - over-alert
  - high heart rate
  - slow habituation to negative stimulus
  - increased awareness
  - avoidance behaviour, avoiding danger
- strongly developed left hemisphere
  - strongly linguistically oriented
  - well able to put thoughts and feelings into words
  - continuous self-reflection
  - constant urge to adjust own behaviour
  - little risk of norm exceeding behaviour
- strong recognition of biological self
  - strong me–other differentiation
  - 'altruistic'
  - empathic
  - strong moral awareness, aimed at care for others and co-operation
  - strong realisation of mine and thine
  - not well able to put own role into perspective
  - guilt feelings
  - need to have contact with others, linked to fear, need to have bosom friends
  - social isolation as a result of avoiding social situations
- risk of conduct problems because of lack of adjustment and limited experience with social situations.

Medication?

Hormones play an important part with anxiety disorders and medication can influ-ence that. There are several psychopharmacologic drugs available for the treatment of anxiety. It is, however, not immediately indicated to use these systematically with children and youngsters who are developing, because of their side effects and their disruption of normal development. Moreover, with psychopharmalogical drugs used against anxiety there is the addictive effect of the medication. The disorder is not remedied with medication and in principle reoccurs after the use of medication has stopped. The advantage of medication, however, is that the anxiety diminishes and a situation is created in which the child can learn how to deal with anxious situations. It can have good effects with social anxiety and panic attacks. Nevertheless, medication is not as easily prescribed as, for example, with ADHD. This has possibly something to do with the fact that hyperactive behaviour is more inconvenient for the environment than anxious behaviour. Anxiety is mainly inconvenient for the person his/herself. Moreover, anxiety seems to be something which is easier to overcome than hyperactivity and the anxious child is expected to control the anxiety. The question is also to what extent the gender has a part to play in it, and it is possible that help will be asked for more quickly for boys than for girls.

With anxiety *behaviour therapy* and in particular *cognitive behaviour therapy* is most successful. Behaviour therapy does not only provide help in the short term but also the strategy to be able to deal with problems in the future. In terms of the locus of control (Rotter 1966) it can be said that medication barely influences the location of the locus of control, while behaviour therapy does. With children with an internalising conduct disorder it can be said that their locus of control is situated extremely internally. They have the feeling that they are guilty of everything and have an extreme need to control themselves and their environment; at the same time they feel powerless in trying to achieve what they really want. With medication the child will attribute the change in behaviour to the medication and will therefore feel less as if they can influence the behaviour; the locus of control will then be situated mainly externally. With behaviour therapy the child will put its own influence, its own role, in an event more into perspective and will move the locus of control to a more realistic, internal position. Behaviour therapy is proven to make an actual change to the working of the brain, just as medication does (Baxter 1996).

Cognitions to label the anxiety

Characteristic for the internalising conduct disorder is a generalised anxiety which is almost always present. The anxiety is caused by an overproduction of hormones in reaction to stimuli. As a consequence the child experiences anxiety. (I have already mentioned this sequence, physical sensation followed by feeling, in Chapter 3.) The arousal is caused by an assessment of danger triggered by the amygdala. The child with the internalising conduct disorder has a strong arousal-response to an (unconscious) assessment of danger, comparable to the one of significant danger for other people. Subsequently the child will look for ways to explain this arousal, as is made clear by the *labelling theory* of Schachter (1968; see Chapter 3). In order to find an explanation the child will connect subjects to the anxiety; the anxiety 'attaches' itself to subjects. Education about the physiological condition and the feeling of anxiety that subsequently attaches itself to subjects can help the child to reduce the anxiety to realistic proportions. Employing the anxiety model of Chapter 3, it can be said that an activity reduces the anxiety, even when the problem is not directly solved because of it. It does mean that the intensity of the anxiety is less, the panic decreases and the child is better able to think over the situation. It is useful to explain this to the child:

> You have an anxious predisposition. That means that a lot of substances in your body are produced which keep you anxious. When you remain seated, your anxiety does not become less, it becomes even more. The best thing is to do something, tidy something up, or pace up and down if necessary. You will notice that the anxiety will diminish.

Activity converts the adrenergic substances. I have already stated that men are more inclined to take action and therefore experience less anxiety and for a shorter period of time. Women are less inclined to take action and therefore feel more anxiety and for a longer period of time.

The child with an internalising conduct disorder finds it hard to relax. The tension decreases somewhat when she is alone, but even then her never-ending self-reflection results in her still feeling uncomfortable.

> An adolescent girl with a generalised anxiety did not know what relaxation was. She had never experienced it. The assignment to relax therefore did not link up to her perception of the world. What she did know was that she experienced a lower level of tension when she was alone in her room. This was even stronger when she had a pet on her lap, the guinea pig or the cat. She was encouraged to do this often and to experience the difference with respect to other situations. In this way a starting point was found to help her learn to relax.

Anxiety has two components. The first one is the metabolism in the body. The other one regards the cognitions made to give the anxiety a place. These cognitions are in line with the anxiety and therefore have a negative character. The cognitions become linked to the anxiety by means of a *conditioning process* and can subsequently independently conjure up fear. In this way the child with the internalising conduct disorder keeps going round in circles.

These are the cognitions that mainly take place internally and are not expressed, causing the child with the internalising conduct disorder to be hindered in her normal functioning. Because the cognitions are not expressed and situations are avoided, they are not tested against reality. The cognitions often concern the self-image and usually take on the form of a disapproval.

> Cognitions to name the anxiety often hinder the social functioning: 'I have nothing interesting to say, so I will not go there.' 'I'll probably have to blush again and then everybody will see that again, I hate birthdays.' 'I will not hold this conversation, because I will stumble over my words again.'

Self-esteem and self-confidence are affected by these cognitions. Changing these cognitions is the aim of cognitive behaviour therapy, which is pre-eminently suitable for these problems.

Behaviour therapy

The behaviour therapies have won their spurs mainly in the field of anxiety. This form of therapy goes back to the researches by Watson (1928), who researched the way in which anxiety develops. Watson's most important experiment was that with 'little Albert', who was 11 months old. Albert was conditioned to be afraid of a white rabbit. While he was sitting in his bed, a white rabbit was placed beside him. Then a loud sound was made, which scared him very much. In this way the presence of and touching the white rabbit was linked to an unpleasant, loud, sudden noise. Albert developed a fear of the white rabbit. Watson discovered that the fear spread from the white rabbit to everything that was white or moved. Following on from these researches Jones (1924) carried out research that became the basis of behaviour therapy. Through the experience of the little boy Peter, who was afraid of rabbits, research was carried out into how the fear could be unlearned. Peter got a positive reinforcer (an element that reinforces behaviour; in this case Peter was given sweets) when seeing a rabbit. The rabbit was brought closer and closer, until Peter lost his fear and was able to stroke the rabbit. Based on this research a new method was developed to unlearn fear through a behavioural change method, *systematic desensitisation*, systematically desensitising a subject. This method means that the person slowly learns to associate a relaxed feeling with the subject of the fear. In this way the fear will gradually disappear. This method was at the basis of the development of behaviour therapeutic techniques to combat anxiety.

These techniques are suitable for treating excesses of internalising problems like *phobias* in general and *agoraphobia* in particular. In his outline of behaviour therapeutic treatments Emmelkamp (1995) indicates that research shows that behaviour therapy works very effectively with anxiety disorders. The current behaviour therapy has developed in the direction of cognitive therapies; Arntz and

Bögels (1995) show in their outline that cognitive therapies prove to be very successful with the treatment of anxiety.

In cognitive therapy the *cognitions*, the conceptions of the person, are at the centre. Behaviour of humans is seen as being directed by their cognitions. These cognitive behaviour therapies are especially useful for the child with the internalising conduct disorder. We should, however, keep remembering that these are aids to learn to live with the disorder and that they do not remove the problem, as is possible with the internalising conduct problem. The hormonal level is not easily affected, although in the long run adaptation and a lower level of response can arise. The contrary is also the case. When long-term stress is experienced the body will adjust to that and give a higher response level (Prins, Kaloupek and Keane 1995). The child can, through cognitive behaviour therapy, learn to cope with the cognitions which are constantly conjured up by anxiety. This can help the child to rein in the anxiety.

The cognitive stream within behaviour therapy, of which Ellis (1973) and Beck (1985) are the founders, takes as a starting point that the person is hindered in his or her behaviour by wrong cognitions, by errors of reasoning. Within this stream Beck (1989) named the *errors of reasoning*, which can affect the self-image, distort reality and conjure up or maintain anxiety. The cognitions of children with an internalising conduct disorder are characterised by frequent use of these errors of reasoning:

1. Black-and-white thinking – categorising your characteristics in absolute, all or nothing categories: 'I never do anything right.'

2. Labelling – equating yourself with your faults or characteristics: 'I am just a sickening person that I could do such a thing.'

3. Exaggerating – seeing one negative event as a repeating pattern of failures: 'I always do that!'

4. Mental filtering – having the tendency to convert neutral or positive events into negative ones and keep occupying yourself with them: 'She looked at me in rather a nice way, but she probably only felt sorry for me.'

5. Mind-reading – assuming negative thoughts about yourself with other people: 'He probably thinks that I'm childish.'

6. Predicting the future – predicting like a 'fortune teller' that something will come to a bad end: 'I will probably stutter terribly when it's my turn to speak in class.'

7. Reasoning emotionally – basing your thoughts on how you feel: 'I *feel* inferior, so I am inferior'; 'I *feel* ridiculous, so I am ridiculous.'

8. Thinking 'should' – criticising yourself or others with commands, obligations, threats, or other strong requirements. This way of thinking is supported by words like 'must' or 'should': 'I should be a bit nicer.'

9. Self-reproach – exclusively blaming yourself for something that you are not, or are not solely, responsible for: 'If only I had not picked a fight, then that accident would not have happened.'

    (Beck, adjusted by Sterk and Swaen 1997 pp.54–61)

I will illustrate a number of errors of reasoning by means of an example:

> A girl does not dare go to the school party because she feels that she looks ugly. This conjures up a number of thoughts which can be classified as errors of reasoning:

They will think I'm ugly.	*Mind-reading*
I am ugly.	*Labelling*
No boy likes me.	*Black-and-white thinking*
No one is as ugly as I am.	*Exaggerating*
I will probably not be invited to a party again.	*Predicting the future*

In cognitive therapies the emphasis lies, among other things, on the internal logic of cognitions and the absence of testing them against reality. In analyses, statistical principles are often used:

> It is possible that you are so afraid of crossing that bridge, but hardly any accidents happen because of a bridge collapsing. It is more dangerous just walking on the pavement. Your fear is not realistic. It is a waste to let your life be determined by a fear which is not based on reality.

When a child learns not to see her cognitions as established truths, but as concepts which can be brought up for discussion, she will not be so weighed down by the burden of these cognitions. What is more important is that she learns to accept that her predisposition causes the forming of substances in her body which feed the cognitions. She will more quickly recognise cognitions formed by anxiety and quash them. It is easier to cope with the realistic cognitions such as 'I am easily scared' than with the socially hampering cognitions such as 'Nobody likes me'.

> Harrowing is the example of the adolescent who was told ever since her earliest childhood that she was a 'scared baby'. She was ashamed of her continuous anxiety, without knowing that her predisposition caused an increased anxiety level. When she had to take a train late one evening in a village, she did not want to sit alone in the lit waiting room. She was afraid because everybody could see her and terrible things could happen. Her anxiety annoyed her, and following her upbringing she told herself not to be such a baby and just go and sit in the waiting room. This, however, proved to be her undoing. She was indeed seen and finally raped. She had 'unlearned' to protect herself and subsequently irresponsibly exposed herself to danger.

One of the reasons why anxiety can be maintained is because there is no or insufficient testing against reality. It is important to offer the child possibilities to test without this increasing the anxiety. The testing should result in an experience which proves that the anxiety was not necessary. It is therefore important to realise this afterwards, so that the cognition can arise: 'I was scared, but later it proved to be without reason', or 'I was scared, but because I took that precaution, the situation proved to be manageable.' Likewise, realistically testing the child's own role in an event by means of cognitions is also important. In this way self-confidence will increase so that the child is able to face anxious situations and the self-image is restored. The image that the child has of the world will then become more realistic and less frightening.

It is also important for children with an anxiety disorder to pay attention to their interaction with peers. Because these children tend to avoid social situations, they will be less able to build up good friendships, because by definition, no matter how limited, this is a social situation.

Finally, it is necessary that the child learns to act in cases of anxiety, so that the anxiety can decrease. The child is not assertive enough and may benefit from assertiveness training or social skills training. The ability to assess social interaction is generally amply present and the training will therefore often successfully offer skills because it falls on grounds of sufficient insight into social situations. The child does not lack insight, but the ability to act accordingly.

Depression

Children with an internalising conduct *disorder* are at risk of developing an *endogenous* depression when they become older. There are two situations that amplify that risk: traumatic situations and the start of puberty, especially with girls. It is necessary to spot this at an early stage, when a change in appetite and a change in desire to sleep are important markers. Extra attention will then have to be paid to two areas: undertaking activities and keeping moving, and the forming of self-criticising cognitions. When a child shows signs of depression, it is wise to look for help, if this has not yet been done.

> A girl, during her childhood, used to be always scared of everything. When puberty started she became depressed and this took on such forms that she took antidepressants from the age of 14. When she was in her early twenties she really wanted to stop the medication. She suddenly stopped and to everyone's surprise it went very well. After a period of about six months the depression started again, with great intensity. It turned out afterwards that at the same time as stopping the medication she got a nice, but physically strenuous job. She worked hard and with a lot of pleasure. Six months later, however, she was off work temporarily due to an injury. The activity had taken over the function of the medication.

In the case of symptoms of depression it is important to break through the situation as soon as possible, because the body adapts to the negative situation and more and more negative cognitions are formed, which in their turn cause stress hormones to be produced and conjure up fear, while the body keeps becoming less able to transfer these substances into activity.

Psychiatric or educational residential help?

There is not much point in attributing a disorder to the parents' childrearing, and an educational approach will be less effective with the internalising disorder just as with the externalising one. Although the disorder may be regarded as a psychiatric problem and there are psychopharmacologic drugs available, a residential setting is often not the obvious solution. A child who is anxious wants to be protected and that is much easier to realise within the childrearing situation than, for example, the structure which the child with an externalising conduct disorder needs. A child with an internalising conduct disorder will more likely be able to stay in a family situation than a child with an externalising conduct disorder, because the child does not get into conflict with its environment in an aggressive manner. Help within the family setting is therefore the best.

Who does what in professional help?

Parents quickly learn, when rearing a child with an internalising conduct disorder, that there is not much point in forcing the child to try to get over its fear. The resistance is great and the anxiety asks for protection. Parents try to find out why their child is so scared and often manage to do so quite well with these children. Children with an internalising conduct disorder are generally verbally skilled and can put into words what affects them, because they themselves are incessantly occupied with it. In order to be able to share it with another person, security and trust are necessary, because the child with an internalising conduct disorder will in general be too ashamed. Besides, it will experience that its anxiety is often trivialised by others. Although it sees intellectually that the other person could be right, it feels its own anxiety and feels misunderstood about that. In this way the child learns not to share its feelings with others.

Because the cognitions are often far from reality and provide a strongly exaggerated image, parents can put the child at ease through their own ability to reason. This can only be done when they do this respectfully, linking up to the child and not trivialising. Parents who are verbally and logically strong have more possibilities of helping their child with this. It goes wrong when parents cannot do this or do not take the child's anxiety seriously enough. Educational help is not prescribed so much with these children because the situation usually does not have anything to do with educational powerlessness of the parents, but more with intellectual powerlessness.

With an internalising disorder the risk that the problem will be translated into educational terms is usually small. Often the shyness of the child has been clear from childhood and there have already been many problems with going to school, sleeping over and playing with friends. The predisposition of the child, in the case of shyness, is generally more often seen as a cause than in the case of antisocial behaviour. The anxious behaviour is more accepted when it concurs with the child's gender. An anxious girl can generally expect more support than an anxious boy.

> Anxious children find it difficult to go to their peers' birthday parties. Mother offers to take the child, but on reaching the front door of the peer's house, the child's heart is in its boots. What often plays a part is that the child leaves the mother on the doorstep in an unfamiliar situation. It often works better when the child is picked up and leaves the mother in a familiar, trusted place.

The principle of *attachment* plays a part with anxious children. They want to stay near their parents, often their mother. They need the closeness to know that there will be help when they are in need. Anxious children are often in need and therefore like to have their parents available. Staying away from home overnight, for example, is a big problem. *Homesickness*, then, is not so much a longing for the people you leave behind, but more the fear that these people are not available when something goes wrong. In the example stated above the availability of a mother whom you leave at the door is less clear than the mother whom you leave at home. In the latter case you know exactly where she is and how you can reach her. This is also the case with working mothers. When the child has seen the workplace of the parent, knows where the phone is and can form a picture of where her mother is, the fear of the mother's leaving to go to work can decrease. When the child has successfully tried to contact her mother, this will work favourably with regard to her anxiety. The arrival of the mobile phone is a solution for children who are anxious, because in this way they can mobilise their parents at any moment – not that they need to talk to their parents all the time, but the fact that the possibility is there is important. It is about the availability of the parent when the child feels in need. The desire to mobilise the parent decreases when the parent remains available.

When a child is hindered to such an extent in its social functioning that medication is thought of, medical help is then the appropriate way. GPs have considerable knowledge about medication for anxiety and depression and it is therefore not always necessary to involve a psychiatrist. It is, however, sensible to let the choice of medication depend on a psychiatric examination. In view of the positive effects which all researches show continuously with respect to behaviour therapy, a medicinal treatment should at least be combined with a behaviour therapeutic treatment, also called 'pills and talks'. With behaviour therapeutic techniques the child has a solution which she can use at all times, also independently and years later. Behaviour therapy also links up well with the idea of 'learning to live' with the disorder. With this help we are in the field of psychology.

Group therapy can help these children by confronting them with the unreality of their concepts. Functioning in a group, however, is, for these socially anxious children, such a big task that, prior to the group therapy, preparation in individual therapy is necessary.

Because the child makes high demands on her parents, it is important to involve the parents in the therapy and to support them in dealing with the child's anxiety.

Table 10.1 The treatment aspects of the internalising conduct disorder
Coping with the disorder
Medication, if necessary
Fighting anxiety
Interacting with peers
Behaviour therapy
Improving self-image
Learning to deal with cognitions
Learning to put own role into perspective
Learning through reality testing
Assertiveness training.

To close off, the treatment aspects of the internalising conduct disorder are listed in Table 10.1.

Summary

A child with an internalising conduct disorder struggles with generalised anxiety, based on a continuous arousal of the body, and with a constant flow of cognitions that affect the self-image and hinder the social functioning. Within psychology, behaviour therapeutic techniques have been developed which can help the child with an internalising conduct disorder to cope with the anxiety and the cognitions which it is struggling with. Extra attention should be paid to the risk that the child with the anxiety disorder has of ending up in a depression.

11

The Treatment of Externalising and Internalising Conduct Problems

After discussing conduct disorders, where learning to cope with the predisposition was at the forefront, I will now look at the conduct problems. It applies to both the externalising and internalising conduct problems that the most important source of the behaviour is the environment. Predisposition always plays a part, but in this case a subordinate one. The role of the predisposition can mainly be found in the nature in which the problem manifests itself. With boys a problem is more likely to be externalised, whereas with girls it is more likely to be internalised. I will discuss the externalising and internalising conduct problems in one chapter because the emphasis in both lies on the environment and the treatment has many similarities.

Treatment areas

In order to put the treatment into context, I will state the characteristics of an *externalising* conduct problem here:

- mainly boys
- situation-bound aggression
- antisocial behaviour.

These problems are, however, *not* accompanied by strong consciousness fluctuations, limited linguistic functioning, an inadequate self-reflection or not being well able to assess one's own role. In contrast to the externalising *disorder*, the child or the youngster with an externalising conduct *problem* has a normal me–other differentiation and is reasonably capable of assessing the consequences of his behaviour for other people.

The characteristics of an *internalising* conduct problem are:

- mainly girls
- situation-bound anxiety
- avoiding specific situations.

These elements are present without an excessive generalised guilt feeling, an insistent lack of assertiveness in all areas or excessive self-reflection, as is the case with an internalising conduct *disorder*. The child or the youngster is generally capable of putting her own role in an event into perspective. Situation-bound anxiety can be generalising when we are dealing with an *attachment disruption*. The child can then in a general sense develop fear of relations or resistance to relations.

Researching the source of the behaviour

For the treatment of children with conduct *problems* it is important to realise that a child with a *disorder* basically wants to be protected, at least when it feels understood; a child with conduct problems usually puts up opposition, especially against specific persons. He or she often regards help as 'interference', which with these children is more likely to result in a situation of 'rebellion'. Forming an alliance is usually more difficult with a child with conduct problems than with the child with the disorder.

The treatment of conduct problems will have to take the source of the behaviour into account. I mentioned four: *childrearing and socio-cultural context*, *puberty*, *traumas* and *divorce*.

With a youngster who, for example, starts to show externalising behaviour because he has difficulty in accepting his stepfather in a father's role, there is not much point in exclusively paying attention to the external behaviours. It is important to pay attention to the source of the behaviour: the difficulty he has with the divorce and with his new 'father'.

The first problem that crops up when choosing the suitable form of help is discovering the source of the behaviour. When it has been established, based on a combination of antisocial behaviour with a normal me–other differentiation, that the behaviour should be interpreted as an externalising problem and not as a disorder, this does not yet explain what the possible source of the behaviour is. The next step will therefore have to be to find out what the possible source of the behaviour is. I will give a few guidelines, without being exhaustive. The diversity of factors in the environment does not allow for that. I therefore refer to Chapter 5, where the environment as the most important source is discussed and where the risk factors are stated in Table 5.2, and also to Chapter 8, where I discussed questions to research the source of conduct problems. Some factors are easier to detach than others. A first indication is the chronology, the order in time, and the moment when the problems started.

> Up to the seventh grade of primary school, Louisa never had serious problems. Suddenly she started to have nightmares and refused to sleep over away from home.

In this example the suddenness of the nightmares and the age at which these occur are indications to suggest a conduct problem; a disorder would have manifested itself much sooner, and nightmares that start all of a sudden do not belong with the age phase in which she finds herself. The combination of nightmares and sleeping somewhere else could point to unpleasant or traumatic experiences connected to the stay-over period. This could be an event that happened during the stay over, or surrounding it – for example, her mother being admitted to hospital while Louisa went to stay over somewhere.

When there is a distinct period in which the child at first did not show problematic behaviour and then later did, we can look for factors that can explain this transition. Childrearing, as a structural factor, is less obvious unless a situation has arisen within the childrearing situation causing the child to be treated differently. And if puberty is not yet an issue then there are two areas left which can be considered: traumas and divorce/separation.

> During the vacation in Sweden, Earnest was caught stealing. Either he never did it before or it was not as obvious as now. His mother could not believe it at first. It was not at all like Earnest to do such things. At school everything was fine – he completed his first year at secondary school well – but at home things were getting worse. In a period of a few months he was stealing from everyone in the house, even from his sister's piggy bank, but remarkably enough not from his stepfather.

The distinct start of the problems and mapping the situation (at home) and the persons (difference between own family and stepfather) points to problems in the relation pattern of Earnest with the family members with whom he lives.

Should we be dealing with problems that started during puberty, without material problems, then this age phase could be a sufficient explanation for the occurrence of the behaviour.

When the behaviour suddenly occurs without demonstrable reason and does not come across as logical to the people around the child, then it is possible that it is based on a trauma. When the problems have started in the start-up phase or after the divorce/separation of the parents or the arrival of a step-parent, then the conduct problems could well be connected with that.

The next two examples, which were brought up by a participant in a conduct problems workshop at a primary school, give a good idea of how problems can be approached.

1. So what!?

> Robert is in the seventh grade. He came to our school in the fifth grade, after a number of heavy collisions at school. In a one-to-one situation Robert is a nice, engaging boy with a lot of interests and is creative. In a group Robert fights with everything and everyone. He has no respect at all for adults. When he is reprimanded or when a simple question is asked regarding his behaviour his normal reaction is: 'So what!?'
>
> Both parents work and there is no co-operation between them and the schoolteachers. Robert lives with his real mother and a 'fake' father. His parents see Robert's behaviour as a school problem. 'At home everything goes all right' is what the parents say. The relationship between Robert's natural parents is bad.

The person who put this forward is a warm, male teacher who has talks with Robert now and again. The first thing that strikes one is that Robert's behaviour does not seem to be generalised. It seems that at home everything goes well but at school things go so badly that a change of school proves to be necessary. The second thing that strikes one is that it is possible to point immediately at a source with regard to conduct problems, namely the divorce of his parents. The parents furthermore do not seem to recognise this behaviour and that indicates that it has not been there since earliest childhood. These are all signs that point to a conduct problem that has arisen on the basis of his parents' divorce. In order to test this it is possible to ask a few questions regarding the situation. The problematic behaviour has started as a result of the divorce. A number of moments can be stated: the moment that it became clear that his parents would get a divorce, the moment that his parents split up, the moment that his mother started a new relationship, the moment that the new relation started to fulfil a father figure role. In the situations where Robert shows difficult behaviour, there must be elements of the divorce of his parents present – for example, it is especially common in situations with men or women with children who have contact with their divorced father and with children who also have divorced parents. The common thread of the situations can make clear in what way Robert is bothered by the divorce. With the help of the task schema by Wallerstein and Blakeslee (1989) (see Chapter 5) it can be seen what stage Robert is at regarding coping with the divorce. If the divorce is indeed the problem that Robert is struggling with, he himself will be bothered by his behaviour and cannot easily be helped to solve the problem. A real solution for him would be that his parents get back together again and stop fighting each other. In a conversation Robert himself had actually said so.

2. Keep your hands off me!

Bernard is in the seventh grade and came to this school in the sixth grade after the situation at his previous school became unbearable. Bernard has 'serious' ADHD and takes Ritalin® six times a day and a sleeping tablet at night. There is excellent co-operation with the parents. When Bernard is working, it usually goes well. He has a place alone, at his own request. In a group situation his behaviour is difficult. The biggest problem is his language. He can suddenly explode and uses the most horrific terms of abuse. The paediatrician's advice is to let him 'rage out'. This is, however, barely manageable in the school situation.

What is striking with this case is the fact that Bernard looks for solutions for his behaviour himself; this is an indication for predisposition problems. A child with a disorder looks for solutions itself and is more or less successful in it. It seems that a diagnosis is made and medication is provided, but with that the behaviour is still not under control. Good co-operation with the parents also points to predispositional problems. The parents feel understood in the fact that there is something wrong with their son and want to co-operate with the persons who are helping him. It is also striking that, despite strong medication and even medication for the side effects, Bernard shows norm exceeding behaviour, notably exploding with serious bad language expressions. As a diagnosis of ADHD has been made there does not seem to be another reason to look for a predisposition or environment source. It is, however, useful to understand Bernard better and to look into it more, particularly because very specific behaviour takes place. Bernard himself indicates that he wants to sit alone. He therefore looks for solutions for his problems and these solutions are atypical for a primary school child in the seventh grade. They prefer to be in groups and with friends than alone. Upon inquiry it appears that Bernard had a talk with the teacher about that. The teacher wanted to put him in a group, but Bernard protested, 'You don't understand me; if I sit in a group everything will go wrong – I have to sit alone.' The serious torrents of abuse are interpreted by the paediatrician as outbursts of aggression. It seems useful to examine this more closely. Is there always a clear cause for an 'explosion'? Is this generalised behaviour? Do the parents also experience this? Under what circumstances does this happen? Are there also other forms of aggressive behaviour apart from swearing? Does it come across as 'involuntary, uncontrollable' behaviour? The answers to these questions could lead to a more detailed specification of the diagnosis. Instead of ADHD, or co-morbidity with ADHD, Bernard could be suffering from *Tourette's syndrome*, the multiple tic syndrome where serious and sudden torrents of abuse and obscene language can occur. When we speak of 'exploding' 'outbursts' and 'swearing' we are more likely to think of directable behaviour than of behaviour that is no longer controllable. The high dosage of the medication that also stems outbursts does not seem to help. In view of Bernard's own activity in coping with his problems it seems more plausible that the behaviour is not directable and not controllable, and this makes us think in the direction of predisposition and in this case of Tourette's syndrome.

When we are dealing with more structural problems, that are not bound to a certain period, without it being the case of a disorder, then it is probable that the childrearing situation as a whole or, for example, the childrearing style plays a part. A diagnosis of the childrearing situation will be able to provide information about the extent of the role. Here there are a number of elements, such as the nature and predisposition of the parents, the degree of attachment, the amount of warmth, the space for autonomy and the degree of structure.

In the development of children I can name a number of main points which belong to the various age phases. Although many points require attention, I aim at limitation so that problematic development areas can be mapped with little effort. I call this the *attention route* (Delfos 1999b). This attention route can be found in Table 11.1.

The first focus of attention is fundamental for the development of children: a good attachment in order to be able to function independently on that basis. Respect for a child means that the parent gives the child space to develop at his or her own pace (Focus Point 2). When a parent has been physically or sexually abused, he or she is at risk of treating their own child the same way despite all their good intentions (Focus Point 3). Bandura (1965) showed how important a moral example is for children (Focus Point 4). The biological origin is important for children, necessary to develop their identity; when they do not get the answers they need, they will start looking during their puberty (Focus Point 5). Although it is of consequence in every phase, the interaction with peers becomes important for the forming of *social identity* (Focus Point 6) at the end of primary school. At the end of primary school, children have a great interest in sex education and this is pre-eminently the period to pay (extra) attention to this (Focus Point 7). The adolescent is proud of his cognitive skills and needs the adult to sharpen them and peers with which to practise them. When an adolescent really feels 'heard' by adults he will have considerably less chance of becoming derailed (Focus Point 8). Interaction with peers is very important during adolescence and at the same time it has some risks (Focus Point 9). A big change in eating and sleeping habits is an indication for serious problems and can be an indication of a psychosis (Focus Point 10). Because youngsters tend to experiment, drug and alcohol use is a focus point (11) during puberty. It can be used as self-medication. Adolescents have more chance of depression and suicide than children (Focus Point 12).

When the upbringing situation is regarded as problematic, the degree to which this can be changed will have to be looked at as well as the degree to which participants in the professional help process can change with the child and are *able*

Table 11.1 Attention route from birth to adolescence

Age phase from birth to five years

1. (a) Was the child able to attach?

   (b) Has the child been able to develop independence?

2. (a) Is the parent aware of the fact that children have their own development?

   (b) Does the parent act accordingly?

3. (a) Is the parent aware of the personal powerlessness that can cause abuse of power?

   (b) Is the way the parent acts towards the child 'clean', and therefore not sexual?

4. Is a positive moral model available for the child?

Age phase from six up to and including eight years

5. Does the child know his or her biological origin?

Age phase from nine up to and including 12 years

6. Does the child have enough opportunities to learn how to cope with peers in a group?

7. Has sex education taken place?

Age phase from 13 years

8. (a) Does the youngster have the opportunity to exchange opinions with the important adult in his or her direct environment?

   (b) Does the youngster feel 'heard' by this adult?

9. (a) Does the youngster have peers for support and solidarity?

   (b) Is the youngster part of a group which has the risk of use of drugs and delinquent behaviour attached to it?

10. Does the youngster have a good eating and sleeping pattern?

11. (a) Has the youngster been informed about the consequences of the use of alcohol and drugs?

   (b) Does the youngster use stimulants?

12. (a) Are there signs that indicate that the youngster suffers from depression?

   (b) Are there signs that indicate that the youngster is at risk of suicide?

to learn. The question is then to what extent the parents are *coachable.* A number of general questions that we can ask within that framework are given below.

Questions about the coachability of parents

- Are the parents intellectually capable of gaining insight?

- Are the parents capable of recognising their own role in the arising, or maintaining, of the child's problem?

- Does the childrearing situation have enough stability?

- Is the family open enough to admit a 'prying' professional helper?

- Is it a matter of a symbiotic or 'tangled' family, where interference may upset a shaky balance and help is not actually tolerated?

For most forms of coaching it is necessary for the parents to be intellectually capable of gaining insight. This applies in particular to psychotherapies, because these are insight-giving therapies, but also most other forms of therapy. Family therapy also requires an intellectual effort from the parents and the family as a whole. There are, however, also forms of childrearing support that can be applied independently from the intellectual capabilities of parents; these are for example *video home training, Families First* and *Intensive Home Support,* where intensive and also concrete help is offered to the family. The Family Group Conference also requires the intellectual insight of the parents, but can be adjusted to the level of the family. The Family Group Conference is based on the principles of the Maori society. 'Family' is understood to mean the direct and more distant family members, but also people who are important for the family. Together the family makes a plan of what the best way is to give shape to the professional help. The results are positive and experience with the Family Group Conference has improved the practical execution of the method (Hudson *et al.* 1996).

Parents have to be capable intellectually, and especially emotionally, to recognise their own role in the arising or maintaining of the child's problem. In the initial stage of recognition people are often flooded by feelings of guilt and they often do not dare to think and feel further, as they are afraid that they will be overloaded with even more guilt. Nevertheless, every person is, as it were, 'unguiltied' when he proceeds and faces the truth. The task of the professional helper is to recognise the pain of the other person and to guide him or her through it. Not everyone is capable of doing that – not the person concerned and also not always the professional helper.

In order to make coaching possible, there has to be enough stability in the childrearing situation. It is, however, not always possible to help immediately, and unstable families especially need help quickly. A path where various levels of help are provided is the right thing in such situations, for example from practical help to support to therapy.

The family has to be 'open' enough to admit a 'prying' professional helper. A professional helper, by his watching, can upset a shaky balance in a family. A closed family can really need help, but not be able to actually allow it. Help can be perceived as interference, as an intrusion on one's privacy, and there may be the fear that the help is not adequate, especially when in the past incompetent and non-successful help has taken place. In particular, a 'symbiotic or tangled' family struggle to admit a professional helper because interference could upset the shaky balance, and the family as a whole could disintegrate. A family like that cries out for help but does not allow it at the crucial moment.

The answers to these questions give an insight into the possibilities for coaching the family and into the extent to which preliminary work is necessary to allow this family to become open for coaching. These questions are often not given enough attention by the professional helpers and people become stranded because of a lack of preparation.

I separated the four areas relevant here (childrearing, puberty, trauma, divorce), but that does not mean to say that they all occur separately. A combination of problems occurs regularly. The chance of problems especially increases with a coming together of various sources, as we have already seen with the *multiple risk model*.

> Ronald was almost ten years old when his parents separated. He was relieved, because the fights were terrible. He stayed to live with his mother, and his father lived alone in an apartment. His mother had had a hard time for the first two years after the divorce and Ronald was therefore happy when she, after three years, found a new relationship. He seemed to get on well with his mother's new friend. His father kept on living alone. When Ronald was 14, he started to show serious problems. Because the first year and a half went well with his stepfather, everyone thought that Ronald's behaviour was caused by puberty and nobody looked at any other factors. Nevertheless, it proved that Ronald had had a delayed reaction. Out of loyalty he had done his best to accept his stepfather. He felt very sorry for his father, who was living alone and grew lonely. After his mother became more stable, Ronald seemed to allow himself his own problems.

Medication?

Because constitutional problems with conduct problems are less to the foreground, the use of medication is generally not indicated. It can be useful in the case of serious anxieties to prescribe sedatives for a period of time, but other ways are more frequently indicated, especially with children and youngsters. If the influence comes mainly from the environmental factors, it is more obvious to try to influence these factors and if possible remove the source of the problem. This becomes most clear when we look at puberty. No matter how many problems puberty can cause, we would not think about stemming this phase, which is essential for development, by altering the hormonal flow with the help of medication.

Influences of the environment and the possibilities of professional help

The various factors, each in their own way, exercise influence. Sometimes the source can be recognised in the child's behaviour, although after some time this is not always that visible. When at first the problem was restricted to a specific situation, in the long run it can extend itself because the child can get into more and more trouble. I will have a closer look at the various influences and some professional help possibilities.

Childrearing

When the childrearing proves to be the source of influence of the child's conduct problem, then we are dealing with educational powerlessness of the parents. In the next chapter I will go into the attitudes of educators and childrearing techniques by concentrating on the situation of a child with ADHD or with hyperactivity as the reactive behaviour.

One of the most penetrating problems in this framework is an insecure attachment which arises because the parents do not respond warmly to the child's needs.

In the case of problematic childrearing, the communication between parents and child has been disturbed. Help for parents and child can then be given in the form of, for example, *childrearing support*, family therapy or individual psychotherapy.

One of the methods used for childrearing support which has become popular is *video home training*. Video home training is a form of ambulatory help for the family. The most important starting point of video home training is, as described by Dekker and Biemans (1994), that children, even when they have been neglected for years, invite their parents to have positive contact. The training with the help of a video camera aims at parents learning to receive the initiatives for contact with the child and building on *positive interactions*.

Basic principles of communication with video home training are:

- receiving initiatives to contact children so that the onus is shared

- giving attention equally in turn to everyone

- consultation

- making conflicts manageable.

The purpose of the video home training is to extend positive interactions. At the centre of this method is the interaction between parent and child.

Help through video home training has increased enormously in the past few years. Scientific research into the effects has, however, not yet got off the ground sufficiently.

We can state in general that children and parents basically want to have a good contact with each other. Making each other's intentions explicit is the ground for the professional help on which new behaviour can be taught. Problems in communication often mean that the family members interpret each other's behaviour wrongly. The task of the professional helper in a family is therefore often the role of 'interpreter-translator'.

In a problematic childrearing situation it is important to map the patterns in the family and the way in which these patterns are maintained by the members. Within system theory, from which family therapy has been developed, this is taken as a starting point.

When the parents are educationally incompetent and professional help cannot make any changes, it may be necessary to look for a different childrearing situation for the child. Initially this will be a family upbringing in a different situation. I speak here of conduct problems, which can in principle be influenced through the environment, so that a different childrearing situation in family form can possibly take the problem away. That is why, in the case of conduct problems, family upbringing is a realistic alternative to growing up with the natural parents. It is of the utmost importance here that the natural parents are behind this foster home placement and 'allow' their children to live there, otherwise *loyalty problems* will prevent the child from starting a relationship with the family. In extreme cases a residential setting may be necessary.

Puberty

Although it may seem strange to categorise puberty under environment factors, in this period the problem is the detachment of the youngster from his or her environment and his or her conflicts with that. During puberty the youngster extends his or her independence and tries to form his or her own identity. This process is often accompanied by resistance to parents, school and authority. Although this behaviour is often difficult for parents and they may be very worried, youngsters usually get through their puberty quite well (Rutter *et al.* 1976). When the source of the problematic behaviour lies mainly in puberty, and the problematic behaviour was not present before, there is little reason to worry. It is in that case especially important that parents are helped to ease the detachment process for themselves and their children.

A democratic upbringing, characterised by consultation, links up better to the adolescent's world. I have already said that the adolescent is proud of his or her intellectual skills. When having a conversation with an adolescent it is important to give him or her the space to develop those intellectual skills. Stimulating the thinking process, instead of giving them your own opinion, will mostly result in an opinion which is close to that of the adult. Imposing an opinion, however, evokes resistance which hinders the thinking process and conjures up opposition. In the latter case the opinion of the adolescent and the adult remain far apart (Focus Point 8 in the attention route).

If parents have great difficulties with the way in which their child detaches itself, they need help to learn to have faith in their child's development. They have to learn to consult and to negotiate with the youngster while at the same time having to set limits. The *moral aggression* (Kapteyn 1985) with which the youngster puts down its wishes has to be placed into a perspective in which the parent does not always feel personally attacked.

During the 1960s and 1970s the conflicts between youngsters and their parents became a spearhead for the policy of professional help. Youth advice bureaux were set up, which directed their attention to the youngster and his or her right to independence. The parents were sometimes ignored too much. Nowadays adolescence problems are viewed more in the perspective of the detachment phase of parents and children. The attention of the professional helper has shifted to the family system.

Trauma

When a child is a victim of traumatic experiences it can react with externalising or internalising conduct. Externalising conduct can sometimes lead to a repetition of the trauma. We can see that, for example, with children who are physically abused. The physical abuse they undergo is painful, and they still show the behaviour that can again provoke the same physical abuse – *revictimisation*. They can also externalise the behaviour to others, such as peers. Research into bullying shows that the ones who bully often undergo serious physical punishment at home. I recall research by Deater-Deckard and Dodge (1997), who discovered that hard disciplinary measures by parents promoted outbursts in their children, especially with boys. During childhood a trauma can mean that a child has a relapse in skills which it already seemed to control. One of the most familiar examples is toilet-training problems:

> A little girl, eight years old, wet her pants regularly during the day. The group leaders of the children's home where she lived could not talk to her about this. She refused to put clean clothes on and have a bath. She would scream blue murder in order not to have to take a bath. She would hide dirty pants in her room. This was a difficult problem for the group leaders that took a lot of energy. The little girl responded to 'nothing'. The group leaders told the girl that they were not angry with her and she did not have

to be ashamed. They tried to make clear to her that she smelt bad and other children responded to that. The little girl ignored everything, even the remarks by the other children in the group. What the girl was in fact doing was strongly denying what was going on. She had a traumatic history behind her with extreme sexual abuse, which gave her a venereal disease for which she had to be treated. With the help of thinking 'ignore it, then it doesn't exist' she tried to ban the negative from her life. In order to solve this problem, advice was given to shift the attention which was paid to the subject she denied to a positive subject. She was allowed to pick a scent for bath foam and the group leader would bathe her and expressly tell her how nice she was smelling and how nice it was to smell her. The little girl was overjoyed and asked to have a bath the next day. She invited the people around her to smell how nice she smelled. She prevented herself from becoming wet and smelling badly. A simple intervention, which caused a shift from denial to a realistic positive alternative, enabled her to feel fine, and the group leaders did not have an energy and time-consuming problem any more. Also, without talking about it any further, the child herself asked for the pills which she had to take, something she had refused before.

With *PTSD, Post Traumatic Stress Disorder,* an increased irritability is a usual reaction with children. This reaction can deter support and comfort from others. People find it easier to deal with reactions like sadness and fear, where a clearer appeal for help is made on the other than with irritability, which is more likely to discourage the other person. Because of that there is the risk that children's traumatisation signals are not noticed in time, and that they are more repelled than helped. This applies even more strongly to boys than to girls. Boys tend to externalise their problems and show difficult behaviour. Where the girl gets help almost as a matter of course, the boy is more likely to get a disciplinary reaction. The traumatic reaction becomes even more difficult to signal when the child undergoes PTE (Pervasive Traumatic Experience) and there is a culmination of effects. In that case a direct cause is not easily discernable, because there are several consecutive causes.

Professional help after a trauma should consist of various steps which take place chronologically. 'Information' is placed at the end of the series. However, it is often the case that it is given earlier, and as a result hinders the processing of the trauma. This is connected with the fact that the information is exactly the thing that the professional helper has at his or her disposal and he or she thinks that it solves his or her powerlessness with regard to the trauma. We can see that at the moment when a child says it feels guilty about the sexual abuse it went through. Adults around it are quick to inform the child that it is not responsible and to tell them how the abuser should be thought about. They wave aside the feeling of guilt, with the best intentions. The child, however, needs attention to be paid to its guilt feelings. The feelings of guilt also work as a form of protection, as we have already seen in Chapter 5. By carefully naming the contents of the feelings of guilt, the child will gain more insight into what happened, slowly discovering how it can protect itself against repetition, and the child itself will in general put into words that it is not the guilty one. I have already observed that the feeling of guilt is not based on a realistic interpretation of the experience. A feeling of guilt is an 'antidote' against the fear of repetition which also goes together with a trauma. The elements for professional help after a trauma are stated in Table 11.2.

Table 11.2 Elements of help when coping with a trauma

Chronological order of actions:

- create physical safety

- take care of physical consequences, such as feeling cold

- look for attachment figures

- pay attention to the nature of the trauma itself

- communicate in verbal and non-verbal sense

- pay attention to feelings of guilt

- pay attention to the consequences

- give information.

Attitude of the professional helper:

- inviting and not telling

- humanity more than professionalism.

Creating physical safety is a prerequisite for giving help in the case of a trauma. Sometimes this is difficult to realise. A child who has been sexually abused by their father can, in fact, not really be brought into safety. We cannot place the father out of the house (Delfos 1995), although people start to think in that direction more and more. Taking the child out of the house means that on the one hand we create safety and on the other danger, because being separated from attachment figures has a traumatising effect. Taking care of the physical consequences is next in line, followed directly by looking for attachment figures. In coping processes attachment figures play a significant role. An arm around you from an attachment figure can often do more good than hours of talking to a professional helper. The core of attachment itself lies exactly at the moment when someone is in need, especially when the quality of the attachment and the reliability of the attachment figure come to light. For example, we attach ourselves immediately to someone who has saved our life, even though before the accident he was a total stranger to us. The rescuer showed by his or her action that he or she is a real attachment figure in the real sense of the word; he or she was there in case of extreme need: life-threatening danger.

In addition, it is important to observe that when a disaster has taken place, sharing the trauma together can work in a healing way, especially in the first hour. A clear example of this is the difference in problems from which Second World War soldiers and Vietnam veterans suffered. The fact that the soldiers from the Second World War spent a few weeks together returning home on a ship helped them with their processing of the war. The Vietnam veterans were thrown back into ordinary life within a day from the war situation by means of modern, faster means of transportation such as planes. *PTSD* proved to occur much more often with these soldiers.

Subsequently attention to the nature of the trauma itself is important. People want to understand what has happened to them, mainly to know how to prevent it recurring. The fear of repetition is great with traumas. In order to understand, all details are important so that finally the main issues can be separated from the side issues and an insight into what happened can be gained. This is a reason why the trauma keeps appearing in one's mind's eye, in order to see all details clearly. Repeatedly talking about it also serves this purpose.

Communication is necessary both in a verbal and in a non-verbal sense. Eye contact and a comforting arm are possibly more important than talking. In professional help and with traumas in particular the task of the professional helper should be more listening than talking. Chaos has arisen in the victim and putting thoughts and feelings into words gives the opportunity to create order in that chaos. When another person puts things into words for you this process cannot take place in that way.

Attention to the guilt feelings is more about giving the other person the chance of putting these feelings into words, and by doing that getting rid of them rather than taking things over and trying to take them away. It is also striking that people seem to cling to their feelings of guilt, no matter how unrealistic they are. This clinging on is an attempt to keep things under control, control which the feelings of guilt seem to offer.

Subsequently, it is important to pay attention to the consequences, and chronological information should be given now, something professional helpers tend to bring forward. As far as the attitude of the professional helper is concerned it can be said that this should be more inviting than telling and more humane than professional.

Individual or group psychotherapy is suitable for the treatment of traumas. Depending on the age of the child this can be play or drama therapy or conversation therapy. Treatment programmes are increasingly being set up for various traumas, as are trauma protocols. There is, for example, a lot of experience with the treatment of sexual abuse – there are reporting centres and protocols to obtain professional help in such cases.

In the case of a traumatic event it is not only that there is a sense of fear regarding the event, but also that the person's faith in the world has been affected. During the treatment attention should therefore also be paid to rebuilding faith in the relative safety of the world (Bower and Sivers 1998).

Divorce

Divorce can be a lengthy process for both parents and children. Even after many years have passed and the influence is not directly visible, children can continue to suffer from their parents' divorce. An extra problem is that children tend not to show their own grief to their parents. They see the grief and despair of their parents and do not want to add their own grief to that. It is very important to the child to get the people whom he or she is so dependent on stable again as soon as possible. Furthermore, the child, by means of its own adaptation behaviour, wants to prevent further problems and often nurses secret hopes that the parents can be brought back together again.

A typical example of an extreme, harmful, adaptation is the story of an adolescent girl who seriously disfigured herself:

> The parents of a young adolescent girl were divorced when the girl was still very young. The joint custody went harmoniously. The girl had always been an intelligent, sweet, social and easy child. She therefore surprised her parents completely when she confessed that nine months before she had scratched 'I hate myself' on her leg. The wounds were still visible and she took a lot of trouble to ensure that nobody would see them, for example during gym class. The occasion that had caused this was a conflict with her mother, in which she considered herself to have been very unreasonable. Her mother did not seem to remember the scene. Every time when her parents asked her to do something, she did it, but inwardly she was complaining. She thought that that was unreasonable of herself and she was very much ashamed that she had had those feelings. Because she had never shared these feelings with anyone, she did not know that it was perfectly normal to hate having to do things that you are asked to do. In this way she started to dislike herself, while on the outside she was a sweet, social and easy child.

In Chapter 5 I discussed what a divorce or separation can mean for children. No matter how much the parents fight, and how relieved the children are after the divorce that the fights have stopped, the children in fact often want their parents to get back together again (without the fighting), and this desire goes on into adulthood. This means that the only real help for the child would be that the parents get back together again, happy and without fights. This is not feasible, but it is good for the parents to realise what the child is thinking. Even if divorce is a 'second chance of happiness' for the parents, as Wallerstein and Blakeslee (1989) put it, it is not so for the child. He or she will have to learn to cope with the reality of the divorce and a different family perspective, often also different parent figures.

Behaviour therapy and behaviour contract

It is often the case that problem behaviour extends itself after a first occasion and starts to live its own life. The behaviour also occurs in the absence of the situation which caused it. The more time has passed, the more the behaviour becomes a normal part of everyday life. This means that taking the original problem away is often not enough to remedy the behaviour problems. In that case behaviour therapy can help to teach new behaviour and unlearn undesired behaviour. The advantage of behaviour therapy with conduct *problems* is that the problem is actually remedied by it; this is unlike the conduct *disorder* where one has to learn to live with the predisposition.

In Chapter 10 it has been described in detail how behaviour therapeutic help can be applied to internalising problems. Cognitions and the way in which these can be changed are central in modern streams of behaviour therapy. Behaviour therapeutic techniques are pre-eminently suitable for offering help with conduct problems, both with the externalising and the internalising form. One should not lose sight of the fact that originally there was a cause for the behaviour, and one should consider whether that cause has been sufficiently worked on and processed. An example of a behaviour therapeutic technique is the *behaviour contract,* which can be very useful with conduct problems. The explanation of a behaviour contract was given in Chapter 9, and an example is provided in Appendix 2. Behaviour contracts can be used where the child has the ability to reach the desired behaviour, but does not execute it enough. It is necessary here that the predisposition does not impede and that the behaviour can be automated by working with a behaviour contract – otherwise the child will fall back into its old behaviour pattern after the contract. In order to make a behaviour contract workable, it will have to be reciprocal. This means that parents and child have to bind themselves to the contract and therefore can also be reciprocally rewarded. The motivation of all partners has to be present in the contract. All partners to the contract should also make an effort to bring about a change in behaviour. Behaviour does not exist in a vacuum; it also exists thanks to the way in which the environment responds to the behaviour. If one wants to accomplish a change in behaviour in a child, then one should also have to start with a change in the parents' behaviour.

Another development of behaviour therapeutic techniques is the *competence model*. The starting point of the competence model is development tasks from which sub-tasks can be derived, up to and including small tasks in the daily routine. In order to execute tasks, skills are needed which the child either has or does not have at its disposal. The skills it already has at its disposal can be employed and new skills can be learned. The competence model is used successfully mainly in residential settings (Gageldonk and Bartels 1990). It makes a group approach possible, while at the same time there is tailored help for each child and each youngster separately. The emphasis is on learning new skills. With each phase of the treatment privileges, the freedoms and responsibilities of the youngster increase, and people work more and more towards the situation which the child will be in after the residential setting.

Psychiatric or educational residential help?

Conduct *problems* do not necessarily lie in the field of psychiatry. Initially the problems lie mainly in the field of education or psychology. If there are problems which seriously disrupt development, and the educational incompetence of the parents is significant, then educational and psychological help may be necessary. First, an effort will have to be made to look for easily accessible social assistance. Professional help should, in order to be effective, be offered at as early a stage as possible, as close to home as possible, in the lightest possible form and for as short a period of time as possible.

Should forms of educational support come to a standstill, then the family as a whole can be helped, for example by means of family therapy. When it is difficult to change the educational incompetence of parents, then it may be necessary to look for a different childrearing situation – foster care or a residential setting. Childrearing support has more chance of success with the conduct problem than with the conduct disorder. Should one choose a residential setting, then this will have to be of an educational nature and not of a psychiatric one. When the concern is behaviour that is not so much included in the child's predisposition, but is caused by the parents' way of childrearing, the new setting will need to aim to remedy the damage of inadequate childrearing. If one wants to place the child back home again, it will also be necessary to offer help to the parents in order to reduce their educational incompetence.

Who does what in professional help?

The form of professional help that should be called in depends largely on the source of influence from the environment. When we are dealing with educational incompetence, then help coming from social work is the most appropriate because social workers are the most familiar with the socio-emotional and economic problems of families.

If there is a disturbed family life, then family therapy is advised. If the child gets stuck to such a degree that individual psychotherapeutic or behaviour therapeutic help is necessary, then we are mainly in the field of the psychologist or maybe the psychiatrist. When a child is seriously suffering from the consequences of a traumatic event, then psychotherapy will be advised. Psychiatric help in the form of medication is not advised in the case of conduct problems, only as a time-out when the situation is not feasible and where peace and quiet has to be created.

In the case of divorce problems help through social work, such as help with the arrangements concerning parental access, is advised.

Van Acker (1995) mentions a few significant characteristics of the professional helper in the case of conduct problems:

1. He or she sees the family members as partners.

2. He or she looks for solutions in the actual here and now.

3. He or she uses the potential possibilities of the family members.

4. His or her attitude is caring and respectful.

I would like to add that a proper analysis of the history of the child or the family can be of the utmost importance in gaining insight into the problems and to set the course for help. Solutions in the 'here and now' have to be anchored in expert knowledge of the history of the problems.

To conclude, the treatment aspects of the conduct problems are given in Table 11.3.

Table 11.3 The treatment aspects of conduct problems

Professional should establish establish environment factor and where appropriate:

- provide help with the childrearing

- provide help with dealing with divorce

- provide help with trauma processing

- provide help with taking puberty seriously and teach how to put things into perspective.

Continued on next page

Table 11.3 continued

Professional should provide the following kinds of help:

- childrearing support

- psychotherapy

- behaviour therapy

- behaviour therapeutic techniques

- family therapy

- trauma protocols.

Summary

With conduct problems the environment is the most important source of influence. There is a difference in the nature in which the problems manifest themselves with the different sexes. Boys usually respond in an externalising way, girls usually in an internalising way. For the correct treatment strategy to be chosen it is important to know what the most important source of influence is within the various environmental factors: childrearing, puberty, trauma or separation/divorce. Conduct problems are mainly in the field of education and psychology. Behaviour therapeutic techniques can make a significant contribution to the solution of conduct problems.

The Treatment of ADHD and Hyperactivity

The discovery of the diagnosis ADHD as a disorder with a biological cause, as a disruption of the maturation of the central nervous system, has furthered the search for an appropriate treatment. When children who were overactive, chaotic and had difficulty in sustaining attention were diagnosed as *MBD*, *Minimal Brain Damage*, help was mainly aimed at curtailing the child's chaotic behaviour. It was thought that more structure might be sufficient. This sometimes proved to have a contrary effect. Now that we know that, among other things, there is a problem with processing stimuli, we are more aimed at how we can help these children to process stimuli. The medication is also tuned to that. The search for the right treatment has, however, by no means been completed; opinion is still divided about the right approach. In addition, there are many incorrect diagnoses based on the externalising, overactive behaviour of children who express their problems in this way.

Treatment areas

Before I discuss the treatment of ADHD, I will state the characteristics of this disorder (for a specific translation into daily actions see Chapter 6 for the criteria of the *DSM-IV* and Chapter 8):

- mainly boys
- immaturity of the central nervous system
  - reduced working of prefrontal brain
  - smaller corpus callosum
  - stimuli not being processed properly

  — unrest, impulsivity

  — inadequate concentration

  — difficulty with letting what is being said sink in

- possible immaturity of hormonal structure

  — generalised anxiety

  — hyperactivity

- risk of conduct problems due to conflicts with the environment

  — situation-bound aggression

  — norm-exceeding behaviour as outlet for problems

- risk of immature development of left hemisphere of brain

  — risk of dyslexia

  — risk of learning disorders

- risk of addiction as self-medication in order to become tranquil.

And, in the case that there is no co-morbidity with the externalising conduct disorder:

- normal me–other differentiation

- normal empathic capacity

  — normal moral sense

  — need to engage in play activities with others

  — normal ability to see one's own role

  — normal self-reflection.

Medication?

When helping children with ADHD combination form, that is to say hyperactivity, impulsivity and concentration disorder, stimulant medication – amphetamines – proves to have good results. Initially this may seem strange, because this is a stimulant and the child needs rest rather than stimulation. In pharmacology it is, however, not always clear how certain medication works. It is suggested that ADHD is a problem with the processing of stimuli which is linked to the stimulus transfer in the brain, notably the dopamine transfer and an underdevelopment of the prefrontal brain. The medication is aimed at stimulating this transfer. As a result

the concentration improves and hyperactivity decreases. The best known medication used with ADHD is methylphenidate (Ritalin®); furthermore clonidine
(Dixarit®) and Dipiperon® are employed, particularly when Ritalin® does not seem
to work or does not seem to work sufficiently. Ritalin® affects the prefrontal cortex,
the area at the front of the brain. In this area the attention function and the
planning ability are supposed to be situated. Because of the fact that the child is
better able to concentrate, the child also becomes less restless.

Some psychiatrists are of the opinion that Ritalin® is an extremely effective
substance; others are a bit more cautious, and see at least the necessity of a
combination with psychotherapy, in particular behaviour therapy. Children can
also become more active due to Ritalin® and the positive effect can decrease after
some habituation. In addition, there is the risk of addiction with higher doses, as is
usual with amphetamines. The use of Ritalin® as a substitute for cocaine and the
lively trade in it encourage more strictness in prescribing Ritalin®. It should be used
only when needed. The amount of Ritalin® prescribed has increased enormously
during the past years. In the Netherlands an estimated 32,000 children take
Ritalin® and every month sees an addition of 1000 young users (ANP 2000). In the
USA Ritalin® is now used in the same way as it was in the boom in stimulant
medication in the 1970s, that is as the 'maths pill', to improve school performances.
From the 1980s onwards it was used as medication for MBD (Koopman 1989).
The school performances of children did improve, but the reason that it was not so
successful in the 1970s was because of the resistance against the medical model in
general and medication in particular, and because of the side effects of stimulant
medication. The side effects of Ritalin® are sleeplessness, loss of appetite and the
'rebound effect', causing the restlessness to become even stronger after the Ritalin®
has stopped working. Ritalin® is mainly used to improve concentration and is
therefore mainly used during school hours. It works for a few hours and
subsequently the restlessness is much greater during free time (see also the 'vicious
circles' of van Dijk below). A countermovement has now started against the use of
Ritalin®. The ANP (2000), for example, reports that a group of parents in Texas are
suing the manufacturers of Ritalin® because of the harmful side effects. Handen *et
al.* (1999) indicate that primary school children with dyslexia and ADHD can
benefit from Ritalin®, but that children at this age are also very sensitive to the
harmful effects.

The behaviour of children who 'bounce through the room' is sometimes barely
manageable, if at all, and medication, combined with therapy, can give parents and
child the 'time out' they need so badly. It can ensure that the child flies off the
handle less quickly and give the parents more space for positive attention.

Because of their continuous conflict with the environment and their own
experience of failing in their functioning, these children have a high chance of
developing conduct problems. In addition to the ADHD-steered behaviour,

behaviours develop through the children's interaction with the environ[ment] is mainly problematic behaviour that is arises from the harmful effect on the self-image that results from conflicts with the people in their environment.

During puberty there is a chance that children with ADHD will start to use drugs as self-medication, especially amphetamines and cannabis. The effect of each of these substances is the opposite of each other. Amphetamines are stimulating and cannabis is relaxing. When we apply van Dijk's model (van Dijk 1979; Noorlander, Rijnders and Wijdeven 1993) to this, it can provide insight into the way this works and how both drugs can have the intended effect, even though they have the opposite effect. Van Dijk states that as with all substances, the body forms a counter-reaction to harmful substances. The body starts to produce antibodies in order to neutralise the harmful substance. The reaction to amphetamines, which work to 'accelerate', is therefore 'decelerating'. The reaction to cannabis that works to 'decelerate' is therefore 'accelerating'. According to van Dijk addiction means, for example, that the body will ask for the drug because it has already made the antibodies against that drug, the 'anticipatory reaction'. You are, as it were, addicted because of the counter-reaction of your body, not because of the substance itself.

When the youngster uses cannabis, then the body will, as a reaction to that, produce 'accelerating', 'restless' substances and he will again feel the need to use cannabis. In this way a vicious circle arises. The use of what initially seemed to be a 'relaxing' substance leads to strong reactions and the urge to smoke cannabis again in order to calm down again becomes stronger. In this way structural use is encouraged. The chances are that the use increases to such a level that during the rebound not only overactivity arises but also aggression. If the youngster uses amphetamines, then the body will produce 'relaxing' substances as a reaction to this, causing the youngster to become relaxed. In order to reach that effect the youngster will have to use them more often and use more of them. This shows that both substances have a 'relaxing' effect, the cannabis directly and the amphetamines through the antibodies.

> The use of alcohol and drugs is subject to conditioning processes. The use gets linked to certain situations and certain actions. The cigarette after the cup of coffee leads to the fact that when trying to stop smoking one should also skip the cup of coffee, if one does not want to be overwhelmed by the need for a cigarette. Just how important the forming of habits is is explained in the experiment with opium use by mice (Noorlander *et al.* 1993). Mice were habituated to opium in a green space. When they were subsequently given opium in a red space their body was not prepared for it and had taken insufficient 'precautionary measures' and not produced any antibodies. The mice died of the opium in the red room, while the same dose in the green room did not cause any problems. A body develops 'programmes' for certain substances. This programme remains in the body and can be active again after a long time of stopping use of a certain substance. This often leads to renewed use.

A 17-year-old hyperactive boy had become addicted to drugs. He 'smoked dope' on a daily basis. This finally enabled him to be able to concentrate. When he was 'stoned' he could, without any problems, put the parts of a moped together in a relaxed manner. If he was not under the influence he could definitely not achieve this. Apart from the psychological addiction, the drug ensured that he was at last able to concentrate, something which he had never managed to do at school. His school career in which he had reading and mathematics problems had become stranded, even though according to his intelligence quotient he should have been amply able to go through secondary school. In the course of time he noticed, however, that he needed more and more 'weed' and that when he did not use any, he became aggressive.

Buitelaar (1994) states that Ritalin® prevents children from starting to use drugs. In the reasoning of van Dijk (1979) this is possible because Ritalin® takes over the task of the above-mentioned 'self-medication'. The use of Ritalin® as a drug instead of medication is, however, increasing; more often it is used in the same way as cocaine. Gunning (1993) warns against risks when using this drug and even talks of a possible risk of suicide. Maybe the latter can be understood in the light of van Dijk's (1979) model. According to that model the body, in the case of Ritalin®, may produce so many 'decelerating' substances that depression may set in. Youngsters who smoke cannabis a lot become alternately aggressive (from a surplus of antibodies) and depressed (a surplus of the drug). There is a risk that all the young person's interests slowly disappear and that nothing appeals to her any more. She will need help to come out of this predicament.

Behaviour regulation

When ADHD is seen as a problem of the maturation of the central nervous system, it is clear that it is important to give these children an optimal chance of maturation. In Chapter 2 I said that it is probably of great importance for the maturation when these children have a quiet, safe night. At the same time it is shown that these children have had trouble sleeping ever since they were babies. At first, after birth it is the maturation of the sleeping phases which is important. The settling, the day and night rhythm, has to be created. The various sleeping phases have to mature. The *sleeping-through phase* is formed during the first years after birth and decreases again at the end of life. Especially *falling asleep* and *sleeping on* can be difficult for children with maturation problems. Children with ADHD often cried a lot when they were babies. When we realise that Ritalin® can have sleeplessness as a side effect, then that casts an extra doubt on its use, which furthers the concentration during the day, but possibly frustrates the maturation at night. In addition, the research by Stickgold *et al.* (2000), which I mentioned in Chapter 2, shows that sleep, and notably the fourth dream stage, is necessary for cleaning up the brain and transferring elements of the short-term memory to the long-term memory. It is the working of the short-term memory that is the problem for children with ADHD.

The two important attention fields in the treatment of ADHD are the *behaviour regulation* in order to get the hyperactivity and impulsivity under control and the *improvement of the attention function* in order to reduce the concentration disorders. Although often with limited success, various treatments have been given structure. One of the most familiar ones is that of Barkley's (1995). His starting point is an inadequate inhibition and his help for the child with ADHD and his parents has been given shape around this principle. Barkley assumes a respectful attitude both toward the child and his parents. His programme, in an American style, is a step-by-step programme aimed at change in behaviour and attitude in child, parents and school. A *multi-model approach* where various behaviour therapeutic techniques are applied is often supported (Prins *et al.* 1999). The various situations in which the child may become stuck have to be tuned into each other, at school as well as at home.

For the behaviour regulation it is important that the child does not end up in a situation where it has to process an excess of stimuli. Structure and an overview of the daily course of affairs can ensure that these children do not have to process too many stimuli. When, however, we are dealing with co-morbidity with the *externalising conduct disorder*, then the chances are that structure also becomes monotonous, the consciousness level drops, and on that basis the child will start seeking danger.

It is important to teach the child to cope with ADHD. Information ensures that he can help himself, but also enables the adults around him to help him. A characteristic of ADHD is, for example, that these children often do not give any feedback when they are spoken to. They will continue with the activity they were engaged in and seem not to hear anything. The adult, however, needs some feedback – eye contact, for example. Without feedback the adult quickly gets the feeling that she does not have any contact, causing her to become irritated. When the child is aware that the adult needs a sign, he will be more easily prepared to oblige. Because giving feedback to the adult from the activity in which the child is caught up often proves to be difficult, a behavioural training may be helpful with this. This is at the same time a training of the attention function. This may be done with the help of a *behaviour contract*. An example of a behaviour contract of a girl with ADHD can be found in Appendix 2. The people around the child will also benefit from education. People often have the impression that the child with ADHD does it on purpose, is indifferent and does not pay attention. When they know that the behaviour bothers the child just as much, that the short-term memory ensures that things do not sink in and the child is flooded with impulses, the irritation will diminish. A lot of the irritation is linked to the fact that the adults think that the child has tuned his behaviour to the adult and therefore that the things he does, he does on purpose. The adult subsequently does not feel taken seriously and is hurt. Education can take away personal pain and promote a more helping and supportive attitude. The hyperactive and impulsive behaviour, however, remains disturbing and undesired and can easily evoke negative reactions from the people around the child.

Children with ADHD attract attention, among other things, because it seems that what they learn does not sink in. Their intelligence can be normal, while their memory does not work properly. This usually concerns the short-term memory. If one wants people to remember things, then 'little roads' have to be 'burned' into the brain neurologically. We recall the importance of sleep here. Forming a neural connection can be reinforced by repetition. Behaviour contracts can be useful for this aspect. Through behaviour contracts neural connections can be reinforced in the brain, causing the learned subjects to sink in. This means that the behaviour contract has to be set up in a very simple manner and have a repetitive nature. The aim should be to go from single to multiple behaviour. This can be achieved by means of *shaping* (see Chapter 9).

Behaviour contracts can be suitable for children with ADHD because these children have trouble regulating their behaviour. It is not a question of lack of motivation, more of not being able to regulate behaviour. Behaviour therapeutic techniques in general are usable to help children with ADHD, including both behaviour therapy and cognitive behaviour therapy (Prins *et al.* 1999). The build-up of the desired behaviour should, however, be simple, because these children would otherwise quickly fail and lose their motivation. Apart from that, the training has to be longer than average for the neural connections to actually be achieved and the behaviour automised. If the training is stopped too early, the child will revert to the old behaviour.

Music seems to fulfil a regulating function with stimulating the attention function with ADHD. We see here an analogy with a different maturation problem, namely stuttering. The stutterer does not stutter when he sings. Stuttering is a co-ordination problem inside the brain regarding control of the vocal cords (Peters and Guitar 1991), and music gives structure there and regulates the tempo.

A different element that deserves attention is *computer games*. Although computer games are exciting and can make the active child even more active, some games, on the other hand, can play a structuring part and also an educational one in the case of ADHD. *Tetris*, for example, a spatial jigsaw puzzle on the computer, can stimulate making connections from left to right in the brain and thus improve the thinking and the capacity to concentrate (Delfos 2003).

Children with ADHD often have the experience that the people around them make all sorts of remarks which are aimed at cautioning the child. The child often does not listen to them because in his experience things usually go well; what the adult is saying then does not sound right. Moreover, children with ADHD are fairly indifferent towards failing. They are not easily discouraged and their *frustration tolerance* in activities is low. Because they are constantly restless, they would rather have everything fast, with a few misses in between, than slow with fewer misses. Children with ADHD are therefore not easily motivated to do things more slowly. Just like another person feels unhappy when there is commotion, a child with ADHD feels unhappy if it has to do things slowly. It can, however, be sensitive to the effects this has on other people.

> A girl with ADHD wanted to do one activity after another during play therapy – everything in a hurry and in a slapdash manner. The therapist tended to go with the pace and felt unpleasant doing that. She explained smiling, 'I'm trying now to do it as fast as you, but I don't have ADHD, so I get nervous from it.' The child was beaming – now her ADHD was an advantage instead of a disadvantage. A few sessions later the therapist was doing something in a hurry and the girl said, very matter-of-fact, 'Take it easy, otherwise you will become nervous.'

These and similar interventions taught her that her ADHD was not always a disadvantage for herself, but could make the people around her restless. She also learned that at a slower pace she could achieve better results. She was told:

> You want a lot very quickly, and that is fine. We've now made a nice doll and you can take it with you now. But you always want to finish everything in one go. That's a pity, because you can make such nice things, and if you take two appointments to do it instead of one, it will become even prettier. The doll is a little messy now.

The girl started to enjoy taking more care of the end result. She was given the opportunity to decide herself whether she wanted to finish a lot of things quickly or take some more time and make fewer but prettier things. After some time she was proud of the fact that she was able to take more time to do something.

A child has to learn to interpret reactions of other people to its behaviour. A big problem with that is the interaction with peers. The child with ADHD needs help with this. The disturbing, chaotic behaviour can deter peers. They do not want to play with the child any more. This is hurtful for the *prosocial* child with ADHD. It needs handles to give structure to the interaction with peers. A children's book about ADHD can be useful for that (Delfos 2001b).

No matter how professional the help is, it still remains very tiring for parents to raise a child with ADHD. In order to prevent burn-out, it is therefore necessary that the parents have people around them who help to take care of the child, for example by staying over. A network for such a family helps to keep the family together. The problem with other people who help can be that the child does not show the behaviour in this situation, due to the fact that it is a new situation that needs attention and the attention function is therefore sharpened. The hyperactive and impulsive behaviour therefore goes into the background. This sometimes means that other people, totally unjustly, point to the parents as the guilty parties for the behaviour. The child does not show the behaviour when it is with them and does when it is with the parents.

Childrearing attitude and techniques

Based on the elements that play a part with ADHD it is possible to give practical instructions about the attitude which is suitable with regard to the child with ADHD. In addition to medication, if any, a number of consequences for childrearing techniques and treatment aspects can be mentioned for the various symptoms: hyperactivity, impulsivity and concentration disorder. Many of the stated attitudes and childrearing techniques are not only suitable for children with ADHD, but can also be used in general.

Attitude

When we are dealing with the undesired behaviour of a child, it is important that the parents and child become *allies* instead of opponents. Adults often have the idea that the child shows the behaviour on purpose, even to annoy the adult. A child with ADHD has little control over his behaviour and does things to a large extent without directing it. The child himself is also overwhelmed by his own behaviour. The parent's attitude is important to the child. It influences the child's *self-image*. A parent who responds negatively to the child will give the child the feeling that the child is not good, not wanted.

> Martin, a hyperactive, enterprising child, had many conflicts with his parents. At school everything went wrong as well. Beneath his tough behaviour was a particularly negative self-image. With the help of his therapist he managed to tell his parents his deepest fear: 'You would prefer to have the neighbours' son Josh as your child instead of me.' Martin had been convinced of that for a very long time, because his parents were very taken with Josh, who was a quiet, serious boy.

Parents can be important in teaching the child to structure his behaviour, but the contact between parents and child has to be good for that to happen. The child, however, has an *effect on his parents*. A baby who cries a lot has a different effect on his parents from a smiling one. A child that keeps having fights with his peers and has conflicts at school can make his parents feel down-hearted. The child also has an *effect on other children*. Peers often have trouble with the child with ADHD because he disrupts their game and is busy. The pluckiness and good ideas on the other hand are very popular.

An attitude of *respect* towards the child, and *acceptance* of the fact that the child would also like to change his behaviour, ensures that parents and child can become allies and that the warmth between them can flow again. Respect does not mean that everything is approved. Bad behaviour is bad behaviour. Respect means that you do not accept bad behaviour, but at the same time do not condemn the child. Respect means interpersonal warmth. The *attachment* between parents and child will be repaired because of that.

Childrearing techniques

With childrearing, the *attention* the child gets is of the utmost importance. Young children in particular are active in mobilising their parents' attention. Childrearing means *giving structure and setting limits* for the child. Setting limits and giving structure are an important support for the child with ADHD (without co-morbidity with the externalising conduct disorder). It takes some time before these things catch on with the child and it is therefore necessary to *persevere consistently* for some time. A basis of *justice* is of great importance with that. Children with ADHD in particular feel short-changed, because they already get so much negative attention. Giving *appreciation, confirmation* and *positive physical contact* has a favourable effect on the child. Punishment, as we have already seen, does not help to teach new behaviour, whereas appreciation and *reward* on the other hand do, and stopping the behaviour can in fact be accomplished by means of *ignoring the undesired behaviour.* That especially is extremely difficult in the case of children with ADHD as the behaviour imposes itself and the environment can hardly ignore it. Nevertheless, it is important to realise that all the attention which is paid to the behaviour will amplify the behaviour instead of diminishing it.

In order to avoid irritations is it wise to *make the house ADHD-friendly.* That means, for example, that breakable objects are put away – the same thing we do with toddlers and pre-schoolers.

In order to direct his behaviour, it is necessary that the child learns to *put his thoughts and feelings into words.* Parents can play an important part here. Parents do have to realise that when they explain something, this only makes sense when they *link up to where the child is* and not explain it from how they themselves understand it.

Because sleep is so important and children with ADHD often have trouble sleeping, notably settling in and sleeping through, a *sleep management programme* is important. The sleep ritual with children with ADHD has to be longer and more extensive than with other children. In order to increase the child's *self-confidence, stimulating the ability to cope* and *giving responsibility* which the child can manage is of great importance.

Because the child has had to suppress his restlessness at school for a long time, it is necessary that he *can blow off steam after school.* It is wise to teach the child to make time for that, instead of getting into conflicts because he is so active. Doing homework should definitely not take place immediately after school, but later in the day.

In view of the genetic factor with ADHD, the odds are that there is an *experienced expert* in the family who could give advice about what helped him to deal with it.

Living with a child with ADHD is often very tiring for a family. It follows from this, that it is sensible *to let other family members and friends help*, by taking care of the child for a while. It is then of great importance that they understand the child's behaviour and not point an accusing finger at the parents.

Because the rearing of a child with ADHD demands a lot from parents, it is sensible to ask for support, like video-home training or other forms of childrearing support.

Treatment for the various symptoms

Hyperactivity

Underneath hyperactivity often lies *anxiety*, and suppressing the activity can make the child more agitated. It is therefore better not to let the child sit still for too long, but *alternate sitting still with moving*.

The child with ADHD can, when he does his best, temporarily suppress his hyperactivity and impulsivity. Because he can only suppress his behaviour for short periods of time and not structurally, it is sensible to teach the child to *'cool it' effectively*. That means to say that it is discussed with the child in what situations extra effort to quieten down will be employed but also extra time to blow off steam. An example where cooling it effectively can be important is *interaction with peers*. At the end of primary school it is learned to a certain degree how to enter into relations later. Striking up friendships influences the forming of relationships later. It is therefore an important subject to pay attention to.

With the help of *computer games* the child can learn to recognise when the activity in his body is mounting and how this can be recognised in time. Computer games can also conjure up excitement and in that way have a contrary effect. Not all games are suitable to practise with for the child with ADHD.

Both in order to generate movement, but also for the interaction with peers, *playing a sport* is an excellent occupation. Because the interaction with peers is not easy, these should be sports that do not require too much team spirit. Looking for a *physical activity* which the child can always engage in when it needs to can have a preventative effect on aggression. It is therefore important *to let the child run around after doing something difficult*, because the tension will increase the hyperactivity. *Stress balls or a comboloi* (a chaplet that is also used as a prayer chain) can help to let go of some unrest in the body inconspicuously. Pinching stress balls or playing with the comboloi means 'using' adrenaline; they are a kind of action. This helps to diminish the level of adrenalinee and as a result the level of anxiety is diminished (see Chapter 3).

Impulsivity

The idea of the 'candy reward' that I mentioned in Chapter 6 can be used to *teach the child to postpone something*. The child has difficulty planning, and learning how to plan is therefore important. The process of *shaping* can be helpful when teaching how to plan. *Behaviour therapy* is a good aid with impulsivity to let the child experience that postponing activities can lead to good results. The same goes for the result of improving by persevering. Here too, a behaviour therapeutic approach can be helpful.

Concentration disorder

Because the memory works best through *emotional congruence* it is necessary to bring the child into a *positive mood* in combination with positive activities. Having tasks executed in a positive mood will teach the child that concentration lies within his reach and motivate him to bring this about himself more often. In order to achieve the neural connections *repetition* is necessary for the child with ADHD.

Also *music* and *computer games* can help to further concentration. I mentioned, for example, the game of *Tetris* that works on furthering concentration.

Hyperactivity as a conduct problem

When we are dealing with hyperactivity on its own, not as a symptom of ADHD, then the professional help should be specifically tuned to this problem. That means to say that the aim is not so much looking for ways of controlling, managing or suppressing hyperactivity, but finding the source of the behaviour. I have already stated that the first reason for this behaviour can be that the child has a problem with which it is struggling. This can be a traumatic experience: physical abuse by a parent, the divorce of parents, a wrong choice of school, a removal, the loss of a friend and there are many more examples. In such cases it is necessary to work on the source of the behaviour. The source makes the child afraid, and with some children this will result in the child becoming hyperactive in order to remove the anxiety, as is explained in the anxiety model. It will not always be possible to remove the source of the behaviour, but teaching the child to deal with the source and to process the problems can calm the child, or rather let the child come to itself, and in this way develop itself at its own pace.

A completely different source for hyperactive behaviour is when the lifestyle of the child, of the family where the child grows up, is such that the child has to do everything at an accelerated pace. In that case the entire childrearing structure will have to change in order to steer the child's behaviour and its development to a quieter path.

With hyperactivity caused by environmental factors the professional help should be different from that with ADHD. It should be not so much aimed at controlling the behaviour or teaching the child to cope with the behaviour, but at taking the behaviour away by working on its source. When the behaviour has started to lead its own life, independent of the source, it is necessary and possible to unlearn the behaviour by means of behaviour therapy. The hyperactive behaviour of the child means basically that the source is still active and this activity will only decrease when the source is actually gone, under control or processed.

Psychiatric or educational help?

A child with ADHD, especially the combination form, is hard to keep at home. It requires a lot of educational capacity of the parents. This applies even more strongly when there is co-morbidity with conduct difficulties. When the child cannot live at home, then being brought up in a foster home is usually also not feasible. We then end up with a residential setting. This can be both psychiatric and remedial educational. The psychiatric setting is, especially with co-morbidity with the externalising disorder, the most advised. In these settings more attention will be paid to the predisposition of the child. The community in psychiatric settings is generally smaller than in remedial educational settings. This means that the child will be confronted less with activity, with stimuli around him. An educational setting will only be able to offer help to the child when the child's predisposition is taken as a starting point and the child is helped to cope with its predisposition, rather than the help being based on the idea that the problems will disappear by means of a structured childrearing. Nevertheless, a psychiatric setting will often refer to a remedial educational setting because of the way in which the child gets into conflict with the environment. Just as with the externalising conduct disorder, it also applies to ADHD that the behaviour comes so much to the foreground that there is a tendency to offer help with regard to behaviour in the sense of an educational setting rather than psychiatric help. In addition, the problem arises that the number of places in psychiatric settings is too small to be able to help the number of children with ADHD.

Here it also applies, just as with the externalising conduct disorder, that a combined treatment, as becomes possible in a remedial psychiatric setting, is preferred.

If it is a matter of hyperactivity and not ADHD, a residential setting will then only be helpful when the source of the behaviour cannot be treated otherwise than through placement in care. We are then dealing with a conduct problem and not a disorder (see the information on the treatment of conduct problems in Chapter 11).

Who does what in professional help?

Especially when we are dealing with ADHD-combination form a combination of help is necessary: psychiatric help, if necessary, for the medication, psychological help for (cognitive) behaviour therapy or psychotherapy, and educational help for the family. In addition it is important, in connection with the risk of burn-out, to form a *network* around the family where other people can take over the care of the child for short periods. Staying over regularly at other members of the family's homes and relief in the neighbourhood can help parents to get their breath back. There exist 'staying-over houses' where children with ADHD can stay for a while, giving them the opportunity to experience other things and unburdening the family for a while. The child with ADHD often functions a little more easily during the relatively short time of a stay over. It is important that the network around the child is also familiar with the child's problems. When people involved have the idea that the child only functions badly at home because the parents are not bringing it up properly, they will form a psychological burden for the parents instead of a help to them.

In therapy the child will have to be helped with various attention areas: learning how to cope with having a disorder; learning how to avoid stimuli; learning to lower the pace; learning how to plan; and learning how to interact with peers.

When we are dealing with co-morbidity with conduct difficulties, then the help will have to be combined with the help for the specific conduct difficulties (see Chapter 9).

To conclude I have set out the treatment aspects for ADHD in Table 12.1.

Summary

ADHD, Attention Deficit-Hyperactivity Disorder, is a disorder where the child has trouble with regulating his hyperactive and impulsive behaviour and directing his attention. The processing of stimuli does not happen optimally and the short-term memory works inadequately. This causes the child to be hindered in its social and intellectual functioning. Concentration is poor, causing the child to function badly at school. Especially in the combination form the effect of this disorder is major. Education, medication and behaviour therapeutic techniques are of great importance for the help given to the child. Parents need to be helped to cope with their child's disorder. In addition, it is also important to prevent the parents from becoming exhausted. They need to have a network of people around them who help to care for the child.

Apart from the hyperactivity which forms a symptom of ADHD, there exists also hyperactivity as an expression of problems or as a result of the accelerated pace of living in which the child exists. In the case of hyperactivity as expression it is necessary that the source of the behaviour is traced and removed if possible, or that the child learns to cope with the source or processes what it has gone through. When the hyperactivity is the result of a childrearing situation within which the child is growing up in an accelerated pace of living, the childrearing situation will have to change significantly in order to let the child get back to himself again and continue his development at his own pace and within his own capabilities.

Table 12.1 The treatment aspects for ADHD

Coping with the disorder

Medication, if necessary

Behaviour regulation:

- structure

- (cognitive) behaviour therapy

- psychotherapy

- behaviour contracts

Attention function:

- behaviour contracts

- feedback when there is contact

Impulsivity:

- learning to postpone satisfaction of needs

- learning to plan and order

Interacting with peers

Education and help for parents

Network around the family

Psychosomatics Model

In this appendix I introduce the psychosomatics model. It is the physical translation of the anxiety model, and in particular it is about what happens physically when the balance of hormones is disturbed. It is published for the first time here, though only in a brief summary.

I indicated in the anxiety model that the human body responds to danger with the production of hormones, but seeks a balance between adrenergic hormones like adrenlaline and androgenic ones like testosterone. I mentioned these two because they are the most important representatives. These hormones are thought to be related to the behaviour components 'being able to take action' and 'actually taking action'. I mentioned earlier the difference in action that arises in the case of danger with men and women. Women prefer to look for safety, take care of the nest and nearest relations and talk to trusted people; men are more likely to react to the danger by fighting, fleeing or working for the nest, as a result of which the nest is protected against the outside world (Taylor *et al.* 2000). The women's behaviour is hormonally supported by oxytocin. Women, when taking action, often remain dependent on others to cope with the danger. They therefore run more of a risk that the substances are not sufficiently converted.

An important problem with the production of stress hormones is adrenaline. This hormone is necessary in order to take action, but at the same time this substance also has to be converted into action, otherwise there will be a toxic amount of adrenlaline in proportion to other substances. I take as a starting point the necessity for a balance with the amount of testosterone. Men have on average nine times as much testosterone in their body as women do (Bernards and Bouman 1993). They can therefore process more adrenaline than women. Women therefore produce less adrenaline than men. The body takes all sorts of measures to restrict the amount of adrenlaline and if necessary stop its production. The first way is to encourage the subject to take action. Even while sitting still the body will subconsciously start wriggling and trembling in order to lose excess adrenlaline when there is insufficient action.

We know the phenomenon where we bravely face danger, but afterwards start shaking. We have then produced more adrenlaline than necessary and the excess substances are converted into action. A second way is to sweat excess adrenlaline out of the body. The adrenlaline leaves the body through the pores. Cold sweat is an example of that.

When the production keeps increasing, the body, through cortisol as a *neurotransmitter* in the brain, will try to curb the production of adrenlaline. This is a paradoxical process, because at the same time the danger has not yet passed and the body will tend to stimulate the production and try, by means of adrenlaline at a *hormonal* level, to stimulate the action regarding the danger. In this way it is possible for there to be two contrary processes going on in the body at the same time: the attempt to keep the right balance between adrenlaline and other substances, and the necessity to produce adrenlaline in order to stimulate action. Testosterone could also be produced, and that does happen in situations which are exciting (Archer 1991); the problem is that the production of this basic hormone is so slow that it does not offer a fast solution. Testosterone is a very basic hormone that has many functions in the body, and the body will therefore, except when in danger, be aimed at having a stable amount of testosterone present. We can see this when testosterone can no longer be produced in the testicles because of castration. The body then starts to produce testosterone through other organs. That is why only chemical castration can stop the production of testosterone. However, large personality changes then take place, like listlessness and depression, and physical changes such as corpulence.

Our starting point is that there must be a balance between testosterone and adrenlaline. We can put this in a quotient, with the numerator being adrenlaline and the denominator being testosterone:

$$\frac{A}{T}$$

The numerator is adrenlaline because this fluctuates more easily than testosterone. In a healthy situation this quotient could be put at:

$$\frac{A}{T} = 1$$

With the help of this quotient we can measure for everyone personally what the right proportion of adrenlaline and testosterone is under normal circumstances. With men we can expect that the denominator and numerator are nine times higher than with women. When this quotient is available we can register a deviating situation. Being 'stressed' is then no longer 'between the ears', but can be measured. When people are under stress for a long period of time, their quotient will start to deviate.

When the balance is disturbed, the human being will notice this first in the behaviour. The activity of the adrenlaline takes on unpleasant forms and this is experienced as a feeling of agitation, of not being able to stop doing something. A phase later, physical symptoms arise, the *psychosomatic* conditions. We speak of psychosomatic conditions because they are not based on a physical, somatic deviation. It is now known that physical deviations can result from them and that long-term stress can have life-threatening consequences. Research showed that physically and sexually abused women had significantly more frequent chronic pain and complaints like fybromyalgia (Finestone *et al.* 2000). The stress reaction can reach a structurally high level, resulting in a general state of anxiety, alertness and physical complaints (Kendall-Tackett 2000).

The diseases that can arise depend on the nature of the disturbance of the balance. Too much adrenlaline in relation to testosterone has different consequences from too much testosterone in relation to adrenlaline. In the first case we might want to take action, but we cannot get round to doing it. In the second case we might get round to doing it, but we cannot perform the action. The latter is always a bit more difficult to understand. The example of an operation explains this. With an operation, when someone is put under anaesthetic, a lot of testosterone is produced by the body. During the anaesthetic and the period afterwards it is hard to take physical action.

In the psychosomatics model represented below in Figure A1.1 we can see the various problems fanned out according to the nature of how much the balance is disturbed. Which disease will break out depends on the physical constitution. The predisposition of the human being has its weak spots. If it is the muscular system then it is more likely that muscular problems will arise; if it is the heart then heart problems may arise. The digestive system is sensitive to any disturbance of the balance. There are two kinds of imbalance: too much adrenlaline for the testosterone available, or too much testosterone for the adrenlaline available:

$$\frac{A}{T} < 1 \text{ and } \frac{A}{T} > 1$$

The reaction of the body under stress is often the same as under a physical exertion. This makes it difficult to distinguish whether a complaint is caused by stress or whether it is based on an actual physical problem. This is an important breeding ground for anxiety. People who are suffering from stress will start to be bothered by physical complaints, which in turn can be a cause for fear of serious diseases. What follows is a simple example of how to cope with this. People who have heart palpitations are often scared that this has something to do with a heart condition. The heart is a muscle and this muscle does not register why it has to work, whether this is because of stress or a physical exertion. When it is a matter of a heart condition, the problem will always occur, both in the case of stress and in the case of a physical exertion. When it is a stress problem, the heart will, in principle, function normally during physical exertion. This normally means that the heart rate increases during exertion, without actual heart palpitations, and that after the exertion the heart rate recovers itself reasonably quickly, with a short period of irregularity in order to reach the average number of beats.

When we put the anxiety model and the psychosomatics model together, the message is clear: stress has consequences for emotional and physical conditions. The most effective thing to do is to take action in relation to the danger, and all kinds of action can help. Even vacuuming or pacing up and down temporarily decreases the anxiety. With many conditions like ME, RSI and tiredness, the tendency and the advice is to rest. However, this proves to weaken the situation rather than curing it. The conditions are a

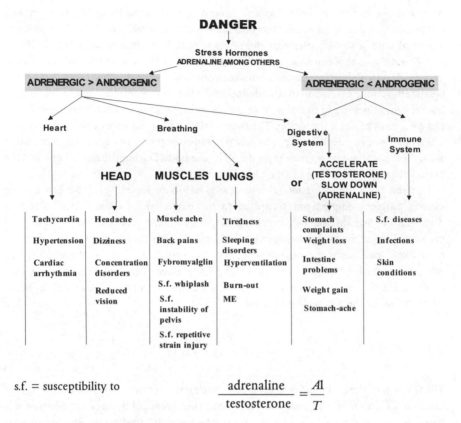

DANGER

↓

Stress Hormones
ADRENALINE AMONG OTHERS

ADRENERGIC > ANDROGENIC   **ADRENERGIC < ANDROGENIC**

Heart   Breathing   Digestive   Immune
                                       System   System

                                                    ACCELERATE
HEAD   MUSCLES LUNGS   or   **(TESTOSTERONE)**
                                              SLOW DOWN
                                             (ADRENALINE)

Tachycardia	Headache	Muscle ache	Tiredness	Stomach complaints	S.f. diseases
Hypertension	Dizziness	Back pains	Sleeping disorders	Weight loss	Infections
Cardiac arrhythmia	Concentration disorders	Fybromyalglin	Hyperventilation	Intestine problems	Skin conditions
	Reduced vision	S.f. whiplash	Burn-out	Weight gain	
		S.f. instability of pelvis	ME	Stomach-ache	
		S.f. repetitive strain injury			

s.f. = susceptibility to

$$\frac{\text{adrenaline}}{\text{testosterone}} = \frac{Al}{T}$$

Figure A1.1 The psychosomatics model

sign of a disturbance of the balance caused by a surplus of adrenalin, which means that the substances have to be converted in order to restore the balance.

The most important danger known to western people is the thought process. The danger is no longer a real bear on the road, but an imaginary one. A thought can conjure up stress, but a constructive thought is an action which reduces it. By experiencing the situation the stress may be varied. Influencing thoughts is therefore of the greatest importance. But sitting still causes problems rather than being helpful. When the situation has already worsened to a high degree, one can hardly force oneself to take action – this is the emotional condition of depression; nevertheless it is important to get the metabolism going again with the help of making small efforts.

Following on from the anxiety model we can see that women tend to act less than men. They will therefore be bothered more by these psychosomatic conditions. In addition, when they are suffering from these conditions they have the tendency to act less and therefore have more chance of the condition dragging on. Having a condition in itself creates stress again and ensures that the adrenergic mill keeps turning.

Behaviour Contract

Example of a behaviour contract

A behaviour contract should first of all be considered as a contract. That means that it should be reciprocal and demand the efforts of all concerned. With children a contract is easily formed as one-way traffic; the child has a task, the adult does not. In this example the child and the adult both have to make an effort and both are being reinforced:

> Janet is an only child. She has ADHD, is intelligent and is a hindrance to herself. She really wants to do well at school, but she cannot manage to show the desired behaviour and to spend sufficient time on her homework. She is resitting the first year of secondary school and is in danger of having to repeat the year again. The therapist who is treating her has drawn up a behaviour contract in consultation with her.

Behaviour contract for Father, Janet and Mother

The contract consists of two stages. When the first stage goes well, the second stage may start. If not, then this contract will lapse.

FIRST STAGE

'Hanging up your coat' has been chosen as the starting behaviour. This behaviour is limited, surveyable and easy to verify. It does not, however, appeal to Janet because it seems so trivial. She would prefer something that would make things better at school. Nevertheless, a simple start is necessary (reading starts with the alphabet).

DESCRIPTION

When Janet comes home from school she hangs up her coat on a coat hook. Because this is easy to verify this means in a practical sense: when her father or mother are at home, Janet will hang her coat on the coat hook; when her father or mother come home and Janet is already at home, then the coat will already be hanging on the coat hook. It is also acceptable if Janet accidentally hangs up her coat a bit later but before father or mother comes home. What it is all about in the end is that Janet learns to programme herself to think of something. Janet's father or mother will check this behaviour.

PERIOD

1 November until 28 November.

SCORE

For each school day that Janet hangs up her coat, she will get one point. If her father or mother forget to check and Janet points that out when she goes to bed, she will also get a point. Janet and her father or mother will check on the spot whether the coat is on the coat hook. For this she will get a point whether she has hung up her coat or not! If she did hang it up, she will get two. Both behaviours of Janet (thinking about hanging up her coat and thinking about whether her parents checked whether she has hung up her coat) ensure that she has to enter 'hang up coat' in her memory. In this way Janet can get a maximum of 40 points: 20 because she hung up her coat and 20 if her father and mother forgot to check it, while she did think about it.

Moving to the second stage takes place when Janet has obtained at least 17 points.

Her mother or father hangs a sheet of paper up at a convenient spot and on which the weeks are entered in squares next to or underneath each other. Janet makes a drawing to go with it so it also looks nice!

REWARD

The final reward is appreciation and access to the second stage.

No other reward is offered like money, a meal out or something similar. This reward has been chosen by Janet herself in consultation with her therapist. It is therefore important to respect this choice.

SECOND STAGE

This stage takes four school weeks and follows directly on from the first stage. The subject Janet chose for the second stage is the homework she has to do, in particular doing exercises, sums and the like. In a next stage learning the theory can be the subject. When the first stage has gone well, the next contract will be entered into.

No matter how childish this may seem, all three parties and the therapist sign this contract, so that it is clear that everyone is bound to it.

Therapist   Janet

Father   Mother

References and further reading

AACAP (American Academy of Child and Adolescent Psychiatry) (1998) 'Practice Parameters for the Assessment and Treatment of Children and Adolescents with Depressive Disorders.' *Journal of the American Academy of Child and Adolescent Psychiatry 37*, 10 (supplement), 635–835.

Aarden, L. (1997) (Personal Communication). Centraal Laboratorium van de Bloedtransfusiedienst van het Nederlandse Rode Kruis, Amsterdam.

Achenbach, T.M. (1978) 'The child behavior profile: I: Boys aged 6–11.' *Journal of Consulting and Clinical Psychology 46*, 478–488.

Achenbach, T.M. and Edelbrock, C.S. (1978) 'The classification of child psychopathology: a review and analysis of empirical efforts.' *Psychological Bulletin 85*, 1275–1301.

Acker, J. van (1995) *Gedrags- en opvoedingsproblemen*. Houten/Diegem: Bohn Stafleu van Loghem.

Adelson, J. (ed) (1980) *Handbook of Adolescent Psychology*. New York: Wiley.

Ainsworth, M.D.S. and Bell, S.M. (1970) 'Attachment, exploration, and separation: illustrated by the behavior of one-year-olds in a strange situation.' *Child Development 41*, 49–67.

Ainsworth, M.D.S., Blehar, M.C., Waters, E. and Wall, S. (1978) *Patterns of Attachment: A Psychological Study of the Strange Situation*. Hillsdale-NJ: Erlbaum.

Albert, D.J., Walsh, M.L. and Jonik, R.H. (1993) 'Aggression in humans: What is its biological foundation?' *Neuroscience and Biobehavioral Reviews 17*, 4, 405–425.

American Psychiatric Association (1994) *DSM-IV. Diagnostic and Statistical Manual of Mental Disorders*. Washington DC: American Psychiatric Association.

American Psychiatric Association (2000) Diagnostic and Statistical Manual of Mental Disorders, Fourth Edition, Text revision. Washington DC: American Psychiatric Association.

Amstislavskaya, T.G., Osadchuk, A.V. and Naumenko, E.V. (1990) 'Pathways of activation and change of the endocrine function of testes elicited by effect of presence of the female.' *Neuroscience and Behavioral Physiology 20*, 6, 549–552.

Angold, A., Costello, E.J., Erkanli, A. and Worthman, C.M. (1999) 'Pubertal changes in hormone levels and depression in girls.' *Psychological Medicine 29*, 5, 1043–1053.

ANP (2000) 'Makers Ritatlin voor de rechter in Texas gesleept ' *De Volkskrant*, 16 May 2000.

Archer, J. (1991) 'The influence of testosterone on human aggression.' *British Journal of Psychology 82*, 1, 1–28.

Archer, J. (1994) 'Testosterone and aggression.' *Journal of Offender Rehabilitation 21*, 3, 3–26.

Arntz, A. and Bögels, S. (1995) 'Cognitieve therapie bij angststoornissen: een overzicht.' In J.A. den Boer and H.G.M. Westenberg *Leerboek Angststoornissen. Een neurobiologische benadering.* Utrecht: de Tijdstroom.

Asher, S.A. and Gottman, M. (eds) (1981) *The Development of Children's Friendships.* Cambridge: Cambridge University Press.

Asperger, H. (1944/1991) '"Autistic psychopathy" in childhood.' In U. Frith (ed) *Autism and Asperger Syndrome.* Cambridge: Cambridge University Press.

Baird, J., Stevenson, J.C. and Williams, D.C. (2000) 'The evolution of ADHD: a disorder of communication?' *The Quarterly Review of Biology. 75*, 1, 17–35.

Bakker-Brouwer, A. and van Wieringen-Kemps, J.B.M. (1991) 'Gordon communicatietraining voor jongeren van 12–20 jaar.' In A.M.L. Collot d'Escury-Koenigs, T. Engelen-Snaterse and L. J.Tijhuis *Gelukkig op school? Emotionele stoornissen en het functioneren op school.* Lisse: Swets and Zeitlinger.

Balans (1994) *Doe normaal. Over MBD/ADHD.* Bilthoven: Balans, landelijke vereniging voor gedrags- en leerproblemen.

Bancroft, J. (1991) 'Reproductive hormones.' In M. Rutter and P. Casaer (eds) *Biological Risk Factors for Psychosocial Disorders.* Cambridge: Cambridge University Press.

Bandura, A. (1965) 'Influence of Model's reinforcement contingencies on the acquisition of imitative responses.' *Journal of Personality and Social Psychology I,* 589–595.

Bandura, A. (1974) *Principles of Behavior Modification.* New York: Holt, Rinehart and Winston.

Banks, T. and Dabbs, J.M. Jr. (1996) 'Salivary testosterone and cortisol in a delinquent and violent urban subculture.' *Journal of Social Psychology 136,* 1, 49–56.

Barkley, R.A. (1995) *Taking Charge of ADHD.* New York: The Guilford Press.

Baron-Cohen, S., Ring, H.A., Wheelwright, S., Bullmore, E.T., Brammer, M.J., Simmons, A. and Williams, S.C. (1999) 'Social intelligence in the normal and autistic brain: an fMRI study.' *European Journal of Neuroscience 11,* 6, 1891–1898.

Barrett, S., Beck, J.C., Bernier, R. Bisson, E., Braun, T.A., Casavant, T.L., Childress. D., Folstein, S.E., Garcia, M., Gardiner, M.B., Gilman, S., Haines, J.L., Hopkins, K., Landa, R., Meyer, N.H., Mullane, J.A., Nishimura, D.Y., Palmer, P., Piven, J., Purdy, J., Santangelo, S.L., Searby, C., Sheffield, V., Singleton, J. and Slager, S. (1999) 'An autosomal genomic screen for autism: Collaborative linkage study of autism.' *American Journal of Medical Genetics 15,* 88, 6, 609–615.

Bartels, A. and Heiner, H. (1994) 'De condities voor optimale ontwikkeling.' *Jeugd en Samenleving 5,* 282–295.

Bates, J.E. and Bayles, K. (1987) 'Objective and subjective components in mothers' perceptions of their children from age 6 months to 3 years.' *Merrill-Palmer Quarterly 30,* 2, 111–130.

Bauman, M.L. (1996) 'Brief report: neuroanatomic observations of the brain in pervasive developmental disorder.' *Journal of Autistic Developmental Disorder 26,* 2, 199–203.

Bauman, M.L. and Kemper, T.L. (1994) 'The neuroanatomy of the brain in autism.' In M.L. Bauman and T.L. Kemper (eds) *The Neurobiology of Autism.* Baltimore: Johns Hopkins University Press.

Baumeister, R.F. (1997) *Evil: Inside Human Violence and Cruelty.* New York: Freeman.

Baxter, L. (1996) 'The mind–brain connection.' *Psychology Today*, July/August, 18.

Beck, A.T. (1985) *Anxiety Disorders and Phobias*. New York: Basic Books.

Beck, A.T. (1989) *Love is Never Enough*. New York: HarperPerennial.

Benton, D. (1992) 'Hormones and human aggression.' In K. Bjorkqvist and P. Niemela (eds) *Of Mice and Women: Aspects of Female Aggression*. San Diego: Academic Press.

Berenbaum, S.A. and Hines, M. (1992) 'Early androgens are related to childhood sex-typed toy preferences.' *Psychological Science 3*, May, 3, 203–206.

Bergman, B. and Brismar, B. (1994) 'Hormone levels and personality traits in abusive and suicidal male alcoholics.' *Alcoholism, Clinical and Experimental Research 18*, 2, 311–316.

Bernards, J.A. and Bouman, L. N. (1993) *Fysiologie van de mens*. Vierde herziene druk. Utrecht/Antwerpen: Bohn, Scheltema & Holkema.

Berne, E. (1996) *Games people play. The Basic Handbook of Transactional Analysis*. New York: Ballantine Books.

Bernhardt, P.C., Dabbs, J.M. Jr, Fielden, J.A. and Lutter, C.D. (1998) 'Testosterone changes during vicarious experiences of winning and losing among fans at sporting events.' *Physiology and Behavior 65*, 1, 59–62.

Biddulph, S. (1998) *Raising Boys. Why boys are different and how to help them to become happy and well-balanced men*. Berkeley, CA: Celestial Arts.

Birmaher, B., Ryan, D., Williamson, D., Brent, D., Kaufman, J., Dahl, R., Perel, J. and Nelson, B. (1996) 'Childhood and adolescent depression: a review of the past 10 years. Part I.' *Journal of the American Academy of Child and Adolescent Psychiatry 35*, 1427–1439.

Boszornemyi-Nagy, I. and Spark, G. (1973) *Invisible Loyalties*. New York: Hoeber & Harper.

Bower, G.H. (1981) 'Mood and Memory'. *Psychology Today*, June.

Bower, G.H. and Sivers, H. (1998) 'Cognitive impact of traumatic events.' *Developmental Psychopathology 10*, 4, 625–653.

Bowerman, C.E. and Kinch, J.W. (1969) 'Changes in family and peer orientation of children between the fourth and tenth grades.' In M. Gold and E. Douvan (eds) *Adolescent Development*. Boston: Allyn & Bacon.

Bowlby, J. (1979) *The Making and Breaking of Affectional Bonds*. London: Tavistock.

Bowlby, J. (1984) *Attachment and Loss: Volume I, Revised Edition*. London: Penguin Books.

Bowlby, J. (1988) *A Secure Base: Clinical Applications of Attachment Theory*. London: Routledge.

Bowlby, J. (1990) *Charles Darwin. A New Life*. New York/London: W.W. Norton & Company.

Braams, R. (1999) 'Stop Jimmy, denk na! Omstreden peppil helpt rusteloze kinderen.' *Intermediair 35*, 18, 25–27.

Bradford, J.M.W. (1988) 'Organic treatment for the male sexual offender.' In R.A. Prentky and V.L. Quinsey (eds) *Human Sexual Aggression: Current Perspectives*. Annals of the New York Academy of Sciences, 528, 193–202. New York: New York Academy of Sciences.

Brezinka, V. (1995) 'Sekseverschillen in diagnostiek en behandeling. Coronaire hartziekten als voorbeeld.' *de Psycholoog*, 1995–7/8, 305.

Brower, K.J. (1992) 'Anabolic steroids: addictive, psychiatric, and medical consequences.' *American Journal on Addictions 1*, 2, 100–114.

Buck, R. and Ginsburg, B. (1997) 'Communicative genes and the evolution of empathy.' In W. Ickes (ed) *Empathic Accuracy*. New York/London: Guilford Press.

Buitelaar, J.K. (ed) (1993) *Diagnostiek en behandeling van ADHD 91–105*. Utrecht: Stichting Onderwijs en Voorlichting.

Buitelaar, J.K. (1994) *Kinderen en hyperactiviteit*. Amsterdam: Kosmos-Z&K.

Buitelaar, J. (2000) 'Open-label treatment with risperdone of 26 psychiatrically hospitalized children and adolescents with mixed diagnoses and aggressive behavior.' *Journal of Child and Adolescent Psychopharmacology 10*, 1, 19–26.

Buitelaar, J.K., Huizink, A.C., Mulder, P.G., De Medina, P.G. and Visser, G.H. (2003) 'Prenatal stress and cognitive development and temperament in infants.' *Neurobiological Aging 24*, 1, 53–60.

Burke, H.L. and Yeo, R.A. (1994) 'Systematic variations in callosal morphology: The effects of age, gender, hand preference, and anatomic asymmetry.' *Neuropsychology 8*, 4, 563–571.

Campbell, S.B., Szumowski, E.K., Ewing, L.J., Gluck, D.S. and Breaux, A.M. (1992) 'A multi-dimensional assessment of parent-identified behavior problem toddlers.' *Journal of Abnormal Child Psychology 10*, 569–592.

Castellanos, F.X., Giedd, J.N., Marsh, W.L., Hamburger, S.D., Vaituzis, A.C., Dickstein, D.P., Sarfatti, S.E., Vauss, Y.C., Snell, J.W., Lange, N., Kaysen, D., Krain, A.L., Ritchie, G.F., Rajapakse, J.C. and Rapoport, J.L. (1996) 'Quantative brain magnetic resonance imaging in attention-deficit hyperactivity disorder.' *Archives of General Psychiatry 53*, 7, 607–616.

Chambers, J., Ames, R.S., Bergsma, D., Muir, A., Fitzgerald, L.R., Hervieus, G., Dytko, G.M., Foley, J.J., Martin, J., Wu-Schyong Liu, Park, J., Elles, C., Ganguly, S., Konchar, S., Cluderays, J., Leslies, R., Wilson, S. and Saraull, H.M. (1999) 'Melanin-concentrating hormone is the cognate ligand for the orphan G-protein-coupled receptor SLC-1.' *Nature 400*, 15 July, 262–265.

Clarke, J.M. and Zaidel, E. (1994) 'Anatomical-behavioral relationships: corpus callosum morphometry and hemispheric specialization.' *Behavioural Brain Research 64*, 1–2, 185–202.

Clarke, M. (1990) *The Disruptive Child: A Handbook of Care and Control*. Plymouth: Northcote House.

CMR-Nijmegen (1997, 2000) Continue Morbiditeits Registratie Regio Nijmegen van de Vakgroep Huisartsengeneeskunde, Sociale Geneeskunde en Verpleeghuisgeneeskunde van de Katholieke Universiteit Nijmegen. [Continuous Registration of Illnesses.] Published by H. van de Hoogen and H. Bor.

Coe, C.L., Hayashi, K.T. and Levine, S. (1988) 'Hormones and behavior at puberty: Activation or concatenation? Development during the transition to adolescence.' In M.R. Gunnar and W.A. Collins (eds) *Minnesota Symposia on Child Psychology 21*, 17–41. Hillsdale: Lawrence Erlbaum Associates.

Coles, M.G.P., Donchin, E. and Porges, S.W. (1986) *Psychophysiology: Systems, Processes, and Applications*. New York: Guilford Press.

Collot d'Escury-Koenings, A. (1998) 'Met de ogen van een kleuter.' In A. Collot d'Escury-Koenings, T. Snaterse and E. Mackaay-Cramer (eds) *Sociale vaardigheidstrainingen voor kinderen. Indicaties, effecten & knelpunten.* Lisse: Swets & Zeitlinger.

Conger, J.J. and Petersen, A.C. (1984) *Adolescence and Youth: Psychological Development in a Changing World.* New York: John Wiley & Sons.

Constant, D. and Ruther, H. (1996) 'Sexual dimorphism in the human corpus callosum? A comparison of methodologies.' *Brain Research 727*, 1–2, 99–106.

Constantino, J.N., Grosz, D., Saenger, P., Chandler, D.W., Nandi, R. and Earls, F.J. (1993) 'Testosterone and aggression in children.' *Journal of the American Academy of Child and Adolescent Psychiatry 32*, 6, 1217–1222.

Cornelissen, P.L., Hansen, P.C., Hutton, J.L., Evangelinou, V. and Stein, J.F. (1998) 'Magnocellular visual function and children's single word reading.' *Vision Research 38*, 3, 471–482.

Csikszentmihalyi, M. (1996) *Creativity. Flow and the Psychology of Discovery and Invention.* New York: Harper Collins

Cyranowski, J.M., Frank, E., Young, E. and Shear, M.K. (2000) 'Adolescent onset of the gender difference in lifetime rates of major depression: a theoretical model.' *Archives of General Psychiatry 57*, 1, 21–27.

Dabbs, J.M. (1990) 'Age and seasonal variation in serum testosterone concentration among men.' *Chronobiology International 7*, 3, 245–249.

Dabbs, J.M. (1992a) 'Testosterone measurements in social and clinical psychology.' Special Issue: Social psychophysiology. *Journal of Social and Clinical Psychology 11*, 3, 302–321.

Dabbs, J.M. (1992b) 'Testosterone and occupational achievement.' *Social Forces 70*, 3, 813–824.

Dabbs, J.M. Jr. (1993) 'Salivary testosterone measurements in behavioral studies: Saliva as a diagnostic fluid.' In D. Malamud and L.A. Tabak (eds) *Annals of the New York Academy of Sciences 694*, 177–183. New York: New York Academy of Sciences.

Dabbs, J.M. (1997) 'Testosterone, smiling, and facial appearance.' *Journal of Nonverbal Behavior 21*, 1, 45-55.

Dabbs, J.M. and Hargrove, M.F. (1997) 'Age, testosterone, and behavior among female prison inmates.' *Psychosomatic Medicine 59*, 5, 477–480.

Dabbs, J.M. and Hopper, C.H. (1990) 'Cortisol, arousal, and personality in two groups of normal men.' *Personality and Individual Differences 11*, 931–935.

Dabbs, J.M., Hopper, C.H. and Jurkovic, G.J. (1990) 'Testosterone and personality among college students and military veterans.' *Personality and Individual Differences 11*, 12, 1263–1269.

Dabbs, J.M., Jurkovic, G.J. and Frady, R.L. (1991) 'Salivary testosterone and cortisol among late adolescent male offenders.' *Journal of Abnormal Child Psychology 19*, 4, 469–478.

Dabbs, J.M. Jr., La Rue, D. and Williams, P.M. (1990) 'Testosterone and occupational choice: actors, ministers, and other men.' *Journal of Personality and Social Psychology 59*, 6, 1261–1265.

Dabkowska, M. and Rybakowski, J.K. (1997) 'Increased allergic reactivity of atopic type in mood disorders and schizophrenia.' *European Psychiatry 12*, 5, 249–254.

Dalton, K. (1961) 'Menstruation and crime.' *British Medical Journal 2*, 1752–1753.

Damasio, A.R. (1994) *Descartes' Error: Emotion, Reason and the Human Brain.* New York: Putnam.

Damasio, A. (1999) *The feeling of what happens. Body and emotion in the making of consciousness.* San Diego/New York/London: Harcourt

Damon, W. (1988) *The Moral Child: Nurturing Children's Natural Moral Growth.* New York/London: The Free Press.

Darwin, C. (1859/1979) *The Origin of Species.* New York/Avenel: Gramercy Books.

Darwin, C. (1872/1998) *The Expression of the Emotions in Man and Animals.* New York/Oxford: Oxford University Press.

Dasen, P., Berry, J.W. and Sartorius, N. (1992) *Cross-cultural Psychology and Health: Towards Applications.* London: Sage.

Dawkins, R. (1989) *The selfish gene.* Oxford: Oxford Press.

Dawson, G. and Fischer, K.W. (eds) (1994) *Human Behavior and the Developing Brain.* New York: Guilford Press.

Deater-Deckard, K. and Dodge, K.A. (1997) 'Externalizing behavior problems and discipline revisited: nonlinear effects and variation by culture, context, and gender.' *Psychological Inquiry 8*, 3, 161–175.

DeFries, J.C., Plomin, R. and Fulker, D.W. (1994) *Nature and Nurture During Middle Childhood.* Oxford/Cambridge: Blackwell.

Dekker, T. and Biemans, H. (1994) *Video-hometraining in gezinnen.* Houten/Zaventhem: Bohn Stafleu van Loghem.

Delfos, M.F. (1993) *Postpartum Mood Disturbances: The Menstrual and Emotional Cycle.* International Marcé Conference, November 1993.

Delfos, M.F. (1994a) 'De ontwikkeling van intimiteit. Een ontwikkelingspsychologisch model gekoppeld aan een model van de gevolgen van seksueel misbruik.' ['The development of intimacy. A developmental model together with a model of the consequences of sexual abuse.'] In *Tijdschrift voor Seksuologie 18*, 282–292.

Delfos, M.F. (1994b) 'Jij bent dood, daar krijg ik mooi 150 punten voor!' *Tijdschrift voor Jeugdhulpverlening en Jeugdwerk, TJJ*, September, 9–13.

Delfos, M.F. (1995) 'Metacognitie en lateraal denken' [Metacognition and Lateral Thinking. The Further House] *TJJ, Tijdschrift voor Jeugdhulpverlening en Jeugdwerk*, Januari/Februari, 51.

Delfos, M.F. (1996a) 'Jongens, de zorgenkindjes van de toekomst.' *Psychologie 15*, 16–17.

Delfos, M.F. (1996b) *Kinderen in ontwikkeling. Stoornissen en belemmeringen.* Lisse: Swets & Zeitlinger.

Delfos, M.F. (1997, 2003) *Kinderen en gedragsproblemen. Angst, agressie, depressie en ADHD. Een biopsychologisch model met richtlijnen soor diagnostick en behandeling.* Lisse: Swets & Zeitlinger.

Delfos, M.F. (1999a) *Ontwikkeling in vogelvlucht. Ontwikkeling van kinderen en adolescenten.* Lisse: Swets & Zeitlinger.

Delfos, M.F. (1999b) *Le parent insaisissable et l'urgence d'écrire.* Amsterdam: Rodopi.

Delfos, M.F. (1999c) *Kind in Ontwikkeling.* Cursusmap versie 1999. Utrecht: PICOWO.

Delfos, M.F. (2000a) *Are you listening to me? Communicating with children from four to twelve years old.* Amsterdam: SWP.

Delfos, M.F. (2000b) *Van alles twee. Over de betekenis van echtscheiding voor jonge kinderen.* Bussum: Trude van Waarden Produkties.

Delfos, M.F. (2001a) 'The developmental damage to children as a result of the violation of their rights.' In J.C.M. Willems (ed) *Developmental and Autonomy Rights of Children: Empowering Children, Caregivers and Communities.* Antwerpen/Groningen/Oxford: Intersentia.

Delfos, M.F. (2001b) *Ze vinden me druk. Over drukke kinderen en ADHD.* Bussum: Trude van Waarden Produkties.

Delfos, M.F. (2003) 'The conquered giant: The use of computers in play therapy.' In F.J. Maarse, A.E. Akkerman, A.N. Brand and L.J.M. Mulder (eds) *Computers in Psychology 7.* Lisse: Swets & Zeitlinger.

Delfos, M. F. (2004a) *A Strange World – Autism, Asperger's Syndrome and PDD-NOS: A Guide for parents, professional carers, and people with ASDs.* London: Jessica Kingsley Publishers.

Delfos, M. F. (2004b) *De schoonheid van her verschil. Waarom mannen en vrouwen verschillend én hetzerfd zijn.* [The beauty of differene. Why men and women are different and the same] Lisse: Harcourt

Dennen, J.M.G. van der (ed) (1992) *The Nature of the Sexes: The Sociobiology of Sex Differences and the Battle of the Sexes.* Groningen: Origin Press.

Descartes, R. (1633/1963) *Oeuvres philosophiques (1618–1637). Tome I, textes établis, présentés et annotés par Ferdinand Alguié.* Paris: Garnier.

Dijk, W.K. van (1979) 'de miskende alcoholist.' *Ned. Tijdschrift Geneesk 123,* 2, 1228–1236.

Doef, P. van der (ed) (1995) *Psychopathologie van kinderen en jeugdhulpverlening.* Utrecht: SWP.

Dolto, F. (1985) *La cause des enfants.* Paris: Laffont.

Donovan, B.T. (1985) *Hormones and Human Behaviour: The Scientific Basis of Psychiatry.* Cambridge: CUP.

Doornen, L. van (1999) *Stress: Mind and Body.* Utrecht: Universiteit Utrecht.

Doornen, L. van (2000) 'Stress: mind the body.' *De Psycholoog 35,* 3, 114–118.

Dorelijers, T.A.H. and Schornagel, W.H.L. (1996) 'Medicatie bij antisociale gedragsstoornissen en agressieregulatiestoornissen.' In F. Verhey and F.C. Verhulst (ed) *Kinder- en jeugdpsychiatrie. Behandeling en begeleiding III.* Assen: van Gorcum.

Dorion, A.A., Chantome, M., Hasboun, D., Zouaoui, A., Marsault, C., Capron, C. and Duyme, M. (2000) 'Hemispheric asymmetry and corpus callosum morphometry: a magnetic resonance imaging study.' *Neuroscience Research 36,* 1, 9–13.

Dumont, J.J. (1990) *Dyslexie.* Rotterdam: Lemniscaat.

Dumont, J.J. (1994) 'Van woordblindheid tot dyslexie.' *Tijdschrift voor Orthopedagogiek 2,* 47–51.

Dunn, A.J. (1995) 'Interactions between the nervous system and the immune system.' In F.E. Bloom and D.J. Kupfer (eds) *Psychopharmacology: The Fourth Generation of Progress.* New York: Raven Press.

Dunn, J. and Plomin, R. (1990) *Separate Lives: Why Siblings are so Different.* New York: Basic Books.

Duveen, G. and Lloyd, B. (1986) 'The significance of social identities.' *British Journal of Social Psychology 25,* 219–230.

Edelman, G.M. (1991) *Bright Air, Brilliant Fire: On the Matter of the Mind.* New York: Basic Books.

Eisenberg, N., Murphy, B.C. and Shepard, S. (1997) 'The development of empathic accuracy.' In W. Ickes *Empathic Accuracy.* New York/London: Guilford Press.

Ellis, A. (1973) *Humanistic Psychotherapy.* New York: McGraw-Hill.

Emmelkamp, P.M.G. (1995) 'Gedragstherapeutische behandeling van angststoornissen.' In J.A. den Boer and H.G.M. Westenberg *Leerboek Angststoornissen. Een neurobiologische benadering.* Utrecht: de Tijdstroom.

Eppink, A., Bok, I. and Taris, T. (1998) 'Sociaal vaardiger in een tweede cultuur.' In A. Collot d'Escury-Koenings, T. Snaterse and E. Mackaay-Cramer (ed) *Sociale vaardigheidstrainingen voor kinderen. Indicaties, effecten & knelpunten.* Lisse: Swets & Zeitlinger.

Erikson, E. (1968) *Identity and Crisis.* New York: Norton.

Evers, A. and Vliet-Mulder, J.C. van (1996) *Documentatie van Tests en testresearch in Nederland.* (COTAN) Nederlands Instituut van Psychologen. Assen/Maastricht: van Gorcum.

Federman, J. (1966) *Media Ratings: Design, Use and Consequences.* Studio City, CA: Mediascope.

Fedora, O. and Reddon, J.R. (1993) 'Psychopathic and nonpsychopathic inmates differ from normal controls in tolerance levels of electrical stimulation.' *Journal of Clinical Psychology 49,* 3, 326–331.

Felsenfeld, S. (1994) 'Developmental speech and language disorders.' In J.C. DeFries, R. Plomin and D.W. Fulker *Nature and Nurture During Middle Childhood.* Oxford/Cambridge: Blackwell.

Field, T. (1987) Quoted in Trottes, R.J. (1987) 'The play's the thing.' *Psychology Today,* January.

Finestone, H.M., Stenn, P., Davies, F., Stalker, C., Fry, R. and Koumanis, J. (2000) 'Chronic pain and health care utilization in women with a history of childhood sexual abuse.' *Child Abuse and Neglect 24,* 4, 547–556.

Fischer, K.W. and Rose, S.P. (1994) 'Dynamic development of coordination of components in brain and behavior: A framework for theory and research.' In G. Dawson and K.W. Fischer *Human Behavior and the Developing Brain.* New York: Guilford Press.

Fishbein, D.H. (1992) 'The psychobiology of female aggression.' *Criminal Justice and Behaviour 19,* 99–126.

Fisher, S.E., Marlow, A.J., Lamb, J., Maestrini, E., Williams, D.F., Richardson, A.J., Weeks, D.E., Stein, J.F. and Monaco, A.P. (1999) 'A quantative-trait locus on chromosome 6p influences different aspects of developmental dyslexia.' *American Journal of Human Genetics 64,* 1, 146–156.

Flaton, J., Hogerbrugge, M., van Haersma Buma, C. and Mocking, D. (1997) *Voeding en gedragsproblemen bij kinderen.* Amersfoort: NVAS.

Fraiberg, S.H. (1959) *The Magic Years: Understanding and Handling the Problems of Early Childhood.* New York: Scribner's.

Freud, A. and Burlingham, D. (1974) *Infants without Families and Reports on the Hampstead Nurseries 1939–1945.* London: Hogarth Press.

Freud, S. (1947) *Abriss der Psychoanalyse. Gesammelte Werke, Band XVII.* London: Imago.

Frey-Wettstein, M. and Cradock, C.G. (1970) 'Testosterone-induced deplation of thymus and marrow lymphocytes as related to lymphopoiesis and hematopoiesis.' *Blood 35,* 257–271.

Friedman, M.J., Charney, D.S. and Deutsch, A.Y. (eds) (1995) *Neurobiological and Clinical Consequences of Stress: From Normal Adaptation to Post-Traumatic Stress Disorder.* Philadelphia/New York: Lippincott-Raven.

Frith, U. (2003, 2nd edition) *Autism: Explaining the Enigma.* Cambridge: Basic Blackwell.

Fulker, W., Cherry, S.S. and Cardon, L.R. (1993) 'Continuity and change in cognitive development.' In R. Plomin and G.E. McClearn (eds) *Nature, Nurture and Psychology.* Washington DC: American Psychological Association.

Furbay, L. and Wilke, M. (1982) 'Some characteristics of infants' preferred toys.' *Journal of Genetic Psychology 141,* 207–210.

Gageldonk, A. and Bartels, A.A.J. (1990) *Evaluatie onderzoek op het terrein van de hulpverlening.* Leiden: Universiteit Leiden, Centrum Onderzoek Jeugdhulpverlening.

Galaburda, A.M. (ed) (1993) *Dyslexia and Development: Neurobiological Aspects of Extra-ordinary Brains.* Cambridge: Harvard University Press.

Galanter, M. (ed) (1995) *Recent Developments in Alcoholism, Vol. 12: Alcoholism and Women.* New York: Plenum Press.

Galjaard, H. (1994) *Alle mensen zijn ongelijk. de verschillen en overeenkomsten tussen mensen: hun erfelijke aanleg, gezondheid, gedrag en prestaties.* Amsterdam: Muntinga.

Garber, J. (1984) 'The developmental progression of depression in female chidren.' In D. Cicchetti and K. Schneider-Rosen (eds) *Childhood Depression.* San Francisco: Jossey-Bass.

Garmezy, N. (1987) 'Stress-resistant children: the search for protective factors.' In H. Groenendaal, R. Meijer, J.W. Veerman and J. Wit (ed) *Protectieve factoren in de ontwikkeling van kinderen en adolescenten.*

Gavaler, J.S. (1995) 'Alcohol effects on hormone levels in normal postmenopausal women and in postmenopausal women with alcohol-induced cirrhosis.' In M. Galanter (ed) *Recent Developments in Alcoholism, Vol. 12: Alcoholism and Women.* New York: Plenum Press.

Gay, P. (ed) (1964) *John Locke on Education.* New York: Bureau of Publications, Teacher's College, Columbia University.

Gayan, J., Smith, S.D., Cherny, S.S., Cardon, L.R., Fulker, D.W., Brower, A.M., Olson, R.K., Pennington, B.F. and DeFries, J.C. (1999) 'Quantative-trait locus for specific language and reading deficits on chromosome 6p.' *American Journal of Human Genetics 64,* 1, 157–164.

Gelder, X. van (1998) 'Klik en Go!' *de Volkskrant,* 10 September

Gent, T. van, Heijnen, C.J. and Treffers, P.D.A. (1997) 'Autism and the immune system.' *The Journal of Child Psychology and Psychiatry and Allied Disciplines 38,* 3, 337–349.

Geschwind, N. and Galaburda, A.M. (1984) *Cerebral Dominance: The Biological Foundations.* Cambridge, Massachusetts and London, England: Harvard University Press.

Geschwind, N. and Galaburda, A.M. (1987) *Cerebral Lateralization: Biological Mechanisms, Associations, and Pathology.* Cambridge: The MIT Press.

Geschwind, N. and Galaburda, A.M. (1995) 'Cerebral laterization, biological mechanisms, associations, and pathology I: A hypothesis and a program for research.' *Archive of Neurology 4*, 428–59.

Gesell, A. (1965) *Developmental Diagnosis: Normal and Abnormal Child Development: Clinical Methods and Pediatrics.* New York: Amatruda, Catherine Strunk.

Gesell, A. and Ilg, F. (1949) *Child Development.* New York: Harper and Row.

Gezondheidsraad, Advies van een commissie van de Gezondheidsraad (1997) *Dyslexie. Afbakening en behandeling.* Den Haag.

Giedd, J.N., Castellanos, F.X., Casey, B.J., Kozuch, P., King, A.C., Hamburger, M.A. and Rapoport, L. (1994) 'Quantitative morphology of the corpus callosum in attention deficit hyperactivity disorder.' *American Journal of Psychiatry 151*, 5, 665–669.

Gijsbers van Wijk, C.M.T., Huisman, H. and Kolk, A.M. (1999) 'Gender differences in physical symptoms and illness behavior. A health diary study.' *Social Science and Medicine 49*, 1061–1074.

Goldstein, A.P. (1973) *Structured Learning Therapy: Towards a Psychotherapy for the Poor.* New York: Academic Press.

Golombok, S. and Fyvush, R. (1994) *Gender Development.* Cambridge: Cambridge University Press.

Gomez, J. (1991) *Psychological and Psychiatric Problems in Men.* London/New York: Routledge.

Gordon, T. (1974) *P.E.T Parent Effectiveness Training: The tested new way to raise responsible children.* New York: Wyden.

Goudena, P.P., Groenendaal, H.J. and Swets-Gronert, F.A. (ed) (1988) *Kind in geding: bedreigende en beschermende factoren in de psychosociale ontwikkeling van kinderen.* Leuven: Acco.

Graaf-Tiemersma, M.J. de (1994) 'Verband niet rechtshandigheid, leesstoornissen en allergieën.' *Tijdschrift voor Orthopedagogiek*, 225–238.

Graaf-Tiemersma, M.J. de (1995) *Linkshandigheid en dyslexie. De testosteron-theorie voor cerebrale lateralisatie.* Utrecht: Proefschrift.

Graham, T. and Ickes, W. (1997) 'When women's intuition isn't greater than men's.' In W. Ickes (ed) *Empathic Accuracy.* New York/London: Guilford Press.

Granger, D.A., Weisz, J.R., McCracken, J.T., Kauneckis, D. and Ikeda, S.C. (1994) 'Testosterone and conduct problems.' *Journal of the American Academy of Child and Adolescent Psychiatry 33*, 6, 908.

Gray, A., Jackson, D.N. and McKinlay, J.B. (1991) 'The relation between dominance, anger, and hormones in normally aging men: Results from the Massachusetts Male Aging Study.' *Psychosomatic Medicine 53*, 4, 375–385.

Gray, J. (1982) *The Neuropsychology of Anxiety: An Enquiry Into the Functions of the Septo-Hippocampal System.* Oxford: Oxford University Press.

Gray, J.A. (1987) *The Psychology of Fear and Stress.* Cambridge: Cambridge University Press.

Gray, P. (1999) *Psychology.* New York: Worth.

Greenberg, M., Cicchetti, D. and Cummings, M. (eds) (1990) *Attachment in the Preschool Years.* Chicago: University of Chicago Press.

Groebel, J. (1998) *Summary of the Unesco Global Study on Media Violence.* Paris: Unesco.

Groenendaal, H., Meijer, R., Veerman, J.W. and Wit, J. de (ed) (1987) *Protectieve factoren in de ontwikkeling van kinderen en adolescenten.* Lisse: Swets & Zeitlinger.

Guilleminault, C. (ed) (1987) *Sleep and its Disorders in Children.* New York: Raven Press.

Gunning, W.B. (1993) 'Medicatie behandelingsmogelijkheden.' In J.K. Buitelaar (ed) *Diagnostiek en behandeling van ADHD.* Utrecht: Stichting Ondewijs en Voorlichting.

Gunning, W.B. (1996) Interview by R Didde. 'Overactive and uninhibited'. *De Volkskrant,* 2 September.

Gunning, W.B. (2001) 'ADHD and foster children.' In, M.F. Delfos and N. Visscher. *(Foster) care and odd behaviour?! On 13 themes.* Amsterdam: SWP.

Habib, M., Pelletier, J., Salamon, G. and Khalil, R. (1994) 'Neuroanatomie fonctionnelle des relations interhemispheriques. Aspects theoriques et perspectives cliniques: 2. Morphometrie fonctionnelle du corps calleux normal et pathologique.' ('Functional neuroanatomy of interhemispheric processes: Theoretical aspects and clinical perspectives: II. Functional morphometry of the normal and pathological corpus callosum.') *Revue de Neuropsychologie 4,* 2, 143–186.

Hadders-Algra, M. and Groothuis, A.M. (1999) 'Quality of general movements in infancy is related to neurological dysfunction, ADHD, and aggressive behaviour.' *Developmental Medicine and Child Neurology* 41, 6, 381–391.

Hadders-Algra, M., Klip-van den Nieuwendijk, Martijn, A. and Eykern, L.A. (1997) 'Assessment of general movements: towards a better understanding of a sensitive method to evaluate brain function in young infants.' *Developmental Medicine and Child Neurology 39,* 2, 88–98.

Halpern, D.F. (1992) *Sex Differences in Cognitive Abilities.* Hillsdale: Lawrence Erlbaum Associates.

Halpern, C.T., Udry, J.R., Campbell, B. and Suchindran, C. (1993a) 'Relationships between aggression and pubertal increases in testosterone: a panel analysis of adolescent males.' *Social-Biology 40,* 1–2, 8–24.

Halpern, C.T., Udry, J.R., Campbell, B. and Suchindran, C. (1993b) 'Testosterone and pubertal development as predictors of sexual activity: a panel analysis of adolescent males.' *Psychosomatic-Medicine 55,* 5, 436–447.

Halpern, C.T., Udry, J.R., Campbell, B., Suchindran, C. and Mason, G.A. (1994) 'Testosterone and religiosity as predictors of sexual attitudes and activity among adolescent males: a biosocial model.' *Journal of Biosocial Science 26,* 2, 217–234.

Hamilton, L.W. and Timmons, R. (1990) *Principles of Behavioral Pharmacology.* Englewood Cliffs: Prentice Hall.

Hamstra-Bletz, E. and Bie, J. de (1985) 'Diagnostiek van het dysgrafisch handschrift bij leerlingen uit het gewoon lager onderwijs.' In A.J.W.M. Thomassen, G.P. van Galen and L.F.W de Klerk *Studies over de schrijfmotoriek.* Lisse: Swets & Zeitlinger.

Handen, B.L., Feldman, H.M., Lurier, A. and Murray, P.J.H. (1999) 'Efficacy of Methyl-phenidate among preschool children with developmental disabilities and ADHD.' *Journal of the American Academy of Child and Adolescent Psychiatry 38,* 7, 805–812.

Hankin, B.L. and Abramson, L.Y. (1999) 'Development of gender differences in depression: description and possible explanations.' *Annals of Medicine 31,* 6, 372–379.

Harasty, J. (2000) 'Language processing in both sexes: evidence from brain studies.' *Brain 123* (Pt.2), 404–406.

Harasty, J., Double, K.L., Halliday, G.M., Kril, J.J. and MacRitchie, D.A. (1997) 'Language-associated cortical regions are proportionally larger in the female brain.' *Archives Neurology 54,* 171–8.

Hare, R.D. (1978) 'Electrodermal and cardiovascular correlates of psychopathy.' In R.D. Hare and D. Schalling *Psychopathic Behavior: Approaches to Research.* New York: John Wiley & Sons.

Hare, R.D. and Schalling, D. (1978) *Psychopathic Behavior: Approaches to Research.* New York: John Wiley & Sons.

Harris J.R. (1998) *The Nurture Assumption – Why Children Turn Out the Way They Do.* New York: The Free Press.

Hart de Ruyter, T. (1968) *Het moeilijk opvoedbare kind in het pleeggezin.* Assen: van Gorcum.

Hassler, M. (1991) 'Maturation rate and spatial, verbal, and musical abilities: a seven-year-longitudinal study.' *International Journal of Neuroscience 58,* 3–4, 183–198.

Health Council (1997) *Dyslexie. Afbakening en behandeling. Advies van een commissie van de Gezondheidsraad* [Dyslexia. Delineation and treatment. Recommendations from a committee of the Health Council].

Hellendoorn, J. (1998) 'Individuele hulp bij sociale problemen.' In A. Collot d'Escury-Koenings, T. Snaterse and E. Mackaay-Cramer (ed) *Sociale vaardigheidstrainingen voor kinderen. Indicaties, effecten & knelpunten.* Lisse: Swets & Zeitlinger.

Hellige, J.B. (1993) *Hemispheric Asymmetry: What's Right and What's Left.* Cambridge/ London: Harvard University Press.

Henry, J.P. and Stephens, P.M. (1977) *Stress, Health, and the Social Environment.* New York: Springer.

Hersov, L.A., Berger, M. and Shaffer, D. (eds) (1978) *Aggression and Anti-Social Behavior in Childhood and Adolescence.* London: Pergamon Press.

Heusmann, R. (1998) 'In Het gevaar na de vechtfilm.' *De Volkskrant,* 12 September..

Heuvel, E. van den (1998) *Anorexia nervosa: een samenspel tussen leken en deskundigen: de sociale representatie van het lichaam en de sociale constructie van de epidemie van eetstoornissen.* Tilburg: Tilburg University Press.

Hoff, A.L., Neal, C., Kushner, M. and DeLisi, L.E. (1994) 'Gender differences in corpus callosum size in first-episode schizophrenics.' *Biological Psychiatry 35,* 12, 913–919.

Holloway, R.L., Anderson, P.J., Defendini, R. and Harper, C. (1993) 'Sexual dimorphism of the human corpus callosum from three independent samples: relative size of the corpus callosum.' *American Journal of Physical Antropology 92,* 481–498.

Horst, W.A. van der (1989) *Gedragsveranderingen op school en in het gezin. Achtergronden programma-ontwikkeling project O.S.M. Gedragsmodificatie.* Rotterdam: project Onderwijs en Sociaal Milieu.

Hrdy, S.B. (1999) *Mother Nature. A History of Mothers, Infants and Natural Selection.* New York: Pantheon Books.

Hucker, S.J. and Bain, J. (1990) 'Androgenic hormones and sexual assault.' In W.L. Marshall, D.R. Laws and H.E. Barbaree (eds) *Handbook of Sexual Assault: Issues, Theories, and Treatment of the Offender. Applied Clinical Psychology.* New York: Plenum Press.

Hudson, J., Morris, A., Maxwell, G. and Galoway, B. (1996) *Family Group Conference: Perspectives on Policy and Practice.* Leichhadt, NSW:The Federation Press

Hugdahl, K. (1993) 'Functional brain asymmetry, dyslexia, and immune disorders.' In A.M. Galaburda (ed) *Dyslexia and Development: Neurobiological Aspects of Extraordinary Brains.* Cambridge: Harvard University Press.

Hugdahl, K., Synnevag, B. and Satz, P. (1990) 'Immune and autoimmune diseases in dyslexic children.' *Neuropsychologia 28*, 7, 673–679.

Huizink, A.C., De Medina, P.G., Mulder, E.J., Visser, G.H. and Buitelaar, J.K. (2002) 'Psychological measures of prenatal stress as predictors of infant temperament.' *Journal of the American Academy of Child and Adolescent Psychiatry 41*, 9, 1078–1085.

Huizink, A.C., Mulder, P.G. and Buitelaar, J.K. (2004) 'Prenatal stress and risk for psychopathology: specific effects or induction of general susceptibility?' *Psychological Bulletin 130*, 1, 115–142.

Hynd, G.W., Semrud-Clikeman, M., Lorys, A.R., Novey, E.S., Eliopoulos, D. and Lyytinen, H. (1991) 'Corpus callosum morphology in attention deficit-hyperactivity disorder: morphometric analysis of MRI.' Special Series: Attention deficit disorder. *Journal of Learning Disabilities 24*, 3, 141–146.

Ickes, W. (1997) *Empathic Accuracy.* New York/London: Guilford Press.

IJzendoorn, M.H. van (1994) *Gehechtheid van ouders en kinderen.* Houten/Zaventem: Bohn Stafleu van Loghem.

INED (Institut National d'Études Démographiques) (1996) Facts and statistics provided by F. Meslé and J. Vallin.

International Molecular Genetic Study of Autism Consortium (1998) 'A full genome screen for autism with evidence for linkage to a region on chromosome 7q.' *Human Molecular Genetics 7*, 3, 571–578.

IWAPV (1984) *Tussen droom en daad. Eindrapport van de Interdepartementale Werkgroep Ambulante en Preventieve Voorzieningen voor Hulpverlening aan jeugdigen* [Between dream and action. Final report of the Interdepartmental Work Group for Ambulant and Preventative Accomodation for Youth Care] Rijswijk: Ministerie van Welzijn, Volksgezondheid en Cultuur.

Jansen, R.J.A. and Wels, P.M.A. (1998) 'The effects of video home training in families with a hyperactive child.' *ACPP Occasional Papers 15*, 63–73

Janssens, J.M.A.M. and van As, N,M.C. (1994) 'Negatieve communicatie in gezinnen.' *Tijdschrift voor Orthopedagogiek 33*, 432–442.

Janssens, J.M.A.M., de Veer, A.J.E. and Janssens, A.W.H. (1991) 'Locus of control ten aanzien van de opvoeding: relaties met opvoedingsgedrag van ouders en de gedragsstijl van het kind.' In J.R.M. Gerris (ed) Ouderschap en ouderlijk functioneren. Amsterdam: Swets & Zeitlinger.

Jiang, H.K., Wang, J.Y. and Lin, J.C. (2000) 'The central mechanism of hypothalamic-pituitary-adrenocortical system hyperfunction in depressed patients.' Psychiatry and Clinical Neuroscience 54, 2, 227–234.

Jones, M.C. (1924) 'The eliminations of children's fears.' Journal of Experimental Psychology 7, 383–390.

Josselson, R. (1980) 'Ego development in adolescence.' In J. Adelson (ed) Handbook of Adolescent Psychology. New York: Wiley.

Jouvet, M. (1992) Le sommeil et le rêve. Paris: Odile Jacob.

Julian, T. and McKenry, P.C. (1998) 'Relationship of testosterone to men's family functioning at mid-life: a research note.' Aggressive Behavior 15, 4, 281–289.

Jung, C.G. (1999) The essential Jung. Princeton: Princeton University.

Juraska, J.M. (1990) 'The structure of the rat cerebral cortex: effects of gender and the environment.' In B. Kolb and R.C. Tees (eds) The Cerebral Cortex of the Rat. Cambridge: MIT Press.

Kalat, J.W. (1992) Biological Psychology. Pacific Grove, California: Brooks/Cole.

Kaplan, H.I. and Sadock, B.J. (1988) Synopsis of Psychiatry. Baltimore: Williams & Williams.

Kaplan, H.I. and Sadock, B.J. (ed) (1995) Comprehensive Textbook of Psychiatry/VI. Volume 1. Baltimore: Williams & Williams.

Kaplan, L. (1990) Das Mona-Lisa-Syndrom: Männer die wie Frauen fühlen. Düsseldorf: Econ.

Kapteyn, P. (1985) In de speeltuin Nederland. Amsterdam: Synopsis.

Kayl, A.E., Moore, B.D., Slopis, J.M., Jackson, E.F. and Leeds, N.E. (2000) 'Quantitative morphology of the corpus callosum in children with neurofibromatosis and attention-deficit hyperactivity disorder.' Journal of Child Neurology 15, 2, 90–96.

Kendall-Tackett, K.A. (2000) 'Physiological correlates of childhood abuse: chronic hyperarousal in PTSD, depression, and irritable bowel syndrome.' Child Abuse and Neglect 24, 6, 799–810.

Ketterlinus, R.D. and Lamb, M.E. (1994) Adolescent Problem Behaviors: Issues and Research. Hillsdale, NY: Erlbaum.

Kirkpatrick, S.W., Campbell, P.S., Wharry, R.E. and Robinson, S.L. (1993) 'Salivary testosterone in children with and without learning disabilities.' Physiology and Behavior 53, 3, 583–586.

Kitterle, F.L. (ed) (1995) Hemispheric Communication: Mechanisms and Models. Hillsdale: Erlbaum Associates.

Kohlberg, L. (1969) 'Stage and sequence: the cognitive-developmental approach to socialization.' In D. Goslin (ed) Handbook of Socialization Theory and Research. Chicago: Rand McNally.

Koomen, H.M.Y., Hoeksma, J.B. and Meerum Terwogt, M. (1998) 'The importance of knowledge about the absent genetic father.' *Zeitschrift für Soziologie der Erziehung und Sozialisation, 70*, 5, 368–81.

Koopman, H. (1989) 'Het medicijn Ritalin. Een mogelijke bijdrage van MBD.' *Balans,* March 2–4.

Kovacs, M. and Timbremont, B. (1992) *CDI, Children's Depression Inventory.* New York: Multi Health Systems.

Kubey, R.L. and Larson, R. (1990) 'The use and experience of the new video media among children and young adolescents.' *Communication Research 17*, 107–130

Lacoste, M-C de, Horvath, D.S. and Woodward, D.J. (1991) 'Possible sex differences in the developing human fetal brain.' *Journal of Clinical and Experimental Neuropsychology 13*, 831–846.

Lahey, B.B., Piacentini, J.C., McBurnett, K., Stone, P., Hartdagen, S. and Hynd, G. (1987) 'Psychopathology in the parents of children with conduct disorder and hyperactivity.' *Journal of American Academy of Child and Adolescent Psychiatry 27*, 163–170.

Lang, R.A., Langevin, R., Bain, J., Frenzel, R.R. *et al.* (1989) 'Sex hormone profiles in genital exhibitionists.' *Annals of Sex Research 2*, 1, 67–75.

Lewine, R.R., Gulley, L.R., Risch, S.C., Jewart, R. and Houpt, J. (1990) 'Sexual dimorphism, brain morphology, and schizophrenia.' *Schizophrenia Bulletin 16*, 2, 195–203.

Lieve, C. van (1990) *Lastige leerlingen. Een empirisch onderzoek naar sociale oorzaken van probleemgedrag op basisscholen.* Amsterdam: Proefschrift.

Locke, J. (1964) 'Some thoughts concerning education.' In P. Gay (ed) *John Locke on Education.* New York: Bureau of Publications, Teacher's College, Columbia University.

Loeber, R. (1998) 'Ontwikkelingspaden en risicopatronen voor ernstige jeugddelinquentie en hun relevantie voor interventies: nooit te vroeg en nooit te laat.' In W. Koops and W. Slot (ed) *Van lastig tot misdadig.* Houten/Diegem: Bohn Stafleu van Loghum.

Loevinger, J. (1990) 'Ego development in adolescence.' In R.E. Muuss (ed) *Adolescent Behavior and Society.* New York: McGraw-Hill.

Loftus, E. and Ketcham, K. (1994) *The Myth of Repressed Memory: False Memories and Allegations of Sexual Abuse.* New York: St. Martin's Press.

Maas, H. van der, Molenaar, P., Hopkins, B. and Kalverboer, A.F. (1998) 'Over de almanak van F.X. Plooij.' *De Psycholoog 33*, 4, 164–165.

Maccoby, E. and Jacklin, C.N. (1980) *The Psychology of Sex Differences.* Stanford: Stanford University Press.

Mahler, M. (1968) *On Human Symbiosis and the Vicissitudes of Individuation.* New York: International Universities Press.

Mahler, M., Pine, F. and Bergman, A. (1975) *The Psychological Birth of the Human Infant: Symbiosis and Individuation.* New York: Basic Books.

Marcia, J. (1980) 'Identity in adolescence.' In J. Adelson (ed) *Handbook of Adolescence.* New York: Wiley.

Martens, W. (1997) *Psychopathie en narijping. Een theoretische terreinverkenning aangevuld met een kwalitatief onderzoek naar het verschijnsel narijping.* Maastricht: Shaker Publishing.

Mathijssen, J. (1998) *Gezinsfunctioneren en probleemgedrag bij kinderen: Een longitudinale studie bij verwezen kinderen en adolescenten.* Rotterdam: Proefschrift Erasmus Universiteit.

Matthijs, W. (1990) *De zelf/ander representaties van gedragsgestoorde kinderen.* Amsterdam: Swets & Zeitlinger.

McAnally, K.I. and Stein, J.F. (1997) 'Scalp potentials evoked by amplitude-modulated tones in dyslexia.' *Journal of Speech, Language and Hearing Research 40*, 4, 939–945.

McBurnett, K., Lahey, B.B., Rathouz, P.J. and Loeber, R. (2000) 'Low salivary cortisol and persistent aggression in boys referred for disruptive behavior.' *Archives of General Psychiatry 57*, 38–41.

Meer, B. van der (1993) 'Een vijfsporenaanpak van het pestprobleem op school.' *Bulletin Nederlandse vereniging voor adolescentenzorg 11*, 3, 20–29.

Meerum Terwogt, M. (2001) 'The power of the degenes.' In M.F. Delfos and N. Visscher (eds) *(Foster) Children and Odd Behaviour?! On 13 Themes.* Amsterdam: SWP.

Meerum Terwogt, M. and Reijnders, C. (1993) 'Afstammingsonrust. Psychische gevolgen van onbekendheid met één of beide genetische ouders.' *Jeugd en Samenleving 10*, 499–508.

Meesters, G. and Singendonk, K. (1994) *Kind en echtscheiding. De gevolgen van echtscheiding voor kinderen vanuit een ontwikkelingspsychologisch perspectief.* Lisse: Swets & Zeitlinger.

Meeuws, W. (1993) 'Psychosociale welbevinden, identiteitsontwikkeling en separatie-individuatie.' In W. Meeuws and H. Hart (ed) *Jongeren in Nederland. Amersfoort: Academische Uitgeverij.*

Merimee, T.J., Russell, B., Quinn, S. and Riley, W. (1991) 'Hormone and receptor studies: relationship to linear growth in childhood and puberty.' *Journal of Clinical Endocrinology and Metabolism 73*, 5, 1031–1037.

Meslé, F. and Vallin, J. (1996) Facts and Statistics provided to INED.

Mesman, J. (2000) *Preadolescent Internalizing and Externalizing Psychopathy.* Rotterdam: Erasmus University.

Meyer-Bahlburg, H.F.L., Feldman, J.F., Cohen, P. and Ehrhardt, A.A. (1988) 'Perinatal factors in the development of gender-related play behavior: sex hormones versus pregnancy complications.' *Psychiatry 51*, 260–271.

Milner, A.D. and Rugg, M.D. (1992) *The Neuropsychology of Consciousness.* London: Academic Press.

Moffit, T.E. (1990) 'The neuropsychology of juvenile delinquency: a critical review.' In M. Tonry and N. Morris (eds) *Crime and Justice: A Review of the Literature.* Chicago: University of Chicago Press.

Moffit, T.E. (1993) 'Adolescent-limited and life-course persistent antisocial behavior: a developmental taxonomy.' *Psychological Review 100*, 674–701.

Money, J. (1980) *Love and Love-sickness.* Baltimore: Johns Hopkins University Press.

Montemayor, R., McKenry, P.C. and Julian, T. (1993) 'Men in midlife and the quality of father–adolescent communication: Father–adolescent relationships.' In S. Shulman and A.W. Collins (eds) *New Directions for Child Development.* The Jossey-Bass Education Series, 62, 59–72. San Francisco: Jossey-Bass.

Montessori, M. (1986) *Discovery of the child.* New York: Ballantine Books

Muuss, R.E. (ed) (1990) *Adolescent Behavior and Society*. New York: McGraw-Hill.

Nagy, M.H. (1948) 'The child's theories concerning death.' *Journal of Genetic Psychology 73*, 3–27.

NIPO-TNS (2004) *Research report*. http://www.nipo.nl

Njiokiktjien, C. (1987) *Gedragsneurologie van het kind. Vol. 1 Klinische principes*. Amsterdam: Suyi Publications.

Njiokiktjien, C. and Verschoor, C.A. (1998) 'Attention deficits in children with low performance IQ: arguments for right hemisphere dysfunction.' *Human Physiology 24*, 2, 145–151.

Noorlander, E., Rijnders, W. and Wijdeven, R. (1993) *De cirkels van van Dijk (volgens Detox Utrecht)*. Utrecht: Detox

Noorlander, P.C. (2000) 'Begrip "Het belang van het kind" onnodig? Omgangsproblemen na helft van scheidingen.' *Uit Balans 122*, 12–13.

Oka, S., Miyamoto, O., Janjua, N.A., Honjo-Fujiwara, N., Ohkawa, M., Nagao, S., Kondo, H., Minami, T., Toyoshima, T. and Itano, T. (1999) 'Re-evaluation of sexual dimorphism in human corpus callosum.' *Neuroreport 10*, 5, 937–940.

Olweus, D. (1977) *Longitudinal Studies of Aggressive Reaction Patterns in Males*. Bergen: Institute of Psychology, University of Bergen.

Olweus, D. (1978) *Aggression in the Schools, Bullies and Whipping Boys*. New York: Wiley & Sons.

Oord, E.J.C.G. van den (1993) *A Genetic Study of Problem Behaviour in Children*. Rotterdam: Proefschrift.

Os, J. van and Selten, J.P. (1998) 'Prenatal exposure to maternal stress and subsequent schizophrenia: The May 1940 invasion of The Netherlands.' *British Journal of Psychiatry 172*, 324–326.

Overmeyer, S., Simmons, A., Santosh, J., Andrew, C., Williams, S.C., Taylor, A., Chen, W. and Taylor, E. (2000) 'Corpus callosum may be similar in children with ADHD and siblings of children with ADHD.' *Developmental Medicine and Child Neurology 42*, 1, 8–13.

Paarlberg, K.M. (1999) *Stress Exposure and Pregnancy Outcome*. Amsterdam: Proefschrift VU.

Paikoff, R.L., Brooks-Gunn, J. and Warren, M.P. (1991) 'Effects of girls' hormonal status on depressive and aggressive symptoms over the course of one year.' Special Issue: The emergence of depressive symptoms during adolescence. *Journal of Youth and Adolescence 20*, 2, 191–215.

Papernow, P.L. (1993) *Becoming a Stepfamily*. San Francisco: Jossey-Bass.

Peters, T.J. and Guitar, B. (1991) *Stuttering: An Integrated Approach to its Nature and Treatment*. Baltimore: Williams and Wilkins.

Piaget, J. (1972) *The Child's Conception of the World*. Totowa, NJ: Littlefield Adams.

Piaget, J. and Inhelder, B. (1966) *La psychologie de l'enfant*. Paris: Presses Universitaires de France.

Pine, D. S., Cohen, P. and Brooks, J. (1996) 'Emotional problems during youth as predictors of stature during early adulthood· Results from a prospective epidemiologic study.' *Pediatrics 97*, 6, 856.

Pinel, J. and John, J.P.J. (1990) *Biopsychology*. Boston: Allyn & Bacon.

Pirooz Sholevar, G. (ed) (1995) *Conduct Disorders in Children and Adolescents*. Washington: American Psychiatric Press.

Piven, J., Bailey, J., Ranson, B.J. and Arndt, S. (1997) 'An MRI study of the corpus callosum in autism.' *American Journal of Psychiatry 154*, 1041–1056.

Plomin, R. (1994) *Genetics and Experience: The Interplay between Nature and Nurture. Individual Differences and Development Series, Volume 6.* Thousand Oaks, London, New York, Delhi: Sage.

Plomin, R. and McClearn, G.E. (ed) (1994) *Nature, Nurture and Psychology.* Washington DC: APA.

Plomin, R. and Rutter, M. (1998) 'Child development, molecular genetics, and what to do with genes once they are found.' *Child Development 69*, 1223–1242.

Plomin, R., DeFries, J.C. and McClearn, G.E. (1980) *Behavioral Genetics: A Primer.* San Francisco: Freeman and Company.

Plooij, F.X. (1990) 'Developmental psychology: developmental stages as successive reorganizations of the hierarchy.' In R.J. Robertson and W.T. Powers (eds) *Introduction to Modern Psychology: The Control-theory View.* Gravel Switch, KY: The Control Systems Group, Inc.

Plooij, F.X. (1994) *Stress en baby's. Inaugurele rede.* Groningen: Universiteit van Groningen.

Premack, D. and Woodruff, G. (1978) 'Does the chimpanzee have a theory of mind?' *The Behavioral and Brain Sciences 4*, 515–526.

Prins, A., Kaloupek, D.G. and Keane, T.M. (1995) 'Psychophysiological evidence for autonomic arousal and startle in traumatized adult populations.' In M.J. Friedman, D.S. Charney and A.Y. Deutsch (eds) *Neurobiological and Clinical Consequences of Stress: From Normal Adaptation to Post-Traumatic Stress Disorder.* Philadelphia/New York: Lippincott-Raven.

Prins, P. (1998) 'Sociale vaardigheidstraining bij kinderen in de basisschoolleeftijd: programma's, effectiviteit en indicatiestelling.' In A. Collot d'Escury-Koenings, T. Snaterse and E. Mackaay-Cramer (ed) *Sociale vaardigheidstrainingen voor kinderen. Indicaties, effecten & knelpunten.* Lisse: Swets & Zeitlinger.

Prins, P., Brink, E. Ten, Eenhoorn, A. and Lootens, H. (1999) *ADHD: een multimodale behandeling.* Houten/Diegem: Bohn Stafleu van Loghum.

Prokasy, W.F. and Raskin, D.C. (eds) *Electrodermal Activity in Psychological Research.* New York: John Wiley & Sons.

Provenzo, E.F. (1991) *Video-kids: Making Sense of Nintendo.* Cambridge: Harvard University Press.

Pynoos, R.S. (1990) 'Children's exposure to violence and traumatic death.' *Psychiatric Annals 20*, 6, 334–344.

Quay, H.C. (1965) 'Psychopathic personality as pathological stimulation-seeking.' *American Journal of Psychiatry 122*, 180–183.

Rahe, R.H., Karson, S., Howard, N.S., Rubin, R.T. and Poland, R.E. (1990) 'Psychological and physiological assessments on American hostages freed from captivity in Iran.' *Psychosomatic Medicine 52*, 1, 1–16.

Raine, A. (1993) *The Psychopathology of Crime: Criminal Behavior as a Clinical Disorder*. San Diego: Academic Press.

Raine, A. (1997) *The Psychopathology of Crime*. Sidcup, Kent: Harcourt Brace.

Raine, A. (2002) 'The role of prefrontal deficits, low automatic arousal and early health factors in the development of the antisocial and aggressive behaviour.' *Journal of Child Psychology and Psychiatry 44*, 4

Raine, A. and Venables, P.H. (1984) 'Electrodermal non-responding, schizoid tendencies, and antisocial behavior in adolescents.' *Psychophysiology 21*, 424–433.

Raine, A., Lencz, T., Birhrle, S., LaCasse, L. and Coletti, P. (2000) 'Reduced prefrontal gray matter volume and reduced autonomic activity in antisocial personality disorder.' *Archives of General Psychiatry 57*, 2, 119–127.

Raine, A., Venables, P.H. and Williams, M. (1990a) 'Relationships between CNS and ANS measures of arousal at age 15 and criminality at age 24.' *Archives of General Psychiatry 47*, 1003–1007.

Raine, A., Venables, P.H. and Williams, M. (1990b) 'Autonomic orienting responses in 15-year-old male subjects and criminal behavior at age 24.' *American Journal of Psychiatry 147*, 933–937.

Raine, A., Venables, P.H. and Williams, M. (1995) 'High autonomic arousal and electrodermal orienting at age 15 years as protective factors against criminal behavior at age 29 years.' *American Journal of Psychiatry 152*, 1595–1600.

Ramaekers, G. and Njiokiktjien, C. (1991) *Pediatric Behavioral Neurology: Vol. 3, The Child's Corpus Callosum*. Amsterdam: Suyi Publications.

Rapport, M.D., Tucker, S.B., DuPaul, G.J., Merlo, M. and Stoner, G. (1986) 'Hyperactivity and frustration: the influence of control over and size of rewards in delaying gratification.' *Journal of Abnormal Child Psychology 14*, 181–204.

Reichart, C.G. and Duyx, J.H.M. (1998) 'Depressies bij Kinderen en adolescenten' [Depression in Children and Adolescents] In W.A. Nolen and C.A.L. Hoogduin (ed) *Behandelingsstrategieën bij depressie*. Houten/Diegem: Bohn Stafleu van Loghem.

Reijden-Lakeman, E.A. van der (1996) *Growing Pains? Psychological Evaluation of Children with Short Stature after Intrauterine Growth Retardation, Before and After Two Years of Growth Hormone Treatment*. Rotterdam: Erasmus University.

Rijt-Plooij H.H.C. van de and Plooij, F.X. (1992) 'Infantile regressions: disorganization and the onset of transition periods.' *Journal of Reproductive and Infant Psychology 10*, 129–149.

Rijt-Plooij, H.H.C. van de and Plooij, F.X. (1993) 'Distinct periods of mother–infant conflict in normal development: sources of progress and germs of pathology.' *Journal of Child Psychology and Psychiatry 34*, 229–245.

Rispens, J., Goudena, P.P. and Groenendaal, J.J.M. (1994) *Preventie van psychosociale – problemen bij kinderen en jeugdigen*. Houten/Zaventhem: Bohn Stafleu van Loghem.

Robins, L.N., West, P.A. and Herjanic, B.L. (1975) 'Arrests and delinquency in two generations: a study of black urban families and their children.' *Journal of Child Psychology and Psychiatry*, 1975, 16, 125–140.

Rose, S., Lewontin, R.C. and Kamin, L.J. (1985) *Not in our Genes; Biology, Ideology and Human Nature*. London: Penguin Books.

Rosenbaum, A. (1991) 'The neuropsychology of marital aggression.' In J.S. Milner (ed) Neuropsychology of Aggression. Boston: Kluwer.

Rotter, J.B. (1966) Generalized Expectancies for Internal versus External Control of Reinforcement. Psychological Monographs, 80, 1, 1–28.

Rousseau, J-J. (1957) Emile ou de l'éducation. Paris: Garnier.

Rovee-Collier, C. and Fagan, J. (1976) 'The retrieval of memory in early infancy.' In L.P. Lipsitt (ed) Advances in Infancy Research, Vol. 1. Norwood, NJ: Ablex.

Rubia, K., Overmeyer, S., Taylor, E., Brammer, M., Williams, S.C., Simmons, A. and Bullmore, E.T. (1999) 'Hypofrontality in attention deficit hyperactivity disorder during higher-order motor control: a study with functional MRI.' American Journal of Psychiatry 156, 6, 891–896.

Rubia, K., Overmeyer, S., Taylor, E., Brammer, M., Williams, S.C., Simmons, A., Andrew, C. and Bullmore, E.T. (2000) 'Functional frontalisation with age: mapping neurodevelopmental trajectories with fMRI.' Neuroscience and Biobehavioral Reviews 24, 1, 13–19.

Rutter, M. (1978) 'Family, area and school influences in the genesis of conduct disorders.' In L.A. Hersov, M. Berger and D. Shaffer (eds) Aggression and Anti-social Behavior in Childhood and Adolescence. Oxford: Pergamon Press.

Rutter, M. (1979) 'Protective factors in children's responses to stress and disadvantage.' In M.W. Kent and J. Rolf (eds) Social Competence in Children; Series: Primary Prevention of Psychopathology. Hanover, New Hampshire: University Press of New England.

Rutter, M. and Casaer, P. (eds) (1991) Biological Risk Factors for Psychosocial Disorders. Cambridge: Cambridge University Press.

Rutter, M. and Rutter, M. (1993) Developing Mind: Challenge and Continuity across the Life Span. London: Penguin Books.

Rutter, M., Graham, P., Chadwick, O. and Yule, W. (1976) 'Adolescent turmoil: fact or fiction?' Journal of Child Psychology and Psychiatry 17, 35–36.

Rutter, M., Macdonald, H., Le Couteur, A., Harrington, R., Bolton, P. and Bailey, A. (1990) 'Genetic factors in child psychiatric disorders: II Empirical findings.' Journal of Child Psychology and Psychiatry 31, 1, 39–83.

Ruwaard, D., Gijsen, R. and Verkleij, H. (1993) 'Chronische aspecifeke respiratoire aandoeningen.' In Volksgezondheid Toekomst Verkenning. De Gezondheidstoestand van de Nederlandse Bevolking in de Periode 1950–2010 [Public health. Future exploration. The health of the Dutch people in the period 1950–2010] Report of the Dutch Ministry of Public Health.

Sacks, O. (1984) A Leg to Stand On. London: Duckworth.

Saito, Y., Nothacker, H-P., Wang, Z., Lin, S.H.S., Leslie, F. and Civelli, O. (1999) 'Molecular characterization of the melanin-concentrating hormone receptor.' Nature 400, 15 July, 265–268.

Scarr, S. and McCartney, K. (1983) 'How people make their own environments.' Child Development 54, 424–435.

Scerbo, A.S. and Kolko, D.J. (1994) 'Salivary testosterone and cortisol in disruptive children: relationship to aggressive, hyperactive, and internalizing behaviors.' *Journal of the American Academy of Child and Adolescent Psychiatry 33*, 8, 1174–1184.

Scerbo, A.S. and Kolko, D.J. (1995) '"Testosterone and aggression": Reply.' *Journal of the American Academy of Child and Adolescent Psychiatry 34*, 5, 535–536.

Schachtel, E. (1973) *Metamorphosis: On the Development of Affect, Perception, Attention and Memory.* New York: Basic Books

Schachter, S. (1968) *The Psychology of Affiliation: Experimental Studies of the Sources of Gregariousness.* California: Stanford.

Schachter, S. and Singer, J.E. (1962) 'Cognitive, social and physiological determinants of emotional state.' *Psychological Review 69*, 379–399.

Schagen van Leeuwen, J.H. (1991) *The Premenstrual Syndrome: Some Diagnostic and Neuroendocrine Aspects.* Utrecht: Ütrecht University Press.

Schiavi, R.C., Schreiner-Engel, P., White, D. and Mandeli, J. (1991) 'The relationship between pituitary-gonadal function and sexual behavior in healthy aging men.' *Psychosomatic-Medicine 53*, 4, 363–374.

Scholte, E.M. and van der Ploeg, J.D. (1998) *AVL, ADHD Vragen Lijst.* Lisse: Swets & Zeitlinger.

Scott, P.D. (1973) 'Fatal battered baby cases.' *Medicine, Science and the Law 13*, 197–206.

Seligman, M.E.P. (1975) *Helpessness: On Depression, Development, and Death.* San Francisco: Freeman.

Selman, R. (1981) 'The child as friendship philosopher.' In S.A. Asher and M. Gottman (eds) *The Development of Children's Friendships.* Cambridge: Cambridge University Press.

Selye, H. (1956) *The Stress of Life.* New York: McGraw-Hill.

Semrud-Clikeman, M., Filipek, P.A., Biederman, J., Steingard, R., Kennedy, D., Renshaw, P. and Bekken, K. (1994) 'Attention-deficit hyperactivity disorder: magnetic resonance imaging morphometric analysis of the corpus callosum.' *Journal of the American Academy of Child and Adolescent Psychiatry 33*, 6, 875–881.

Shekim, W.O., Asarnow, R.F., Hess, E. and Zaucha, K. (1990) 'A clinical and demographic profile of a sample of adults with attention deficit hyperactivity disorder, residual state.' *Comprehensive Psychiatry 5*, 416–425.

Shimomura, Y., Mori, M., Sugo, T., Ishibashi, Y., Abe, M., Kurokawa, T., Onda, H., Nishimura, O., Sumino, Y. and Fujino, M. (1999) 'Isolation and identification of melanin-concentrating hormone as the endogenous ligand of the SLC-1 receptor.' *Biochemical and Biophysical Research Communications 261*, 622–626.

Silberg, J., Pickles, A., Rutter, M., Hewitt, J., Simonoff, E., Maes, H., Carbonneau, R., Murelle, L., Foley, D. and Eaves, L. (1999) 'The influence of genetic factors and life stress on depression among adolescent girls.' *Archives of General Psychiatry 56*, 3, 225–232.

Silverman, P.R. (1989) 'The impact of parental death on college-age women.' *Psychiatric Clinics of North America 10*, 387–404.

Simonnet, D. (1992) *Révélations sur le sommeil et les rêves.* L'Express international, 2120, 46–53.

Skinner, B.F. (1974) *On Behaviorism.* New York: Knopf.

Slabbekoorn, D. (1999) *Effects of Sex Hormones on Cognition and Emotion.* Utrecht: Proefschrift.

Slap, G.B., Khalid, N., Paikoff, R.L., Brooks-Gunn, J. and Warren, M.P. (1994) 'Evolving self-image, pubertal manifestations, and pubertal hormones: preliminary findings in young adolescent girls.' *Journal of Adolescent Health 15*, 4, 327–335.

Slot, N.W. and Spanjaard, H.J.M. (1999) *Competentievergroting in de residentiële jeugdzorg. Hulpverlening voor kinderen en jongeren in tehuizen.* Baarn: Intro.

Sommerhoff, G. (1990) *Life, Brain and Consciousness: New Perceptions through Targeted Systems Analysis.* Amsterdam: North Holland.

Spee-van der Wekke, J., Meulmeester, J.F. and Radder, J. (1998) 'Gezondheidsverschillen tussen leerlingen in het reguliere en het speciaal onderwijs.' *Tijdschrift voor Orthopedagogiek 37*, 87–96.

Speece, M.W. and Brent, S.B. (1984) 'Children's understanding of death: a review of three components of a death concept.' *Child Development 55*, 1671–1686.

Spencer, T., Biederman, J. and Wilens, T. (1998) 'Growth deficits in children with attention deficit hyperactivity disorder.' *Pediatrics 102* (2, Pt3), 501–506.

Spitz, R.A. (1945) 'Hospitalism: an inquiry into the genesis of psychiatric conditions in early childhood.' *Psychoanalytic Studies of the Child 1*, 53–74.

Spitz, R.A. (1965) *The First Year of Life.* New York: International Universities Press.

Steerneman, P. (1997) *Leren denken over denken en leren begrijpen van emoties. Groepsbehandeling van kinderen.* Leuven/Apeldoorn: Garant.

Steerneman, P. (1998) 'Een sociale cognitietraining voor kinderen met problemen in sociale situaties.' In A. Collot d'Escury-Koenings, T. Snaterse and E. Mackaay-Cramer (ed) *Sociale vaardigheidstrainingen voor kinderen. Indicaties, effecten & knelpunten.* Lisse: Swets & Zeitlinger.

Steiger, A., Bardeleben, U. von, Wiedemann, K. and Holsboer, F. (1991) 'Sleep EEG and nocturnal secretion of testosterone and cortisol in patients with major endogenous depression during acute phase and after remission.' *Journal of Psychiatric Research 25*, 4, 169–177.

Steiner, G. (1965) *Children's Concepts of Life and Death: A Developmental Study.* New York: Columbia University.

Steinmetz, H., Jäncke, L., Kleinschimdt, A., Schlaug, G., Volkman, J. and Huang, Y. (1992) 'Sex but no hand differences in the isthmus of the corpus callosum.' *Neurology 42*, 749–752.

Steinmetz, H., Staiger, J.F., Schlaug, G., Huang, Y. and Jancke, L. (1995) 'Corpus callosum and brain volume in women and men.' *Neuroreport 6*, 7, 1002–1004.

Sterk, F. and Swaen, S. (1997) *Denk je sterk! Meer zelfvertrouwen! Meer zelfwaardering!* Utrecht/Antwerpen: Kosmos.

Stickgold, R., Whidbee, D., Schirmer, B., Patel, V. and Hobson, J.A. (2000) *Journal Cognitive Neuroscience 12*, 2, 246–254.

Stone, L.J. and Church, J. (1973) *Childhood and Adolescence.* New York: Random House.

Storey, A. (2000) *'Pregnant' Men.* Memorial University, St. John's, Newfoundland, Canada. www.abcnews.go.com/sections/living/DailyNews/pregnant_men000105.html

Sullivan, H.S. (1953) *The Interpersonal Theory of Psychiatry*. New York: W.W. Norton & Co.

Sullivan, M.W. (1982) 'Reactivation: priming forgotten memories in infants.' *Child Development 53*, 516.

Swaab, D.F. (1999) *Ontwikkeling van de hersenen*. Rotterdam: Stichting Bioweten-schappen en Maatschappij.

Swaab, D.F. and Hofman, M.A. (1995) 'Sexual differentiation of the human hypothalamus in relation to gender and sexual orientation.' *Trends-Neuroscience*, June 18, 6, 264–270.

Swets-Gronert, F. (1986) *Temperament, taalcompetentie en gedragsproblemen van jonge kinderen. Een longitudinaal onderzoek bij kinderen van een half tot vijf jaar*. Lisse: Swets & Zeitlinger.

Tan, U. (1990a) 'Relationship of testosterone and nonverbal intelligence to hand preference and hand skill in right-handed young adults.' *International Journal of Neuroscience 54*, 3–4, 283–290.

Tan, U. (1990b) 'Relation of testosterone and hand preference in right-handed young adults to sex and familial sinistrality.' *International Journal of Neuroscience 53*, 2–4, 157–165.

Tan, U. (1990c) 'Testosterone and nonverbal intelligence in right-handed men and women.' *International Journal of Neuroscience 54*, 3–4, 277–282.

Tan, U. (1991) 'Serum testosterone levels in male and female subjects with standard and anomalous dominance.' *International Journal of Neuroscience 58*, 3–4, 211–214.

Tan, U. and Akgun, A. (1992) 'There is a direct relationship between nonverbal intelligence and serum testosterone level in young men.' *International Journal of Neuroscience 64*, 1–4, 213–216.

Tan, U. and Tan, M. (1997) 'The mixture of left minus right hand skills in men and women.' *International Journal of Neuroscience 92*, 1–2, 1–8.

Tan, U., Akgun, A. and Telatar, M. (1990) 'Relationships among nonverbal intelligence, hand speed, and serum testosterone level in left-handed male subjects.' *International Journal of Neuroscience 71*, 1–4, 21–28.

Tannen, D. (1990) *You Just Don't Understand*. New York: William Morrow.

Tanner, J. (1978) *Fetus into Man: Physical Growth from Conception to Maturity*. Cambridge: Harvard University Press.

Taylor, E. (1994) 'Syndromes of attention deficit and overactivity.' In M. Rutter, E. Taylor and L. Hersov (eds) *Child and Adolescent Psychiatry: Modern Approaches*. Oxford: Blackwell.

Taylor, S.E., Klein, L.C., Lewis, B.P., Gruenewald, T.L., Gurung, R.A. and Updegraff, J.A. (2000) 'Biobehavioral responses to stress in females: tend-and-befriend, not fight-or-flight.' *Psychological Review 107*, 3, 411–429.

Teyler, T.J. (1994) *A Primer of Psychobiology*. New York: Freeman.

Thibaut, F., Cordier, B. and Kuhn, J.M. (1993) 'Effect of long-lasting gonadotrophin hormone-releasing hormone agonist in six cases of severe male paraphilia.' *Acta Psychiatrica Scandinavia 87*, 6, 445–450.

Thomas, A. and Chess, C. (1977) *Temperament and Development* New York: Brunner & Mazel.

Timiras, P.S., Hudson, D.B. and Segall, P.E. (1984) 'Lifetime brain serotonin: regional effects of age and precursor availability.' *Neurobiology of Aging 5*, 235–242.

Tolan, P.H. (1998) 'Voorspellers van geweldadig gedrag bij jongeren.' In W. Koops and W. Slot (ed) *Van lastig tot misdadig.* Houten/Diegem: Bohn Stafleu van Loghum.

Treffers, P. and Westenberg, P.M. (1997) *CZAL, Curium Zinaanvullijst.* Kinder-psychiatrisch instituut Curium. Lisse: Swets & Zeitlinger.

Treffers, P.D.A., Boer, F. and Meijer, M. (1995) *Capita Selecta uit de Kinder- en Jeugdpsychiatrie.* Leiden: Boerhaave Commissie voor Postacademisch Onderwijs in de Geneeskunde.

Tremblay, R.E. (1999) ' When children's social development fails.' In D.P. Kearing and C.Hertzman (eds) *Developmental Health and the Wealth of Nations.* New York: Guilford Press.

Ude, G.R. (1977) *Locus of Control as both a Predictor and Outcome Measure of Therapeutic Success in an Alcoholic Population.* Atlanta: Emory University.

Udry, J.R. (1990) 'Biosocial models of adolescent problem behaviors.' *Social Biology 37,* 1–2, 1–10.

Udry, J.R. (1991) 'Predicting alcohol use by adolescent males.' *Journal of Biosocial Science 23,* 4, 381–386.

Uhl, G.R., Sora, I. and Wang, Z. (1999) 'The mu opiate receptor as a candidate gene for pain: polymorphins, variations in expression, nociception, and opiate responses.' *Proceedings of the National Academy of Science 96,* 14, 7752–7755.

Valk, I. van der (2004) *Family Matters. Longitudinal Studies on the Association between Family Structure, Family Process, and the Adjustment of Adolescents and Young Adults.* Utrecht: ISED.

Valkenburg, P. (2004) *Children's Responses to the Screen: A Media Psychological Approach.* Mahwah, N.J.: Laurence Erlbaum.

Velle, W. (1992) 'Sex differences in sensory functions.' In J.M.G. van der Dennen (ed) *The Nature of the Sexes: The Sociobiology of Sex Differences and the Battle of the Sexes.* Groningen: Origin Press.

Venables, P.H. and Christie, M.J. (1973) 'Mechanisms, instrumentation, recording techniques, and quantification of responses.' In W.F. Prokasy and D.C. Raskin (eds) *Electrodermal Activity in Psychological Research.* New York: Academic Press.

Verhulst, F.C. (1986) *Mental Health in Dutch Children: An Epidemiological Study.* Meppel: Krips Repro.

Verhulst, F.C. (1987) *De toekomst van het kind.* Inaugurele rede, Rotterdam: Erasmus universiteit.

Verhulst, F.C. and Akkerhuis, G.W. (1986) 'Mental health in Dutch children. III: Behavioral-emotional problems reported by teachers of children aged 4–12.' *Acta Psychiatrica Scandinavia 73,* 330.

Verhulst, F.C. and Versluis-den Bieman, H.J.M. (1989) *Buitenlandse Adoptiekinderen; vaardigheden en probleemgedrag.* Assen/Maastricht: van Gorcum.

Verhulst, F.C., Akkerhuis, G.W. and Althaus, M. (1986) 'De gedragsvragenlijst voorkinderen 4–16 jaar: criteriumgerelateerde validiteit.' *Tijdschrift Orthoped. Kinderpsych. 11,* 24–30.

Verhulst, F.C., Versluis-den Bieman, H.J.M., Ende, J. van der, Berden, G.F.M.G. and Sanders-Woudstra, J.A.R. (1990) 'Problem behavior in international adoptees: diagnosis of child psychiatric disorders.' *Journal of the American Academy of Child and Adolescent Psychiatry 29,* 420–428.

Vink, T., Hinney, A., van Elburg, A.A., van Goozen, S.H., Sandkuijl, L.A., Sinke, R.J., Herpertz-Dahlman, B.M., Henebrand, J., Remschmidt, H., van Engeland, H. and Adan, R.A. (2001) 'Association between an agouti-related protein gene polymorphism and anorexia nervosa.' *Molecular Psychiatry 6*, 3, 325–328.

Virgilio, G. (1986) *Maturation of the CNS and Evoked Potentials.* Amsterdam: Excerpta Medica.

Virkkunen, M. and Linnoila, M. (1993) 'Brain serotonin, Type II alcoholism and impulsive violence.' *Journal of Studies on Alcohol 11*, 163–169.

Virkkunen, M.K.E., Rawlings, R., Tokola, R., Poland, R.E., Guidotti, A., Nemessof, C., Bissette, G. and KAlogeras, K. (1994) 'Personality profiles and state aggressiveness in Finnish alcoholic, violent offenders, fire setters, and healthy volunteers.' *Archives of General Psychiatry 51*, 1, 28–33

Voort, T.H.A. van der and Valkenburg, P.M. (1994) 'The impact of television on children's fantasy play.' *Developmental Review 14*, 27–51.

Vries, M.W. de (1984) 'Temperament and infant mortality among the Masai of East Africa.' *American Journal of Psychiatry 141*, 1189–1194.

Vrij, A. (1998) *De psychologie van de leugenaar.* Lisse: Swets & Zeitlinger.

Vygotsky, L.S. (1978) *Mind in Society: The Development of Higher Psychological Processes.* Cambridge: Harvard University Press.

Vygotsky, L.S. (1988) *Thought and Language.* Cambridge: MIT Press.

Vygotsky, L.S. (1993) *The Collected Works of L.S. Vygotsky, Volume 2: The Fundamentals of Defectology (Abnormal Psychology and Learning Disabilities).* Edited by R.W. Rieber, and A.S. Carton: New York: Plenum Press.

Wallerstein, J.S. and Blakeslee, S. (1989) *Second Chances; Men, Women and Children a Decade after Divorce.* New York: Ticknor and Field.

Wansink, H. and Veen, O.S. van der (1996) 'Hulpverleners over jongeren met een slechte prognose.' *Tijdschrift voor Jeugdhulpverlening en Jeugdwerk, TJJ*, mei, 42–46.

Ward, O.B. (1992) 'Fetal drug exposure and sexual differentiation of males: Sexual differentiation.' In A.A. Gerall, H. Moltz and I.L. Ward (eds) *Handbook of Behavioral Neurobiology, 11.* New York: Plenum Press.

Warren, M.P. and Brooks-Gunn, J. (1989) 'Mood and behavior at adolescence: evidence for hormonal factors.' *Journal of Clinical Endocrinology and Metabolism 69*, 1, 77–83.

Watson, J.B. (1928) *The Psychological Care of the Infant and Child.* New York: Norton.

Weerth, C. de, Van Hees, Y. and Buitelaar, J.K. (2003) 'Prenatal maternal cortisol levels and infant behavior during the first 5 months.' *Early Human Development 74*, 2, 139–151.

Weinberg, W., Rutman, J., Sullivan, L., Penick, E. and Dietz, S. (1973) 'Depression in children referred to an educational diagnostic center: Diagnosis and treatment.' *Journal of Pediatrics 83*, 1065–1072.

Weiss, G. and Hechtman, L. (1993) *Hyperactive Children Grown Up.* New York: Guilford Press.

Wels, P.M.A., Jansen, R.J.A.H. and Penders, G.E.J.M. (1994) 'Videohometraining bij hyperactiviteit van kinderen.' *Tijdschrift voor Orthopedagogiek 9*, 363–379.

Westenberg, P.M., Cohn, L.D. and Blasi, A. (eds) (1998) *Personality Development: Theoretical, Empirical, and Clinical Analyses of Loevinger's Conception of Ego Development.* Mahwah, NJ: Erlbaum.

Westenberg, P.M., Jonckheer, J., Treffers, P.D.A. and Drewes, M. (1998) 'Ego development in children, adolescents, and young adults: another side of the Impulsive, Self-protective, and Conformist ego levels.' In P.M. Westenberg, L.D. Cohn and A. Blasi (eds) *Personality Development: Theoretical, Emprical, and Clinical Analyses of Loevinger's Conception of Ego Development*. Mahwah, NJ: Erlbaum.

Westenberg, P.M., Treffers, P.D.A., Jonckheer, J., Drewes, M.J. and Warmenhoven, N.J.C. (1995) 'Angst(stoornissen) en sociaal-emotionele ontwikkeling bij kinderen vanaf acht jaar.' In P.D.A. Treffers, F. Boer and M. Meijer *Capita Selecta uit de Kinder- en Jeugdpsychiatrie*. Leiden: Boerhaave Commissie voor Postacademisch Onderwijs in de Geneeskunde.

Wiegman, O. (1995) *Kind en computerspelletjes: relaties en vrijetijdsbesteding, agressie, sociale integratie en schoolvaardigheden*. Enschede: Vakgroep Psychologie Universiteit Twente.

Wilkins, L., Fleischman, W. and Howard, J.E. (1940) 'Macrogenitosomia precox associated with hyperplasia of the androgenic tissue of the adrenal and death from corticoadrenal insufficiency.' *Endocrinology 26*, 3, 385–395.

Willems, J.C.M. (1998) *Wie zal de opvoeders opvoeden? Kindermishandeling en het recht van het kind op persoonswording*. Den Haag: Asser Press.

Williams, T.J., Pepitone, M.E., Christensen, S.E., Cooke, B.M., Huberman, A.D., Breedlove, N.J., Breedlove, T.J., Jordan, C.L. and Breedlove, S.M. (2000) 'Finger-length ratios and sexual orientation. Measuring people's finger patterns may reveal some surprising information.' *Nature 30*, 404, 6777, 455–456.

Windle, M. (1994) 'Temperamental inhibition and activation: hormonal and psychosocial correlates and associated psychiatric disorders.' *Personality and Individual Differences 17*, 1, 61–70.

Wit, C.A.M. de (2000) *Depressie bij kinderen en adolescenten. Theorie en onderzoek, diagnostiek en behandeling*. Houten/Diegem: Bohn Stafleu van Loghum.

Worden, J.W. (1996) *Children and Grief: When a Parent Dies*. New York/London: Guilford Press.

Zahn, T.P. (1986) 'Psychophysiological approaches to psychopathology.' In M.G.P. Coles, E. Donchin and S.W. Porges *Psychophysiology: Systems, Processes, and Applications*. New York: Guilford Press.

Zaidel, D.W. (1994) *Neuropsychology: Handbook of Perception and Cognition*. San Diego: Academic Press.

Zaidel, E., Aboitiz, F., Clarke, J., Kaiser, D. and Matteson, R. (1995) 'Sex differences in interhemispheric relations for language.' In F.L. Kitterle (ed) *Hemispheric Communication: Mechanisms and Models*. Hillsdale: Erlbaum.

Zee, S.A.M. van der, Molen, H.T. van der and Beek, D.T. van der (1989) *Sociale vaardigheden voor zwakbegaafde jongeren; praktijkboek Goldsteintraining*. Deventer: van Loghem Slaterus.

Zeiger, R.S. and Heller, S. (1995) 'The development and prediction of atopy in high-risk children: follow-up at age seven years in a prospective randomized study of combined maternal and infant food allergen avoidance.' *Journal of Allergy and Clinical Immunology, 95*, 6, 1179–1191.

Zlotnik, G. (1993) *Ferme jongens, stoere knapen? Verschillen tussen jongens en meisjes vanaf conceptie tot aan de puberteit. Jongens als het zwakke geslacht*. Rotterdam: Ad. Donker.

Subject Index

Author Index